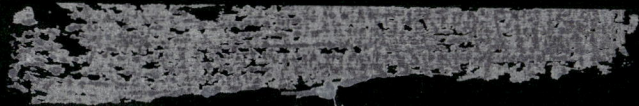

Adolf Loos. Works and Projects

## Adolf Loos about Design and Architecture

I do not need to draw my designs. A good architectural concept of how something is to be built can be written down. The Parthenon can be written down.

I am against photographing interiors. The results are always different from the original. There are architects who design interiors not so people can live in them, but so they will look beautiful in the photographs. These are so-called drawing-board designs which, with their mechanical combination of light and shade, correspond most to a piece of mechanical equipment, in this case the darkroom. My interiors cannot be judged from photographs or reproductions. I am sure that in photographs they will look awful, make no impression at all.

Photographs dematerialize reality, but precisely what I want is for people in my rooms to feel the material around them, I want it to have its effect on them, I want them to be aware of the enclosing room, to feel the material, the wood, to see it, touch it, to perceive it sensually, to sit comfortably and feel the contact between the chair and a large area of their peripheral sense of touch, and say: this is sitting as it should be. How can I demonstrate on a photograph how good my chairs are to sit on? How can I make a person who sees the photograph feel it, however well the chair is photographed?

So you see, photography says nothing. Photography produces pretty or not so pretty pictures, it diverts people from the real object, miseducates them, it is photography's fault that people want to furnish their rooms not for living in but to look nice. Photography cheats. I have never tried to cheat anyone with my things. It is a method I condemn. But our architects have been educated in this method of illusion alone and develop out of it. They make their reputation with pretty drawings and beautiful photographs. They do it deliberately, because they know that people are so helpless that a graphic, a photographic illusion is sufficient to get them to live in the interior and even be proud of it. And the clients are so dishonest even to themselves, that they accept in an act of self-denial to live in all this drawings and photographs. [...]

I don't like people call me "architect". Simply "Adolf Loos" is my name.

Adolf Loos, "On Thrift" (1924), in *On Architecture*, Ariadne Press, Riverside 2002, pp. 178-9, 180

*To Julius, Elias, Amadeus and Susanne*

Ralf Bock

# Adolf Loos
## Works and Projects

SKIRA

*Cover*
House on Michaelerplatz, detail
Photograph by Philippe Ruault

*Back cover*
Loos, 1922, 52 years old

*Page 2*
Adolf Loos in 1924
Photograph by Trude Fleischmann
(ALA 2111)

*Editor*
Luca Molinari

*Design*
Marcello Francone

*Editorial Coordination*
Francesca Ruggiero

*Editing*
Monica Maroni

*Layout*
Paola Ranzini

*Translations*
Lorenzo Sanguedolce

*Photographs*
Philippe Ruault (colour photographs)
Albertina Archive, Vienna (b/w photographs)

*Drawings*
Irene Ciampi
Thiys Pulles

The publisher wishes to thank the Albertina Museum
of Vienna for their kind permission to use their
archive images

In the captions, the initials ALA are added to images
that come from the Albertina Archive, followed
by the inventory number

The author wishes to thank the Science and Research
Fund of the Department of Culture of the City
of Vienna for their precious support to his research
on Adolf Loos

First published in Italy in 2007 by
Skira Editore S.p.A.
Palazzo Casati Stampa
via Torino 61
20123 Milano
Italy
www.skira.net

© 2007 by Skira editore
© 2007 by Albertina Archive for archive photographs

Printed and bound in Italy. First edition

ISBN: 978-88-7624-643-2

Distributed in North America by Rizzoli International
Publications, Inc., 300 Park Avenue South,
New York, NY 10010
Distributed elsewhere in the world by Thames
and Hudson Ltd., 181a High Holborn,
London WC1V 7QX, United Kingdom

# Contents

# Introduction

This book was instigated in 2001 when Philippe Ruault telephoned me to ask me to collaborate on a small project for a Japanese architecture magazine. For its last issue of the year, the magazine traditionally publishes a supplement booklet. Taken together, the booklets make up a series on major architects of the 20th Century. The booklet that year featured Loos and, in addition to the text, the editor was hoping to get some photographs of Loos' houses. I spontaneously accepted the offer from Philippe Ruault, not knowing what was ahead of me or whether it would be possible at all to take the photographs since his objects are all inhabited and are private property. I took on the challenge, because ever since my arrival in Vienna, I wanted to know more about this Adolf Loos and the myth surrounding him up until this day. Now, a window of opportunity had opened up to learn more about his work.

The project had to be finished within six weeks – a short and easily broken down period of time which provided me with an additional argument to offer Philippe my assistance without any hesitation. I got right to work and established as many contacts to the houses' present owners as possible. Initially, I searched for an organization dedicated to Loos and his legacy. I imagined there would be a Loos foundation, but I soon learned there was none. That would have been too easy. Next, I called different institutions dealing with architecture in Vienna and the Albertina, which houses the "Loos archive". From all these I got some direct contacts or hints to the identities of the present owners. Thanks to the friendly assistance of many people, all of whom I would like to express my gratitude to. If I finally made contact with the owners of some of Loos' houses. I always spoke with very friendly and open people and they gratefully showed their homes to us and gave us permission to take photo-

graphs. Without this readiness on the owners' part, this book would have never come about. Therefore, I would like to express my most sincere thanks to them here.

This is how we could visit and photograph 10 objects in six weeks. We saw the interiors of several Loos houses one after the other within a very short time, and we were repeatedly fascinated by the spatial effect and atmosphere, which seized and emotionally affected us even 80 to 90 years after their realization. We were both surprised because the rooms were much more up-to-date and more alive than in the black-and-white archival photos we had seen; additionally, the interiors were usually close to being in their original condition thanks to some complex restorations their current owners had undertaken; and they were inhabited by individuals who all felt content in the Loos ambiance. The houses were not museums or exhibition spaces; they were not scarcely used second or third home dwellings. Families lived here and found the focal point of their lives in these houses.

When Philippe Ruault and I saw the first prints of his color photographs, Loos' work suddenly appeared completely up-to-date – a wholly different impression from the archival pictures in black and white which have been shown as the primary illustrations in the existing literature on Loos. These photographs of a consistently high quality by Martin Gerlach Jr. from 1928-30, which he had taken on the occasion of the first monograph on Loos by the Schroll publishing house in Vienna, had accompanied us throughout the past years and had always served us as a benchmark and a point of reference.

Naturally, they are documents of their time, although in some cases 20 years passed from the completion to the photographic appointment. At

Duschnitz Villa, 1915-16: view from inglenook to dining room with winter garden
Photo by Philippe Ruault, 2004

9

that time nearly all of the objects were still inhabited by the original owner, who had created them with Loos. To the extent that his health permitted him, Loos supervised the produaction and the selection of the pictures. In some cases, he intervened and corrected them by means of photomontage or retouching of the original diapositives on glassplates. The production of the first monograph on Loos in 1931 is attributed to his faithful coworker of many years, Heinrich Kulka, who had taken on the oversight for the production of the book.

Now, holding some large format color slides in our hands, we were still full of the impression of what we had seen and experienced, and for a long time we discussed in depth what it was that moved us to such an extent in these works of Loos. We analyzed it, setting up hypotheses and questions which remained unanswered.

Afterwards, I made the decision to engross my thoughts into Loos' work in order to get to the bottom of what had emphatically affected me. The myth surrounding Loos had enveloped me and would not let me go. Thus, I embarked on my task by getting in touch with all the current owners of Loos' objects.

I am happy about the fact that I could no longer recall Loos' texts in detail upon my first visits to the residences. I had read his texts as a student. My faded memory of them allowed me to be directly affected on an emotional level by these interiors rather than employing reason in discovering them. The feelings I had were my own and stemmed from my own perception, leading me in search of explanations.

It was satisfying to read Loos' texts again after revisiting and learn that he regarded it his goal to produce feelings and moods with his work.

As one discovers Loos' writings and work, one quickly uncovers their complexity accompanied by initially felt contradictions. Soon thereafter, one thinks one can decipher him with premature readings and one-sided interpretations if one compares his writings with his constructed works in terms of his fight against ornamentation – the cause he is commonly associated with. But one has to get rid of stereotypes and prejudices, reading the text exactly and regarding his objects with equal innocence. This way, contradictions in content are no longer present. What remains are perhaps different stylistic means, which the fields of architecture and literature employ to get their statements across; but the core of the message is conveyed coherently in both fields.

It was some years later, after I had seen and analyzed many further objects, after I had read many primary and secondary sources, after I had spoken with some Loos specialists, descendants of the original owners and the current residents, that I wanted to document my fascination with Loos in this book. Which is the attempt to understand and explain the fundamentals and the philosophies of Adolf Loos and his work. It seeks to document and shed light on the subject from several points of view. Perhaps it will allow for a better comprehension of his personality and his work.

This approach is being employed through the photographs of Philippe Ruault who, with his technique and experience, succeeds to transfer the moods of the interiors he had experienced into two-dimensional images. He has always worked without any artificial illumination, without flash and without any arrangements, which may compromise the authenticity of the pictures. The photographs attest Loos' gift to produce certain moods in interiors through light, construction, material and selection of furnishings. We photographed interiors and exterior views in which Loos' basic concept was recognizable, even if not every article was original, so long as they were furnished according to the principles of "comfortable living". If the original impression was changed due to extensive renovations or missing interior arrangement, we did not take photographs, and instead I show the condition as it was around 1930.

Besides the pictures, plans also represent the objects. One of Loos' principles was that a drawing for a design must be second to architecture itself because it may only be an instrument or technical aid, but never more than that. Therefore, in his studio, Loos only produced the necessary number of drawings and he discussed his requests directly with the owners and craftsmen, outlining the solutions with them. Furthermore, Loos ordered that all drawings and construction documents be destroyed in his Viennese office when he moved to Paris in 1924. Only a part of them were secretly saved by his coworkers. Additionally, the building permit drawings submitted to the City department were preserved, but in the period of execution, some of the details were changed of which, so far, there has been no documentation.

It was difficult to determine the solutions implemented by Loos based upon the different available construction documents I could find in publications, archives and in the private documents of current owners. This I evaluated, by visiting the objects, in conversations with the owners and by the archival photos provided in good quality by Gerlach. During this process Irene Ciampi and Thijs Pulles digitized and relentlessly redrew all floorplans, sections and elevations with many revisions and meticulous elaborations, so that today we have now compiled for the objects' comparative analysis a comprehensive collection of the construction documents together with a digital archive of Loos' plans.

A further facet is the personal data on Adolf Loos as an individual, as the biographical explanations and the analysis of his written work help us in understanding Loos as a human being and as an essayist. His works were informed by his view of man, and he applied his experiences and analyses of everyday life to his works. He never wished to be called an architect, and many considered him a reformer of life, an educator, a benefactor, etc.

Furthermore, I have attempted to overlay his world of thinking, which is delivered to us through his written sources with the constructed objects. Also, I have laid out approaches to interpretation, which result from my research into his work, and I have discovered some issues that had not been dealt with in earlier Loos publications.

After the completion of his projects, his clients cultivated a life-long friendship with Loos and commissioned him for successive jobs. He was able to establish numerous contacts thanks to his circle of friends, including Karl Kraus, Arnold Schönberg and Peter Altenburg. All of this is evident when the clients biographies are examined. To depict this exceptionally good relationship between the "architect" Loos and the client was of special importance to me, since reality usually deviates from this ideal: perhaps the example of Loos can show today's architects that it is possible to deal with the client on an intimate level if one's own perspective is accordingly closer to living than to design.

I now wish you much pleasure in reading and regarding this book.

Finally, I would like to cordially thank the cultural department of the municipality of Vienna for its financial support, which made this complex research possible. Special thanks to my wife Susanne and my children Julius, Elias, and Amadeus, whose patience and understanding was crucial in the realization of this project, which I therefore dedicate to them.

*Ralf Bock*

Dieses Bild ist ähnlicher
wie ich selbst!    Adolf Loos

OK    13. II. 1916

# Biography

Loos, 1887-88, 17 years old
(ALA 2058)

Loos, 1892, 21 years old
Photo by Otto Mayer, Dresden
(From Rukschcio/Schachel, p. 10)

### Childhood, Youth and Education

On 10 December 1870, Adolf Loos was born as the first of three children to Adolf Loos and Marie Hertl in Brünn (Czech Republic); his sisters Hermine and Irma were born after him. He was baptized a Christian. His father ran a sculpting and a stone-cutting workshop and his work was generally recognized in Brünn. The house, workshop and stone warehouse were located on one single property. Loos witnessed the daily work of his father and grew up with stone masonry. Loos greatly esteemed and admired his father, who died suddenly, in March 1879 at age 48. His father's passing was a dramatic experience for the eight-year old boy. The event put an end to his protected childhood and his performance at school sharply declined as a consequence. His mother and his strict guardian, initially a man named N. Nedved, lost their emotional bond with the boy. Adolf Loos was increasingly pressured by educational measures, which, however, made him more and more headstrong.

His mother took over and successfully ran the business. In 1881, she sent Adolf to her parents in Iglau (Bohemia) where he attended the local high school and became acquainted with Josef Hoffmann, of the same age. He had to repeat the first year but then received an excellent school report. In 1883, his mother brought him back to Brünn and re-enrolled him at the local high school.

His conduct and behavior repeatedly got him into trouble; however, his academic achievements were noteworthy all throughout school. The frequent change of schools and the tense relationship with his mother made his social integration more difficult; he had to fend for himself.

It was only in 1884 that his academic performance declined at the high school in Melk an der Donau, a school led by Benedictine monks. He was removed by his mother and enrolled in the vocational school in Reichenberg (Bohemia), which he later continued in Brünn. In 1889, he graduated from a technical high school, already determined to become an architect.

He moved on to the Technical University of Dresden as a guest auditor. He could not enroll as a regular student as he did not graduate from the Gymnasium. He was ex-matriculated after two semesters for not paying his enrollment fees. It must have been during the two semesters in Dresden that he was exposed to the work and the writings of Gottfried Semper who worked and taught in Dresden until 1848. Semper's work became a substantial basis for Loos' written, theoretical and architectural work.

In 1890 he enlisted in the army as a volunteer. Subsequently, in 1891, he went to Vienna to commence his architecture studies at the Academy of Arts, which, in the end, he did not choose to attend for unknown reasons. During this period, an event took place which Schachel described as follows: "His godfather [...] had led him into the brothel. Some time later, Loos got sick with syphilis. He only went to the doctor when a high fever broke out and his illness had already progressed. The result was a severe inflammation of the testicles. Loos was bound to his bed for many months and was in great pain. He was healed, but the illness had rendered him sterile."[1] His mother agreed to house him and care for him. Immediately upon his recovery, Loos returned to Vienna; however, in 1892 he briefly resumed his studies in Dresden, and then decided, in 1893, to travel to America. He wanted to visit his uncle in Philadelphia and the world exhibition in Chicago.

He traveled to New York alone and without the support of his family, and from there he continued to Philadelphia, where his uncle's family lived. From Philadelphia, he continued his journey and visited the world exhibition in Chicago. Loos described his lasting impression of this exhibition as follows: "When, years ago, I left my native region. [...] I was still fully convinced of the superiority of German arts and crafts. In Chicago I went with a proud feeling inside of me through the German and the Austrian section. With pity I smiled as I looked at the American examples of 'arts and crafts'.

"And how my view has changed since then! The year-long stay over there triggers nothing but shame if I consider the embarrassment the German arts and crafts had earned themselves in Chicago. The proud and splendid achievements, the stylish pieces of splendor, they were nothing but barbaric pretentiousness [...]. At that time, however, I experienced a silent rage over these (American) things. There were purses, writing utensils, suit-cases, bags etc. All of which were plain, without ornamental decorations [...]. I was ashamed of these works [...]. Today, I realize that, at that time, the stupidest *Gigerl* [Austrian word for a man whose clothes serve only to make him stand out against his environment] had a more refined taste than me."[2]

After the death of his son, his uncle moved to the country where Loos performed some unskilled labour in his service, but the situation did not satisfy him, therefore he decided to go to New York. However, in the family life with his uncle, he became aware of the emancipated role of the American woman and thé small cultural difference between country dwellers and city dwellers in the American life of that time. The country dwellers dressed in urban fashion and clothes outside of the working hours. They lived in small mansions, the so-called "farmhouses", and in active exchange and contact with the city.

In New York, he initially made a living with odd jobs and there were hardly any records of his activities. According to Loos' own account, it was only after more than a year of this that he finally took a job as a draftsman in an architectural office.

The three years in America and the journey back via England left a lasting impression on Loos, serving as a kind of self-liberation. His comparison of the American and English with the Austrian and German culture would re-shape his life.

In 1896, he returned to Brünn but not without stopping over in England and London in order to be outfitted with custom-tailored clothes. This is how Loos re-entered the Viennese cultural life as a well-

dressed gentleman. He would keep his love for custom-made clothes throughout his whole life; he documented the meaning good clothes held for him in many essays, which he published starting in 1898 in the *Neue Freie Presse* [*New Free Press*], which, at that time, was the most renown daily paper in German-speaking countries. Loos noted that: "Somewhere an American philosopher says, 'A young man can count himself rich if he has a brain in the head and a decent suit in his wardrobe.' That is a philosopher who knows the world. He knows people. What use is a brain if one doesn't have the decent clothes to set it off? The English and the Americans expect everybody to be well-dressed."[3]

His mother disowned him during his stay in America and placed him under guardianship, as he had refused her entreaty to leave America immediately to take on his paternal legacy and to support his mother in the family business. After this incident, he broke all contact with her.

From Vienna he tried to annul the guardianship, which turned out to be extremely complex and difficult. Loos noted on this topic: "The thing ended with a settlement. It annoys me that I agreed to it. I never received any money anyways. I would still be under guardianship today, but the thought to live in this condition was intolerable to me [...]. But the abolition of the guardianship was of no use. It was already too late."[4]

With these circumstances, he could not have an academic career, as Josef Hoffmann did, and it was impossible for him to receive any public work in this status in the foreseeable future. Particularly, the fact that he had no prospect of teaching loomed large on his mind, because the education of people had always been a great concern of his.

Thus, it remains to be stated that at the end of his education period, Loos was an autodidact who neither completed a degree nor possessed any other apprenticeship training.

### The Beginning of his Professional Career
In 1896, Loos took on a job in the office of Professor Carl Mayreder in Vienna, whose wife Rosa was an active member of the Women's Emancipation Movement. Carl Mayreder had a high regard for classical architecture and dealt mainly with problems relating to urban development.

It was during this time that he formed friendships with the poet Peter Altenberg, the essayist

Loos, 1898-99, 28 years old
Photo by Otto Mayer, Dresden
(From Rukschcio/Schachel, p. 34)

Loos' first wife, Lina Obertimpfler, 1904
Portrait by Pietzner
(From Rukschcio/Schachel, p. 79)

Karl Kraus and the composer Arnold Schönberg. In the beginning of their friendships, they frequently met at Café Griensteidl. Deep and open lifelong friendships grew from these acquaintances, and although each of these four personalities set out on a lonely path in his own artistic field, they mutually supported each other again and again. Kraus and Schönberg also brought work to Loos through their own contacts.

In 1897 Loos began to create his first objects. The decor of the premises of the royal tailor Ebenstein is thought to be his first work.

In 1898, on the occasion of the Viennese jubilee exhibition, he wrote a series of articles for the *Neue Freie Presse*. He reported on exhibitions, questions of fashion and culture as well as tools and consumer goods. His reviews became very popular and form the foundation of his written work and the basis of his later architectural work. The series of articles in the *Neue Freie Presse* helped him to achieve a certain popularity, and he thus reached a high level of recognition for his opinions and his character.

He now applied the significance of clothes for cultured people to his essays on architecture. He searched for parallels in facade design and in the furnishing of apartments and shops. Additionally, he utilized clothes in the representation of his own person – he only wore English cuts and models, which were custom-made by the best tailors in Vienna. He did not wear ready-made. Bessie Bruce always said: "Loos was better dressed than an English gentleman." Elsie Altmann-Loos, recalling her memories described him as follows: "Loos looked like a typical Englishman and had good manners, it was easy to love him."

His preference for high quality clothes made him a customer of the best tailor shops of the city, who in turn became his clients. After having finished the project for the Ebenstein tailor shop, this was how he was able to work with Kniže, Erich Mandl and Goldman & Salatsch.

Also in 1898, the building of the Secession was finished by Olbricht, under the presidency of Gustav Klimt. Josef Hoffmann was commissioned to furnish some of the rooms in this building, and Loos asked his schoolmate to let him furnish the meeting room pro bono. Josef Hoffmann denied him this request. Not only did this incident signify Loos' emancipation from the Secession, but also the end of his personal ties with Josef Hoffmann. A lifelong

antagonism developed from this incident, and Loos attacked him repeatedly in public and with him the Wiener Werkstätten [Viennese Workshops], founded and run by Hoffmann.

Retrospectively, Loos commented at the end of the 1920s: "[...] now I laugh at it. But at the time it harmed my fight against ornamentation – the fact that a draftsman of six picture postcards, 'artist postcards', he called them, due to this achievement could become professor at the college of arts and crafts [Kunstgewerbeschule], that the same person could jettison his principles after visiting the Stössler residence and then, owing to the possibility his exhibitions provided him, which he always arranged himself (and never invited me to, the unpleasant, plundered competitor) he would become known as the smooth propagator of the new style, a short-lived stage. Because in reality his non-ornamental style of then and now (since that Paris embarrassment in 1925) is pure ornament."[5]

In 1899, Adolf Loos received much attention for his design of the Café Museum, and the critics recognized his clear opposition to the Secession in the direct proximity of the newly established exhibition building. Some critics assessed his skills as forward-looking and they discussed his views and his attitude at length.

In 1902, Adolf Loos married Lina Obertimpfler, just 20 years old, who had also been admired by his friend Peter Altenberg and stylized as a goddess. On 22 December, he rented a small apartment on the fifth floor of the building at Giselastrasse 3 (today Bösendorferstrasse 3), close to the Ring. Loos kept this apartment until the end of his life and it became a focal point to which he returned again and again after many journeys and longer stays abroad.

He remodeled and furnished his own apartment in 1903 according to his ideas. He maintained this same design until the end of his life. It is noteworthy that almost all principles he developed here would resurface in his later work. This speaks to the inner maturity of the 33-year-old architect, who had already found his own concepts of building and habitation early on in his career.

Likewise in 1903, the two editions of the magazine published by him, called *Das Andere - Ein Blatt zur Einführung der abendländischen Kultur in Österreich* [*The Other - Periodical for the Introduction of the Western Culture in Austria*], were released. Loos commented: "[...] I also believe that I am able to say everything I have to say in 24 issues a year. The purpose of the magazine is to make my job easier for me. I furnish apartments. I can only do this for people who possess a western culture. I was lucky to have been exposed to western culture for three years in America. Since I am convinced of its superiority, I personally hold it to be characterless to descend to the Austrian level – subjectively speaking. This leads to fights. And I am alone in these fights."[6]

In 1904 he had already separated from Lina Loos, who had been cheating on him for several months with Heinz Lang. Lang took his life after the affair became known; the prompt was the utterance: "Die, she is a goddess!" by Peter Altenberg. Lina accepted an engagement in America and left Vienna for some time. In 1905, after her return, the divorce was made official.

In 1905, Loos, in a lecture, stepped up for the abolishment of national funding of the arts, reasoning that art can be revolutionary, whereas the state cannot. Loos: "[...] The concern for art is an individual matter; it is the duty of the state to make it the concern of each individual [...] my conclusion appears to me concisely: if the state is already forced to concern itself with matters of art then it can only happen that preferences are given to inability or the genius is limited."[7]

At the end of the year Loos met the 19-year-old dancer Bessie Bruce, from England, on his nocturnal tour with Peter Altenberg at the Casino de Paris. She was also adored by Peter Altenberg. Loos was again successful and conquered the heart of the young woman, which made Peter Altenberg incredibly jealous. As a result, Loos' friendship with Peter Altenberg suffered a crisis which lasted for a few months. Bessie, in spite of her youth, was already sick with a lung ailment and had to give up her stage career. Out of the passionate love, a devoted life partnership developed.

After Loos had furnished some apartments equipped over the last years, he invited the public to two "housing migrations" in December 1907. In these migrations, he led an interested public through the apartments and two business premises designed by him to bring his work to the attention of others.

In 1908, Loos wrote his essay "Ornament and Crime", which was printed, however, in German for the first time only in 1929. In France it already appeared (in French translation) in 1913 in the magazine *Cahiers d'aujourd'hui*; thus, Le Corbusier had already taken note of Loos' thoughts and used them in his publications as a basis for his own thoughts. In this essay, Loos summarized his whole theory in a shortened literary form. "Ornament and Crime" probably developed on the occasion of the first art fair in Vienna, which was organized by Josef Hoffmann and curated by Gustav Klimt. The fair gave an overview of contemporary art forms: beaux-arts and applied arts.

Loos used the contents of the essay for lectures, and those held in Vienna and Munich were documented. Besides his written essays, he used his gift for lecturing to communicate his endeavor to the public. In whatever city he was, he would always be certain to find himself in front of large audiences and overcrowded halls. The audience did like very much the style of his lectures. He spoke freely and used no manuscripts, thus he could communicate intimately with the public. In the end, he would always prompt his audience to ask him questions in order to engage in a discussion with them. Later, when his hearing impairment progressed, he had slips of paper distributed during the lecture, on which one could write the questions.

Oskar Kokoschka was invited to exhibit at the first *Kunstschau*, but he was scornfully dismissed by critics as being over the top, raw and wild. Loos was immediately supportive of him, and promoted him from this moment on, throughout his life, wherever he could. He introduced Kokoschka to his circle of acquaintances and to his clients, and he convinced many of them to have themselves portrayed by Kokoschka. If the painting was not to the client's liking, Loos bought it, and so he always had a collection of the artist's paintings in his possession, which he gradually sold later, whenever he needed money urgently.

Bessie was in a sanatorium in Switzerland during this time, being treated for a severe tuberculosis. Loos paid for her stay and went to visit her frequently. He also sent Kokoschka to keep her company for a longer period of time.

## Loos Began Building in Vienna

In 1910, a public controversy was sparked concerning the smooth, exterior, plaster facade with simple cut-out windows on the Goldman & Salatsch building. The building is located on Michaelerplatz in the center of Vienna opposite the imperial Hofburg. The

Loos, 1903, 32 years old
Photo by Otto Mayer, Dresden
(From Rukschcio/Schachel, p. 80)

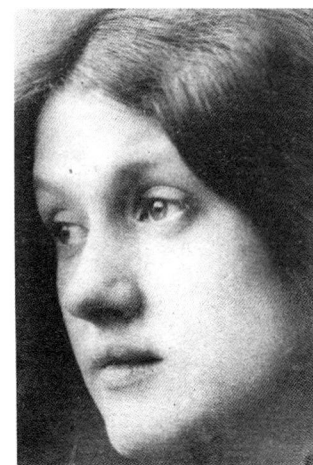

Bessie Bruce, 1905
(From Rukschcio/Schachel, p. 105)

Loos, winter 1912, 42 years old
(From Rukschcio/Schachel, p. 172)

Loos, 1914
(ALA 2073)

Loos and Grethe Hentschel, 1916
(From Rukschcio/Schachel, p. 208)

city council and the media attempted to force Loos to change his plans for the facade design. When he and his clients Leopold Goldman and Emanuel Aufricht refused to comply with the instructions, the city announced the renovation of the facades in the style of historicism. If the clients and builders did not agree on this style the city would call a competition for the construction of the facade. At the same time, the city threatened the client with high penalties should he implement Loos' design. The local press reported extensively on this case and made central contributions to the polemic tendencies of the debate.

Due to the ongoing stress caused by this project, Loos suffered another outbreak of his stomach condition, which had affected him previously in 1905 and 1908. He had to undergo treatment in a sanatorium. His recovery became very lengthy. Years later, he still nourished himself almost exclusively on ham with cream.

In the summer of 1911, a compromise was reached by Loos when he agreed to have flower pots attached to the window sills of the Goldman & Salatsch building.

In 1912 he founded the Adolf Loos Bauschule after he had been asked by a group of Otto Wagner's last students, led by R.M. Schindler, to apply as his successor for the professorship at the Academy of Arts. Otto Wagner had already exceeded the maximum age limit of 70 and was sent into retirement. Loos commented: "A ray of light in my life! [...] Of course, I was convinced of the futile nature of such an undertaking. But the confidence of our best youth gave me the energy needed to bring my own school into existence. This is how the 'Adolf Loos Bauschule' was conceived."[8]

This proved how much importance Adolf Loos attributed to teaching and education. It was a preference which propelled and motivated him his whole life and equally depressed him, because he could never reach the public status of a professor and thus general acknowledgment by the public.

The teaching was subdivided into the *three fields* of *art history*, *interior building* and *material science*, complimented by regular study trips whose scope was precisely specified in Loos' first curriculum.

Rudolf Schleicher, who hailed from Stuttgart, Germany, and who attended Loos' school of building, remembered his first discussion with Loos in his office: "Already on the stairs, a smooth metallic entrance door to the office struck me, which was painted with mirror-smooth, red tin paint. To me, that was the new spirit. [...] We spoke first about the furniture of the room, in which we stood: an old gothic cabinet, a conventional Biedermeier commode, even a baroque mirror on the wall – all objects originating from completely different times, which each held a special significance for Loos. That was new to me. So, the red tin door was, for me, the new world."[9]

Several times, Loos tried to create a private building school, whose permanence as an institution, however, did not stand a chance without national support.

In the year 1914, Loos furnished a small apartment for the young and beautiful former pupil of the Schwarzwald Schule, Grethe Hentschel. He had been in close contact with her for some time now. In 1915, Loos proposed to her, but she refused, probably due to her strictly Catholic upbringing and not having received her father's blessing. Both remained in touch all throughout their lives and maintained a good friendship.

In the year 1917 Loos' friendship with the 17-year-old Elsie Altmann began, also a student of the Schwarzwald Schule. She was taking dance classes with the Wiesenthal sisters, whose studio was in the same house where Loos had his office. In 1918 the two wished to get married and tried to obtain the necessary consent and documents. They succeeded in July 1919 and Elsie Altmann became Loos' second wife in his 48th year.

In May 1918 Loos suffered a hemoptysis, losing consciousness, and was brought to the hospital. The diagnosis was a possible occurrence of cancer. The doctors decided to perform surgery immediately and to remove Loos' entire stomach, his appendix and a large piece of his intestine. Loos' convalescence lasted over six months. Erich Mandl put him up at his house, which Loos had converted for him in 1916, and Mandl took care of him with the help of his family until Loos had regained complete health.

## After World War One

After the war, the monarchy dissolved and new nation states were founded. Loos took on Czechoslovakian citizenship and the first Austrian republic was founded.

His friend and client Gustav Scheu, whose family participated in the establishment of the social-democratic party in Austria, asked Loos to formulate new *Guidelines for a Ministry of Art*, in order to raise these suggestions during the discussion preceding the establishment of this office.

Loos availed himself of the help of Max Ermers, Karl Kraus, Leopold Liegler, Ludwig Münz and Arnold Schönberg, and on 28 March 1919 the *Guidelines for a Ministry of Art* were published by Richard Larny. The fundamental idea underlying these guidelines was the obligation of the state to bring the people as close to the artist as possible. Loos voiced his opinion, much in line with the principles of evolution, which he had always represented, that society was to develop and be cultivated until it would understand art and thereby stand in opposition to the concept of "applied art", which tries to bring art into society, thus making art useful. Loos put emphasis on the fact that the genius, who is mentally ahead his time, is obstructed by the useless promotion of the average. In his opinion, the state should aspire to increase the general education in order to follow the thoughts of the genius. Loos noted: "The resistance of mankind against their most prominent spirits will be stronger if the gap between society and artist is large. [...] The contemporaries of the artist belong to different periods. In the recent monarchy, the inhabitants situated themselves over the last thousand years [...]. The intellect of the state should create such an environment for the 'artist-being' [*Künstlermensch*] which offers him the smallest resistance. The smallest resistance will be posed by people who are his contemporaries, not just physically but also mentally: people of the twentieth century. The state, hence, has the obligation to bring society as close to the artist as possible. The state cannot provide any other support of the arts but this one."[10]

Also in 1919 R.M. Schindler once again contacted Loos from America and asked him to present the manuscript of Louis Sullivan's book entitled *Kindergarden Chats* to European publishers, because there was no opportunity to get the book published in America at the time. Louis Sullivan was completely impoverished at this time, which is why Schindler tried to help him. Loos accepted the manuscript but did not find a publisher. Later, Loos offered Sullivan to run his building school after the move from Vienna to Paris. Sullivan was interested but felt too old and instead wished to see photos of Loos' projects.

The same year, Loos organized an exhibition of the Swiss painter Johannes Itten. Itten, who had come to Vienna after his studies, was in touch with Arnold Schönberg, because he was searching for parallels between his color theory and the tone theory. Itten became acquainted with Walter Gropius in Vienna, who was married to Alma Mahler at that time. Gropius engaged Itten for the Bauhaus in Weimar, which was under construction at the time.

Loos advised his student Richard Neutra to go to America, where he met Schindler in Los Angeles. Schindler had been inspired to emigrate to America as well by Loos' favorable opinion and tales.

In 1920, Loos participated in the Salon d'Automne in Paris. He presented his project Hotel am Semmering.

Toward the end of the year, Bessie Bruce asked Loos to bring her back to her mother in England and together they traveled to London in early 1921. Up to that point Bessie had spent her time in lung sanatoriums in Switzerland, all of which had been paid for by Loos. In July Bessie died at the age of 35 at her mother's house in London.

After the first city council elections in Vienna in 1919, with the victory of the Social Democrats, Gustav Scheu became the city councilor for housing under mayor Reumann in Vienna. He immediately asked Loos to assist him in the department of housing by serving as his advisor. The department of housing was directed by Max Ermers, who had already cooperated with Loos on the *Guidelines for a Ministry of Art*. As Ermers later reported in his memoirs, he was completely fascinated with Loos' eagerness and enthusiasm in this task – a task for which he did not even receive payment in the first years. Only in 1921 did Scheu's push for Loos' paid employment succeed. In 1921 Loos was appointed chief architect in the department of housing – but he was only hired for the duration of one year. In the year 1922 Max Ermers resigned from the department of housing after internal disputes with the civil servants of city hall, whereupon Loos was offered his position. Loos did not wish to accept the offer to become a civil servant, because he felt the constant need to express his opinion freely. He did not talk it over with Elsie Altmann, but it was his housekeeper, Mitzi Schnabl, who convinced him to take on the position for financial reasons. Thus, Loos became the head of the department of housing but remained doubtful and reluctant to fully embrace this decision. In June

Loos with his second wife, Elsie Altmann, 1919
(From Rukschcio/Schachel, p. 238)

Loos, 1919, 49 years old
Photo by Franz Löwy, Vienna
(From Rukschcio/Schachel, p. 228)

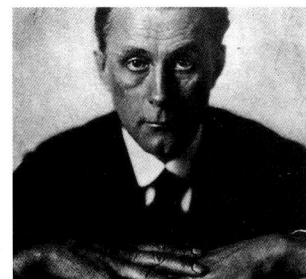

Loos, 1922, 52 years old
(From Rukschcio/Schachel, p. 258)

Loos, 1925
Photo by Trude Fleischmann
(ALA 2115)

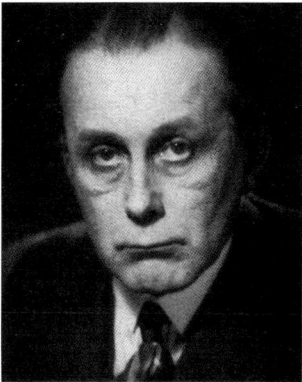

Loos in a photograph taken by Man Ray
in 1926 in Paris
(From Rukschcio/Schachel, p. 316)

Adolf Loos in his apartment, 59 years old
Photo by Claire Beck, 1929
(ALA 2116)

1924 there was a falling out with the municipality of Vienna, as the new emphasis in the department was affordable, multi-floor mass housing. Loos suggested a new typology, the so-called "terraced building". It consisted of a row of houses comprised of duplex units stacked on top of each other, each with its own terrace. The typology was a compromise, since Loos was convinced that people prefer to live in small houses. The "terraced building" did not find any supporters. Scheu, Ermers and Loos were inspired by the garden city and settler movement; however, mass housing in palace-like blocks of apartments became generally accepted at this time in Vienna. For Loos, it posed not an architectural or design question but a social, democratic question. In his view, the private possession of house and garden give the individual family more independency from economic crises.

In 1922, Loos participated in the competition for the new office building of the *Chicago Tribune* and submitted his legendary draft of a monumental Doric column in polished black granite.

## Leaving Vienna

In the summer of 1924, after the division with the City of Vienna, Loos decided to settle in Paris. He left Vienna with the hope and belief that his ideas would find a more fertile soil in Paris, as the culture there was more advanced than in Vienna. He wished to finally realize larger constructions, in which he could better apply his works within the spaces. He lived in Paris without a steady address, rather with regular stays in guest houses, hotels and the homes of friends. Loos was appreciated in Paris and had many contacts, mostly with emigrants; but he could not build in France, the only exceptions known till today are the Tzara House and the furnishing of the branch of the firm Kniže. During a visit to his Viennese studio in 1925, Loos ordered that the office at Beatrixgasse 25 be dissolved and all plans and documents be burned.

In March 1926, Elsie Altmann filed for a divorce and accepted an engagement in New York. Until then, Loos had always tried to convince her to move to Paris with him, although he had no work there, which didn't make the offer an interesting prospect for her. The sudden news of their divorce was a heavy blow to him, and in a letter to Mitzi Schnabl, he related how lonely he felt in Paris, where he did not understand the language. His hearing was greatly diminishing by the end of the 1920s, such that even with the aid of an ear-trumpet, conversation was difficult – from this point on, he was nearly deaf.

In 1928, Loos frequently stayed in Pilsen, where his long-time admirer, Otto Beck, a wire-fence manufacturer, arranged jobs for him from within his circle of acquaintances. By 1908, Loos had already furnished the homes of Otto Beck and his partner, Wilhelm Hirsch, in Pilsen. Loos was thus commissioned for the furnishing of a number of homes in Pilsen, and in this period he became acquainted with the Pilsener building contractor, Frantisek Müller, who planned to build a villa in Prague. Through these visits to the Beck home, Loos and Claire, Otto Beck's daughter, soon fell in love. At the time, the girl was 23 years old. Otto Beck was strictly opposed to this relationship, but Adolf and Claire were married nonetheless in July 1929.

In 1928 it happened that Loos was arrested by the police and released on bail four days later. According to Loos' statement, he casually addressed two young, bedraggled girls, whom he took into his home for a conversation, as he was the co-founder of a charitable foundation ("Haus in der Sonne" ["House in the Sun"] of Eugenie Schwarzwald), which made it possible for poor Viennese children to experience a vacation in France. But first, he invited them to take a bath, as cleanliness had always been a concern of his. This was Loos' account. The girls related the story to their parents, who consequentially made report and the police had Loos arrested. The press immediately publicized the case, which was widely discussed in Vienna. In the trial on 4 December, Loos was charged according to penal law §132/III, punishing the exposure of a minor to an obscene act, and sentenced to four months of strict arrest on probation. He was ultimately allowed to go home, as he was tried not guilty of the other charges.

At the end of 1929, Loos fell very ill after his return from Frankfurt, where he had hoped to obtain work in home and settlement construction, as Grethe Klimt, born Hentschel, who was living in Frankfurt at the time, took a strong interest in him. She introduced him as the successor of Ernst May, who intended to move to Moscow in 1930.

Loos was admitted to a sanatorium in Vienna and spent three months confined to bed, during which time Claire took care of him. In the spring of 1930, he once again had to undergo a longer cure in

Zuckmantel (Schlesien). In December 1930, there was a great celebration in Prague of his 60th birthday. Loos received countless recognitions and praises for his life's work from the press, from public representatives and, of course, from his friends and acquaintances. He was endowed from the Czechoslovakian government with an annuity to the tune of 10,000 crowns. In the evening, a ceremony was held at the Müller Villa.

In 1931 he again brought Claire to Paris for a longer stay, in which they made many long stops in Germany, Italy and southern France. His hopes of receiving new jobs were not fulfilled, and Loos focused all of his expectations on his arrival in Paris; however, when promised projects were again cancelled, Loos broke down inside with disappointment and bitterness. Thereby, his relationship with Claire came to an end in 1931.

In late summer, his health again declined drastically, and he had to be admitted to a sanatorium for nervous and emotional disorders near Prague.

In February 1932 his divorce with Claire ensued. Loos again returned to Vienna and later spent time in various institutions in Austria and in Czechoslovakia. On 3 December 1932, during a trip to Vienna, he suffered a heart attack and was admitted to the Rosenhügel sanatorium. His friends and former clients, such as Scheu, Moller, Steiner and more plus Mitzi Schnabl, took care of him, although he hardly recognized them any more. He died in Vienna in utter poverty on 23 August 1933 at the age of 62, probably due to remote damages from the contraction of syphilis.

Loos, 1931-32, 61 years old
Photo by Emil Theis, Dessau,
from Gustav Schindler's legacy
(From Rukschcio/Schachel, p. 380)

[1] Burkhardt Rukschcio, Roland Schachel, *Adolf Loos. Leben u. Werk*, Residenz Verlag, Salzburg 1982 [from here on R+S], p. 20 (Engl. trans. L.S.).

[2] Adolf Loos [from here on A.L.], "Der Silberhof und seine Nachbarschaft", in *N.F.P.*, Wien, 15 May 1898, R+S, p. 24 (Engl. trans. L.S.).

[3] A.L., "Men's Fashion" (22 May 1898), in *Ornament and Crime*, Ariadne Press, Riverside, 1998, p. 39; original text "Die Herrenmode", in *N.F.P.*, Wien, 22 May 1898; R+S, p. 27.

[4] A.L., "Das Luxusfuhrwerk", in *N.F.P.*, Wien, 1898 (Engl. trans. L.S.).

[5] A.L., undated manuscript fragment from R+S (Engl. trans. L.S.).

[6] A.L., "Das Leben, Ein Blatt zur Einführung der abendländischen Kultur in Österreich", Classified ad in *Die Zukunft*, Berlin, 30 January 1904; R+S, p. 85 (Engl. trans. L.S.).

[7] A.L., unpublished manusscript, R+S, p. 102 (Engl. trans. L.S.).

[8] A.L., "Meine Bauschule", in *Der Architekt*, 29, 10, Wien, October 1913 (Engl. trans. L.S.).

[9] Gustav Schleicher, *Antworten auf 9 Fragen*, typoscript from 10 June 1970, in R+S, p. 172 (Engl. trans. L.S.).

[10] A.L., "Richtlinien für ein Kunstamt", in *Der Friede*, vol. III, no. 62, Wien, 1919 (Engl. trans. L.S.).

Loos with his third wife, Claire Beck, 1929
(From Rukschcio/Schachel, p. 350)

Loos in front of his fireplace with an ear-trumpet in his hands, 1929
Photo by Claire Beck

Loos on the terrace of the Rosenhügel Sanatorium, Vienna, 1932
(From Rukschcio/Schachel, p. 387)

Covers of the two issues of Loos' magazine *Das Andere* and of the brochure *Wohnungswanderungen*

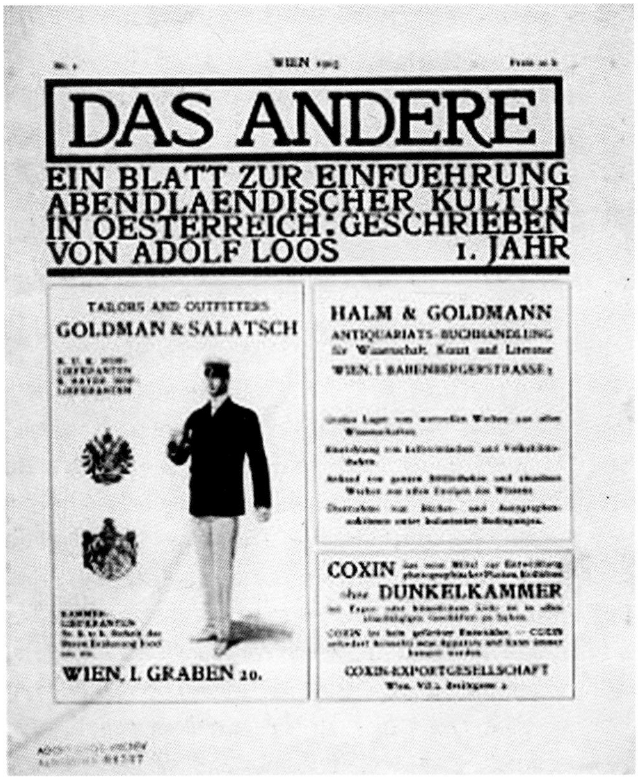

WIEN 1903

DAS ANDERE

EIN BLATT ZUR EINFUEHRUNG ABENDLAENDISCHER KULTUR IN OESTERREICH: GESCHRIEBEN VON ADOLF LOOS 1. JAHR

TAILORS AND OUTFITTERS
GOLDMAN & SALATSCH

WIEN, I. GRABEN 20.

HALM & GOLDMANN
ANTIQUARIATS-BUCHHANDLUNG
für Wissenschaft, Kunst und Literatur
WIEN, I. BABENBERGERSTRASSE 1

COXIN
DUNKELKAMMER

COXIN-EXPORTGESELLSCHAFT

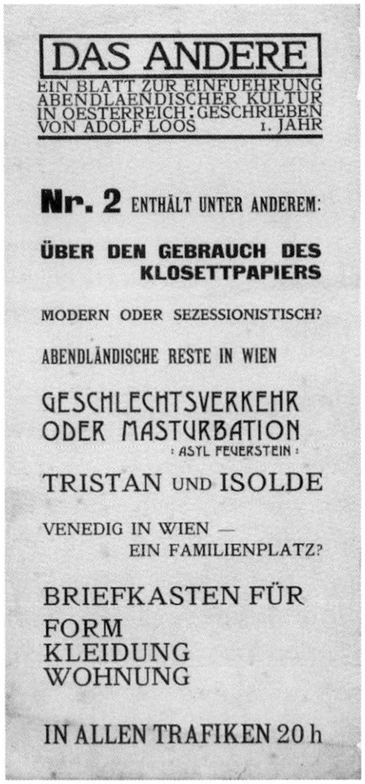

DAS ANDERE

EIN BLATT ZUR EINFUEHRUNG ABENDLAENDISCHER KULTUR IN OESTERREICH: GESCHRIEBEN VON ADOLF LOOS 1. JAHR

**Nr. 2** ENTHÄLT UNTER ANDEREM:

ÜBER DEN GEBRAUCH DES KLOSETTPAPIERS

MODERN ODER SEZESSIONISTISCH?

ABENDLÄNDISCHE RESTE IN WIEN

GESCHLECHTSVERKEHR ODER MASTURBATION
: ASYL FEUERSTEIN :

TRISTAN UND ISOLDE

VENEDIG IN WIEN —
EIN FAMILIENPLATZ?

BRIEFKASTEN FÜR
FORM
KLEIDUNG
WOHNUNG

IN ALLEN TRAFIKEN 20 h

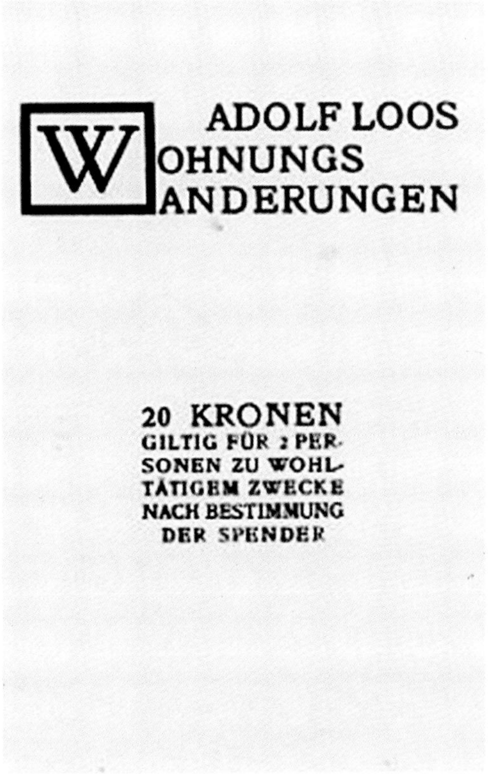

ADOLF LOOS
WOHNUNGS
WANDERUNGEN

20 KRONEN
GILTIG FÜR 2 PERSONEN ZU WOHLTÄTIGEM ZWECKE NACH BESTIMMUNG DER SPENDER

# Written Work

*I don't like people call me "architect".*
*Simply "Adolf Loos" is my name.*[1]

## General

Loos' body of written work is made up of essays, articles and speeches. Although it is not a coherent theoretical work, the collection does illuminate Loos' perspectives and findings on a variety of topics. Taken together, his writings present a complex perspective on creative themes and cultural questions. I recommend that everyone read these short essays, which are written in a simple, clear, and humorous language. Using understandable, everyday examples, they reveal like an X-ray the essence of things as Loos viewed them, resulting in surprising and clear insights.

Robert Scheu, brother of Gustav Scheu and a longtime friend of Loos, expressed his fascination with Loos' writing: "[…] Loos actually never made jokes and was dead serious about everything. And despite that [his words] had an unspeakably amusing effect. To me, Loos was the most amusing person that I had ever met. Wit and truth in a form that made them both bearable. […] I differentiate among three types of writers. With the first type, I say to myself, 'If that had occurred to me, I would have stopped myself from writing it down.' As to the second type: 'Why didn't I write that? I had the very same thought.' The third type makes me think, 'Why didn't I ever think of that?' Only the last type is truly interesting, and Adolf Loos belongs to this group. His thoughts do not summarize in words that which has long wrestled within us for expression, but instead they are surprises that put us to shame."[2] It must be noted that Loos had already written the basis of his essays between 1897 and 1900, before he began his work as an outfitter and architect. In the years between his return from America and the construction of the House on Michaelerplatz (1910), he limited his assignments to the interior design of apartments, shops, cafés and bars. Even for the renovation of Villa Karma, he was hired only to do the interior decoration. He delivered the renovation and the facade designs without payment. Up to its building phase, which began in 1910, he wrote most of the articles, using them as a basis for his architectural work.

The profound analytical capacity and farsightedness that characterized Loos' experience of his early years demonstrate an astounding maturity. He laid out his formal agenda in writing before having any building experience. The essays served as an opportunity to explain his viewpoint, beginning with the critique of existing conditions. But beyond the criticism, which could be devastating, he presented his view from the ground up and demonstrated new paths. He succeeded in equally dismantling the "preservationists" as well as the "rebels" with his critique, and he forged a new path that not only respected tradition, but even inevitably built itself upon it, taking into consideration the necessary improvements regarding use and function. These thoughts were built upon the theory of evolution that today scientifically and indisputably describe the basic principle of biological development. By transferring the principle of evolution to architecture and the arrangement of spatial areas and objects, he placed himself not only in opposition to the conservative guard, which wished to secure the situation, but also against the radical new thinkers, who searched for independent, new, and unique solutions by breaking with the past.

He had no qualms in copying everyday objects that had emerged in the past and which continue to completely satisfy our demands, utilizing them just as they were intended in their own times. An example would be the Chippendale dining-set chair that Loos felt was the quintessential and most comfortable chair for sitting while eating, which he therefore used repeatedly. We find things from every cultural epoch in his interiors, from an Egyptian stool to a naked light bulb. According to Loos: "[...] everything created in earlier times can be copied today provided it is still usable. For the form of new phenomena in our culture (railway carriages, telephones, typewriters, etc.) solutions must be found that *do not consciously echo* a past style. Changing old objects to adapt them to modern needs is not permissible. We must either copy or create something completely new. By that, however, I do not mean the new must be the opposite of what was before."[3]

Loos emphasized English culture, which he found superior. For him, this was based on several facts. English industry aimed to manufacture high-quality objects that were perfect and appropriate to their purposes. The product was convincing because of its quality and therefore marketable worldwide. It was likewise economically advantageous because the manufacturer could sell a high-quality, well-adapted product at a higher price. For the buyer, the advantage was that the product lasted substantially longer than a cheaply produced or fashionable product that one would be forced to replace after a short time. Because English products fit their purpose, one had in one's wardrobe – to use Loos' example – many suits that one could wear according to the occasion, without wearing them out quickly. To Loos, this was thriftiness: preserving the resources of material and expended labour by creating a product with a long life expectancy.

He believed that in this way, people who could afford objects with top quality materials and workmanship would become richer and those who purchased cheap and fashionable objects would become poorer. Loos wanted to educate people by raising their culture so that they would understand these connections and create a basis that would allow them to be able to purchase high-quality products. In this context, Loos saw it as essential for workers to secure their own property and house. With garden work and animal husbandry, they could, to a large extent, care for themselves independently and better withstand times of crisis. With

financial savings, they could buy quality products and furnishings, or use the money for their education or that of their children. He was convinced that owning a house with land was the natural ambition of free people because it made them independent.

This is the intellectual background that motivated Loos to engage himself in the settler movement. He did not tire of stressing that formal design played a secondary role; everything had to be tied to its purpose and developed from there. The budget available to the settler was small and the houses had to be partially completed with one's internal labour. The settlement and the house had to be planned according to the fruit and vegetable garden's specifications, because self-sustaining and the therein related community uses were the central facts. This is one main idea of the ethical concerns that underlay the educational ideas of Loos.

Loos saw that people always strove for better and higher standards; hence the leading social class, or the aristocracy,[4] was responsible for providing the population with good examples with which to orient themselves. Expressed in Loos' words: "Every barber wants to look like a count, while a count would never strive to look like a barber."[5] In this manner, Loos also established his villa work and his clientele from among the cultivated and influential upper middle class. Luxury items also justified themselves and fell into his economic considerations: "Luxury is a very necessary thing. Quality craftsmanship has to be paid for by someone. And this luxury industry, which only serves a select few, is similar to what I have said about the best runner and the best high jumper – that for this perfection of production, at least a small handful of the most capable craftsmen has to arduously succeed – through talent and persistence. That must be exemplary of the best human ability. Otherwise, each and every field goes downhill. [...] Without outstanding people, we would never achieve anything above the average."[6]

This is a short summary of some substantial trains of thought which, during a continuous reading of Loos' articles, assemble into an all-encompassing thought pattern like a puzzle, piece by piece.

Next I would like to give an overview of written works and afterwards, the key concepts that Loos employed, illustrated by citations and short com-

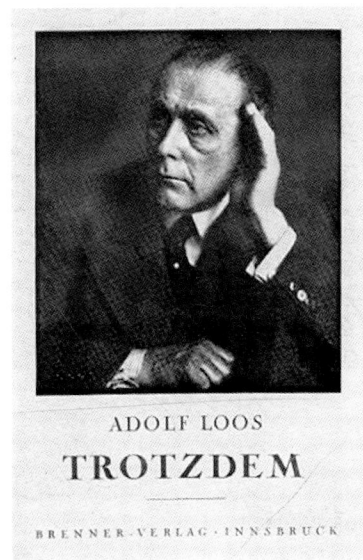

First-edition covers of the two volumes
of essays and articles by Loos

ments. In the following chapters, these key concepts, in relationship to his creative work, will be thoroughly addressed.

The writings of Loos are gathered in three editions:

1: *Ins Leere gesprochen*, first edition 1921, Georges Crès & Cie, Zürich-Paris

These are the articles published by Adolf Loos between 1897 and 1900, which he wrote immediately after returning to Vienna from America. In 1898 Loos wrote a series of articles related to the Viennese Anniversary Exhibit for the Austrian newspaper *Neue Freie Presse*. It is not known how Loos, without references, managed to gain this opportunity to write for what was at the time the most famous (and rather conservative) paper. In these articles, he expressed his understanding and opinions to numerous readers and established his position among architects in all German-speaking countries. They form the basis of his written work.

Before this, he had published essays in *Die Wage* and in *Die Zeit*, and later in the *Wiener Tagblatt*.

This essay collection, assembled by Loos, was first published in German in 1921 by Georges Crès & Cie, based in Zurich and Paris. This was more than 20 years after the articles' original appearance, because initially no publisher had been ready for it, and later Loos put it off.

In the preface to the first edition, Loos explained why the edition first appeared two decades later: "Over the years many German publishers have made me offers to publish these articles. But I was against it. These essays were written for one time and in one newspaper, and I had a thousand things to think about. For didactic reasons, I had to express my true opinions in sentences that years later still cause me to shudder as I read them. But even this watered-down way of writing has earned me the reputation, not from the philistines but from the 'modern' artists, of attacking the *modern* through a paradoxical way of writing. Only at the insistence of my dear students, especially the architect Otto Breuer, have I decided to consent to the publication of these essays."[7]

The title, *Spoken into the Void*, revealed a bit of resignation on the part of Loos, who suffered a lack of recognition for his ideas and as a result, jobs as an architect. He knew that much of what he had analyzed and prophesized had already been realized or had changed its direction; however, he desired public acknowledgment, since it was he who had begun the public discussion about modern society in Austria.

2: *Trotzdem*, first edition 1931, Brenner, Innsbruck

These are his writings from 1900 to 1930. The articles had been printed in various publications over the years or were extracted from Loos' lectures. They were not intended as a cohesive work, but were written for individual occasions.

This volume also contains the famous essay "Ornament and Crime", which was written in 1908 as a lecture on the occasion of the first *Kunstschau* in Vienna, created by Josef Hoffmann and headed by Gustav Klimt. However, the article was first published in German in the 24 October 1929 edition of the *Frankfurter Zeitung*.

Loos compiled the articles, his publisher friend Ludwig von Ficker, owner of Brenner Publishing Innsbruck, accepted them, and Karl Kraus suggested the title: *Trotzdem* [*Regardless*] in reference to a quote from Nietzsche: "Das Entscheidende geschieht trotzdem", that is "The essential happens regardless". Loos had first considered the titles, "Wer Ohren hat der höre" ["Who has ears hears"] and "Ins Volle getroffen" ["Direct Hit"].

3: *Die Potemkinsche Stadt*, first edition 1983, Georg Prachner Verlag, Wien

This volume contains essays from the years 1897 to 1933 – Loos' entire creative period – that were not included in the first two volumes, *Ins Leere gesprochen* [*Spoken into the Void*] and *Trotzdem* [*Regardless*].

All these essays had already been printed in newspapers or magazines during Loos' lifetime. Among the volume's contents are the two issues of the magazine *Das Andere* and the *Guidelines for a Ministry of Art*.

## Stylistic Device

The dominating stylistic device in Loos' writings was the polemic with which he attacked the groups who opposed his thinking. One can account for it through his personality, but it was also a result of his position. Without holding a public office, it was difficult for an architect in Vienna to be heard. He could not gain the professorship position he desired because he had never completed the academic requirements, and because he was temporarily legally incapacitated in his youth. The polemic was aimed particularly at architects, professors of applied arts (especially Josef Hofmann), academically trained artists, and members of the Secession and the Deutscher Werkbund. *against architects.*

(As an example, I would like to present the polemic about architects: "The mason and the master builder were also placed under tutelage. The master builder just built houses and that was called building in the style of his own times. The one who took control was the man who could build in the style of every past age, the man who had lost contact with his own times, the rootless man, the warped man, in a word, the architect.)

"Books meant little to the craftsman. The architect took everything from books. An abundance of works of reference provided everything and anything worth knowing. People have no idea of the way this mass of slick publishing ventures has poisoned our urban culture, the way it has prevented us from remembering who and what we are. [...] The effect was always the same: an abomination. And there was no end to the abomination. Everyone was desperate to see their things perpetuated in the new publications and a large number of architectural periodicals appeared to satisfy the vanity of architects. And so it has remained to the present day.

"There is another reason why the architect has ousted the craftsman. He has learned draftsmanship, and since that is all he has learnt, he is good at it. The craftsman is not. He has a heavy hand. [...]

("The architect has reduced the noble art of building to a graphic art. The one who receives the most commissions is not the one who can build best but the one whose work looks best on paper. And these both are antipodes."[8])

Organizations, societies, and professional groups were not the only target of his polemic. He also repeatedly snubbed the Viennese, Austrians, and the Germans with international comparisons, saying that they must be more open in order to gain international competitiveness. Loos always wanted to open the markets – local thinking was not successful with his demarcated politics. Someone who manufactured products that were in international demand would have long-term success. But to achieve this economic goal, the education of the people to a higher cultural level had to be reached first. Loos regarded this as his mission.

## Themes in his Criticism

In order to approach the themes of his written work, I would like to briefly sketch the historic background that Loos faced when he returned from America in 1896. This will explain what he stood for and who he challenged in order to create tolerance for his thoughts so that he could build as an architect.

At the time, buildings in Vienna were being constructed in the style of historicism and eclecticism, which was promoted by academics. Loos considered those architects and professors "philistines". They were well educated in art history and drawing skills, and they could imitate all styles of historical architecture and adapt them to their purposes and needs.

Opposing them were the "modernists". Just as well educated with drawing, they were members of the Secession, which would later join with the Wiener Werkstätten. Around the turn of the century, the movement would be led by Gustav Klimt and represented through the architects Josef Hoffmann, Joseph Maria Olbrich, and Josef Plecnik. All three architects were Otto Wagner's students. The Secession followed the Jugendstil movement and was inspired by the ideal of the total work of art (*Gesamtkunstwerk*). Everything should be created by artists' hands through the integration of arts, from architecture to interior design, from every day objects to clothing and jewelry. The Wiener Werkstätten wanted to bring art close to the people, by bringing it into everyday life with products developed by artists and executed by good craftsmen at the highest level of quality.

Standing over these movements was Otto Wagner, who was a generation older and had already created a large body of work. He, too, sensed that a change was going to be necessary in architecture. Indeed, he sought his own path, which he also explained at length in 1896 with the book *Moderne Architektur* (*Modern Architecture*). Loos did not attack Wagner, but respected him. ("But in the face of Otto Wagner's genius I capitulate."[9])

## Art and Culture

Loos was convinced that, penetrated by arts and crafts, no useful everyday object could be produced,

Stoclet Palace by Josef Hoffmann, Brussels, 1906: breakfast room as total work of art (*Gesamtkunstwerk*)

Stoclet Palace, Brussels, 1906: tableware of breakfast room designed by Josef Hoffmann

because under the dictate of the artist, it would not be conceived according to functional criteria, nor would the appropriate materials be used. To Loos, every useful form had an evolutionary development and arose with the knowledge and experience of generations. This knowledge was passed on through craft guilds. Therefore, Loos was for the strict separation of art and craftsmanship. According to Loos, every generation will conform everyday objects to its own requirements, but this occurs through experience and necessity over the course of time and needs no originating artistic blueprint.

"I say the work of art is eternal, the handcraft is fleeting. The effect of the work of art is spiritual, the effect of the practical object is material. The work of art is consumed by the spirit, and is therefore not subject to deterioration through use; the practical object is used materially and thereby consumed."[10]

He wanted to limit the term "art" in architecture, and thereby limit the activity of the architect as an "artist" to a few building assignments: "A building should please everyone, unlike a work of art, which does not have to please anyone. A work of art is a private matter for the artist, a building is not. A work of art is brought into the world without there being a need for it, a building meets a need. A work of art has no responsibility to anyone, a building to everyone. The aim of a work of art is to make us feel uncomfortable, a building is there for our comfort. A work of art is revolutionary, a building conservative. A work of art is concerned with the future and directs us along new paths. A building is concerned with the present [...] So the building has nothing to do with art and architecture is not one of the arts? That is so. Only a tiny part of architecture comes under art: monuments. Everything else, everything that serves some practical purpose, should be ejected from the realm of art."[11]

Loos thus stripped the art academy-trained architects, the "philistines" and the "modernists", of their ascendancy in the field of architecture.

He wanted to free not only the craftsmen, but all of humanity from the dictates of the artists. He wanted to inform them about culture so that for their everyday life, they would no longer need the "academic artists", whom he painted as "cultureless". With Loos, the term culture implies the inclusion of tradition; simply creating something new is a pure

artistic act. The cultural education of the people was his primary goal. Therefore, he wanted to give them examples or hold talks on "going, standing, sitting, lying, sleeping, eating, living and dressing! Learn to dwell! The elimination of furniture! Ornament and crime!" and so on. The mundane was a frequent theme in Loos' lectures and writings, and it was the everyday actions and objects, such as clothing, that he would use as examples to illustrate the current state of western culture in other countries, mostly in England and in America. His elegant clothing and his appearance lent him the credibility of a cosmopolitan.

In one of his theses, Loos said that if the people were made familiar with 20th-Century culture, as he had seen it in America, ornament would disappear through this evolutionary development: "The inability of our culture to create new ornament is a sign of its greatness. The evolution of humanity goes hand in hand with the disappearance of ornamentation from objects of everyday use. Whatever our applied artists, prompted by the survival instinct, may say, for people of culture a face without a tattoo is more beautiful than one with a tattoo, even if it has been designed by Kolo Moser himself. And the people of culture also want not only their skin but also their book bindings and bedside tables protected from the Indian ornamental frenzy of these state-appointed cultural barbarians."[12] And elsewhere: "The evolution of culture is synonymous with the removal of ornamentation from objects of everyday use."[13]

In 1919 he also attacked the academic training of artists in *Guidelines for a Ministry of Art*. In it, he spoke out against any kind of artistic funding because the "great spirits" would prevail regardless, as they have received their gift from God. Therefore, their works and actions would be applied equally to a mission that they are obliged to follow, overcoming all opposition. In order to keep society's resistance against genius as slight as possible (because the spirit is also bound to the body and therefore not eternal), it is the singular duty and assignment of the state to teach people about culture so that they can follow the "great spirits". Loos saw the "great spirits" as prophets and bound their work with God's mission. He drew up the hierarchy of design as follows: "[...] With that, I was referring to the correlation between the inner and outer culture. The way is: God created the artist, the artist creates time, time creates the craftsman, the craftsman creates the button. If from a folk nothing is left but a button, then it is possible for me to conclude something, through the form of this button on the clothing and objects of this people, regarding their customs and their religion, their art and their spirituality. How important this button is!"[14]

Taking the thought further, it follows that one cannot be trained as an artist; one must be born as an artist. That is why he, with exaggeration, called artists trained in applied art "prostitutes of art", to which he also counted architects.

Loos' second argument as to why true art cannot be taught by the state is that art can be revolutionary, and therefore stand against the state's interests. Thus when teachers are chosen, the best artists are not taken into account, and therefore the results of an artistic education are only mediocre. The consequence for society is that all the objects drafted by applied artists and architects and turned into products by handworkers are uneconomical, since their natural sense of adapting to a situation has been lost through their training; capital and labor are senselessly wasted. They instead always follow loftier theories and artistic ideals, as Loos explains in the following excerpt on architects: "May I take you to the shores of a mountain lake? [...] But what is this? A discordant note in the tranquility. Like an unnecessary screech. Among the locals' houses, that were not built by them, but by God, stands a villa. The creation of an architect. Whether a good or bad architect, I don't know. All I know is that the tranquility, peace and beauty have vanished. [...] And therefore I ask, why is it that any architect, good or bad, desecrates the lake? The farmer doesn't. Nor does the engineer who builds a railway along the shore or scores deep furrows in its clear surface with his ship. [...] Like almost all city dwellers, the architect lacks culture. He lacks the sure touch of the farmer, who does possess culture."[15]

One could summarize Loos' view of the dilemma of state training for artists with the following description: not called to a higher cause, deprived of natural innocence, and therefore superficial. Through his initiative of cultural education and his understanding of the role of the higher classes of society in setting examples, Loos pursued his goal of liberating the people to the degree that they could then make decisions for themselves in furnishing their apartments.

Reading the attacks on the applied artists and the praises of artists freely chosen by God, one senses that this perspective reveals parallels to Loos' own life, particularly to his lonesome struggle against the Secession and later the Wiener Werkstätten under Josef Hoffmann, professor of the academy of applied arts. Seen from this perspective, the *Guidelines for a Ministry of Art* also served as a justification of his own personal situation and a defamation of his opponent. Loos himself did not wish to be called an architect; he described himself as a mason who had studied Latin. Clearly, at the bottom of this is the reproof that his occupation concerned craftsmanship and Roman culture rather than academic training.

### Tradition and Progress
*And what I've said against the "historic sickness" I said as one who learned to recover from it slowly and painfully; and by no means was I going to abandon "history" in the future because I had once suffered from it.* (Friedrich Nietzsche)[16]

Loos believed that tradition and truth in the last centuries in Austria and Germany had been hidden and blocked by "academic applied artists" and "philistines". He wanted to lead people back to the tradition that they had lost in the 19th Century. To him, our tradition had roots in Roman antiquity: "At the beginning of the 19th Century we departed from tradition. That is where I want to go back to."[17]

In terms of architecture, these starting points were the works of Fischer von Erlach, Gottfried Semper, and Karl Friedrich Schinkel. "Our culture is founded on the recognition of the all-transcending greatness of classical antiquity. Our manner of thinking and feeling we have adopted from the Romans, who taught us to think socially and discipline our emotions. [...] The present should build on the past, just as the past built on previous generations. It was never otherwise, nor will it ever be. It is the truth that I am teaching [...]."[18]

Loos used tradition as a basis for his consideration that the fundament of our origin gives us our inner security, but he avoided accepting tradition as an absolute truth; when the development of the culture is already advanced, the adaptation of formal elements from past styles to modern objects is ridiculous. As an example, he points to costumes as well as facade decorations.

His conception of tradition was less directed at formal concerns; it interested him far more to understand the thought processes used by Roman culture to achieve their solutions. The Romans thought logically, constructively, and efficiently; they were well organized and could thus build and administer the great Roman Empire. Were this not the case, Roman culture would never have been implemented in so many provinces, and it certainly would not have left such contributions in these former provinces as have persisted through the present day.

For Loos, it was certain that every era has to find its own solutions, especially in times of rapid technical progress. Indeed, this can not be achieved with a uniform, formal, artistic style that is stuck onto everything: "They are so much in the style of our age that – and this is the only criterion – we do not see them as being in a 'style'."[19]

The forms of everyday objects can not be determined by single artists or by artistic organizations. Hence, the 1908 founding of the Deutscher Werkbund, in which applied artists and architects joined in cooperation with industry to develop their products, was, in his opinion, redundant.

Loos dismissed this attempt as a false path with the same reasoning he used to reject the influence of artists on craftsmen, in terms of the total work of art, through the integration of the Secessionist artists with the Wiener Werkstätten: "We have our culture, we have the forms in which our life takes place, and the utensils that make those lives possible. No individual, nor any organization, created our cupboards for us, our cigarette cases, our jewelry. Time created them for us and they change from year to year, from day to day, from hour to hour. From hour to hour we change too, our opinions, our habits; and that leads to changes in our culture. But the members of the Werkbund are confusing cause and effect. We do not sit in a particular way because a cabinetmaker has made a chair in this or that way, the cabinetmaker makes the chair in a particular way that we can sit comfortable, because that is the way we want to sit. And that means – to the delight of everyone who loves our culture – the activities of the Werkbund are completely ineffective".[20]

Loos developed the designation "the redundants" in reference to the members of the Deutscher Werkbund (incidentally, Josef Hoffmann actively took part in its founding).

Loos also clearly defined for himself when something was allowed to be copied and when something had to be created new: "My pupils know that change from the traditional way of doing things is only permissible if the change is an improvement. And the improvements, the new inventions are tearing huge holes in the tradition, in the traditional way of building. The new inventions – the electric light, the *Holzzement* roof [wood-cement roof; a first construction type for a flat roof]– do not belong to one particular region, they belong to the whole world."[21] And elsewhere: "[...] everything created in earlier times can be copied today provided it is still usable. For the form of new phenomena in our culture (railway carriages, telephones, typewriters, etc.) solutions must be found that do not consciously echo a past style."[22]

Loos' position on progress on the basis of tradition, which also appeared in his work, earned him the criticism of the "modernists", for whom Loos' architectural work was not radical enough in breaking with tradition. Indeed, Loos considered critiques such as the following as praise, since it was his desire to achieve exactly that for which the critics reproached him: "And in this delusion I am further strengthened by the hostile criticism of the modern artist, who says, 'He thinks he's a modern architect, yet he builds a house like the old Viennese.'"[23]

The following remarks, made on the occasion of his 60th birthday, support just how seriously Loos' work and writings were regarded by other high-ranking representatives of the "classic modern".

*Walter Gropius*

"Adolf Loos is a seer. At a time when everything still lay in the slumber of shallow eclecticism, he predicted, from the loneliest of positions, the future developments whose realizations we are now approaching in what is today called functional building. [...]Just how much the Imperial era held his battlesome courage against him is attested by the fact that *Spoken into the Void*, his far-seeing and still valid essays written between 1897 and 1900 for the *Neue Freie Presse* in Vienna, did not find a publisher, neither in Austria nor in Germany. Only after the War did they appear in the German language, published by Crès in France in 1921.

("Loos himself built little. He did not gain recognition, but when he sums up his life on his 60th birthday, he will have the satisfaction that his most important demands, 'spoken into the void' at the end of the last century, have already been heard by a whole generation."[24])

Gropius praises only the theoretical work of Loos and recognizes his courage in the lonely struggle against historicism that he was the first to lead. He portrays him as the one who paved the way for functional construction, an appraisal that Loos fiercely fought against in his lifetime. Already in 1924 he wrote: "By that, I did not mean what some purists have carried ad absurdum, namely that ornaments should be systematically and consistently eliminated."[25]

Loos was forced to qualify the criticism that he had polemically and radically formulated in writing in 1908 with "Ornament and Crime", since in his own work, he always aimed to create a mood appropriate to the use of the interiors, which for him was not possible with plain, white walls. The essay "Ornament and Crime" was widely disseminated, and it resonated with a great echo. It drew a picture of Loos as a radical, uncompromising rebel, a picture that did not quite coincide with his architectural and written work. Herein certainly lies buried a large part of his personal tragedy. Everyone rightly recognized that the predictions he made at the end of the 19th Century had come to be; yet nevertheless, he felt misunderstood and that his architectural work found little international attention and was barely publicized.

The quick, worldwide rise of the "classic modern" as a new style was certainly partially responsible for this. As with all other earlier architecture-collecting movements, he would not let himself be taken in by it. The common theoretical foundation of the classic modern movement was, among other things, the complete break with traditional styles as a countermovement to historicism, and here Loos' more complex perspectives on tradition and progress no longer fit the new picture. Mies van der Rohe did not invite Loos in 1927 to the Werkbund housing exhibition *Am Weissenhof* in Stuttgart, although Loos had absolutely counted on it, having, from his own point of view, something truly new to contribute to "residing in space".

## Le Corbusier

"In the middle of our architectural problems in 1913, Loos suddenly appeared with a splendid article, 'Ornament and Crime'. We found ourselves at the closing of a sentimental period: we had found the connection to nature again and had completely conquered the new technologies (iron and concrete construction, new machines, new materials). All that meant the crucial break with the past, which had been tended artificially by the academies, and a longing preparation for a future. Loos swept beneath our feet with a Homeric cleansing – strict, philosophical and lyrical. In this way Loos influenced our architectural fate."[26]

Le Corbusier refers only to Loos' written work and its impact in overcoming historicism; he does not once mention Loos' architectural work. With the phrase, "Loos swept under our feet," he expressed that Loos no longer stood on the same level with the modernist movement in 1930 since, unlike Le Corbusier, he did not entirely consummate the break with the past. The revolutionary, idealistic standpoint that Le Corbusier took up in his writing and work was foreign to Loos, whose thoughts were certainly evolutionary, concrete, and above all oriented towards the well-being of the user. This manifests the difference between the works of these two important architects at the beginning of the 20th Century and also the heterogeneity within the so-called "modernist" movement.

## Sigfried Giedion

Sigfried Giedion was a proponent of what in the 1920s was called "New Construction". Educated as an engineer and art historian, he was not only a member of this movement but also its spokesperson and living historian. His major work, *Die Herrschaft der Mechanisierung* [*Mechanization Takes Command*], appeared in 1948. In it he presents a large, historical treatise on the effects of increasing mechanization in all areas of life, and how it has fundamentally changed our culture: "We invited Loos to Brussels. Untraceable. Always on the road. One cannot get a hold of him. Neither personally nor objectively. He is a prophet. He is ingenious to an end in itself. Kindred with Michelangelo, but also with Oscar Wilde. A rental house on Michaelerplatz. Below: powerful columns and green-speckled marble. Above: smooth, scraped off! One can sense how he thought, 'They are going to be so annoyed!' But at the same time, he cleaned up architecture. He helped many, primarily the most important ones today, because he showed them, 'that's the way'. A pathfinder. His work is not continuous, [...] but he has moments. In these moments he saw more boldly, cogently, and further than any who began with him. There is no architect living today who doesn't carry a piece of Loos in him. Is that enough?"[27]

Giedion also sees Loos' theoretical work first and foremost; he is either not thoroughly familiar with his architectural work, or it does not suit his branded and representative picture of "functional style" and therefore is not "continuous" to him. Just like Le Corbusier, he sees Loos only as a "forerunner" because in the House on Michaelerplatz he used, in appendages, in the upper portion, the functional facade. An examination of the complexity of Loos' works has not yet taken place at this point. It is rather a selection of Loos-like thoughts to represent his own conviction, and everything that does not suit his own realm of thought is left out.

Thus Loos' international recognition remains reduced to a few ideas. An understanding and acceptance of the complete work of Adolf Loos is still lacking at that time.

## Material and Quality

Two impressive characteristics in his architectural work are the choice of material and the high quality of craftsmanship in the treatment of the materials used. To this point, Loos writes in his essays: "I have formulated the following principle: The form of an object should last as long as, that is, we find it tolerable as long as, the object itself lasts."[28]

With this, Loos means the quality of the processing and the formal composition must be chosen so that, for example, a wooden desk lasts as long as the life expectancy of the wood from which it is manufactured. In this endeavor, the object must remain fashionable for this entire period, while still fulfilling its functional requirements – requirements which must be considered in its formal design. Correspondingly, a superior craftsmanship is sought in the processing of materials.

Therefore, the goal is to always strive for the best quality and the most suitable material for the required use. In the projects presented at the end of this book, one sees that the interior wall finishing in marble or wood is still in its original condition, approximately 90 years after its completion, and that the rooms are still used daily by today's owners. Marginally maintenance is necessary for these materials. This example impressively shows the economical thoughts behind all the beauty and functionality in Loos' work.

"One should remember that quality materials and good workmanship do not simply make up for a lack of ornamentation, they far surpass it in luxuriousness. More than that, they make ornamentation redundant. Nowadays, even the most vulgar person would hesitate to decorate a fine wood with inlay work, engrave over the natural patterns of a marble slab, or cut a magnificent silver fox into small squares to make a chessboard design with other furs. [...] Fine material is God's own wonder."[29]

Here Loos emphasizes that well chosen and properly handled natural material makes every further ornament superficial, and the accordant effect desired by the architect is achieved best through the uniqueness of the natural surface. A fine, natural material produces in the viewer a reverence for God's creation and therefore heightens its effect. Beyond this, one saves work and time by avoiding ancillary ornamentation.

"[...] But for each certain occasion, the Englishman has a suit, a bed, a bicycle. Alterations to the form do not stem from a desire for innovation, but from the desire to perfect the best. Because it is not the new chair that deserves our time, but rather the best one."[30]

For Loos addresses the quest for the qualitatively best products to always be given priority over quantity. A completely comfortable chair in which one can quickly unwind and relax is more valuable than four uncomfortable chairs. The quest for improving products to meet personal requirements should always be one's motive and not an innovation for pure formal reasons. This only leads to rampant consumerism and not to the satisfaction of requirements. If people's demands are determined by requirements of quality and improvement, then the available products will also be oriented accordingly.

"The artist has only one ambition: to master his material in such a way that his work is independent of the value of the raw material. Our architects, however, have not heard of this ambition. For them, a square meter of wall surface out of granite is more valuable than a square meter out of plaster. [...] Fischer von Erlach did not need granite to make himself understood. He created works out of clay, limestone, and sand, works that capture our attention as powerfully as the best buildings made out of materials that are the most difficult to handle."[31]

In this quote Loos addresses a personal gift that distinguishes him in his architectural work: corresponding to the client's budget and situation, he could utilize less expensive materials but still produce an impressive atmosphere in a room. However, Loos draws attention to the fact that the use of one of those materials demands that architects know that each material has its particular expression and thereby can only give rise to certain effects. Therefore, the intended room feeling or spiritual effect is determined first, followed by the material choice, and then its handling and the surface treatment. "Every material possesses its own language of forms, and none may lay claim for itself to the forms of another material. Forms have been constituted out of the applicability and the methods of production of materials. They have come into being with and through materials."[32]

Loos saw imitation materials, mimicking precious materials with surrogates, as a great evil of his time. One cannot attain a room feeling with imitations because the human spirit will not let itself be cheated and recognizes the deception. Admiration and reverence do not arise as they would when triggered by natural materials. Loos introduces Nietzsche's concept of parvenu for people who, through the accumulation of imitations and surrogates, want to appear more than they are. To Loos, these people can never be carriers of our culture: "[...] For those people whom he wants to deceive, those, that is, endowed with the means to surround themselves with diamonds, furs, and stone facades, cannot be fooled. They find his efforts laughable. And his efforts are further unnecessary vis-à-vis those of a lower standing, if one is conscious of his own superiority anyway."[33]

In his essay "Die Baumaterialien", Loos further points out that it is not the quantity of work-time, but the quality of the workmanship that determines the subsequent value of the object. He is conscious that in our system, time is an easily measurable factor and can therefore be readily evaluated. In this way a material's worth can be determined at the initial purchase, but the quality is not objectively measurable, because this judgment requires specialized or previous knowledge. However, the subsequent generations recognize only the value of the qualitative workmanship, and this determines the long-term value of an object or furnishing.

As has already been explained in prior paragraphs, in addition to using artistic and cultural arguments in his stand against Historicism and the Secession, Loos repeatedly used economic reasons to demonstrate that his recommendations and views were a national economic imperative. Thus he leads his concerns away from a pure art-and-culture political debate to a socio-economic question of survival.

Some quotations from Loos on this subject: "Ornament that does not arise organically from the human soul, as it did with the old masters and still does with the modern Oriental, is worthless. Worthless, a waste of labor and materials. And its worthlessness is increasing daily. [...] And make no mistake about it, those objects which are currently being produced in today's uncultured – that is anachronistic, means unmodern – style will suffer the same fate in a few years' time."[34]

"But in respect to economic it is a crime, in that it leads to the waste of human labor, money, and materials. That is a damage time cannot repair."[35]

"The changing of ornaments by fashion results in a premature devaluation of the product; the worker's labour-time and the materials used are wasted capital."[36]

"[...] if you have two people living next door to each other who have the same needs, the same aspirations, and the same income, but who belong to different cultural epochs, you will find the man of the 20th Century getting richer and richer, and the man of the 18th Century getting poorer and poorer. [...] The man of the 20th Century needs much less capital to supply his needs, and can therefore make savings. [...] Decorated plates are very expensive, while the 20th-Century man likes his food on simple white crockery, which is cheap. The one saves money while the other throws it away. And it is the same with whole nations. Woe betide the folk that lag behind in their cultural development. The English are getting richer, and we poorer..."[37]

## Fashion and Clothing

Loos engages himself in this theme on two levels: first with people's clothing, especially men's fashion; second with the "Principle of Cladding", a theme stimulated by Gottfried Semper, which is characterized by the meaning of textile arts in architecture. The German expression "Bekleidung" used by Loos and Semper has both meanings: clothing as well as cladding.

I would like to begin with the theme of men's fashion and its application to Loos' architecture.

## Clothing and Architecture

Loos addresses clothing and the related question of fashion in great detail. Loos wore only tailor-made clothing with a classic, English cut. On the basis of his clothes and manners, which can be likened to those of the Prince of Wales, the best tailors, shoemakers and milliners described him as a gentleman. This demonstrates his personal relationship and predilection for the topic. Loos knew and patronized the best men's tailors in Vienna. Ebenstein, C.M. Frank, Goldman & Salatsch, Kniže, and Mandl all offered nearly exclusively English cuts and models and, at least according to Loos, had the highest distinction of being allowed to supply the court of the English king. Not only was Loos a customer of the aforementioned tailors, but Ebenstein, Goldman & Salatsch, Kniže, and Mandl also became his clients, hiring him to design their shops and workshops as well as their private homes. This is simply explained as the intensity of Loos' relationship to this profession. In his writings we find numerous essays that pertain to clothing; just to name a few titles of representative samples: "Men's Fashion", "Gentlemen's Hats", "Footwear" and "Ladies' Fashion".

Regarding English men's fashion, Loos explained from the beginning that "modern" is not a temporal term but a qualitative one: "One is only dressed modernly if he can be in the center of culture at a specific occasion of the highest society – and not stand out."[38]

With this definition Loos creates a prerequisite in order to carry over the theme of clothing to architecture, because in the classical sense architecture does extol the claim of perpetuity, which is not allowed to be fashionable, temporary or trendy.

Before 1910, in the time during which he mainly furnished apartments and pubs, Loos saw himself as an "outfitter" and did not want to regard his activities as architecture. "Tailors & Outfitters" was Goldman & Salatsch's designation in advertisements. In addition to custom tailoring they also handled retail clothing for men and accessories of the highest quality, which they sought out in England and then, in their shop, composed to complete personal arrangements for each customer.

Loos approached the interiors of his apartments in a somewhat similar manner: "When he arranged an apartment, he asserted: 'It is always the same. The way a dress coat cannot look otherwise. The lining will be different, naturally, and the pockets will vary according to need, but a dress coat is a dress coat. That is my credenza, that is my desk. And yet every room looks entirely different. The variety is infinite.'"[39]

In actuality, Loos used only a limited quantity of furniture pieces from several cultural epochs on which he had already tested his demands. From these, he made a selection and arranged them into a complete interior according to the customer's needs and preferences.

To Loos, the English gentleman style did not entail being attractively dressed, but rather being correctly dressed. The term "gentleman" is not limited to a particular class or strata. An aristocrat, a member of the middle class, or an artist can be a gentleman; he defines himself not primarily by his origins, but by his manners and clothing. In this way clothing transcended – at least on the surface – the monarchy's class system at that time.

Loos used this in architecture in a double sense: the house had to appeal to everyone and the facade protected intimacy from the public: "Those who go around in velvet jackets today are not artists, but clowns or house painters. *We have become more refined, more subtle.* When men followed the herd they had to differentiate themselves through color, *modern man uses his dress as a mask.* His sense of his own individuality is so immensely strong it can no longer be expressed in dress."[40]

With the following sentence, Loos applies his

ideas about clothing for the modern man to architecture: "[...] The house should be discreet on the outside and show its great wealth within. [...]"[41]

Additionally, here is Adolf Loos' view on women's fashion: "The noble side of womankind has only one desire, to take her rightful place at the side of a great, strong man. At the moment this desire can only be fulfilled if she wins a man's love. Love makes her subject to the man... But a naked woman has no attraction for a man. Unclothed, she can arouse a man's love, but not retain it... [...] A woman must hope to arouse a man's lust, his desire. The position he has achieved in human society allows a man to dominate a woman [...]. Thus the woman is compelled to use her clothing to appeal to the man's sensuality [...].

"But we are heading toward a newer, greater age. Women will no longer have to appeal to sensuality to achieve equal status with men, but will do so through their economic and intellectual independence, gained through work. A woman's value will not rise and fall with fluctuations in sensuality. Silks and satins, ribbons and bows, frills and furbelows will lose their effectiveness. They will disappear."[42]

Loos, who always stood for women's emancipation, saw a future of economic independence for the woman, in which she would be free to make her own decisions and no longer forced to subordination by a man out of necessity.

The emancipation of the woman would also require that her clothing be transformed to more closely resemble that of a man. However, to Loos women would always flirt with sensuality, and for that reason, ornament and jewelry would remain forever; but women would no longer be exclusively dependent upon them.

## The Principle of Cladding

The principle of cladding came from architect and theorist Gottfried Semper (1803-1879), who publicized it in his architectural theory book, *Der Stil* [*Style*] (1860-63).

Highly esteemed by Loos, Semper provided evidence of the polychromy of ancient Greek and Roman temple structures, based on his study of antiquity and participation in excavations in his youth. Loos encountered Semper's work during his studies in Dresden, where Semper first taught and

built. Semper had to flee Dresden after the May 1849 uprising, which was part of the 1848 revolutions. He went to London, Zurich, and finally Vienna, where he was commissioned to create the Kaiserforum.

Semper summarized all his experiences and insights in *Style*, which gained wide circulation. Even Otto Wagner used Semper's writings as a foundation in his work *Modern Architecture*. He did not agree with all of Semper's points, but Semper's influences are unmistakable.

Loos, on the other hand, had a closer relationship to the model and so some of the standpoints in his essays are taken directly from *Style*. Indeed, they are simply shortened and coated with Loos' polemic.[43]

Semper divided architecture into the following order, according to importance:
1. Textiles: relating to the wall
2. Ceramics: relating to the hearth
3. Tectonics (Carpentry): relating to the roof
4. Stereotomy (Stone Construction): relating to the supports
5. Metallurgy (Metalwork): joining all four 4 prior classes

The fifth chapter was elaborated in a later version.

To this point, Semper writes: "Probably the most powerful teachings that have affected our cultural circumstances are those which give instructions on mastering materials for building and structural purposes. They correspond to the general practical direction of our time and are supported and carried out through the great construction projects, which railway construction initiates in particular. A reproach to these teachings is that the idea has been too forged to the material by accepting the false tenet that architectural forms have arisen exclusively from material, constructive conditions. And it can only further develop in this way, because material of the idea is much more subservient, and in no way solely controls the sensual prominence of the latter in the physical world. The form, the physically realized idea, is not allowed to contradict the material out of which it is made. [...]

"In every time period, the principle of cladding has exercised a great influence upon construction styles and other arts.

"[...] it remains always certain that the beginnings of construction coincide with the beginnings of textiles."[44]

Here, Semper refers to the importance of textile design from the beginning of history up to the implementation of our contemporary ideas. He dissents from the thesis represented by Otto Wagner, among others, that architecture develops out of constructive possibilities. To Semper and Loos, the first question is which feelings, moods, and effects does one want to create, that is the idea. And only then does one ask oneself, "How can I translate these?" The second step is to think of a construction for it. With Loos, it sounds like the following: "[...] Stability and practicality demand materials which may not harmonize with the function of the building. The job of the architect is to create a warm, cozy room. Carpets are warm and cozy, so he decides to spread one over the floor and hang up four to make the four walls. But you cannot build a house from carpets. Both floor carpets and wall hangings need a construction to keep them in place. Designing this construction is the architect's second task.

"That is the correct way, the logical way architects should go about their business. That was the order in which mankind learned to build. In the beginning we sought to clad ourselves, to protect ourselves from the elements, to keep ourselves safe and warm while sleeping. We sought to cover ourselves. Originally consisting of animal furs or textiles, this covering is the earliest architectural feature."[45]

**Mood and Effect**
*The true artist, the great architect, however, first of all gets a feeling for the effect he wants to produce and then sees in his mind's eye the rooms he wants to create.* (Adolf Loos)[46]

Here we reach a theme in Loos' essays that has a central meaning in his architectural work.

Loos wanted to create moods, arouse feelings, and one can see in his architectural work that he was consistent in realizing this. This is in no way about provocation, but rather to emphasize and characterize the targeted use.

"Architecture arouses moods in people, so the task of the architect is to give these moods concrete expression. A room must look cozy, a house comfort-

able to live in. To secret vice the law courts must seem to make a threatening gesture. A bank must say, 'Here your money is safe in the hands of honest people.'"[47]

One does not expect this in such explicitness from Loos, who preached the renunciation of ornament in "Ornament and Crime" (1908). In that article he wanted to curb only the useless embellishment of surfaces and structural parts at a time in which historicism and Jugendstil, preservationism and rebellion alike, vigorously ornamented everything. For that reason, the call was louder and more glaring so that he would be heard at all. He was heard, and ornament, including all paneling and colors, was removed more quickly and thoroughly than even he expected. The bare, naked surface of functional, purist, white modernism became the emblem of a new era. "Machine aesthetics" and "industrial age" became the predominant catchwords. In 1924 Loos felt himself forced to compose a clarification to his 1908 essay because people were driving his concerns "ad absurdum". These were not his aims, but it was already too late.

Here then are the essential quotations from the essay he composed in 1924, "Ornament and Education", in which he presents his position regarding his architectural work and concerns: "Lack of ornamentation does not mean lack of attractiveness, but is a new attraction and rouses the public from its lethargy. It is when the mill stops clacking that the miller wakes up."[48]

"26 years ago I maintained that the use of ornamentation on objects of practical use would disappear with the development of mankind, a constant and consistent development, which was as natural a process as the atrophy of vowels in final syllables in popular speech. By that I did not mean what some purists have carried ad absurdum, namely that ornamentation should be systematically and consistently eliminated."[49]

It was not in order to erect something new or even provocative that he chose the abstract, matter-of-fact facades that he put on most of his new structures. As explained in the preceding paragraphs, that would have stood contrary to his writings. Rather, there are two motives: one is the Mediterranean origin of our culture, which the Romans brought over the Alps; the other is the mask, comparable to the proper English suit, that we, as with our men's fashion, overlay to protect our insides – that protective layer between public and private life.

"So much Italian air has blown over the Alps to us that we should build like our fathers in a style that shuts the house off from the outside world. [...] The house should be discreet on the outside and show its great wealth within. [...]"[50]

In reality, the interior space, as opposed to the plain facade, is exquisitely and richly outfitted with materials and spatial compositions. After passing through the facade layers, the visitor is surprised because the outer facade raises different expectations of the house's inner life. Throughout the entire visit, the views and attention are directed to the house's interior and the residence. The outer space is effectively excluded through Loos' clever staging. The window serves only as a light source. On this topic, here is an important quote by Le Corbusier: "Loos m'affirmait un jour: 'Un homme cultivé ne regarde pas la fenêtre. La fenêtre est en verre dépoli; n'est là que pour donner de la lumière, non pour laisser passer le regard.'" Which could be translated as: "Loos once asserted to me: 'A cultivated person does not look out the window. It is made of frosted glass. The window is only there to let light in, not to allow the gaze to wander.[51]

I will come to this important sentence again with the discussion of his architectural work.

## Craftsmanship

*These competitions are not for artists. They are for the factory owners and craftsmen. Only from the working and making people do I expect a recovery of the commercial relationships, a raising of culture and taste.* (Adolf Loos)[52]

Loos was firmly convinced of the recovery of craftsmanship, as he had freed it from the "applied artists" and "architects" who delivered the craftsmen the specifications of their work with their drawings. Loos went the opposite path: he provided no drawings, he went to the craftsmen in the workshops or met with them at the construction site to discuss everything in consultation. Because to Loos, craftsman had a natural knowledge of handling material which was transmitted over centuries of experience. Loos believed that this tradition-based knowledge, familiarity with material, and the proper use of material at the appropriate place would achieve the best effect and a long-lasting quality.

The inner certainty of the "unspoiled" craftsman will always produce the proper object that is best suited to its use and application. In this way he is "modern" according to Loos' definition.

Loos contrasts the "creative" craftsman with the "thinking" draftsman, who at the drawing table designs a formal creation in his head and uses his pencil to put it on paper. His product is the pretty drawing, not the high-quality, long-lasting, useful object.

There had already been movements before Loos that championed the revival of craftwork. In England, William Morris (1834-1896) began his Arts and Crafts movement around 1860 when, in order to oust mechanically produced "arts and crafts products", he built for his own house handcrafted, simple, functional furniture that recalled the Middle Ages. However, Morris saw himself as an artist and his motto declared that artists are craftsmen and craftsmen are artists. Thus arose Arts and Crafts schools that taught crafts and applied arts. The style of the products that he marketed from his own firm, and augmented by letting other artists develop them, became increasingly more ornamental. Hence some students became the forerunners of the Jugendstil and movements such as the Wiener Werkstätten developed, invoking Morris and English crafts. For this reason, Loos obviously distanced himself from Morris.

Loos had this to say about Ruskin, the theorist of the Arts and Crafts movement: "The sole important factors for aristocrats are the materials and perfect workmanship. All this was a difficult process for me. Why? Because people felt it was shameful to say that was what was right. It is Ruskin, by the way, who is to blame for all this. I am his sworn enemy. [...]"[53]

Because of the situation in Vienna around 1900, Loos' battle was directed against academic artists and not against industry; later he ridiculed the Werkbund's goal of influencing industry through artists as the wrong method. A direct attack on industry does not ensue in Loos' writings.

Arts and crafts work disappeared again quickly, just as Loos had said before. Since industry already offered and manufactured functional, practical and – importantly – cheaper bulk goods, craftwork could no longer gain the status that Loos had intended.

From the beginning, industrial production attempted to manufacture the craftsman-like products industrially; it was only slowly that articles developed that could be produced mechanically in larger quantities, with less labor. Additionally, industry seldom had the need to manufacture a long-lasting, high-value item since they were interested in a large production volume. In this way, Loos' belief in craftwork was justified.

Loos himself recognized the emerging industrialization. One of his last articles was written in 1929 on the occasion of the death of his furniture craftsman, Josef Veillich. For many of Loos' projects, he had made copies of Chippendale chairs, which Loos called the most comfortable and perfect chairs for the dining room. In the 1929 article Loos wrote: "Since the chairmakers have died out, chairs, wooden chairs, have gone the same way. That is how things die. If they were needed there would be a worthier younger generation to follow them. The successor to the wooden chair will be the Thonet chair which I described as the only modern chair thirty-one years ago. Jeanneret (le Corbusier) realized that too and promoted them in his buildings but, unfortunately, the wrong model. [...]"[54]

### Beauty

*What do we understand by beauty? Complete perfection. It is, therefore, out of the question that something not satisfactorily performing its intended function can be beautiful. The first basic condition any object must fulfill, if it is to be considered "beautiful", is that it does not contravene the rules of practicality. But being functional alone does not make it beautiful. There is more to it than that. The artists of the* Cinquecento *probably gave the most precise definition: "An object is beautiful if it is so perfect you could not add anything or take anything away without spoiling it. That would be the most perfect, absolute harmony."* (Adolf Loos)[55]

For objects of use, beauty is the result of the usefulness and the development of its functions through exact conformity to its requirements. It reaches perfection if all parts and functions meld into a whole. In "Glass and Clay", Loos cites an example from Gottfried Semper, which he used in his book *Style*. Semper explains that the form of a Greek water clay jug arose solely from the way water was drawn, the way women transported it on their heads, and the way it was stored.

Based on this, Loos formulates the following conclusion: "The foot, the body, the handles, the size of the mouth were all dictated by the use they were put to? That means these vases were practical! And we always thought they were beautiful! We have been misled. We had always been taught that practicality and beauty were mutually exclusive.

"[...] the ancient Greeks also knew a little about beauty. And they were led by practical considerations alone, without taking beauty into account at all, without wanting to satisfy some aesthetic need. And when an object was so practical it could not be made any more practical, they called it beautiful. [...]

"Are there still people who work in the same way as the Greeks? Oh, yes. As a nation, the English; as a profession, the engineers. [...] These Greek vases are beautiful, as beautiful as a machine, as beautiful as a *bicycle*."[56]

### Conception of Man, Ethics

Loos wanted to protect people from the revolutionary ideas of the modernists as well as from the eternal yesterdays of the preservationists.

He became individually involved with each of his clients, as we will see in the projects. This is the only explanation of how he came to a lifelong friendship with all of his building owners. They were obliged to him and thankful for what he had personally made for them. His lectures and writings were directed to the individual, whom through education and encouragement he wished to help make independent from the dictates of artists and fashion: to be sufficiently secure inside to evaluate the quality of his everyday products and to make conscious decisions – independently and freely. This was the liberation that Loos, through his personal engagement, wanted to give people, whether they were aristocrats, middle-class citizens or laborers. Everyone was to decide for himself about his surroundings and his furnishings, "[...] I want to try to make you face your own tastelessness; whoever wants to learn fencing must first take up the rapier in his hand."[57]

As a teacher Loos wanted to do something for everyone and act on their behalf. He repeatedly requested that letters be sent to him, which he then answered publicly. "All children should receive the same education. Above all, there should be no difference between town and country. [...]"[58] Breaking down the cultural and social differences was also a central demand of his. In his youth, the slight cultural difference between city and countryside in America had deeply impressed him in comparison to the Austrian situation, where in Loos' opinion, people lived in different centuries right next to one another.

The search for absolute truth was not his; for Loos, everything ordinary and contemporary is always subordinate to a natural change or development.

Loos believed in the unique person and his inner attitude. Like his friend Karl Kraus, he was an ethicist. Respect and responsibility to every individual and to society are important, and not the social conventions that act as morals and obstruct the view of things.

## Conclusion

Loos concerned himself with the present and was certain that his thinking would prevail in the future. With his insights, he foresaw certain things. But by no means did he want to declare modern life a utopia. In contrast to the representatives of "modernism", tradition remained important to him due to his belief that everything develops in an evolutionary manner – architecture as much as objects of use. The roots of our culture lie in tradition.

He had a positive image of the individual; he spent his entire life advocating that people be brought to a higher cultural level, which would lead to deliverance from immaturity. He fought paternalism by the state, special interest unions, and the "academic artists" and saw his greatest feats not in the area of art, but in the service of humanity and the economy.

Shortly before his death, Loos wrote this foreword to the first edition of *Trozdem* in 1931: "After a thirty-year struggle, I have emerged victorious: I have liberated humanity from superfluous ornamentation. Ornamentation was once the epithet for 'beauty'. Today, thanks to my life's work, it is the epithet for 'rubbish'. Sure enough, the echo that sounds believes it is the voice itself. [...] I know that humanity will only thank me when the time they save will pay off the ones that have been until now excluded from the goods of the world."[59]

To this conclusion of his life's work, he adds the following quote from Friedrich Nietzsche: "The essential happens regardless."

Kärntner Bar by Loos, 1908
Photo by Philippe Ruault, 2004

[1] A.L., "On Thrift" (1924), in *On Architecture*, Ariadne Press, Riverside, 2002, p. 180; original text "Von der Sparsamkeit", in *Wohnungskultur*, issue 2/3, in *Die Potemkinsche Stadt*, 1924.

[2] Robert Scheu, "Adolf Loos", in *Prager Tagblatt*, 25 August 1933 (Engl. trans. L.S.).

[3] A.L., "The New Style and the Bronze Industry" (29 May 1898), in *Ornament and Crime*, Ariadne Press, Riverside, 1998, p. 46; original text "Der neue Stil und die Bronzekunst", in *N.F.P.*, Wien, 29 May 1898.

[4] Before the monarchy and World War One ended in 1918, the aristocracy was the highest strata in Austria. Loos' writing largely took place before 1918, therefore he spoke of the exemplary function of the aristocracy for the population.

[5] A.L., "Ladies' Fashion" (1898-1902), in *Ornament and Crime*, cit., p. 107.

[6] A.L., "Von der Sparsamkeit", cit.

[7] A.L., Preface to first edition, *Ins Leere gesprochen*, Editions Georges Crès & Cie, Zürich 1921 (Engl. trans. L.S.).

[8] A.L., "Architecture" (1910), in *On Architecture*, cit., pp. 76-7; original text "Ornament u. Verbrechen" (1908), in *Trotzdem*, Brenner-Verlags, Innsbruck 1931.

[9] A.L., "The Interiors in the Rotunda" (12 June 1898), in *Ornament and Crime*, cit., p. 62; original text "Interieurs der Rotunde", in *N.F.P.*, Wien, 12 June 1898.

[10] A.L., "Antworten auf Fragen aus dem Publikum" (1909), in *Trotzdem*, cit. (Engl. trans. L.S.).

[11] A.L., "Architecture", cit., pp. 82-3.

[12] A.L., "Guided Tours of Apartments" (1907), in *On Architecture*, cit., p. 54; original text "Wohnungswanderungen" (1907).

[13] A.L., "Ornament and Crime", cit., p. 167; original text "Ornament u. Verbrechen", cit.

[14] A.L., "Antworten auf Fragen aus dem Publikum" (1909), cit. (Engl. trans. L.S.).

[15] A.L., "Architecture", cit., p. 73.

[16] Friedrich Nietzsche, Forward, *Menschlich all zu menschliches* II, 1879 (Engl. trans. L.S.).

[17] A.L., "My School of Building" (1913), in *On Architecture*, cit., p. 119; original text "Meine Bauschule", in *Der Architekt*, 29, 10, Wien, October 1913.

[18] Ibid., pp. 119-20.

[19] A.L., "Surplus to Requirements" (1908), in *Ornament and Crime*, cit., p. 154; original text "Die Überflüssigen" (1908), in *Trotzdem*, cit.

[20] A.L., "Cultural Degeneration" (1908), in *Ornament and Crime*, cit., p. 163; original text "Kulturentartung", 1908.

[21] A.L., "Heimatkunst" (1914), in *On Architecture*, cit., pp. 112-13; original text "Heimatkunst" (1914), in *Trotzdem*, cit.

*Holzzement* is a first type of flatroofing using layers of paper, sand and gravel stuck together with *Holzzement* (60% coaltar, 25% sulphur, 15% asphalt), *note of the translator*.

[22] A.L., "The New Style and the Bronze Industry", cit., p. 46.

[23] A.L., "Eine Zuschrift" (1910), in *Trotzdem*, cit. (Engl. trans. L.S.).

[24] Walter Gropius, "Adolf Loos zum 60. Geburtstag", in *Frankfurter Zeitung*, 10 December 1930 (Engl. trans. L.S.).

[25] A.L., "Ornament and Education" (22 August 1924), in *Ornament and Crime*, cit., p. 187; original text "Ornament u. Erziehung" (1924), in *Trotzdem*, cit.

[26] Le Corbusier, "Adolf Loos zum 60. Geburtstag", in *Frankfurter Zeitung*, 10 December 1930 (Engl. trans. L.S.).

[27] Siegfried Giedion, "Adolf Loos zum 60. Geburtstag", in *Frankfurter Zeitung*, 10 December 1930 (Engl. trans. L.S.).

[28] A.L., "Ornament and Crime", cit., p. 172; original text "Ornament u. Verbrechen", 1908.

[29] A.L., "Hands off" (1917), in *Ornament and Crime*, cit., p. 182; original text "Hands off" (1917), in *Trotzdem*, cit.

[30] A.L., "Kunstgewerbliche Rundschau 1", in *Die Wage*, 1898 (Engl. trans. L.S.).

[31] A.L., "Building Materials" (28 August 1898), in *Spoken into the Void*, Institute for Architecture and Urban Studies and

M.I.T., 1982, p. 63; original text *Bauma-terialien*, in *N.F.P.*, Wien, 28 August 1898, in *Ins Leere gesprochen*, cit.

[32] Ibid., p. 64.

[33] Ibid.

[34] A.L., "Guided Tours of Apartments" (1907), in *On Architecture*, cit., p. 54; original text *Wohnungswanderungen* (1907).

[35] A.L., "Ornament and Crime" (1908), cit., p. 169.

[36] Ibid., p. 172.

[37] Ibid., p. 170.

[38] A.L., "Kleidung", in *Das Andere*, 1903 (Engl. trans. L.S.).

[39] Ludwig Hevesi, in *Altkunst - Neukunst*, Wien, 1908 (Engl. trans. L.S.).

[40] A.L., "Ornament and Crime" (1908), cit., p. 175.

[41] A.L., "Heimatkunst" (1914), cit. (Engl. trans. L.S.).

[42] A.L., "Ladies' Fashion" (1898-1902), cit., pp. 106-11; original text, "Die Damenmode" (1902), in *Ins Leere gesprochen*, cit.

[43] Friedrich Kurrent, *Raumplan-wohnungsbau*, Akademie der Künste Berlin, 1983, pp. 92 ff.

[44] Gottfried Semper, *Der Stil*, 1860 (Engl. trans. L.S.).

[45] A.L., "The Principle of Cladding" (4 September 1898), in *On Architecture*, cit., p. 42; original text "Das Prinzip der Be-kleidung", in *N.F.P.*, Wien, 4 September 1898.

[46] Ibid.

[47] A.L., "Architecture" (1910), cit., p. 84.

[48] A.L., "Ornament and Education" (22 August 1924), cit., p. 186

[49] *Ibid.*, p. 187.

[50] A.L., "Heimatkunst" (1914), in *Trotz-dem*, cit. (Engl. trans. L.S.).

[51] Quoted in Beatriz Colomina, *Privacy and Publicity*, The MIT Press, Cambridge (Massachusetts), 1994.

[52] A.L., *Das Andere, unsere konkurrenzen*, 1903 (Engl. trans. L.S.).

[53] A.L., "On Thrift" (1924), cit., p. 183.

[54] A.L., "Josef Veillich" (1929), in *On Architecture*, cit., p. 188; original text *Josef Veillich*, 1929.

[55] A.L., "Chairs" (19 June 1898), in *Ornament and Crime*, cit., p. 63; original text *Das Sitzmöbel*, in "N.F.P.", Wien, 19 June 1898.

[56] A.L., "Glass and Clay" (26 June 1898), in *Ornament and Crime*, cit., p. 69; original text *Glas und Ton*, in *N.F.P.*, Wien, 26 June 1898.

[57] A.L., *Das Andere*, 1903 (Engl. trans. L.S.).

[58] A.L., "Ornament and Education" (22 August 1924), cit., p. 188.

[59] A.L., Preface to the first edition of *Trotzdem*, 1931 (Engl. trans. L.S.).

# Shops, Cafés and Bars

## General

In their catalog, Schachel and Rukschcio count 32 completed works among Loos' shops, cafés and bars. This is clearly less than the number of apartments and houses that Loos finished, but quite noteworthy nonetheless. Some of his most significant works fall under this category, as he could masterfully apply his art of "room-moods" (*Raumstimmungen*) to produce certain psychological effects. First of all, one notices that there is hardly any mention in his writing of themes that are specific to shops or similar, as opposed to the thematic of dwelling. However, he began his career in this category, with the Ebenstein Tailor's Salon, 1897, today undisputedly accepted as his first work after returning to Vienna from America at the age of 27. Subsequent to this were the Goldman & Salatsch Tailor's Salon in 1898 and the Café Museum one year later. With the Café Museum he received his first public critiques in the daily newspapers, and his recognition as an architect began to spread, parallel to his essays in the *Neue Freie Presse*.

While his apartments were only accessible to the acquaintances of the clients who had them built, this type of job gave Loos the opportunity to create publicly accessible and visible places within Vienna, thereby making it possible for the public to become interested in his works. The first apartment tour, which Loos organized in order to show his works to an interested public, took place in 1907.

Loos' jobs in the field of shops, cafés and bars were restricted by his clients to a few specific categories, which I would like to briefly describe with examples in the following section.

## Cafés: Café Museum, 1899

Loos' Café Museum lays at the intersection of Secession Building by Olbrich, which was at that time newly constructed, the Opera, the Technical University, the Theatre an der Wien, the Academy of Beaux-Arts, the Künstlerhaus and the Hall of the Musikverein – a location in the heat of conflict of art and intellect of the time. From the exterior Loos transformed the base of a traditional Viennese corner house in historism style from a heavy natural stone imitation in the kind of Italian renaissance palazzo into a smooth, plain plaster finish, and he built in large, rectangular, transparent window panes with mahogany frames. He took over the raster and proportion of the windows in the upper facade, thereby maintaining the building's base area in its static function, to respect it, so as not to contradict the natural sensation of load transfer. This example illustrates the complexity of Loos' ideas, being respectful of the existing structure, its tradition and its logic, but formal he unmasked through small interventions, the decoration of the heavy plaster material on the rest of the building, representing an imitation of the natural stone facade. Through this purposeful unmasking of Vienna's *Zeitgeist*, Loos provoked the establishment.

As horizontal dividing line between the upper facade and the base-facade he used awnings of canvas which shaded the interior as well as the outdoor seating against the facade facing Karlsplatz.

Beneath this were the words "CAFÉ MUSEUM" in Loos' favorite font, Antiqua, in large, golden letters, affixed on both facades.

Vienna's café culture at the beginning of the 20th Century was legendary: cafés were places where people went to communicate, to read newspapers, for meeting groups and other regular encounters, to play and to eat light meals.

Loos considered this in his partitioning of the interior rooms and created a clear zoning, which was unfortunately no longer respected in the reconstruction attempt of 2003. In fact, he constructed a double-winged great room, which was divided into areas that led to additional rooms. Entering the café on the diagonal of the corner building, one could see two approaching side wings of quite equal length with a slightly arched ceiling. The lower part of the walls was finished in mahogany up to the height of the chairs, and above them, up to the base of the arch, they were covered with a broadly striped, light green, English velour wallpaper. The ceilings were painted light yellow-white. They were articulated by polished strips of brass, behind which were housed the wires for the ceiling lighting.

In the right wing were round and rectangular, white marble tables with light Thonet-style chairs, which were stained red. This was the area for reading newspapers, meeting and talking while drinking a coffee or enjoying a light meal. The left wing, on the other hand, was dominated by three billiard tables with small, round, two-person tables around the perimeter – the game was the center of focus here. Behind this, separated by a room divider, was the game room for card and board games, furnished with comfortable seats and game tables. The walls were decorated with red English tapestries, which provided a muted light, creating a more intimate ambience for the players, often regular customers who remained there for hours.

A door off of the right wing led to the Gibson Room, furnished with various yet comfortable wicker seats from Prag-Rudniker and serving as the meeting place for societies and regular meeting groups. On the wall were hung images by Charles Dana Gibson, whose image of an emancipated, glamorous, athletic, dainty, delicate and rangy woman was highly promoted by Altenberg and Loos, of which there was even a fashion trend, the so-called Gibson-Girls, between 1890 and 1910.[1]

Large mirrors were installed on the front end of the main wings. In the right wing, there were three large, framed wall mirrors, and in the left wing there were mirrored room dividers.

Through the addition of these mirrors, the main room seemed even larger than it actually was; also, they allowed the cashier, centrally located at a round counter opposite the entrance, to better observe the entire main room. At the intersection between both wings and in front of the entrance door, the cashier could greet the guests upon their arrival, as he was located directly in their line of vision upon entering. This is precisely the central point that Loos later employed with increasing frequency in his apartments and villas, to which he led the guest, making it a critical element in his orientation. Exactly in this situation of momentary insecurity in orientation, Loos placed the guest under the observation of the owner. The owner could then decide how and when to enter the scene. The entrance situation in the Café Museum was like a staged appearance put on by Loos for the guest in arrival, which was also witnessed by the entire main room. Loos designed this space with no furniture so that a small stage was truly created, especially well suited to the regulars, who, aware of the situation, could use the opportunity to celebrate their entrance in the café.

The guest seated at the window had the possibility of withdrawing from the public eye; although the panes were transparent, directly along the window frame was a thin fabric curtain, which could be drawn in two levels. With the lower level drawn, one could avoid gazes from the street, and with the upper level, direct sunlight could be shaded. This type of interior curtain stems from England, where they are called "short blinds". Loos had the window frames installed flush to the facade so that the 80 cm thick embrasures provided only narrow glimpses of the interior through open curtains. With this choice, he forwent seating in the window niches. The furniture of the main room was very comfortable, but not upholstered. To Loos, the café was a public place in which one openly and formally displayed one's role in society. Only in the back rooms would the furniture become more casual and the atmosphere more intimate.

In Loos' own comments on his work, we find two fundamental assertions. Firstly, he did not want to create anything new, but rather to connect with the tradition of Viennese coffee houses in the Biedermeier style, as he expressed in his speeches at the Schwarzwaldschule in 1912-13.[2] Hence, the two-winged layout of the corner building, with the entrance directly on the corner, typical of the traditional Viennese Biedermeier café; and also the central cashier's counter, from which the entire room and personnel could be discretely observed and monitored.[3] Secondly, his design was specifically aimed against the trend of the Secession, which was popular in that period.

In a later text, Loos spoke of the Café Museum's popularity, even after more than ten years, as

Café Museum, 1899: entrance situation,
billiard and reading room
(ALA 2495)

Café Museum, 1899: billiard room
(ALA 2495)

a significant criterion compared to the fugacity of the Secessionist style: "That was twelve years ago when I did the Café Museum in Vienna. The architects called it 'Café Nihilism'. But my Café Museum still stands today while all the modern joinery of the thousands of others has long since been consigned to the junk room. Or they are ashamed of it. That the Café Museum has had more influence on modern joinery work than all previous projects put together can be proved by a quick glance at the 1899 volume of the Munich journal, *Dekorative Kunst*, where this interior was reproduced, presumably due to a mistake by the editor. But these two photographic illustrations had no influence; at the time they were completely ignored. Thus, as you can see, it is only the power of the example that has influence. It was by this power that the influence of the old craftsmen spread more rapidly to the most distant corners of the earth despite or, rather because of the fact that there was no postal service, no telegraph or newspapers."[4]

Ludwig Hervesi, one of the most renowned Viennese architectural critics of the period, said of the Café Museum: "With his Café Museum, Adolf Loos proclaims himself a genuine non-Secessionist. Not as an enemy of the Viennese Secession, but as something else, as both are effectively modern. [...] From now on Loos is salvaged, as he truly did his job well. It is indeed something nihilistic, something very nihilistic, but very appetizing, logical and practical. And this is quite a reward...

"As far as Loos may be considered an artist, or if he is one at all, only the future will tell. In this debut work, everything that is known as art is far removed from his approach. He wishes to create an object of pure practicality. [...] Again, we shall see in a few years what remains of his system."[5]

Loos renounced gaudiness in this work, remaining open and concise, without resulting in coldness or in pure functionality. In the words of the contemporary Viennese architect, Robert Örley: "Whoever wishes to visit the Café Museum in Vienna, which was furnished in an exemplary manner by the architect Adolf Loos, can see for himself that it cannot be considered bleak or sober."[6]

**Bars: Kärntner Bar (American Bar), 1908**
The conceived plans for the day and night bar, modeled after the American bar, where drinks are enjoyed while standing, were originally intended only for the admission of men, but because of the bar's great popularity, after some time, the pressures of women finally succeeded in gaining their admission. With the Kärntner Bar, Loos cultivated a popular type of American bar in Vienna. The small area of only 6.15 × 4.45 m afforded the opportunity for a noble, dignified and intimate atmosphere, which Loos created through his design and his choice of materials.

The straight bar counter occupied almost half of the entire space, and there were two niches for seating on the other side, with three small, octagonal bar tables illuminated from beneath. The seat trimming was originally intended to be upholstered in green automobile leather, but since this was not available, English tapestry linen with floral patterns was used instead.[7] The height of the seats was low, in correspondence with the design of modern automobile seats, a detail that Loos would later use with greater frequency. The walls above the backrests, to the height of heads, were cladded with satin-finished, varnished mahogany panels, over these were large, undivided mirrors. The walls and the ceiling were divided into three equally sized case-bays, whose structures were created from marble pilaster strips and joists. The ceiling was composed of a rectangular, coffered marble ceiling, and the floor was laid with black and white marble slabs in a chessboard pattern.

Up to the height of the wood paneling, the inner entrance facade was composed of mahogany frames with glass and mahogany fill. Above this, in the area of the wall mirror, a backlit, translucent onyx wall in a grid of small squares rose to meet the ceiling. This had a golden glow and created a warm, subdued atmosphere in the room. The wall lighting in the entire room was comprised of light bulbs shaded by curtain fabric, creating the same kind of subdued light. The entrance facade area was about one meter deep and composed of the inner facade and a space in between with the load bearing columns of the house facade, outside they were cladded as four superior marble pillars with three glass elements between. The entrance door is centered. Above it was the colorful, backlit, glass mosaic of an American flag with the name "Kärntner Bar". The outward thrusting, illuminated cube of the glass mosaic in the facade provided a strong announcement effect. To top it off, within the level of the existing house, was the writing "American

Bar" in individual, backlit lettering upon a background of broken black glass.

The bar was intended to convey a sense of intimacy, and from the street it was only possible to catch a glimpse of the figures inside through thin fabric curtains hung directly behind the glass, which were sufficient to provide the desired privacy. The curiosity of passers-by was awakened by the insight view above the fabric curtains to the wall mirrors and the coffered ceiling. To enter the bar one had first to surmount an inhibition threshold in the form of an opaque door and an approximately one-meter deep portal area with a second facade and again a fabric-covered door. Loos provided the guests with this small, tight buffer area, despite the bar's already reduced size, so that upon entering the small bar room beyond the second door, it would suddenly seem much larger. Along with the intended effect, Loos used the space created by the structural columns both as a wind breaker and a coat-check area. Inside, one's eyes were immediately drawn into the effect of the room's illusion, which was created by the three-sided, large-surfaced wall mirror above eye-level and beneath the coffered ceiling, which reflected ad infinitum the room, subdivided by three marble beams and pilaster strips, making the space seem many times larger than it actually was. The mirror was used purely as an illusionary room effect; because of its overhead position, people were intentionally not reflected.

Standing at the bar, the customers' view of entering guests was framed by the backlit onyx wall and the glass facade, once again creating a theatrical situation. The audience watched the lit stage and the actor, the entering guest, as he walked into the room of spectators, which to him seemed expansive, because of the mirror's optical enlargement of the room, and dark because of the intimate lighting. The audience sat to the sides and in front of him in the seating niches, as in loges, lit by the internally illuminated tables in the middle, with their frosted glass tabletops. "Behind the bar, the bottles sparkled upon glass tiers and the glasses glittered upon the narrow shelf before them."[8] These are some of the psychological stylistic ele-

Kärtner Bar interior, 1908
Photo from 1910

Goldman & Salatsch I, 1898: ground floor interior view from the entrance (From *Das Interieur II*, 1901)

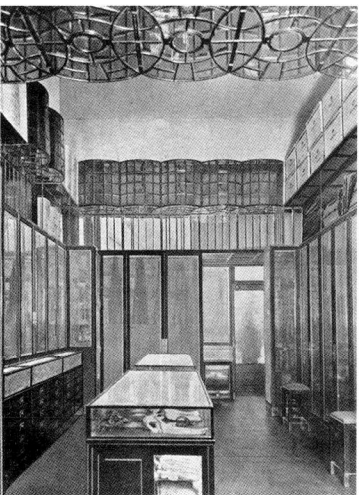

Goldman & Salatsch I, 1898: ground floor interior with view towards the entrance (From *Das Interieur II*, 1901)

ments and theatrical effects which Loos used in this sort of project in order to create this grandiose room-mood.

Münz and Künstler (1964) wrote on the Kärntner Bar: "Compared to the other cases where Adolf Loos used mirror glass to remedy the impression of spatial confinement – the silky polished mahogany walls below don't arise a restricting feel – the aim here was rather to create a subtler staging: this almost miraculous touching display of a twofold beauty – that of regular form and of that of precious material. A mild glow fills the room, warm and intense; and this does not remain without an impact upon the visitor who, fallen silent, unselfconsciously and wholeheartedly abandons himself to the eye's experience.

"With pleasure, the eye meets the soft mahogany shine of the panels, which extend beyond half of the room's height, sliding and sinking, surprised by newness at every turn, in the interweaving of reality and pure reflection of the solidly formed yet unladen marble coffers of the ceiling and of the wall made of translucent onyx slabs."[9]

Loos uses rarely highly glossy and reflective surfaces in living areas, if he does it, he does it very discretely and selectively, but never so excessive as in his bars or tailor's salon.

Already in 1908, before the plans for the House on Michaelerplatz and its interior furnishing, and before he began furnishing villas, the Kärntner Bar showed how masterfully and artfully Loos was associated with the creation of room-moods and how he consciously applied the architectural elements of space, material and light in the process. By all means he used traditional elements, such as marble coffered ceilings and the structuring of rooms with marble beams and pilaster strips in pilings, etc., for a clear, formal order; however, the results were always astounding and above all, fascinatingly new.

### Tailor's and Men's Fashion Salons

Ebenstein Tailor's Salon, Vienna, 1897; Goldman & Salatsch Tailor's Salon I, Am Graben 20, Vienna, 1898; Goldman & Salatsch II, House on Michaelerplatz, 1909; Kniže Tailor's Salon, Am Graben, Vienna, 1910; Grethe Hentschel Tailor's Salon and Residence, Vienna, 1914; P.C. Leschka & Co. Men's Fashion Salon, Vienna, 1923; Erich Mandl Men's Fashion Salon, Vienna, 1923; Kniže Tailor's Salon, Berlin, 1924; Kniže Tailor's Salon, Paris, 1927.

The accumulation of tailor's and men's fashion salons in Loos' work is without doubt a facet worthy of observation. The reasons are mostly based on Loos' infatuation with England's classic, custom-made men's fashion. He was a client of the best tailors and outfitters in Vienna, whose interior designs he created, sometimes as payment for received or new clothing.

Vienna at the turn of the century blossomed with English fashions, which originally arrived with Jewish tailors who specialized in men's clothing, and counted as their clients aristocrats and other high clientele from the Emperor's court. C.M. Frank, the leading men's clothing outfitter in Vienna, himself served at the British court. As we learn from recent studies by Elana Shapira, Goldman & Salatsch did not merely provide general men's clothing, but also uniforms and clothing for exclusive sports and the fast-growing market of aficionados of new recreational activities, such as those organized by the Austrian Automobile Club and Yacht Club, as well as those related to skiing and other winter sports. Apart from custom-made clothing, Goldman & Salatsch - Tailors & Outfitters, also provided high-quality articles of clothing and accessories – often made in England – which they composed for their Viennese clients to complete arrangements.[10]

The interior design for such elite tailors, who enjoyed a select clientele would become a specialty of Loos. He provided the desired atmosphere for these noble, elegant outfitting salons. It was his love for high-quality, classic, practical British fashion, as well as his appreciation of English culture that drove him to such work.

It was already during his first independent work, after returning from America in the year 1897, that he had furnished the interior rooms of the Ebenstein Tailor's Salon in the center of Vienna. In so doing, he used those essential, characteristic features, which would appear in his later works – the darkly stained oak paneling, the room with a fireplace, the stucco frieze in which the tailor's symbol, the scissors, was inlaid.[11] He reused these elements later in his home furnishings and houses. His second project in this line of work from the following year (1898), the Goldman & Salatsch Tailor's Salon I, Am Graben 20, in the center of Vienna, is better documented. The customer entered at the ground floor directly from the street, through a deeply set, narrow, low and small entranceway, with a view of the minimal area of the sales room. Again, we have the effect of the small, narrow and high-ceilinged main room, which is dramatically increased through Loos' use of room sequences.

We then follow a contemporary tour through the rooms of the store: "Smooth reflective walls, spare forms, and bare metal – these are the central elements used in creating such an impeccably fashionable room. From the street one enters the clothing salesroom. On every wall one is surrounded by high, darkly framed rectangles – the display cases. On the left side as one enters, they contain ties, hats and canes, which one can view through faceted panes like in a display window. The borders are made of snakewood, a hard, beautifully coloured patterned material, the handles are made of bare brass. [...] Display cases with movable doors are set up in the middle of the showroom, which also function as countertops. The white, vaulted ceiling is covered in rough plaster. To disguise the structural beams, and to make a virtue out of a necessity, two rows of cage-like structures made of brass with faceted panes of glass are aligned with them. These house the electrical lighting, and are used quite effectively.

"Also the wall cupboards and display cases have brass bases, [...] and through the lattice of a small, deftly adapted side room, the proprietor or the bookkeeper, sitting at his desk, can observe the entire room through a blind pane without being noticed. Everything is practical, perfectly finished, top quality.

"From the outfitting department described here, one ascends a spiral staircase to the tailoring department located on the first floor. In the office and reception room, the desks are evident, furnished with sliding glass surfaces so that they may also be used as standing desks. [...]. In the broad bay-window niches are peculiar fauteuils and tables, and to the left there is a gas fireplace with a striking facing in red bricks. The fitting rooms are constructed of free-standing walls in white varnished wood with square panes of *ajour*-blue Tiffany glass."[12]

The long sides of the showroom on the ground floor were furnished with wall mirrors on the one side of the room, and glass display cases on the other. The reflections served to expand the space and work also as dressing room mirrors for the customers. The entire space was monitored by the clerk or manager from the right rear corner of the room. This workspace, enclosed in the lower half but separated only by balusters in the upper half, functioned as follows: the manager remained unseen while seated. He could, however, monitor and oversee the showroom and the staircase leading to the dressing rooms on the first floor by means of a "blind" window and wall mirrors behind him. While standing, he could observe the situation directly through the vertical balusters. Loos later took up this feature as a central motif – the subtle supervision of the space by the owner, as we have already analyzed in the Café Museum and in the House on Michaelerplatz. At Kniže, he provided us with an even more sophisticated example, over two floors. This motif was carried over to the residential space and applied in many of his projected villas.

The staircase leading from the showroom to the first floor was only hinted at by one single extending step, so that the customer first had to slowly orient himself with his surroundings. While his eye wandered about the room discovering the illusions formed by the wall mirrors and the reflections of the glass showcases, the manager and his sales associates could evaluate his reaction to the situation. They could offer a new customer to help him and escort him to the upper floor; in this way, contact with the customer was pre-established. In the top photo on page 47, we can identify an employee who is stepping forward from behind the wall-mirror in order to greet the incoming customer.

After having his needs attended in the reception area, the customer would proceed to the first floor waiting area, designed as a homelike suite with armchairs situated on a Persian rug next to an open fireplace in front of a large curtained window overlooking the street below. Loos would later apply these elements of comfort in a similar way in his apartment house furnishings as well as in other men's tailoring salons, such as Kniže and Goldman & Salatsch in the House on Michaelerplatz. It is one of his main motifs, which he used here for the first time, in order to provide the customer a comfortable and relaxing atmosphere before and during the fitting.

Goldman & Salatsch I, 1898: office and reception area on first floor (From *Das Interieur II*, 1901)

Goldman & Salatsch I, 1898: waiting area on first floor (From *Das Interieur II*, 1901)

Goldman & Salatsch I, 1898: changing rooms on first floor (From *Das Interieur II*, 1901)

Goldman & Salatsch II, 1912:
tailoring workshop interior
(ALA 1526)

Goldman & Salatsch II, 1912: sewery
(ALA 1526)

Goldman & Salatsch II, 1912: ground floor
interior with stairs to men's tailor salon
(ALA 1526)

In the following, large, representative, historical fitting room, Loos placed a small privacy screens as a subtle room divider. This again achieved the intimate effect that he desired, which the large room had not afforded for this function. The fitting room's walls were very reminiscent of a traditional Japanese room divider – light, mobile and translucent. The small, square, white, wood frames were fitted with blue glass. Light from the window in the rear wall of this space illuminated the glass from within. This must have provoked a nearly magical atmosphere in the fitting room. Loos' most private and intimate spaces were white and soft, feminine and vulnerable, corresponding to the bedrooms in his apartments. This was again accented by the Persian rug on the floor of precisely the same dimensions as the fitting room.

In this example, one can recognize how Loos once again, at age 28 and in his second work, with the elements applied by himself, was able to create room-moods with an almost instinctive certitude of human needs from his personal analysis of Roman, American, English, Japanese and Viennese culture.

Already in 1909-12, with planning and furnishing the new Goldman & Salatsch Tailor's Salon, located in the House on Michaelerplatz, Loos brought the aforementioned ideas to masterful perfection.

Through a concave entranceway of large display windows and a small, centered doorway, the square showroom was reached. On both sides, glass showcases directed the customer to the center of the room. From this central departure point the customer could choose either to visit the showroom of the outfit department on the ground floor, the seasonal goods on the lower level, or the tailoring salon on the mezzanine via the broad and inviting staircase, which lay straight ahead. Also to be found in this central convergence area were two cash registers, one on each side of the funnel-shaped start of the stair.

Should the customer wish to visit the tailoring salon, he would have to walk up the stairs to a platform where the main staircase branched off into two separate side staircases, both of which led up to the mezzanine. Only this dividing platform extended beyond the building's facade, and was therefore covered by a skylight. Large, square, ornamented, glass bricks were mounted on the ceiling,

which, through their wave-textured surface, gave the light entering the room a blue-green hue. Suddenly, the fascinated visitor was inevitably immerged in a calm, underwater atmosphere. The surrounding mirrors and highly polished wall surfaces enlarged the somewhat small skylight, reflecting the light throughout the room and amplifying its effect to envelop the whole area in a "mystical" light.

On the way back there is another impressive effect: while descending the curved staircase, which was finished in rich mahogany, much like a precious stringed instrument, one could see the ceiling reflected in the wall mirror just above the shelves in the ground floor showroom, creating the impression of an infinitely large space, much akin to Loos' Kärntner Bar.

The tailor's book-keeping desk and the cashier were situated opposite the landing in the mezzanine. With mahogany paneling up to eye-level and an enclosure of brass poles, this was analogous to the store manager's alcove in his first parlors. But in the landing area, the wall paneling was lower, so when the customer stood on the central point of the ground floor, he could easily be seen from these workspaces, allowing the employees to make the necessary preparations for his reception in the mezzanine.

After being received in the mezzanine central hall, the customer was led directly to the elevated, homelike waiting room overlooking Michaelerplatz and the large interior space, with the various, multi-leveled workspaces of the mezzanine all connected to each other through the central hall.

Next to the clearly attestable citations and copies of English furniture and furnishing details, this area, the first one to be constructed according to Loos' sense of *Raumplan* also featured light room dividers in the mezzanine, reminiscent of the Japanese tradition.

The workshop area was separated from this presentation area and could only be accessed by way of a barrier. Whereas the walls and pillars of the showroom were furnished with polished, shiny, smooth mahogany veneer, whose luster created a mirror-like surface (as did the brilliant brass handrails and large, illusory wall mirrors), the tailor's workshop area, in contrast, was simply kept white, to have best daylight conditions for the labors, and cozy, by using low ceilings, white soft shining marble and white curtains, etc. Here is yet another parallel to the intimate furnishing of the private rooms in Loos' villas, which are in intentional contrast to the areas of the house intended for presentation.

## Shops

Of the few shops furnished by Loos, perhaps the two Ornamental Plumage Shops of the Steiner family are most exemplary of the development of Loos' architectural elements in his early phase of work (from 1904 to 1906-07).

The entrance to the shop was again kept very narrow and restrained, while deeply recessed. Thus, on one hand, Loos created an enlarged display window for the products being sold, and on the other, an enlarging effect on the rather small shop.

Concerning the assertion of the shop facade's Heinrich Kulka wrote the following: "[...] Loos' shop facades have the characteristic of allowing one to immediately guess the type of store it is, even without a sign. This is achieved through the selection of materials and the forms. The stretched S of the sign, now commonly used, was first made here. Loos says: 'The important thing is not to make legible signs, but rather to create a characteristic image with materials and symbols. The illegibility is often only a trick.' People stop at this entrance and ask themselves what the sign could possibly mean. But that is exactly how it should be."[13]

In the first Steiner Ornamental Plumage Shop (1904) a striking feature were the flower boxes on top of the shop facade, as a transition to the building's facade. Loos used this same motif on other shop facades in the inner-city area, so at the Manz bookshop or the House on Michaelerplatz, which was therefore not the first Loos' work in which he used flower boxes.

The interior of the Steiner Ornamental Plumage Shop II appeared frugal and modest. Loos used some of the same elements that he employed in his apartments: visible wood ceiling beams, tapestries as room dividers and an open fireplace.

The mirror, which in this dimension was only used in his shops, here served as an element of room-illusion, a room divider and a dressing mirror.

## Conclusion

The shops furnished by Loos were almost exclusively from his early period of work, before he could begin with the creation of single family houses or villas in 1910. The works showed typical characteristics, which were repeated among themselves, and simultaneously we witness the appearance of many elements and motifs that Loos later used in his villas.

Among these typical characteristics were the emphasized entrance area with a small sequence of rooms, the precise flow of movement, the perfect staging for the customers and the simultaneous control of the activity by the owner. The surface materials were generally more polished and shinier than in the living spaces, as presentation and display were naturally of primary importance in the showrooms. With the customer's attention, room-illusory elements were always employed, often through wall mirrors and highly polished, reflective surfaces. The stimulation of the senses and the pursuit of effect allowed the customer to dive into his own distinctive world in which the public life on the streets was very rapidly forgotten, and one soon found oneself spiritually complete in the shop's or bar's interior, easily forgetting the passage of time beyond its walls. For this reason, Loos also commonly provided homelike elements, which served for comfortable relaxation. This was especially evident in Loos' tailors and men's fashion salons.

Steiner Ornamental Plumage Shop I, 1904: exterior view
(From *Moderne Wiener Geschäftsportale*, 1914)

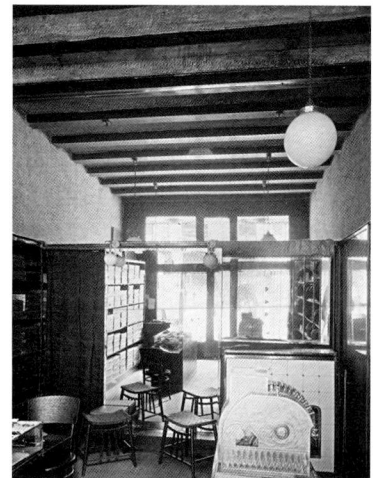

Steiner Ornamental Plumage Shop II, 1906-07: interior view
(From *Moderne Wiener Geschäftsportale*, 1914, plate 19a)

Steiner Ornamental Plumage Shop II, 1906-07:
view to shop front with plants in pots
(From *Moderne Wiener Geschäftsportale*, 1914)

[1] R+S, p. 67 (Engl. trans. L.S.).
[2] Ibid.
[3] Ludwig Münz, Gustav Künstler, *Der Architekt Adolf Loos*, Anton Schroll Verlag, Wien, 1964, p. 35 (Engl. trans. L.S.).
[4] A.L., "Architecture" (1910), in *On Architecture*, Ariadne Press, Riverside, 2002, pp. 78-9.
[5] Ludwig Hervesi, "Kunst auf der Straße", in *Fremden-Blatt*, Wien, 30 May 1899 (Engl. trans. L.S.).
[6] R+S, p. 67 (Engl. trans. L.S.).
[7] R+S, p. 459 (Engl. trans. L.S.).

[8] Münz, Künstler, *Der Architekt Adolf Loos*, cit., p. 40 (Engl. trans. L.S.).
[9] Ibid.
[10] Elana Shapira, *Assimilating with Style*, Wien, 2004, University Dissertation at Universität für angewandte Kunst (Engl. trans. L.S.).
[11] R+S, p. 412 (Engl. trans. L.S.).
[12] *Das Interieur*, Wien, 1900, II, pp. 145 ff. illustrated documentation (Engl. trans. L.S.).
[13] Heinrich Kulka, *Adolf Loos*, Anton Schroll Verlag, Wien, 1930, p. 29, Schmuckfedergeschäft Steiner, Wien, 1907 (Engl. trans. L.S.).

Josef Vogl Apartment in Pilsen, 1929: salon
Photo by M. Gerlach Jr., ca 1930
(ALA 3143)

# Apartments

## General

As of today we know of 56 apartment interiors completed by Adolf Loos. However, it is likely that there were more, as the Loos archive has only survived in fragments. This illustrates the importance that this body of work had in his life. Especially at the beginning of his career in the years between 1898 and 1909, before realizing his first constructed work in Vienna with the House on Michaelerplatz, private interiors were his means of existence.

"[...] It is so kind of you to characterize my earlier work in Vienna as 'architectonic'. Unfortunately, it is not. We live in a time when every wallpaper hanger calls himself an architect. It makes no difference. In America every stoker calls himself an engineer. But interior decorating has nothing to do with architecture. I have supported myself with it because I can do it. It is exactly the same as when I washed dishes for a time in America in order to survive. I have fitted out interiors and I am still fitting out interiors. I give suggestions. Wallpaper? We'll go to Schmidt at the "Neuen Markt". Do you want stripes or solid colors? Do you like this one? I would suggest that one. Some come to me because they do not understand it, some because they do not know the sources, some because they do not have any time. But an individual lives in his own space according to his own individuality."[1]

Loos characterized his occupation with private interiors in this text and clearly dissociated it from architecture. He saw himself rather in the role of an outfitter and a consultant to the client. In the second part of the quotation, however, he indicated that this occupation meant far more to him than mere means of existence. It was the transcending cultural and social concern of guiding man to his "own" apartment via cultural education. It was the practical realization of what he started in his essays. Despite this pedagogical component to his work,

Loos responded to the various preferences and characters of his clients without dogma and with remarkable precision, which led both to close friendships after the completion of his work as well as follow-up commissions. This close relationship to his clients is a characteristic worth mentioning within the body of his constructed work and can also be attributed to his ideas formulated in writing.

It was also a reaction to the idea of the total work of art (*Gesamtkunstwerk*) as it was promoted by the Wiener Werkstätten with Josef Hoffmann. Loos did not wish to use his clients' insecurities, unwittingness and lack of time to illustrate his own artistry, as he charged the "applied artists" of doing in designing and building something unique for their clients only for the sake of later publishing it in architectural magazines.

"The spokespersons for modern artists tell you that they decorate all living spaces according to your individual taste. That is a lie. An artist can only decorate a space in his way. Only you can decorate your own home. Because thereby, your home will become your own."[2]

Loos emphatically resented this superficiality of design, which was solely concerned with the effect of the drawing and the photographic reproduction, through which the artists presented their ideas in magazines. The responsibility of designing an apartment for the specific personality of a client and his family was a highly intimate task for Loos and required a great degree of empathy and restraint in order to respond to the clients' needs. Moreover, the furnishing of an apartment was not a finished work, but had to be able to respond to its inhabitants' life and as such be conceived as an open system, which could be changed and added to. A once-and-for-all finished design including all the fixtures was not suitable for life's changes. The apartment was a lifelong stage for the appearance of its inhabitants and their guests, in which they could show their feelings, backgrounds and preferences, and where life's complexities could develop. It was the private realm of the modern citizen in which he could nurture his personal inclinations and preferences, as opposed to the public realm, where he had to hide these behind the mask of modern clothing.

Loos on the total work of art of the Viennese Workshops in the satire "Von einem armen, reichen Mann" ["The Poor Little Rich Man"]: "The architect did not wait for him to say it twice. He went into the rich man's home, threw out all his furniture, called in an army of [craftsmen ...] and presto, quicker than you could blink an eye, Art was captured, boxed in, and taken into good custody within the four walls of the rich man's home.

"The rich man was overjoyed... The art journals extolled him as one of the leading patrons of the arts; his rooms were reproduced as models, commented upon, and explained. [...]

"The home was comfortable but it taxed the owner's brain. Therefore, the architect supervised the inhabitants in the first weeks so that no mistake might creep in. The rich man gave his best efforts. [...] However, it must not be kept a secret that he preferred to be home as little as possible. [...] Who would blame him for gathering new strength in a café, in a restaurant, or among friends and acquaintances? He had thought things would be different. But art requires sacrifice. [...]

"Once it happened that he celebrated his birthday. His wife and children had lavished gifts upon him. The things pleased him exceedingly and were a source of true joy to him. The architect arrived soon thereafter to look after the correctness of things and to make decisions on difficult matters. [...]

"'I have called you, my dear architect, so that you can give us some advice as to how we can best display these things.'

"The architect's face grew noticeably longer. Then he exploded, 'How do you come to allow yourself to be given gifts! Did I not design everything for you? Did I not consider everything? You don't need anything more. You are complete!'

"[...] 'But what if my grandchild gives me something he has made at kindergarten?'

"'Then you must not accept it!'

"The master of the house was crushed. But he did not yet give up. An idea, yes, an idea!

"'And what if I wanted to buy myself a painting at the Secession?' he asked triumphantly.

"'Then just try to hang it somewhere. Don't you see that there is room for nothing more? Don't you see that for every picture that I have hung for you here I have also designed a frame on the partition or the wall? You can't even move a picture. Just try to find a place for a new picture!'

"Then a transformation took place in the rich man. The happy man suddenly felt deeply, deeply unhappy. He imagined his future life. No one was allowed to give him pleasure. He would have to pass by the shops of the city impervious to all desires. Nothing more would be made for him. None of his dear ones was permitted to give him a picture. For him there were to be no more painters, no more artists, no more craftsmen. He was precluded from all future living and striving, developing and desiring. He thought, this is what it means to learn to go about life with one's own corpse. Yes indeed!! He is finished! He is *complete*!"[3]

This satire by Loos most clearly illustrates his inner convictions. The inclusion of the authentic and the personal, as well as the extension and alteration of the apartment's interiors were clearly more important than the artistic idea.

## As You Like

In the following excerpt, Loos describes his parents' home and notes that the objects within the apartment were tied to personal memories and experiences of its inhabitants. This personal relationship to one's own apartment could not originate from a completely, newly designed apartment, which is why Loos often tried to integrate family heirlooms into his designs. One's own apartment must be able to grow. This notion of evolutionary development is a fundamental idea to Loos. Man lives in the present, the past shapes his experiences and memories, which cannot be erased, and he projects his hopes and developments into the future. An apartment's interior ought to take all of this into consideration, and this cannot be achieved by a design in which all objects are created at the same instance. This would accomplish merely a momentary image, a photographic representation, or as Loos puts it: a hotel room, a "caricature of an apartment", without any personal relationship or potential for development.

"I did not, thank God, grow up in such a 'stylish' apartment. In those days they were unknown.

Rudolf Kraus Apartment, 1907: annex to the
living room with integrated plants in pots
and aquarium
(ALA 3121)

Rudolf Kraus Apartment, 1907: annex
to the living room
(ALA 3120)

Wilhelm Hirsch Apartment, 1907-08: view from
dining room to living room; showing transition
zone as "winter garden" with integrated plants
in pots and wall mirror
Photo by M. Gerlach Jr., ca 1930
(ALA 3113)

Now, unfortunately, things have changed in my family as well. But in those days! Take the table: a crazy jumble of a table with some dreadful metalwork. But our table, *our* table! Can you imagine what that meant? Can you imagine what wonderful hours we spent at it? By lamplight! In the evening when I was a little boy I just could not tear myself away from it, and father kept having to imitate the night watchman's horn to make me scuttle off in fright into the nursery. My sister Hermine spilled ink on it when she was a little tiny baby. And the pictures of my parents! What dreadful frames! But they were a wedding present from father's workmen. And this old-fashioned chair here! A leftover from grandmother's home. And here an embroidered slipper in which you can hang the clock. Made in kindergarten by sister Irma. Every piece of furniture, every object, every thing had a story to tell, the story of our family. Our home was never finished, it developed with us, and we with it. It was certainly without 'style'; that is, it had no alien, no old 'style'. But it did have a style, the style of its occupants, the style of our family. [...]

"We want to be lords and masters within our own four walls again. If we lack taste, that's fine, we'll furnish our homes in a tasteless manner. If we have good taste, all the better. But we refuse to be tyrannized by our own rooms any longer. We will buy everything, as we happen to have need of it and as we like.

"As we like! There we have the style we have been seeking for so long, the style we wanted to bring into our apartments."[4]

An apartment that included such personal references in its furnishing would be authentic and would show very much of the personality of its inhabitants.

Subconsciously perceived moods played an important role for Loos in furnishing his apartments. One was fascinated upon entering these rooms; there was an immediate sense of security, an immersion into the inner world of the apartment. One could relax and lose all connection to the outside world.

None of the archive photos of Loos' apartments show views out of a window. On the contrary, if windows were shown at all, they were draped with curtains or made of opaque glass and served solely as light sources to illuminate the rooms with the desired effect. In the same way, one often notices drapes in front of the doorways to other rooms – membranes that amplify a sense of security and of being enveloped, much in the sense of Semper's theory, who identified this need as the origin of the evolution of architecture.

### Mood and Effect

*Architecture arouses moods in people, so the task of the architect is to give these moods concrete expression. A room must look cozy, a house comfortable to live in.* (Adolf Loos)[5]

I have already discussed these sentences in the chapter "Written Works". This is his theoretical statement, but did he implement this in his apartment?

Moods must be experienced for feeling the effect, this could only be done by using or visiting a Loos' apartment interior. Unfortunately, there is not a single complete apartment interior preserved, unlike his houses, of which we have numerous, nearly complete interiors. With regards to the apartments, there are only single rooms or fragments of the furnishings preserved, which are no longer used for the purpose of living. By the same token, no personal description of an apartment's furnishing has remained to us from which one could derive the impression that the inhabitants or visitors gained from the apartments.

In his apartments, Loos began to apply his concept of *Raumstimmungen* ("room moods"), which he had already developed in theory in his writings. Later, with his villas, where Loos made the further addition of the *Raumplan*, having the possibility to control the construction as well as the directed lighting, he naturally developed these "room moods" more impressively and with greater complexity than the apartment furnishings; but his stylistic devices as well as materials, wall coverings and furniture remained the same.

I do wish to describe one example of how Loos made an effort to achieve what he called a "home feeling" for the inhabitants.

Referring to Semper, who defined the lining of rooms with textiles as a basic human instinct, he wrote: "Job of the architect is to create a warm, cozy room. Carpets are warm and cozy, so he decides to spread one over the floor and hang up four to make the four walls."[6]

In his work on apartment interiors he typically implemented this by choosing hardwood floors, which he covered with either wall-to-wall rug or Persian rugs. The windows and door openings could be covered with movable textile curtains. Above the wall paneling in wood or natural stone, he also liked to use wallpapers, even of textile or grass, besides using paint and plaster finishes. Upholstered benches in fabric were integrated into the wall paneling. The wallpapers, rugs, curtains and upholsteries also had patterns that could be identified as ornaments by a strict interpretation of the word. But as Loos already wrote in 1924: "Lack of ornamentation does not mean lack of attractiveness, but is a new attraction [...].

"26 years ago I maintained that the use of ornamentation on objects of practical use would disappear with the development of mankind, a constant and consistent development, which was as natural a process as the atrophy of vowels in final syllables in popular speech. By that I did not mean what some purists have carried ad absurdum, namely that ornamentation should be systematically and consistently eliminated."[7]

This shows the difference between his essays – which aimed to reveal the alienation of the prevailing contemporary styles from usability and everyday use by means of polemic, satire and pointed phrasing, and to encourage his contemporaries to reconsider their stance – and his actual realizations. Therefore, it is not to be expected to find a full implementation of his written words in every aspect of his realized objects, as both belong to different categories of art. It is however inadmissible to imply that Loos' written work contradicts his actual buildings.

In Loos' own short descriptions, or in those of the critic Hervesi, we find clues concerning his endeavors to better control the light in the various areas of his apartments and to use it more effectively.

In the Rudolf Kraus apartment at Nibelungengasse 13, 1010 Vienna, which he finished in 1907, he added an annex to the dining room, which he described as "half inglenook and half winter garden". Hervesi, however, called this annex an "enchanted grotto". Loos lined the whole niche with skyros marble to the full height of the room, concluding the upper part of the wall with a Donatello frieze around the annex. The window reveal was built as an aquarium through which light penetrated. Next to the window the marble paneling stepped down to form planters for exotic plants. The open fireplace was conspicuously placed in the central axis of the salon in front of the wall. A "U"-shaped, upholstered bench was placed within the niche around a small table, which remained hardly visible from the salon.

Loos repeated the water motive in relationship to the marble paneling in the apartments for Bellak and Friedmann by including a room fountain with a water outlet placed in the wall and a floor basin for goldfish, lined with blue mosaic tiles. In the Duschnitz houses and in the famous Müller Villa in Prague, Loos again used the aquarium motive in connection with the marble wall panels. A theme I will examine closely in the chapter "Villas with Gardens".

Another way to control the light in the apartment and the views from the neighboring houses was Loos' solution to furnish the interior window pane with small squares (approximately 10 × 10 cm) or horizontally oriented rectangular pieces of transparent with cut border or translucent, glass. The accomplished effect was similar to the light parchment wall of the traditional Japanese house. For the following apartments this type of window treatment is documented: Georg and Else Weiss', 1904; Alfred Kraus', 1905; Arthur and Leonie Friedmann's, 1906; Bellak's, 1907; Rudolf Kraus', 1907; Leo Brummel's, 1929; Wilhelm Hirsch's, 1929.

The atmosphere that is communicated in the archive images that have survived, and which I also found in my personal experience while visiting some of these rooms, is enhanced by the limited visibility through the windows. Loos focused the views to the interiors; the relationship to the exterior is lost. There is an immediate sense of security. The inhabitant has the feeling that he can move freely, without being observed by the exterior world, even while located in a dense urban environment.

The pronounced detachment from the urban exterior and also from nature is countered by bringing the natural elements inside the apartment: water (fountain, aquarium), fire (fireplace) and earth (plants). Nature is also represented in a highly abstract manner by the natural grain of the materials used, which are large marble or wood panels. This motif was perfected by Loos in his houses in combination with his concept of the space plan [Raumplan] to an inner landscape.

Bellak Apartment, 1907: the fountain in the living room
(ALA 3101)

Bellak Apartment, 1907: living room and music room
(ALA 2046)

Georg Weiss Apartment, 1904: living room (ALA 2159)

A. Kraus Apartment, 1905: bay with bench in the dining room (ALA 2336)

Wilhelm Hirsch Apartment, 1929-30: garden room (ALA 3115)

## Apartment Furnishing

In furnishing an apartment, Loos distinguished between movable furniture and immovable furniture that stood against a wall. To the latter he included closets, bookshelves, couches, sideboards and glass cabinets. It was the architect's role to include these immovable fixtures into the design of the walls, following English and American examples. With this he liberated the room from unnecessary furniture and increased the space to arrange the movable furniture, which was not to be designed by an architect, but to be built by a craftsman. Loos wrote in his 1924 essay "Die Abschaffung der Möbel" ["The Elimination of Furniture"]: "Any cabinetmaker can make the objects I use for my interiors. I am not an architect who wants to patent his ideas. Any craftsman in marble or textiles, any manufacturer can make my things and they do not have to beg my permission. The main thing is that he does honest work. And there is nothing I have avoided in my life so much as producing new forms.

"Architects are there to get to the bottom of life, to think through people's needs to the very end, to help the disadvantaged in our society and to equip as large a number of households as possible with perfect objects of everyday use. Architects are not there to invent new forms."[8]

Loos addresses the absolute necessity for the architect to understand the "depth of life" in designing an apartment interior in the second part of this quotation, as was already discussed at the beginning of this chapter. And he emphasized his thesis that it is not the architect's duty to design new forms in furnishing an apartment, but that his role is merely to guide the client in the selection of the furniture, as a consultant. For Loos this consultation was based on a repertoire of furniture designs from various centuries that he determined as comfortable and functional, and therefore "modern". Loos ordered these design copies by craftsmen or firms like Friedrich Otto Schmitt, who produced handmade custom furniture. This method aimed to avoid the constraints of contemporary fashion, which could very quickly become unfashionable, and the inhabitants would want to change within a few years. Loos published a response to a reader's question in *Das Andere* in 1903 in this regard: "A resigned letter to Loos: 'I have now been married for thirty years. I have had to let the house be newly refurnished three times [...]'.

"Loos' reply: 'You see, you could have saved yourself the trouble. You should have furnished your house modernly the first time. Then you would have always lived modernly and comfortably. It's true that the apartment from 1873 has no similarities to today's apartment. But for the most part, the furniture would have remained the same. Positioned differently, organized differently. It would have allowed for new discoveries. Electric light, the possibility of providing illumination in any point, would have been enough to revolutionize the disposition of your furniture. Much would have been annihilated and replaced. Much would have been created anew. Gifts, souvenirs, pictures, books and sculptures, gas heating, everything – everything would have helped, worked, mined and exploded in your apartment. People expand, rise to new heights, set higher expectations in life. The old furniture from 1873 would have gone quite well with the new furniture from 1903. Just as in an old castle the furniture from 1673 goes quite well with the furniture from 1703. Your apartment could have offered a reflection of your character. You would have had an apartment where no one but yourself could live – only you alone. You would have possessed your apartment. But now you may begin to work on your apartment. It is never too late. You have children. They will thank you for it.'"[9]

## Living Area

The interiors that Loos furnished were typically large apartments with high ceilings, located on one floor of a multi-story residential building of an upper-middle class type, known as *Zinshaus*, in Vienna and Pilsen.

The apartments of his Viennese clients, who were from the upper-middle class and by all means affluent, were built in the late 19th Century during the period of the Viennese historicist style. The structural system of these houses was based on a load-bearing central wall that ran parallel to the street elevation. This layout generated a sequence towards the street facade of the apartment of almost square rooms that were for the most part interconnected as suites by double-winged doors. The rooms facing the courtyard were for circulation, as well as bathroom, kitchen and adjoining rooms.

Loos used generous openings to connect the single rooms in the living area, or he had them enlarged. He typically had the wings of the doors removed between the living, dining and music rooms as well as the room containing the fireplace. If a separation was requested he replaced the doors with textiles.

He worked room by room, which meant that each room had a particular use and therefore a specific interior that generated the desired mood. As a result, the individual rooms were treated as separate entities and were furnished quite differently from each other, although visually connected. Loos later used and further developed this principle in the space plan in his houses. For Loos the living areas typically included the salon, derived from the English drawing room, the study with library and work desk, the music room, the dining area and the inglenook. This layout corresponded approximately to that of the English country house, which served as an inspiration for Loos' interpretation of the living area.

The walls were paneled to two-thirds or half of the full height of the room. The materials were selected as required for the client's needs for representation, and varied from marble and travertine, to dark oak or mahogany, to softwood panels painted white. Above the paneling were mostly English or Japanese wallpapers with slight ornamentation, or plain and rough plaster with sometimes a stucco frieze beneath the ceiling painted in a single color. Paintings or graphics were to be seen on the paneling as well as above. For the stucco frieze that terminated the intersection of the wall towards the ceiling, he occasionally used copies of antique figurative friezes, or friezes with a "Donatello"-motif from the Italian Renaissance in more representative apartments. Built-in cupboards, seating corners and benches were integrated into the wall paneling. By integrating many elements into the wall paneling, Loos accomplished many horizontal surfaces for multiple possibilities for arranging the inhabitants' personal goods .

Loos liked to use visible wooden beams in the ceiling, which typically had no structural function and could be regarded as decorative, serving exclusively to induce a certain mood. Depending on the furnishing of the room, he used either dark oak timber or wooden beams painted white. The decorative motive of the exposed ceiling beams that Loos often used in his houses was derived from the English country house.

Lighting was usually located at the sitting ar-

eas. The ceiling lighting was replaced with wall lighting except in the dining area, which was illuminated from the ceiling, centered on the dining table.

The existing hardwood floor was preserved and covered with Persian rugs. One variation to this was a light green felt covering stretched over the whole floor, again covered with Persian rugs.

The few free-standing pieces of furniture could be family heirlooms or tables and chairs as recommended by Loos, which were for the most part furniture of English origin that was seemingly very comfortable.

An important quote by Loos as reported by Kulka in his monograph of 1930: "Loos explains the frequent use of corner benches in his apartments as well as the positioning of the other furniture along the walls as follows: 'Nowadays, the layout of the room is centrifugal, as we are being influenced by Japan. The furniture is placed in the corners of the room (not tilted, but straight). The center is left free (space for movement). The artificial light belongs where we need it. There is no emphasis on the center." [10]

## Inglenook

The open fireplace is a feature we find in almost every apartment furnished by Loos. Its design may vary, from the cast of a hearth of a French Renaissance castle, to marble paneling, to a fireplace laid in brick.

If the space allowed for it, an inglenook was created with a large opening towards the living room. Around this fireplace, which was predominantly gas-burning, Loos arranged comfortable armchairs. If there was not sufficient space to separate this area, the fireplace was integrated into the wall paneling of either the living room or the dining room.

From 1905 onwards, Loos liked to combine the motif of the mirror with the fireplace, often placing a mirror over it, preferable above the heads of the sitting people. His intention, most likely more than anything, was to create the illusion of an extended space. The open fire belongs to the primitive hut and is a symbol of warmth, shelter and nurturing. It is the center around which people gathered. This symbolic significance and the relaxing atmosphere most likely determined Loos' choice to use this element of the English country house in his urban interiors, as the apartments

Bellak Apartment, Vienna, 1907-13: salon
Photo by M. Gerlach Jr., ca 1930
(ALA 2045)

Beck Apartment, Pilsen, 1928: salon
Photo by M. Gerlach Jr., ca 1930
(ALA 2040)

Friedmann Apartment, Vienna, 1906-07:
fireplace in the study
(ALA 2157)

were already equipped with a much more efficient and sophisticated heating system.

Heinrich Kulka on this matter: "The 'Adolf Loos Apartment' breaths the spirit of English comfort. He often used the open fireplace, as is typical in England and France [...]. The animated fire is also a comfortable focal point for an apartment house."[11]

### Dining Area

The dining area was an individually designed space for Loos and had its own room if the size of the apartment allowed for it. The dining room was essentially different from the living area (drawing room) where everyone should find his individual relaxation in a comfortable posture and activity, and where conversation was being entertained on light and moveable easy chairs. The dining room, however, was the place where the family gathered every day to eat and was therefore of spiritual and mythical importance, as it also was for Frank Lloyd Wright. Every member of the family should have the same chair and sit up straight. Loos usually used copies of Chippendale chairs that he had built by the furniture maker Josef Veillich in Vienna. In Loos' opinion they were perfect and could not be surpassed for this function.

The dining table was always in the center of the room. The whole room was focused on this area. The dining room always felt more intimate than the living area and was dimensioned to fit the size of the family.

The walls, floors and ceiling were designed with the same elements as already described in regards to the living room.

Löwenbach Apartment, Vienna, 1913: living room and study with inglenook
Photo by M. Gerlach Jr., ca 1930
(ALA 3125)

Mayer Apartment, Vienna, 1913: inglenook
Photo by M. Gerlach Jr., ca 1930
(ALA 3132)

Leopold Langer Apartment, Vienna, 1903: inglenook in the dining room
Photo by M. Gerlach Jr., ca 1930
(ALA 3124)

Loos liked to use a lower reaching wall mirror in the dining room that often came down to eye level with the seated inhabitants, so that the heads and faces were mirrored. With this Loos utilized the mirror not only to create the illusion of extended space but also to hold a mirror up to the family, which could mean on a moral level that one can only sit down with the other family members with a clear conscience, and that one's actions in life should be in accordance to this.

## Bedroom

Loos' reply to his third wife, Claire, who asked him why there should only be one double bed in the bedroom: "[...] The bed, the bedroom is the most sacred, most private affair, no outsider may desecrate this sanctuary. [...] The bedroom should not have a door to the common rooms."[12]

The master bedroom was furnished with light colored precious woods (e.g. maple, ash), softwood painted white and with light and bright textiles. Its appearance was therefore much softer and more delicate and seemed much more feminine than the rather masculine living areas. It was the most intimate room in the apartment and Loos' design emphasized this. The textile cover with animal skin was for Loos the oldest architectural detail, as man sought for his sleep warmth and shelter from the harsh weather. This was already described in "The Principle of Cladding". The most obvious and most sensual implementation of this principle was Loos' own bedroom, which he designed for his first wife, Lina Loos, in 1903. Its appeal was not only sheltering but in fact also very sensual.

He also used wall paneling or textile curtains in the bedroom and covered the walls around the room to less than the full height; behind the curtains or in the walls were integrated wardrobes or built-in cabinets.

The master bedroom always had a double bed, which was centered on one wall, often with a little niche built into the paneling at the headboard, dominating the room. A separate day bed or little couch for resting was predominantly placed at the foot of the double bed. The master bedrooms were typically very special and always contained the woman's dressing table, in some cases also the woman's writing desk at the window. Loos abstained from using mirrors in the bedroom with the exception of the small mirror on the woman's dressing table, which had no special effect on the room.

## Bathroom

Loos attributed great importance to the care of the body and its cleanliness. Thus, to him the bathroom is not only an extremely important element of the modern apartment, but also a tool for measuring the degree of cultural development of a population.

"The plumber is the pioneer of cleanliness. He is the first craftsman in the state, the billeting officer for civilization, for the civilization of today. [...]

"To increase the amount of water we use is one of the most urgent tasks facing our civilization. Let us hope the plumbers of Vienna will do their utmost to bring us closer to our goal of achieving the same level of civilization as the other advanced nations of the West. [...]"[13]

For the cultural development of the Austrian and German people, it was a major concern of Loos' to improve hygiene and cleanliness. Compared to the English and American standard of the time, only a few apartments were equipped with running water and bathrooms.

"An apartment without a bathroom! An impossibility in America. The idea that there is a country of millions at the end of the 19th Century, whose inhabitants cannot bathe daily, is a monstrous one for Americans. [...] Actually we do not need art at all. We do not even have a culture yet. The state could act as a savior in this regard. Instead of putting the cart before the horse, instead of using money for the creation of art, it should be used for the creation of culture. Next to academies they should build public baths, and next to professors they should hire bath attendants. A higher art will follow the creation of a higher culture, which will reveal itself, with or without the help of the state."[14]

## Adolf and Lina Loos Apartment, 1903

Of the two-and-a-half room apartment that Loos furnished on the occasion of his marriage to Lina in 1903, with her parents' money, one has been preserved in the Museum of the City of Vienna, where the living room with the adjacent inglenook are located. The second room we know of is the bedroom, which is only documented through a publi-

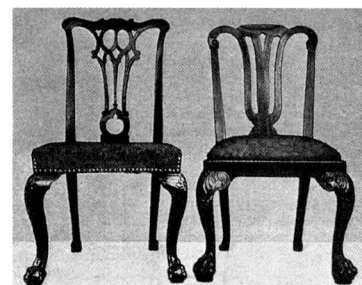

Original Chippendale chairs
(From H. Muthesius, *Das englische Haus*, vol. III, 1906)

Hermann and Eugenie Schwarzwald
Apartment, Vienna 1905-09: dining room
Photo by M. Gerlach Jr., ca 1930
(ALA 3137)

Paul Khuner Apartment, Vienna, 1907:
dining room
Photo by M. Gerlach Jr., ca 1930
(ALA 3116)

Mayer Apartment, Vienna, 1913: dining room
Photo by M. Gerlach Jr., ca 1930
(ALA 3131)

Otto Beck Apartment, Pilsen, 1928: bedroom
Photo by J. Hanus, ca 1930
(ALA 2039)

Sobotka Apartment, Vienna, 1904: bedroom
(ALA 2549)

61

cation and description. The exact layout of the whole apartment is unknown, but it can be assumed that in addition to these rooms there was only a kitchen, a bathroom and the hallway. It was a small apartment in which Loos lived throughout his entire life in Vienna.

Loos was 32 years old and had furnished about half a dozen apartments when he began to design his own. Here he was able to clearly articulate his ideas about interiors – ideas that he had already formulated in writing five years earlier in his newspaper essays for the *Neue Freie Presse* in 1898, and that he maintained and developed in his further work.

Dark oak wall paneling on all the walls in the living room to the height of the door. A built-in corner bench upholstered in pigskin with a square dining table. A flat white ceiling with non-structural, exposed beams in dark stained oak. Hardwood floors covered with Persian rugs. A wide opening with a wooden lintel and a tapestry curtain towards the inglenook. An open fireplace made of brick, with a pyramidal copper hood. Next to the fireplace, bookshelves with Loos' library. To the right of the fireplace, a U-shaped, upholstered bench with a backrest in the full depth of the niche. To the left of the fireplace, stools in front of the set of bookshelves and a window to the street, which had in its upper part colored glass inlays, a motif that he used a little later for the distinct outdoor advertising of the Kärntner Bar.

The ceiling in the inglenook was suspended lower, and therefore the height of this small room was reduced, corresponding to its proportions and its more intimate quality. The ceiling beams were also dark stained oak, which reinforced the association with the English country house of the late 19th Century.

The bedroom walls were draped all around with a loosely hung, white batiste-rayé to about door height. Behind this drapery were cabinets made of softwood, lacquered white, and also a window towards the street. The floor was covered with a light blue colored stretch carpet topped with a huge rug made of white angora rabbit skins that extended over the bed, which projected into the room. All furniture pieces, like the dressing table and nightstands, were also upholstered with white batiste.

The contrast between the private area – intimate, light colored and soft – and the more public, representative, darker colored and harder area was made very obvious in this interior. This distinction was found again and again with his objects, also in his business interiors, where he articulated this differentiation with different means but with the same statement.

These rooms inspired moods by means of the materials used as well as the controlled lighting. Here, Loos had already defined his most important concerns regarding inhabiting.

## Comfortable Living

The most important quality of a piece of furniture in the living room was its comfort and its ability to allow for fast and effective relaxation; this was the

main criterion for Loos, and not its aesthetics or date of design. Loos found this demand for comfort fulfilled, above all, in English furniture. He was deeply impressed that the English had developed different kinds of furniture for different ways to relax in one's home; Loos used this in his own designs. In America, however, Loos was able to experience the carefree attitude the Americans had towards their sitting postures, which did not comply with European education and customs. As a result, he appealed for a reconsideration of the European posture, also for economic reasons: "At the moment we not only demand of a chair that we can rest our bodies in it, but also that we can recover our energy quickly in it. Time is money. Thus resting has become specialized. After mental labor, one needs a different position for resting than after exercise in the open air; different after gymnastics than after riding; different after cycling than after rowing. And there is something else: different degrees of tiredness demand different techniques of resting, and this, in order to accelerate recuperation, is achieved by using several different types of seating one after the other, with several different positions and postures. Have you never felt, especially when you were extremely tired, that you wanted to hang one foot over the armrest? In principle, a very uncomfortable position, but at times a real relief. In America this relief is always obtainable because no one thinks that sitting comfortably, that is, recovering quickly, is inelegant. There you can even rest your feet on a table, as long as it is not used for food. Here, however, there are still those who are offended by other people making themselves comfortable."[15]

The notion of comfort in living had a very high significance for Loos. He made his own observations and experiences and arrived at refined solutions.

"The English and the Americans, free of such pettiness, are real virtuosos in relaxation. In the course of this century they have invented more types of chair than all nations put together, in all countries, since the world began. Following the principle that every type of tiredness requires a different chair, an English room is never furnished with one type of seat alone. Any room will have all kinds of seating. Everyone can choose the one that suits him best. The exceptions are those rooms used only occasionally, and then for the same purpose by all occupants of the house, for example the ballroom and the dining room. But the drawing room, in accordance with its purpose, will have light chairs, that is, chairs that can be easily moved. They are not there for resting on, but to provide flexible seating to stimulate conversation. It is easier to chat on small, unpredictable chairs than in a comfortable old high-backed armchair, and that is why the English make them. [...] The Viennese, either because they did not recognize their purpose, or perhaps because they had a patent chair for all sitting requirements in mind, called them impractical."[16]

Loos also explained the development of our sitting postures as compared to those of the Greeks. The antique chair of the Greeks was therefore not modern anymore and should no longer be used: "The Greeks, who demanded of a chair that it provide plenty of room to accommodate the curvature of the spine [...] would find our chair backs uncomfortable, since we want to have something to lean our shoulder blades against."[17] He also explained the use of the American rocking chair, so that the Europeans would use it properly in the future: "And what would they say to the American rocking chair, which even we have no idea at all what to do with! We think that in a rocking chair one has to rock backwards and forwards. I think this misunderstanding probably comes from the American name rocker. Rocking is a see-sawing movement, but, basically, the rocker is a chair with two back legs in which the feet of the person sitting on it perform the function of the front legs. It arose from the comfortable position you get when you shift your center of gravity backward, lifting the front legs of the chair off the ground. The rear rockers are to stop the chair tipping over backward. The American rocking chair does not have rockers at the front like ours, since it would never occur to anyone over there to rock back and forward in the chair. For that reason some rooms in America have nothing but rockers, while over here they are still very unpopular."[18]

Aside from the notion of comfort regarding seating furniture, Loos once again demands, towards the end of his essay, that it simply be practical: "So every chair should be practical. If manufacturers made only practical chairs, then people would be able to furnish their rooms perfectly without the assistance of the interior designer."[19]

Adolf Loos Apartment, Vienna, 1903:
inglenook
Photo by M. Gerlach Jr., ca 1930
(ALA 3128)

Adolf Loos Apartment, Vienna, 1903:
bedroom
(ALA 2389)

## English Furniture

"The English are bad musicians but they are good chair-makers. English carpenters have already kept the secret of a good seat and proper repose well-guarded for a century. We would be idiots not to use their methods. While we fritter our time away trying to create a newer chair, the English are diligently working on a better one. Let us therefore begin with the English model, whose effectiveness has already been established. We may attempt to find the better chair. It will not be much different from the English variety, as the English variety is already very good. In fact, it will resemble it to the millimeter. Furniture sets are finished; the personal, individual chair now belongs in our living space. There is only one exception: the dining room. In this room, all members of a family congregate briefly for the same activity. There, every individual gives up some amount of personal comfort in order to create a communal dining experience. [...] As for other rooms, we should ask that they be furnished in such a way as to allow for other objects without disturbing the effect, regardless of the style, material and period to which they might belong. [...] The English armchair is an absolutely complete object. There are many such perfect examples in every category of furniture in England and America. I believe that every year only one make of furniture is created in the entire world with extended staying-power. All the others become as unbearable to people as an old hat and are disposed of in a few years."[20]

## Criticism

Loos criticized the interiors designed by the architects of the Secession and the later Wiener Werkstätten, as well as interiors that were completely designed in one historic style: "When I visit such an apartment, I pity the poor people who spend their lives there. Is this then the backdrop that these people have had created for the small pleasures and the great tragedies of this existence?!!! This??

"Alas, you wear these apartments like a Pierrot-costume from a mask pawn shop!"[21]

And elsewhere: "The painters, whom we had thought of as such paragons of taste, when they did paintings of interiors, ignored our magnificent apartments and painted the homes of the stupid peasant, or the poor laborer, or the old spinster. How can anyone find such things beautiful? For, as we have been taught, the beauty of an apartment lies in its 'style'.

"But the painters were right... [they] have always recognized the superficial, pretentious, alien, unharmonious nature of our 'stylish' apartments. The people do not fit in with the rooms, nor the rooms with the people. And how could they? The architect or the interior designer hardly even knows by name the person for whom he is working. Even if the occupant has paid for the rooms a hundred times over, they are still not his rooms. In spirit they will always remain the property of the one who created them. That is why they do not, cannot appeal to the painter. They lack any inner connection with the people who occupy them, they lack that certain something he finds in the rooms of the stupid peasant, the poor laborer, the old spinster: *a feeling of intimacy*."[22]

In this quote Loos addressed an issue that was crucial in creating his interiors: intimacy. And he succeeded in generating this emotion. It should be pointed out that Loos recognized this longing for intimacy as a cultural asset that was still shared and given natural expression among the lesser educated and simpler people, like farmers and laborers. A highly developed culture and knowledge of the issues involved were needed in order to consciously generate this emotion, as it was difficult to communicate the natural, traditional and insouciant to a more highly developed form of existence through intellectual effort once it was lost. However, the objective, as declared by Loos, was for everyone to reach this cultural level, where they could decide for themselves how they wanted to live, without being subjected to the dictates of fashion, art or industry.

"May the seriousness of life never so consume you that you suddenly become aware of your own borrowed rags! Your grandiloquence, which preens itself with the fashionable name 'applied artist', is crushed under the inexorable march of fate. Out from behind your pens, you scribes of men and souls! Write for once of birth and death, of how the cries of pain from a wounded son, of how the last breaths of a dying mother, of how the last thoughts of a daughter who wants to die, take place in a bedroom by Olbrich. One image singles itself out: the young girl, who has taken her own life. She lies prone on the floorboards. One hand still clutches the smoking revolver. On the table a letter. The suicide

Friedmann Apartment, Vienna, 1906-07: study (ALA 2165)

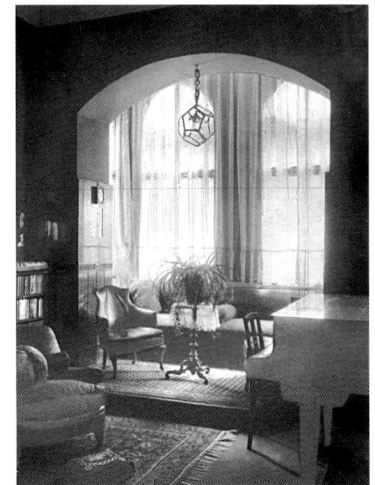

Wilhelm Hirsch Apartment, Pilsen, 1907-08: bay window in gentlemen's room (ALA 3112)

Paul Khuner Apartment, Vienna, 1907:
studio with view into salon
Photo by M. Gerlach Jr., ca 1930
(ALA 3117)

Goldman Apartment, Vienna, 1911: salon
Photo by M. Gerlach Jr., ca 1930
(ALA 3107)

note. Is the room, in which this unfolds, tasteful? Who would ask? Who would care? It is simply a room!"[23]

## Conception of Man, Ethics

"I believe it is a great mistake for people to acquire pieces of furniture made of fine woods and costly fabrics. They will have to keep a permanent eye open to make sure nothing is damaged. There are eternal materials for really living, even if only pigskin, oak or wool.

"An apartment must never be completed. Are we human beings ever finished, complete in our physical and psychological development? Do we ever come to a standstill? And if a human being is in constant movement and development, if old needs disappear and new ones arise, if Nature as a whole and everything around us is always changing, should the thing that is closest to a human being, his home, remain unchanged, dead, furnished for all time? No. It is ridiculous to lay down to people where a thing should stand, design everything for them from the lavatory pan to the ashtray. On the contrary, I like people to move their furniture round so that it suits them (not me!), and it is quite natural (and I approve) when they bring the old pictures and mementos they have come to love into a new interior, irrespective of whether they are in good taste or bad. That is not at all important to me, but for them they are charged with emotion and intimacy. *That is to say, I am an architect who designs his interiors from a human perspective and not from an inhuman artistic one*. I am astonished how many people let themselves be tyrannized by so-called 'architects for interior design'."[24]

"What does the architect really want? He uses materials to arouse feelings in us which are not inherent in those materials themselves. He builds a church. People should be put in a reverent mood. He builds a pub. People should feel at ease there. How do you do that? You see what buildings aroused those feelings in the past. That is where you must start out from..."[25]

## Conclusion

While Loos generally argued in his writings for the emancipation of the people and called on them to furnish their own apartments, and while he understood his role towards his clients as a consultant in their choice of materials and furniture, all his interiors nonetheless shared a clear handwriting. They were indeed different from the Viennese apartments of the time by their choice of heterogeneous materials and furniture, and the discrete treatment of materiality. Ultimately, they did feel homogeneous, animated, comfortable and warm. One could imagine rearranging one's furniture and relaxing, whereas Loos gave a fixed framework through his wall niches and built-in benches, that was definitely not intended to be neutral and endlessly flexible. The rooms were supposed to create moods and effects, and for this Loos' expertise and experience was necessary. Sometimes he went so far as to embed paintings or graphics into the paneling or to create niches for certain pieces of art. Loos' apartments were different from each other. They were not stereotypical, even though Loos worked with a limited vocabulary, which he deftly arranged and skillfully adapted in order to respect his clients' expectations and wishes. How skillful he was may be obvious by the fact that many of his clients gave him consecutive commissions, and that he often enjoyed lifelong friendships with them. I believe this could be taken as an argument for the fact that Loos managed to convey to his clients a sense of living in their own apartment in the same way as he expressed it in his writings. Driven by his sense of mission, Loos wanted to set good examples, for he was convinced that people always looked for examples in the higher social classes. In this sense, his interiors were an educational program for the elevation of Austrian culture rather than an architectural challenge. However, he did suffer from the fact that his works could not be disseminated through photographs in magazines; as impressive and full of atmosphere they were in reality, so they appeared unspectacular in reproduction.

## Photography and Drawing

Loos had a very critical stance towards the media of drawing and photography in architecture, as has already been indicated. For him they were merely means to help communicate the ideas of the architect; however, he witnessed how these elements became more and more independent and influenced the actual outcome of the constructed object. They no longer served to find a solution, but rather they determined it. With regards to drawing, he denounced the education of the academies of fine art, as was described in the chapter on his written work, and he held the lack of practical experience responsible for the exceeded fantasies among the architects and applied artists, who removed themselves more and more from the actual needs of the users. This was particularly apparent in the furnishing of the apartment, a space that was surrounding daily family life and was intended to serve simultaneously as a commodity and as a personal envelope with requirements of safety, a representation of one's character and interests, and a place for relaxation away from the outside world.

"But I repeat: a true building makes no impression as a picture, reduced to two dimensions. It is my greatest pride that the interiors I have created are completely lacking in effect when photographed; that the people who live in them do not recognize their own apartments from the photographs, just as the owners of a Monet would not recognize it at Kastan's? The honor of seeing my works published in the various architectural journals is something I have had to do without. The satisfaction of my vanity has been denied to me.

"Does this perhaps mean my work is without effect? Nothing of mine is known. But this is where the power of my ideas and the rightness of my teachings become apparent. I, the unpublished, am the only one among thousands who has real influence."[26]

To the same extent as Loos condemned the effect that other architects provoked with photographs of their interiors, as he accused them of being self-serving, he suffered from the fact that his works lacked the necessary impact by means of photographic reproduction and that he was therefore unable to effectively propagate his ideas through his work.

How important the photographing of his objects was to Loos, however, was made evident by the pho-tographic work of Martin Gerlach on the occasion of Loos' first monograph, which was published for his 60th birthday in 1930, and of which the original glass plates still exist. These photographs were indeed controlled, and they followed a distinct set of rules, which we can assume have been directed by Loos. If the desired effect was not achieved he, resorted to retouching and photomontage, as for instance with the street facade of the Tristan Tzara House in Paris, where the upper story, which was not built, was retouched into the photograph and the view from the window of the drawing room in the Khuner Country House, which was achieved too through montage.

The fact that Loos was also present at some of the photo shoots is documented by photographs of the Rufer House and the Moller Villa, where Loos can be seen in the pictures.

Martin Gerlach photographed with an extreme wide-angle lens, which allowed him to capture large sections of interrelated spaces and therefore the entirety of the interiors. However, using this lens distorted the actual proportions, and the depth of the spaces was sacrificed for the width of field. Gerlach typically chose a slightly higher position for his camera than human eye-level.

Loos experienced the paradigm of photography in a similar way as he experienced Josef Hoffmann's appointment as professor, and the recognition and influence on public opinion that came with it. Loos battled against the education of the School of Applied Arts and considered the whole institution as dispensable, lobbying for its disestablishment. On the other hand, it had always been his personal goal to achieve such a position and to use its potential for his own ambitions or mission. He suffered dearly from this, as could be felt through the ferocity of his personal attacks on Josef Hoffmann.

Tristan Tzara House, 1925-26: photomontage of the street facade with one additional floor on top
(From H. Kulka, *Adolf Loos*, 1931, plate 203)

Khuner Country House, 1929-30: drawing room
with photomontage of the window view
(From H. Kulka, *Adolf Loos*, 1931, plate 250)

[1] A.L., "Briefkasten Allgemeines", in *Das Andere*, 2, 1903 (Engl. trans. L.S.).

[2] A.L., "Das Heim", in *Das Andere*, 1903 (Engl. trans. L.S.).

[3] A.L., "The Poor Little Rich Man", in *Spoken into the Void*, Institute for Architecture and Urban Studies and M.I.T., 1982, pp. 125-7; original text "Von einem armen, reichen Manne", in *Neues Wiener Tageblatt*, 26 April 1900, in *Ins Leere Gesprochen*.

[4] A.L., "The Interiors in the Rotunda" (12 June 1898), in *Ornament and Crime*, Ariadne Press, Riverside, 1998, pp. 58-9; original text "Die Interieurs der Rotunde", in *N.F.P.*, 12 June 1898.

[5] A.L., "Architecture" (1910), in *On Architecture*, Ariadne Press, Riverside, 2002, p. 84.

[6] A.L., "The Principle of Cladding", in *On Architecture*, cit., p. 42; original text "Das Prinzip der Bekleidung", in *N.F.P.*, 4 September 1898, in *Ins Leere gesprochen*.

[7] A.L., "Ornament and Education" (22 August 1924), in *Ornament and Crime*, cit., pp. 186-7; original text "Ornament u. Erziehung", in *Trotzdem*.

[8] A.L., "On Thrift" (1924), in *On Architecture*, cit., p. 183; original text "Von der Sparsamkeit", in *Wohnungskultur*, issue 2/3, 1924, in *Die Potemkinsche Stadt*.

[9] A.L., "Briefkasten, Wohnung", in *Das Andere*, 1903, in *Trotzdem* (Engl trans. L.S.).

[10] Heinrich Kulka, *Adolf Loos*, Anton Schroll Verlag, Wien, 1930, p. 28 (Engl. trans. L.S.).

[11] Ibid.

[12] Claire Loos, *Adolf Loos - privat, Warum bist du nur für ein Bett*, Verlag der Johannes Presse, Wien, 1936, p. 42 (Engl. trans. L.S.).

[13] A.L., "Plumbers" (17 July 1898), in *Ornament and Crime*, cit., pp. 86-8; original text "Die Plumper", in *N.F.P.*, 17 July 1898.

[14] Ibid., p. 84.

[15] A.L., "Chairs" (19 June 1898), in *Ornament and Crime*, cit., pp. 64-5; original text "Das Sitzmöbel", in *N.F.P.*, 19 June 1898, in *Ins leere gesprochen*.

[16] Ibid., p. 65.

[17] Ibid., pp. 65-6.

[18] Ibid., p. 66.

[19] Ibid., p. 66.

[20] A.L., "Von der Sparsamkeit", in *Wohnungskultur*, issue 2/3, 1924, in *Die Potemkinsche Stadt* (Engl. trans. L.S.).

[21] A.L., "Das Heim", cit. (Engl. trans. L.S.).

[22] A.L., "The Interiors in the Rotunda", cit., pp. 57-8.

[23] A.L., "Das Heim", cit. (Engl. trans. L.S.).

[24] A.L., "On Thrift" (1924), cit., p. 182, italics mine.

[25] A.L., "The Old and New Style in Architecture" (1898), in *On Architecture*, cit., p. 33; original text "Die Alte und die neue Richtung in der Baukunst", in *Der Architekt*, 1898.

[26] A.L., "Architecture" (1910), cit., p. 78.

Strasser Villa, 1918-19: garden view
(ALA 3245)

# Villas with Gardens

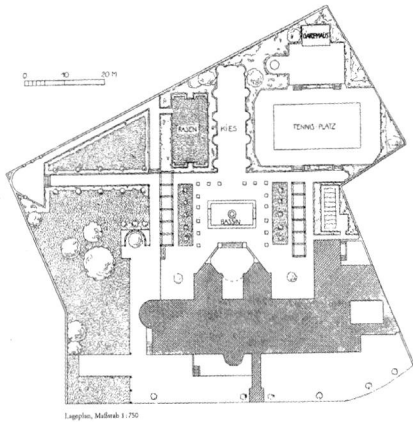

Site plan of Villa Stoclet, Brussels, 1906 by Josef Hoffmann, complete design of villa and garden
(From J. Spalt, *Gartenhäuser von Josef Hoffmann*, Hochschule für angewandte Kunst, Wien, 1985, p. 10)

## General

In Loos' works, he distinguishes between two fundamentally different approaches on this subject: the first was the design of villas in an urban environment, which were situated very close to each other along the street, with little distance to the neighboring lot, like beads on a necklace; the other regarded free standing country houses, integrated into the landscape. Loos responded accordingly to both situations with great precision and sensitivity.

At the center of his occupation were the bourgeois villas for Jewish clients in urban environments, with both new constructions as well as renovations, or more precisely, transformations of existing villas.

The urban villas of the upper-middle class that were being built in the very green and newly developed residential districts around the end of the 19th Century on what was then the outskirts of the city were shaped by historicism and the prevailing country house style, which was known as "cottage-style" in Vienna. The building lots in Vienna were typically around 700-1200 square meters. Up until that time, the middle class was living in large apartments around the newly built inner Ring or in the city center. With the beginning of the 20th Century, many of these families moved out of their urban apartments and into their own houses with gardens on the periphery of Vienna. This trend triggered questions of garden design and garden usage. As this movement was based on the model of the English country house, a typical approach was to try to create an English landscape garden; however, the lots were decidedly too small to achieve the illusion of a wide, sculpted landscape. On some occasions, particularly with some architects of the Jugendstil movement and the Wiener Werkstätten, like Josef Hoffmann and Josef Maria Olbrich, deliberate attempts were made to design decidedly

modern gardens. In these projects, the garden was conceived as continuation of the architecture, blurring the transition between house and garden. The architectural design elements (axis, tea pavilions, pergolas, benches, planting geometries with colored flowers, etc.) were carried through in the garden design. The published plans of these architects always showed the villa with the complete garden design as a whole.

Loos did the opposite, simply said. He showed only the plans of his houses without the gardens. There were no architectural elements whatsoever in his gardens. This, however, should not mean that he did not concern himself with the gardens of his villas. To assume so would be contradictory to the fact that his gardens shared many similarities and that he was acquainted with many well-known contemporary garden designers like Camillo Schneider, Leberecht Migge, Karl Förster, and Grete Salzer. He was also familiar with modern English garden designs, as the landscape garden was already out of fashion in England around the turn of the century, according to Hermann Muthesius, who in the second volume of his book *Das englische Haus* [*The English House*] from 1904, gave a thoroughly illustrated description of the new goals that the modern gardens of English villas were trying to achieve.

Loos defined a completely different type of urban villa that appeared to be very cubic and straightforward on the outside, by using plain and smooth plaster for the facade finishes. The inside, however, revealed a safe, comfortable and homelike atmosphere through refined and opulent spatial effects and moods. The various living areas were interconnected, while their differentiation was no longer by rooms but by areas. In later designs, these areas corresponded to different levels, creating the space plan [*Raumplan*] concept, propagated by Loos. All seating was oriented towards the interior spaces, which deliberately emphasized the distinction between the exterior space, which for Loos was equivalent to the "public" and the interior space, with the notion of "intimacy". Another eminent feature of Loos' work was his skillful and clever sequencing of spaces through which he guided the visitor in the house.

His work distinguished itself in that his design characteristics were defined very early in his career and continuously reused, improved, developed and adapted to his clients' characters. Loos was already 40 years old when he realized his first urban villa in Vienna for the Steiner family in 1910. He worked on this villa parallel to his first and only larger commission, the House on Michaelerplatz. Prior to that he had established his design principles very early in writing and had completed many apartment and business interiors. He carried this experience and the applied principles of his prior work forward to his villas and country houses that he continued to build until the end of his life.

## Villa and Garden Relationship

In Loos' existing architectural drawings, he did not include any garden designs, with the one exception of the small site plan for the building permit of the Horner House in 1911, in which we find traces of a garden design (scale 1:1000). However, the archive photos of the garden elevations of his villas generally show the same structure in the layout of the gardens, which was apparently determined by Loos; otherwise, this consistency could hardly be explained. Two vital characteristics support this assumption. Firstly, his sense of mission included not only architecture but targeted the education of mankind to higher culture and as such included all realms of life. Secondly, Loos maintained close, life-long friendships with his clients, which would make it inconceivable that he should not have been engaged in the finishing of his objects, including the gardens and outdoor designs.

The involvement of well-known garden architects is only documented in writing in one instance. This regarded Camillo Schneider and Karl Förster for the Müller Villa in Prague, who were hired by the client on Loos' recommendation. In 2002, in the course of an extensive renovation of the villa, the gardens were reconstructed in their original layout, thanks to the recovery of the original drawings.

In his biography, Heinrich Kulka mentioned Grete Salzer as the garden architect for the project for the Khuner Country House.

Despite extensive research, it has not been possible to identify the authorship of any of the other original garden designs of Loos' urban villas. He did not touch on the subject of garden design of villas in his writings or letters. I was able to find only very few other sources that even mentioned the garden design of his villas. It can be assumed that Loos' attitude towards garden design was similarly driven by his rejection of the idea of the total work of art that generally kept him from designing any furniture himself, while being very involved in advising his clients of their selection. As a consequence, both his interiors as well as his gardens were very similar to one another, while being distinctly different from other contemporary design solutions in Vienna.

Around the turn of the century, tendencies emerged in England in opposition to the landscape garden, which was thought to be outdated. It was to be replaced by flat or terraced topography with graveled paths, lawn and rose and flower beds around the house. The whole garden was hedged; the vegetable and fruit gardens were separately located to the side of the house, next to the kitchen area. These design principles directly coincided with the concept of the gardens of Loos' villas. Loos was certainly aware of these developments, at least through Hermann Muthesius' book *Das englische Haus*, published in German in 1904, which included a comprehensive description and commentary on this subject.

Loos' villa garden was comprised of a large lawn with few free-standing trees, but densely hedged with trees and shrubs along three sides of the property line. Typically, a narrow graveled path led around the garden between the lawn and the hedge with rose and flower beds planted along the lawn side.

The lawn, with its few primarily fruit-bearing trees, was easy to maintain and it was not so expensive. It invited play and offered shade for sitting beneath the trees. At the same time, the architecture was elevated by the flat horizontal plane of the lawn, and in this sense the garden certainly had a representative function for the architecture. The garden's function as a whole was to provide

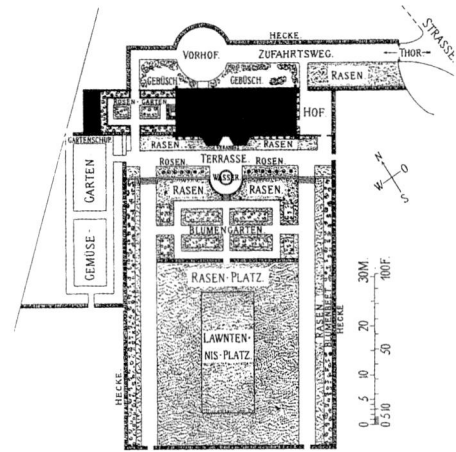

Garden composition of the Prior's Field House, Compton (Surrey), by the architect C.F.A. Voysey
(From H. Muthesius, *Das englische Haus*, vol. II, 1906, plate 37, p. 84)

the family with space for private recreation, with an intimacy that abstained from any further representational garden elements.

As the garden sizes were usually not very large in relation to the size of the villa, a high and densely planted hardwood hedge around the perimeter of the property ensured privacy and distance from the neighbors.

Loos abstained from using designed sitting areas or, for that matter, from using any architecturally designed elements in the garden. The outside sitting area was located on the terrace, which was protected by the house on higher ground and not located in the garden.

The garden terrace was always on the same level as the raised ground floor connected to the living area, and therefore clearly above the garden level. It was decidedly part of the house and not an element for blurring the transition between the house and the garden. This differentiation in height between house and garden was an aristocratic element that Loos held onto for all his life.

The terraces of the living areas were typically set slightly into the house, with additional awnings to screen the view and provide protection from the sun and from indiscreet looks. Furthermore, the terrace was framed by particular plants, like flowering clamberer. Another typical attribute of Loos' garden terrace was a closed parapet separating the garden from the terrace. The parapet was wide enough to accommodate large flower pots (Loos was fond of boxwood trees in oak pots). Moreover, the facade was often covered with vines (Japanese ivy; botanical name: *Parthenocissus tricuspidata*), so that the terrace became a "little nest", protected by the house and framed by plants. One felt secure and protected from the neighbors' gazes and from the public eye.

The stairs leading into the garden were typically always placed parallel to the exterior facade, leaning against the house rather than projecting an axis into the garden, as was preferred in the classical period. Access to the garden was therefore not staged, and was not meant to serve representative purposes, but rather as refuge for the recreation and relaxation of the family.

The Steiner House had the motif of the pond with water lilies and goldfish, which was partially submerged underneath the terrace. Loos opened up a large vertical opening beneath the terrace for this purpose. He replicated this motif of a large opening beneath the terraces in other villas, but the existence of ponds in these cases has not been documented. The contemplative element of the water lily and goldfish pond appeared both in the contemporary English garden as well as the traditional Japanese tea garden.

The interior rooms, however, did not open up towards the garden. It was not the intention of Loos to connect the garden with the living area. He created the possibility of outdoor seating in a very sensitive and atmospheric manner, just as he did with his rooms. Nonetheless, his principle of strict separation between the public and the intimate led to a "internalization" of his concept of living. From this orientation towards the interior and the creation of rooms that emanated an atmosphere of security, Loos developed the "inner landscape" of the space plan (*Raumplan*) step-by-step and in a linear process.

The deliberate separation between the house and the garden in Loos' work is particularly noteworthy in the context of his time. Since the publication in 1907 of Hermann Muthesius' *Landhaus und Garten* [*Country House and Garden*],[1] the idea of unity of house and garden was widely pursued by the architects of the Werkbund and the Secession. The book described in great detail examples in Germany, among others, from Mies van der Rohe, Peter Behrens and Josef Maria Olbrich. The plans naturally showed the whole property, including the garden designs and the positioning of the villa. Plan solutions were adjusted to the garden and vice versa. The transitions between the interior and exterior spaces were staged in a generous and fluent manner.

The pioneers of the Modern Movement like Mies Van der Rohe and Le Corbusier increasingly opened up their buildings to the garden over the course of their careers. However, their well-known villas were situated on large, green parcels of land, without any visual contact to neighboring houses. They tried to capture as much as possible of the surrounding natural features and the daylight for their interiors. This became especially clear comparing the three villas built around the same time in 1928: Mies van der Rohe's Tugendhat Villa in Brünn; Le Corbusier's Savoy Villa in Poissy, near Paris, and Loos' Müller Villa in Prague.

An important aspect for the garden layout of villas at the beginning of the 20th Century was the economy of maintenance, as the villa garden was mainly conceived as recreational and adorning, unlike the fruit and vegetable gardens of the settlements. Loos was on the vanguard in this aspect of the economy of maintenance and design.

He shared many convictions with Leberecht Migge, the great German garden reformer, regarding the cultivation of the garden. Loos' villa gardens were very easy to maintain as compared to the above mentioned gardens by Muthesius, Olbrich and Hoffmann, which all required professional maintenance by at least one gardener. Leberecht Migge on this aspect of garden design in 1927: "In the future, we will want to and we will have to work in our garden. We have to, because the standard of living for most people prohibits them from having their gardens worked on by others. We want to, because natural law compels us to love this duty. Only through thoughtful, dutiful action will nature reveal itself in our little garden. Honest labor produces true leisure and vice versa."[2]

Only around 1930 were Loos' maxims regarding garden design to become the new and universally accepted model: "The need for frugality that has arisen from our economic situation has become a useful aid. It has allowed for the quick and painless elimination of costly pre-war decoration and further compels us to express ourselves in clear, uncontrived forms, so that neither by its arrangement nor by its maintenance should excessive costs arise and elements be suffered that are of artistic burden to the garden. The arrangement of the garden is of special importance with regard to its future maintenance. Maintenance requires new costs on a yearly basis, and when these costs exceed reasonable limits, the garden becomes a burden, if not neglected and overgrown. The simplest composition and most economical application of materials and plants belong to the fundamental tenets of modern garden design."[3]

### Relationship of Country House and Landscape

In all three of his constructed country house projects, Villa Karma at Lake Geneva, the Spanner Country House above the vineyards of Gumpoldskirchen near Vienna and the Khuner Country House in the Alps, Loos was very conscientious in orienting the views from the houses in their specific surrounding

landscapes. Particularly in the projects for Spanner and Khuner he created various terrace levels from the garden to the roof allowing for a multitude of view points to enjoy the landscape, depending on the time of day and season.

The above mentioned projects were truly free-standing houses, without any neighboring buildings, situated in beautiful natural landscape settings.

While the concept of the Villa Karma was very introverted, there was still a summer dining terrace, the so called "sala terrena", below the main floor and a large and spacious roof terrace with pergolas and elevated seats in corner spires towards the garden. Loos was also said to be involved with the construction of the villa's elaborately designed, large garden with a little harbor and outbuildings that were built at the time of the renovation. The garden allowed for staged views from the house of the lake and the nearby mountains.

The Spanner Country House, on the other hand, was realized with very limited means and had a comparatively simple structure. It was situated on a topographically charming spot where the last shallow foothills of the Alps boarder on the Pannonian plane. The small country house was placed above sloping vineyards overlooking the wide and flat landscapes. There were altogether four terraced levels – two in the garden and two on the roof of the house.

The Khuner Country House had three terrace levels. First, a large roof terrace with a shower above the steeply sloped roof; second, a large terrace directly in front of the living room over the whole width of the house; and last, a garden terrace level below the house. The latter two were connected by stairs, in which Loos very skillfully controlled the views of the surrounding mountains by repeatedly changing the direction of the stairs.

From its formal and construction aspects, the Khuner Country House followed the regional tradition, with only very few elements deviating from this traditional form. Apart from the roof terrace and the green sliding shutters, it was the large two-story window on the front end of the living room hall with an imposing view of the mountains that breached the regional canon. The whole lower part of this window could be slid up so that the separation between the terrace and the interior would almost disappear. Loos lowered the terrace by three

Khuner Country House, 1929-30: open window of the hall with view of the mountain panorama
Photo by M. Gerlach Jr., ca 1930
(ALA 3184)

Strasser Villa, 1918-19: view from street
(ALA 3244)

Rufer House, 1922: garden view
(ALA 3217)

steps to allow an open view of the landscape from the furniture suite in the living room over the top of the terrace's necessary parapet. He typically reversed this relationship in his urban villas, in that the parapet secluded the view from a seated position at the terrace window, eliminating the visual relationship with the garden.

The terrace parapet of the Khuner Country House was made from flower boxes, hinting at a detail used by Loos on many occasions and in different settings, as for instance to terminate the top of the portal of the shop entrance of the Manz bookstore in Vienna's inner city, on the facade of the House on Michaelerplatz towards the urban square, on the terrace in front of the living room of the Tzara House in Paris and on the entrance terrace of the duplex-house of the Vienna Werkbundsiedlung.

### Facades (Exterior Shell) and Volume

Looking at Martin Gerlach Jr.'s archive photographs, which were shot around 1930 for Loos' first monograph, one recognizes that apart from the Moller Villa, every newly built villa had one or two facades that were greened with vines, or at least new planting was discernible.

The facade was typically covered with wild vine (*Parthenocissus tricuspitata*, Japanese ivy), which could clamber up a plastered facade by itself. It had a dense cover of large leaves that were green in spring and summer, turning red in autumn. During the winter, the leafless branches covered the facade like a net.

The original plan for the garden design that was recovered during the renovation of the Müller Villa in 1998 showed this type of planting on one facade. For this reason, the facade was replanted with Japanese ivy. By now, these vines have already spread across to the neighboring elevations.

The green facade was an element that was also initiated by Loos in his other villa projects, emphasizing on the one hand the symbolic notion of shelter that the house offered, on the other hand embodying a sort of natural "skin" covering for the house that functioned according to the nature of clothing, much like the fur of an animal for the human body. This pointed directly back to Loos' notion of the archetype of architecture, in which the animal fur was the first measure to protect one's personal intimacy. Loos voiced his opinion on this subject as follows: "Lime plaster is a skin. Stone is constructive."[4]

It seems that his aim was less to symbolize the never-ending struggle between wild and untamed nature with the culture of mankind, but rather the protection of the private from the public. This may also be seen against the backdrop of the struggle his

Steiner House, 1910: garden side
(ALA 2577)

Scheu House, 1912-13: garden side
(ALA 3230)

friend Karl Krauss was leading for a reformation of criminal justice in regards to moral conduct, which is documented in his book *Sittlichkeit und Kriminalität* [*Morality and Crime*]. In this book, he accused the state of investigating private people's lives under the pretense of morality, and subsequently publicizing these highly personal intimacies in the press. An instrument capable of destroying a man or his family, as happened in the case of Theodor Beer, one of Loos' first clients.

Loos' intent in planting might have been to make the house look even less conspicuous from the outside than it already did with its simply plastered facades, revealing even less information about the client to the public eye. This should be considered in relation to what Loos wrote in regards to the clothing of the modern man in his legendary essay "Ornament and Crime", as discussed in the chapter "Written Work" and once again below: "Those who go around in velvet jackets today are not artists, but clowns or house painters. *We have become more refined, more subtle*. When men followed the herd they had to differentiate themselves through color, *modern man uses his dress as a mask*. His sense of his own individuality is so immensely strong it can no longer be expressed in dress."[5] This statement on the clothing of the modern man was then transferred to architecture: "[...] The house should be discreet on the outside and show its great wealth within."[6] This meant for Loos that one opened up to one's friends and acquaintances in one's private rooms, that were designed to express one's passions and preferences, while the exterior of the house was designed to provide protection from the rest of the public and its nosiness. However, this outer facade had to be correct and in accordance with the culture of the specific local culture. It had to communicate that there was a cultivated family living in this house, in analogy to the custom tailored English suit, which characterized the cultivated citizen, the gentleman.

The metaphor of the mask was even literally translated in some of Loos' street elevations, where the facade would almost take on the physiognomic appearance of a face, as for instance in the Horner House (short elevation) or the Moller Villa (street elevation), where it was most distinct.

Following the above quoted passage, Loos continued in his text by also presenting the role of tra-

dition in his requirements, writing: "So much Italian air has blown over the Alps to us that we should build like our fathers in a style that shuts the house off from the outside world."[7]

For Loos, the outer appearance of the house constituted a part of public culture: "A building should please everyone, unlike a work of art, which does not have to please anyone. [...]

"This neurotic vanity, this vain neurosis of having to do things differently from one's fellow craftsmen at all costs was unknown to the old artisans. Tradition determined the forms. And it was not forms that changed it, but the craftsmen, who found conditions under which they could not remain true to the fixed, hallowed, traditional form. New tasks changed the forms and thus the rules were broken, so new forms arose. But the people of those times were in harmony with the architecture of their times. The new building that had gone up pleased everyone. Today, however, most buildings only please two people: the architect and his client."[8] And also: "When I finally received a commission for a building, I said to myself, 'In its external appearance a building can at most have changed as much as a tailcoat. By not very much, that is.' And I saw how our ancestors built and I saw how, century by century, year by year, they had freed themselves from ornamentation. So, I had to go back to the point where the chain had broken. One thing I did know: in order to continue the line of this development I had to be appreciably simpler. I had to replace the gold buttons with black ones. *The building had to look unobtrusive*. Had I not once said, modern dress is that which draws least attention to itself. It sounded paradoxical. [...] What was true of clothing was not true of architecture [...].

"Just try to visualize it. Everyone is wearing clothing from some past age or other, or from some distant, imaginary future. You see men from the mists of antiquity, women with piled-up hair-styles and farthingales, exquisite gentlemen in Burgundian trousers. And among them will be a few roguish moderns in purple pumps and apple-green silk jerkins with appliqué work by Professor Walter Scherbel. And now a man in a plain overcoat appears among them. Would he not arouse attention? Even more, would he not cause offense? And would not the police come, whose job it is to remove anything and anyone that causes a public nuisance?

Spanner Country House, 1924
(ALA 3232)

Bauer Villa (Factory director's villa), Hrusovany near Brünn, 1918

Rufer House, 1922: street view
(ALA 3223)

The Red House, 1859, by Philip Webb for William Morris in Bexley Heath near London (From H. Muthesius, *Das englische Haus*, 1904)

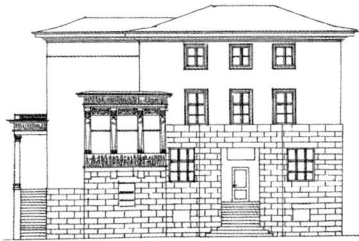

Plans by Adolf Loos for Konstandt Villa, 1919

Brummel House, 1928: today's exterior view

"Exactly this has happened in the fancy dress ball of architecture and my houses cause public nuisance."9

The greening of the facades might have been motivated as well by the English country house, as suggested in a picture of the house that the architect Phillip Webb built for William Morris, and which was also included in Hermann Muthesius's book *Das englische Haus*.

Two noteworthy particularities should be pointed out: besides the famous, newly built cubic houses that were directly influenced by Mediterranean sensibilities, such as the Scheu House, the Moller Villa and the Müller Villa, there were projects like the Stoessl House and the Khuner House that seemed to be rather traditional from the outside, almost unobtrusive, or at least not attracting attention.

Then, there were some designs for villas, which were not executed (Konstandt Villa; Samuel Bronner Palace; Stross House), but had a very strong resemblance to classicism and emphasized the traditional element following Roman antiquity and the classical architects Schinkel and Semper, who were held in such high regard by Loos. The interiors of these houses, however, again followed the concept of the space plan (*Raumplan*). These "classical, volumetric designs" were scattered all through his professional life and could not be tied to a certain period of his development. This indicates that Loos was indeed accommodating his clients needs and expectations very precisely, as was also evident in his many interior designs, while not compromising the principles he had formulated in his writings.

Loos was rather cautious with the facades of existing structures, at least towards the street, in his renovation projects for existing villas. Examples of this were the Rosenfeld House, the Duschnitz Villa and also the Mandl Villa, where both the original volume and the additions were still recognizable as such from the street elevation.

In contrast to these examples, the Strasser Villa did not reveal the original form of the house in any way.

Loos was in the habit of finishing the facade with a smooth and uniform plaster finish on both the existing and the new surfaces after completing a renovation project, in order to unify the appearance of the house and to give it a calm and inconspicuous exterior.

The Brummel House constituted an exception to this approach, in that he changed the character of the existing house towards the street by adding a large parapet, screening off the existing high pitched roof. The existing window partitions were kept, while the plaster finish of the old building was altered. Loos abstained from a uniform treatment of the new and existing structures in this project.

In regards to the facade one may conclude that Loos was preoccupied with protecting the intimate from the public, as well as with a distinct appearance of the exterior following the local traditions. In the urban environment of Vienna this meant a particularly classical antiquity, Italian architecture and the smooth plaster finishes of the bourgeois apartment buildings from around the end of the 18th century. Abstract formal aspects did not motivate his work in the sense of the purism of the white modernists or with the intention of provocating a public interest. This was made most obvious by planting vines to cover the facades by Loos and his clients.

Loos' concerns with the public aspects of architecture were comparable with those, which his long-time friend, Karl Kraus, demanded in regards to language. Paul Engelman, an architect and philosopher who was in close contact with both in his early years, summarized Karl Kraus' intent as follows: "Karl Kraus aims to protect the purity of language born of the poetic experience in a world in which public life (through a combination of factual reports and expression of opinion in the press and through the falsification of true thoughts by empty rhetoric) is in a state of spiritual and ultimately physical collapse. The power of this language is also available in the simple words of any uncorrupted individual. [...]"10 Transposed onto architecture it rendered Loos' own convictions.

It is in this sense that Loos also addressed the very traditional architecture in the countryside along with his work with highly cultivated and intellectually precise concepts in his urban villas. He wrote: "Be true! Nature is always on the side of truth. [...] Do not build in a picturesque manner. Leave that kind of effect to the walls, the mountains and the sun. A person who dresses picturesquely is not picturesque, but a clown. Farmers do not dress picturesquely, but they are picturesque.

"Build as well as you can. Not better and not worse. Do not be arrogant! Do not deliberately descend to a lower level than one on which birth and education has placed you. Even when you go to the mountains. Talk to the country folk in your own language...

"Take note of the forms in which the farmers build. They are wisdom from our forefathers, essence made manifest. But seek the reason from the form. If technical advance has made it possible to improve the form, then the improvement is always to be used. The flail is replaced by the threshing machine.

"Do not think about the roof, but about rain and snow. That is how the country folk think and why in the mountains they give their roofs the shallowest pitch their technical experience tells them is possible. In the mountains the snow should not slide off whenever it feels like it, but when the inhabitants want. For that reason they must be able to climb up on the roof without endangering their lives to get rid of the snow. And we should create the shallowest roof possible according to *our* technical experience.

"Do not be afraid to be criticized for being old-fashioned. Changes in the old way of building are permissible only when they are improvements. Otherwise stick to things as they always have been. For truth, even if it be hundreds of years old, has a closer connection with our inner being than the untruth marching along besides us."[11]

## Interior Rooms

*Loos said: "The frugal room is beautiful", but here everything is embellished, sensual and warm with life as well. It "flaunted," as Peter Altenberg said, "with simplicity." (Heinrich Kulka)[12]*

*The true artist, the great architect, however, first of all gets a feeling for the effect he wants to produce and then sees in his mind's eye the rooms he wants to create. (Adolf Loos)[13]*

*The job of the architect is to create a warm, cozy room. Carpets are warm and cozy, so he decides to spread one over the floor and hang up four to make the four walls. But you cannot build a house from carpets. Both floor carpets and wall hangings need a construction to keep them in place. Designing this construction is the architect's second task. (Adolf Loos)[14]*

*Their projects had to be designed from inside outwards, floors and ceiling (parquet and coffering) were the primary elements, the facade secondary. Great weight was laid on precise axes dividing and on the right furnishings. In this way I taught my students to think three-dimensionally, in the cube. Only few architects today can do that; thinking in surfaces seems to be the be-all and end-all of an architect's education. (Adolf Loos)[15]*

The preceding quotations, which were already commented on previously, briefly circumscribed precisely that with which Loos concerned himself in designing interior spaces, and points to the vital importance of this aspect in his work.

In principle, Loos perpetuated the design approaches he developed for his early apartment and business interiors in the work of his houses. Only now he had the opportunity to decide on interior relationships and on the situating of the areas and rooms through construction, which accordingly resulted in more complex solutions for the interiors of his houses.

His first villas still featured continuous horizontal floor slabs. The mezzanine floor of Goldman & Salatsch Tailor's Salon in the House on Michaelerplatz (1909-11) is the first project where a *Raumplan* solution is documented.

The simple and very compact outside volumes were contrasted and complemented by a rich and complex interior.

The interior volumes of the buildings were basically divided into three functional areas. The central areas were representative and dedicated to general family functions. They were openly connected to each other and also served to entertain guests. The second entity were the private rooms of the inhabitants, that could be closed with a door. The third set of spaces were service and staff areas that were placed conveniently in the background and could service the house without disrupting its life.

The villas that included service personnel had their kitchen and storage rooms in the basement, along with the utility rooms, the garage and the boiler room for the central heating system. The kitchen was connected with the living area and often with the upper floors by a dumbwaiter and usually the service personnel had their own internal stairs to move around the house.

The living and dining area was located on the raised ground floor, distinctly above street and garden level. It was organized, following the example of the English country house, as a series of areas (zones) that were articulated by variable interconnections, bay-windows, furnishing and in his later projects by changes of the floor levels. The dining room was exceptional in this ensemble as it always could be separated, mostly by sliding doors or curtains, and in his later work by having its own floor level. Only the library (gentlemen's room) and the boudoir (ladies room) had lockable doors.

An open stair led from the living area to the second floor where the bedrooms and bathrooms were located. Here, every room could be closed with doors. If there was a third floor, it was typically used for guest rooms, studio, accommodation for service personnel or utility rooms. It was always accessible by a very narrow stair which was hidden behind a normal door and could not be recognized as such by a visitor.

## Raumplan, the Interior Landscape

The term "Raumplan" was not coined by Loos himself. Heinrich Kulka, his student and closest assistant first used it in his monograph on Loos, published in 1931, and explained its design principle at great length: "From Adolf Loos came a substantially new and better way of conceiving space: Free thinking in three dimensions! The design of rooms that lie on different floors and are unbound by a continuous structural plane, the arrangement of interrelating rooms as a harmonious whole and with an economy of space. The rooms not only have different sizes according to their meaning and purpose, but different levels and heights as well. Loos can thereby create more residential area (*Wohnfläche*) with the same construction materials, and he can accommodate more rooms with this method in the same space, on the same foundation, under the same roof, and between the same walls. He exploits the material and construction area to its fullest possible extent. Expressed differently, one could say: The architect who only

thinks in terms of a single level requires a larger area in order to create the same amount of residential space. The traffic routes in the house would become unserviceably longer, the management of the space unprofitable, the comfort level less and the construction costs higher, also requiring more maintenance.

"Columns and beam cross-sections are created today with the highest precision. No construction element may be over-sized so as to create unnecessary material expenses and building costs. Building statistics is the science concerned with this. Generations of specialists have been working on it. The architectural space, however, is ignored and confidently squandered.

"One person created the basis of this architectural economy: Adolf Loos. Just as we have spoken of floor plans until now, with Loos, we can now speak of a room plan. The result is this principle: not until structural analysis is coupled with an economy of architectural space can one speak of a modern (economical) building. This new, space-oriented room plan, with its abundance of practical challenges and requirements, demands the highest levels of concentration from a designing architect. In creating his room structure, he must simultaneously consider the purpose, the construction, the traffic routes, furnishings, cladding and the harmoniousness of the rooms. Adolf Loos has this ability, this gift for conceiving of space, in great quantity. No one resolves these innumerable, contradictory challenges like Loos. One almost forgets the greatness of the work because of its matter-of-course. What one generally designates as 'cubic architecture' arose from another ethos – the attempt to create an outwardly plastic arrangement of building volumes. This is only empty facade architecture. The new, space-oriented *Raumplan* has nothing to do with such outward plasticity. *For Loos the inner space is the primary*. It determines the outward form. That is not to say, however, that the control of building volumes are irreconcilable with the arrangement of inner space. Loos brings to life the clearest forms, the cube and the ideal construction of step pyramids."[16]

This clear and ostensibly formulated description of the *Raumplan* in relation to Loos' design principles was preceded by the following sentence that should be considered more closely: "We have always the intention to connect (link) rooms with each other, but we never thought to do this as only in one direction. In this way, a suite of rooms arose in the living space. A theatre has galleries or annexes (loges) layered on top of each other, that interrelate openly with the main room. Loos recognized that the constriction of the loge was intolerable, if the view of the large main room was suppressed; but with the combination of one higher main room and lower annex rooms, space was economized. Loos applied this knowledge to his construction of housing."[17]

It was precisely upon this sentence that Beatriz Colomina formed the basis for one chapter of her book, *Privacy and Publicity* (1994), in which she described the aforementioned effect in great detail in her analysis of the Moller Villa. She noticed that the family's living area was positioned in an elevated sitting niche within the bay, just below the window. One sat with one's back towards the street, facing the interior of the room, which was in this case the great hall in the center of the house. She therefore described the arrival of a guest or the passing through the space in analogy to entering a stage.

Daylight penetrated into the hall from the window above the seating cove. The visitor entered with his back to the seating cove after ascending the stairs from the lower entrance area, a multitude of directional changes causing him a slight disorientation. His entry would be watched by the family from the cove. As he entered he would try to reorient himself, looking around towards the seating cove. However, he would be slightly blinded by the light, almost like an actor in stage lighting, and he would only be able to discern the silhouettes of the "audience" – in this case the family – until his eyes adapted.

This type of staging and spatial control was a typical and recurring motive in Loos' work. It can be found already in one of his first projects in 1898 for Goldman & Salatsch Tailor's Salon, Am Graben 1, in Vienna and after that it can be found in other two-level refurbishments of tailor shops before he used the theme in his residential work for the first time in the Mandl Villa (1916). While he had formulated his ideas concerning spatial planning already around 1907 and had used them subsequently first for the tailor's salon in the House on Michaelerplatz (1910-11), Loos implemented elements of his spatial concept of the *Raumplan* in residential design for the first time in the renovation of this villa. After the completion of the Strasser Villa (renovation, 1919) and the Rufer House (new construction, 1922) he used the *Raumplan* regularly in his residential designs.

Back to the placement of the seating area below the window and the orientation of the views towards the interior of the room. It was a standard motif that Loos repeatedly used in his urban villas. Together with the detailing of his windows – Martin Gerlach Jr.'s archive photographs showed all windows covered with closed opaque curtains – the attention was concentrated towards the interior, which developed more and more into an inner landscape as Loos was elaborating his *Raumplan* idea during the course of his career. This focus on the interior and the intimate is also documented by a quotation on Loos that Le Corbusier published in *Urbanisme* in 1925: "Loos m'affirmait un jour: 'Un homme cultivé ne regarde pas la fenêtre. La fenêtre est en verre dépoli; n'est là que pour donner de la lumière, non pour laisser passer le regard.'"[xviii] Which could be translated as: "Loos once asserted to me: 'A cultivated person does not look out the window. It is made of frosted glass. The window is only there to let light in, not to allow the gaze to wander.'"

And Loos did indeed use, translucent glazing for windows facing the neighboring lots in his urban villas; or he placed the window parapets above eye level and covered the window panes with thin stretched fabric, or divided the pane into small squares or rectangles. In this way, the window became a source of light that could manipulate the mood of the space, in the spirit of the traditional Japanese house.

Loos structured the living area by articulating different zones for various needs and requirements, following the English example. These zones were distinguished by furniture and furnishings, and by the mood created in each space. Subsequently, he provided separate levels for these spaces in developing his *Raumplan* idea and connected these different levels spatially, composing an interior landscape that could be perceived from different vantage points where Loos had provided seating areas.

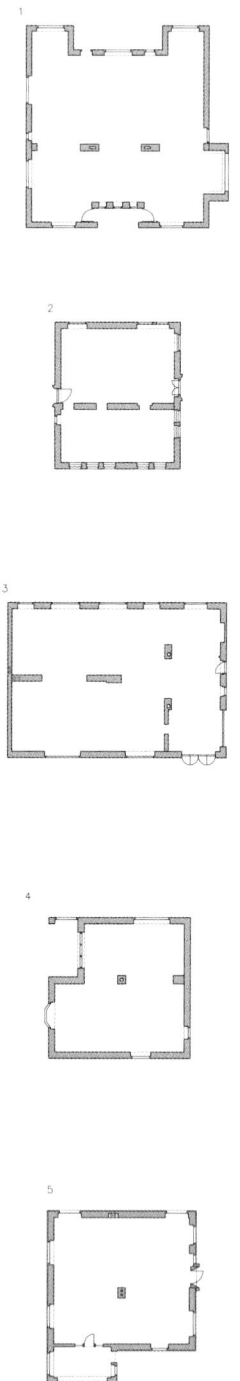

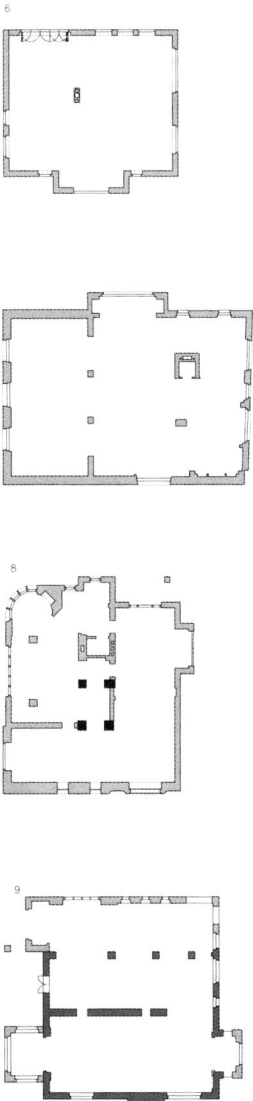

Structural schemes of houses by Loos
1 Steiner House
2 Stoessl House
3 Scheu House
4 Rufer House
5 Horner House
6 Moller Villa
7 Müller Villa
8 Strasser Villa
9 Mandl Villa

Planted winter gardens closed the spatial perspectives to prevent gazing out of the window, to filter the daylight, and to provide a presence of cultivated nature within the house (Steiner House and Duschnitz Villa). The exits to the terrace were low and narrow, and in his early works he had placed them off the main axis of the house (Steiner House) or the terrace was not accessible from the living room at all (Scheu House). With this approach he consciously used the terrace doors to mark the threshold between the outer and the inner world, which had to be crossed deliberately and not by chance.

Natural landscape was also depicted in paintings that were hung on the walls. The elements of nature like fire and water were symbolized. Fire was present in the open fireplace, which was typically always a part of Loos' designs. For Loos the fireplace emphasized the feeling of security that his interiors were intended to convey. Water could be present through the use of marble surfaces or by including fish tanks in his design: "The slabs rest upon long tables, but they are gray and colorless! I am disappointed. Loos laughs. They are not yet polished. Look here! He takes some water and pours it over the gray stone himself. A miracle occurs! The green marble glows with a dark, deep green; blue, violet and reddish-yellow veins run through it in soft waves. *It looks like the ocean.*"[19] And also: "[...] 'Here,' he said, 'is where the illuminated aquarium will be.' [...] No one understands him. The property owner wants to pull him aside, there are important things to discuss. 'Here is where the man of the house will have his favorite spot; when he comes home tired from work, he will watch the fish play silently. All the colors will sparkle in the light of the lamps.'"[20]

## Construction

Loos' point of departure was always the mood and effect he wanted to achieve with his rooms; only thereafter would he consider its furnishing, its function within the living space and its proportions. For this reason he strived to be as independent from structural restraints as possible. The construction aspects of the building that should contain these rooms were merely secondary. Loos established his own concept of precedence of cladding over construction along the line of thought of Semper's theory of cladding. In Loos' own words: "Both floor

carpets and wall hangings need a construction to keep them in place. Designing this construction is the architect's second task.

"That is the correct way, the logical way architects should go about their business. That was the order in which mankind learned to build. In the beginning we sought to clad ourselves [...].

"There are architects who did it the other way round. Their imagination creates not rooms but walls, the rooms being the spaces left inside the walls. Then they clad the internal walls with the material that seems most appropriate. [...]"[21]

He approached his houses with rather simple construction principles that allowed him to realize his spatial ideas in an economically affordable way. The exterior walls were always constructed as bearing walls out of massive brick. The interior loads in his newly constructed buildings were first supported by an interior wall, while his later houses utilized one or more interior columns depending on the size of the building. The basic form remained very compact in plan, and typically approximated a square.

Loos gained his first building experiences with a column grid in planning the House on Michaelerplatz (1909-11), where a grid of sixteen columns in the main sales area gave him the freedom to realize his first *Raumplan*. The columns and floor in this project, as well as parts of the facade, were already built in reinforced concrete.

In his residential houses, however, he resorted to traditional, familiar and cheaper materials, like bricks for bearing walls and columns, and wooden beams for the ceilings. Only in 1928 did he return to reinforced concrete columns and ceilings for the villa of Frantisek Müller, a building contractor who had at that point already gathered a considerable amount of experience in complex concrete construction on various large projects.

He had used the solution of one central column for the first time already in 1912 in the design for the Horner House, which was constructed with relatively moderate means. In this project he succeeded in sustaining all the loads with only one walled column, which was at the same time utilized as a chimney, and which was placed in the center of an almost square plan and cubic volume, with no structural beams visible. Loos had to size the building volume (10 × 11 m) in order to accommodate the typical span of about 5 m of a wooden ceiling construction. The Horner House had no features of the *Raumplan*.

Loos brought this principle to perfection with his design for the Rufer House in 1922, where he developed the spaces on various levels spiraling around a central column, which once again functioned simultaneously as chimney. The house had a square area (10 x 10 m) and was cubic in volume. Loos deemed this the ideal *Raumplan*, as it was economical in its use of the interior space of a simple cubic volume because every room only had the height that was appropriate to its inner nature. With this construction and design method, which was very economically realized, he minimized the space necessary for circulation and maximized the usable area while maintaining the same volume. Another example of a house with only one single, central bearing column is the Moller Villa. For the Müller Villa in Prague, which had a larger volume and area, he used the same principle by hiding four columns in the middle of the house, which could not be perceived by the house's inhabitants or visitors.

With this simple construction principle Loos achieved the necessary freedom to develop his plans in three-dimensional space.

He tried to arrive at the same construction principles in his renovation projects, like the Mandl Villa or the Strasser Villa, by inserting central columns into the existing structure.

## Orientation of Movement

I have already discussed the theatrical quality of the entrance situation at the Moller Villa. This project stands, however, in a sequence of houses designed by Loos that resulted from a specific orientation of movement through the house.

In a simplified description, one entered the house through the main entrance, mostly on the middle axis of the facade. By changing direction more times Loos guides guests near the side facade and after that directly in the center of the house: Loos took the visitor through narrow entrance rooms with low ceilings to the center of the house which opened up to a large spatial volume that seemed bright and big. Loos skillfully increased the spatial effect and size of the living area by creating a longer entrance way leading up to the living area.

Once the visitor arrived at this central point of the house, entering the living area, he would re-

main there for a while to orient himself as he was now confronted with a large spatial volume with multiple annexed areas, all designed to make an impression. This was the moment for the host to greet his visitor after already having the opportunity to secretly watch his ascent through mirrors or small internal windows. Loos set up an aid for the host and hostess to discreetly exert control in their house concerning the presence of their guest. He used this in the following residential projects: Mandl, Strasser, Rufer, Tzara, Moller and Müller. The sphere of representation ended at the open stair leading to the bedrooms and bathrooms on the upper level. In short, one could say that the higher up one ascended within Loos' spatial arrangements, the more intimate the rooms became. The stairs leading to the top floor and to the roof terraces were merely steep ladder-staircases or extremely narrow spiral stairs that were hidden behind doors and not visible from the hallway.

At the beginning of his career, Loos joined the dining and living areas on the same level, as in his designs for apartments. Later on, he developed specific levels and ceiling heights for each partial area through his *Raumplan*, adding bays to the rooms like theater loges, in order to provide a specific space for every activity, such as dining, drinking tea, sitting in front of the fireplace, conversing with guests, reading, relaxing, and playing music.

## Mood and Effect

Loos knew how to create moods and effects through surface treatment and materials. He used them according to the character of his clients and their family. He was able to enhance or to correct the spatial effects as needed. It is therefore not possible to show a linear development in his interior designs. However, there were tendencies that can very well be shown. Loos accumulated a pool of materials, elements and surfaces that he was able to tap into repeatedly, and that could be rearranged in order to match the desired character of his houses with the personalities of his clients and their families. Loos had the gift, like Oskar Kokoschka, to capture his clients' soul and express them creatively.

Only by purposefully choosing the basic materials, and by refurbishing and using them in a masterful way, Loos managed to elevate the character of the materials used. For instance, by using large marble blocks with a distinct grain, that he had cut, polished and installed seamlessly, he created an homogeneous, grained and ornamented surface, which was achieved only through the material and not through applied ornamentation.

In his first houses Loos started out by using the traditional method of a square module for the wood paneling, with large frames and infill panels. The addition of modules resulted in a structured wall surface. An exception to this was the wall treatment in the Steiner House, where the surface was structured by vertical cleats; this was also a traditional technique of wood paneling. Typically, the surface finish was rather matt, even with the softwood panels painted white.

From the Tzara House (1926) onward, Loos almost exclusively used large plywood panels that were assembled in a flush condition next to each other. He liked using wood with distinct grain that provided a lively surface texture. However, he had previously used large format wood panels with exotic wood veneer for his shop designs before using them in a residential context. The very first time Loos used the large wood panels without ledges and frames in a residence was for the library of the Rufer House (1922).

The walls on the floors of the living areas in his larger villas were typically made of hard and dark materials (marble or hardwood), which made these somewhat large and high rooms seem both representative yet very livable at the same time. The area where guests were welcomed was, in these projects, rather "masculine", while the private areas were rather "feminine", as for instance the master bedroom on the upper floor, which was furnished with white painted softwood, wallpaper, or stretched fabric, resulting in an overall "softer and more sensual" character of the room. This symbolism could also be noticed in comparing the man's library and the woman's boudoir. While the man's library was always furnished in darker hardwood (oak or mahogany), the walls of the woman's boudoir had lighter and softer wood or were covered with stretched fabric.

The exposed ceiling beams were not always structural and served to create a spatial effect. There were dark wood beams accompanying dark panels, and white lacquered beams with white paneling. Both ceiling beams as well as wood paneling originated from the English country house tradition.

The floors in the living areas were always oak hardwood floors covered with Persian rugs. The bedrooms could also be made of lacquered softwood floorboards, which were also covered with rugs.

Loos' living areas were not only impressive through their sheer size and richness of materials, but also through their complexity and the competent realization of how the client wanted to leave an impression on his guests.

The dining area of the Scheu House, designed in oak with a matt finishing, seemed puritan and stressed the vital meaning of family in Dr. Gustav Scheu's life. He descended from a family of labor leaders and founders of the Social Democratic movement. He himself was the leader of the Workers' Settlement Movement in Vienna, and a staunch member of the Social Democratic Party and councilman in the first socialist government in Vienna after World War One. Loos designed and furnished the house according to his character.

The client for the Müller Villa on the other hand, Frantisek Müller, was a successful general contractor with a large building firm, who relocated his residence from Pilsen to the country's capital, Prague, in order to be closer to his political contacts, corresponding to the size of his firm. He wanted a house that was suitable to maintain these contacts and that could hold social receptions and Loos chose the spatial effects and means accordingly. In this project the walls were even finished with a shiny lacquer finish on mahogany panels to express the elevated position in society the Müllers aspired to. Other than in this project, this combination of material and surface treatment was only used by Loos for the high-end interiors of the sales area in his men's fashion salons or in bars, as for instance in the American Bar.

At the center of the main level with the living area we find, in many of his villas, the music room, following the passion of many of his clients for music and art. One example is the large and unfurnished music room in the Moller Villa. Mr. Moller liked to play the violin in his spare time and to privately perform music with his friends. He was acquainted with Schönberg and some of his students, and his wife Anny had also been a student of Schönberg as well as a student of the Bauhaus under Johannes Itten. Loos designed the floor of the living area in the spirit of the Japanese tradition, with plain wall paneling, sliding elements to separate the rooms, without furniture, and a window wall towards the terrace that could be completely opened, offering a view into the large garden.

These three examples illustrate how Loos was able to vary his design elements in order to meet his clients' needs. He had the sensibility to respond to his clients' personalities and their social environment through the spatial effects and moods he created. This was his gift and his concern throughout his career, and certainly a vital reason why Loos was often commissioned for follow-up projects and was able to enjoy lifelong friendships with all the clients for whom he had realized projects.

## Comfortable Living

### Furnishings

*The property owner has an entire lifetime ahead of him to "grow into" the house and he has the room to acquire many beautiful things that suit it. That is what Loos thinks and does not search for any further wooden figures.* (Claire Beck-Loos)[22]

Loos did not design furniture, but acted as a consultant for his clients, as was already described above in the chapter "Apartments". His criteria in selecting the chairs was to find the best one for each kind of comfortable relaxation. He exploited the mobility of pieces such as chairs and armchairs so that they could be grouped in different arrangements within the room.

Loos justified the variety of chairs by the different circumstances that cause exhaustion. Every cause of fatigue requires a different way to relax, as Loos argued in reference to English culture.

A strife for security and comfort, and the informal arrangement of furniture awarded the apartment interior with a particular charm. This resonated with the English notion of living as opposed to the Viennese salon, which was influenced by French sensibilities, where the furnishing was unified and all seats within a suite were made in the same style and upholstered with the same fabric – living was embodied in this one furniture suite and was consequentially stiff and not very differentiated.

In Loos' houses, however, a seating suite typically consisted of a bench, either in a corner of a room, a bay or a niche, a round table and different chairs, ranging from Egyptian style stools, to wicker chairs, to armchairs, to different versions of upholstered English easy chairs of utmost comfort.

Loos was much more stringent in regards to the dining area, however. Here we typically find a heavy, round dining table with Chippendale-style chairs.

The wall belonged to the architect in Loos' opinion, as it was a crucial instrument in creating the desired mood for a particular room, as well as integrating the immobile fixtures like cabinets and shelves.

Upon closer inspection, one notices that Loos created various horizontal ledges and offsets by integrating glass cabinets, shelves and built-in cupboards into his walls, which could be used by the inhabitants to place their personal objects. The freedom that he desired and achieved for his inhabitants through the flexibility in arranging moveable furniture and personal belongings, made it in fact very difficult for Loos to communicate his spaces through architectural photography, as they did not correspond with the visual habits and expectations of the readers of magazines of architecture.

Loos knew this, and he always showed his clients and possible clients the houses and apartments he had designed, to allow them to directly experience the atmosphere and intimate mood of the spaces, which gave an immediate impression. Still, he felt personally unsatisfied and frustrated that his method of spatial design, which was his prime interest, was successful in satisfying the client, but could not be communicated to a wider audience through means of publication.

To hang pictures on the walls designed by Loos was not without problems; however, looking at the archive photographs, the houses seemed to be full of pictures and the inhabitants seemed to find places to hang their art, which was certainly encouraged by Loos.

Typically, though, Loos brought the wood paneling only up to the height of the door, which left free space above, or the inhabitants hung their pictures directly on the panels, which had a lively effect as one can see in the archive photos. In cases where Loos already knew of artwork that the clients wanted to install, in particular large format paintings, he liked to directly integrate them into the wall panels, which made it more difficult to change the pictures or to re-hang them. In some cases, like in the library of the Rufer House, he integrated small graphics into the wood paneling which had full ceiling height, and thus made them part of the permanent wall layout.

Even though the idea of the "total work of art" as promoted by Hoffmann and the Wiener Werkstätten was rejected by Loos and discredited in the satire, "The Poor Little Rich Man", it was nonetheless also difficult to hang pictures at will on the architecturally designed walls of Loos; however, he tried to manage to give his clients opportunities.

## Heating

The open living spaces that were also connected to the upstairs sleeping quarters by an open staircase posed a considerable challenge to a comfortable heating system. First of all a rather large volume was to be heated, and secondly draft from rising air was to be avoided. Loos wanted a modern solution for his clients, so he decided for central heating in the basement which was fueled by coal or coke. The rooms were furnished with radiators, and the larger rooms had additional air heating, which was supplied by a centrally located ventilator in the basement blowing warm air through heating shafts and air grills distributed throughout the house. In addition, he placed an open fireplace in the living and dining room, that supported the spatial feeling and comfort rather than having solely a heating function.

## Influences of Other Cultures

Loos had a gift to instantly understand certain foreign cultures analytically, in some cases without ever visiting the country, as was the case with the Japanese culture. He invoked Gotfried Semper in this matter, who he held in high esteem: "'Show us the pots people have produced, and in general you can tell what kind of people they were and their level of culture,' says Gottfried Semper in the preface to his section on pottery."[23]

## English Culture
*Basic conception of interior spaces*
Dietrich Worbs on this subject: "Hermann Muthesius – similarly to Loos – studied the residential architecture of England in great detail and published his precise descriptions and analyses in his multi-volume book *Das englische Haus* in 1904-07.[24] Adolf

Loos was interested in particular characteristics of this architecture: the differentiation of room heights and floor levels, the open transitions between rooms both in horizontal as well as vertical direction, in particular the generous open staircases with their large landings, the inglenooks and bays in the living rooms, the galleries in the halls, the split-level layouts, and the joining of rooms with different room heights.

"These particular characteristics of American and English house-building – in large and small free-standing houses, in row houses, in townhouses, even in city tenements – seem to him to be the attributes of modern residential construction, because they allow for free, more liberated occupancy. With their floor plans and spatial concepts, these buildings are geared towards the practical and economical demands of middle-class life at the end of the 19th Century. Loos employs this approach, among others, in the development of his room plan, but only for the conceptualization of the interior space. Other sources are of influence to him when it comes to the formation of the external structure. Picturesque, elaborately conceived and often widely expansive external structures strike Loos as uneconomic; he seeks instead to integrate his increasingly complicated and sophisticated interior design as seamlessly as possible into rectangular or cubic external structures."[25]

Loos transferred the distribution of functions and rooms of the English house to the Viennese plan typology. In Hermann Muthesius' above mentioned book from 1904 we find exact descriptions of the various rooms. Their meanings, functions and furnishings were explained, so that one could learn, for instance, the importance of the dining room in everyday family life for the English bourgeois family of the late 19th Century, its dimensions in relation to the family size, and that it was never to be dimensioned for entertaining larger parties as it was an essential part of daily family functions. Furthermore, we learn about the library, the boudoir, the business room for the man, the inglenook, the layout of the drawing room with multiple seating suites, partially built into bays, and the central significance of the fireplace for this room, as well as the possibility of merging living and dining areas in smaller houses.

Also, the separation between the open area on the raised ground floor, which was accessible to guests, and the private quarters with bedrooms on the upper levels was thoroughly described by Muthesius.

Loos introduced an innovation to the 19th-Century English country house by moving the kitchen and service rooms from next to the living area to a location below it. If necessary, he added more rooms for service and service personnel on the top floor above the sleeping area. By doing this he raised the living area above the garden level and achieved an overall compact volume, typically with about four levels.

With this approach he created a type of urban villa that was suited for narrow and relatively small sites, as were common in Vienna.

*English Furniture*
Loos offered a few descriptions of comfortable English chairs in his writings, among them the following: "At the moment we not only demand of a chair that we can rest our bodies in it, but also that we can recover our energy *quickly in it. Time is money.* [...]

"The English and the Americans, free of such pettiness, are real virtuosos in relaxation. In the course of this century they have invented more types of chair than all nations put together, in all countries, since the world began. Following the principle that every type of tiredness requires a different chair, an English room is never furnished with one type of seat alone. [...]"[26]

Loos did not limit himself to the use of the English types of the 19th Century, but also employed models from various other centuries which were still included in the Liberty catalog or which he had seen and tried out in museums. The guiding principal for Loos was that he find the chair to be comfortable and appropriate. Loos had these chairs duplicated, or he used exact replicas provided by furniture makers such as F.O. Schmidt in Vienna. A multitude of different types of chairs modeled on English examples was characteristic for Loos' interiors.

Only the dining room table had a single type of chair, again following the English example, to symbolize the unity of the family. The dining room chairs were commissioned for handcrafting by the furniture maker Josef Veillich, following original designs of Chippendale chairs, which Loos deemed as unsurpassed for this task. There was only one type of chair used for the dinning room table, and these chairs could be found throughout all of Loos' projects.

*Exposed Ceiling Beams, Wood Paneling, Built-in Closets and Small, Square Window Partitions, Seating Benches Beneath Bay Windows*
The wooden wall paneling, the exposed ceiling beams, and the small window partitions of the English houses were published in Hermann Muthesius' book *Das englische Haus* in 1904, and could have been seen by Loos in this publication or during his

Motcombe Country House: hall
(From H. Muthesius, *Das englische Haus*, vol. I, 1904, pp. 41-2)

Motcombe Country House: hall
(From H. Muthesius, *Das englische Haus*, vol. I, 1904, pp. 41-2)

New Place House in Haslemere, Surrey, built and furnished by C.F.A. Voysey: billiard room with bench in bay window
(From H. Muthesius, *Das englische Haus*, vol. II, 1906, p. 47)

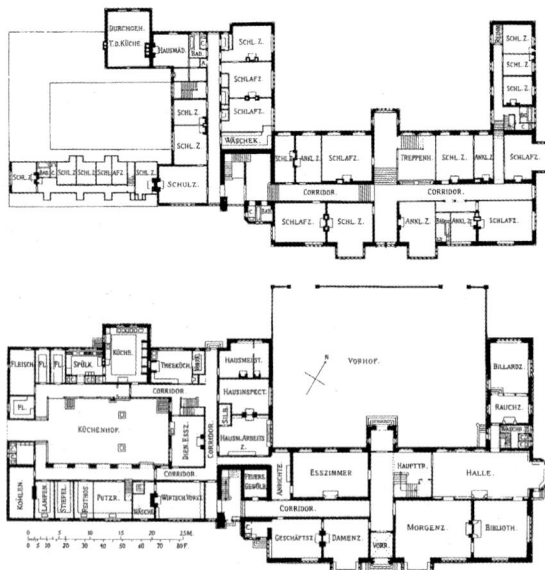

Motcombe Country House in Dorsetshire, built by E. George and Peto: ground floor and first floor
(From H. Muthesius, *Das englische Haus*, vol. I, 1904, p. 39)

Latticed framework bay in courtyard
of the Old Moreton Hall in Cheshire
(From H. Muthesius, *Das englische Haus*,
vol. I, 1904, p. 193)

Garden hall with chessboard floorpattern
in a Scottish country house by R. S. Lorimer
(From H. Muthesius, *Das englische Haus*,
vol. III, 1907, p. 126)

Dining room in The White House in Helensburg
near Glasgow (arch. M. H. Baille Scott)
(From H. Muthesius, *Das englische Haus*,
vol. III, 1907, p. 131)

Bedroom with dressing room from R. Norman
Shaw's House, Lowther Lodge
(From H. Muthesius, *Das englische Haus*,
vol. II, 1906, p. 55)

House in Edgebaston near Birmingham
by W. H. Bidlake
(From H. Muthesius, *Das englische Haus*,
vol. III, 1907, p. 171)

House in Edgebaston near Birmingham
by W. H. Bidlake
(From H. Muthesius, *Das englische Haus*,
vol. III, 1907, p. 170)

short stay in England. It is highly likely that his designs were influenced in this regard, as the similarities of these elements are striking.

The small window partitions were a traditional element of the English house, particularly used in the bays, which could be enlarged as bay windows.

The built-in bench underneath the bay window oriented towards the interior was shown by Muthesius numerous times and described as a typical element of the modern English house.

The built-in closet was also mentioned by Muthesius as the great innovation of the modern English house of the late 19th Century in regards to the bedrooms.

*Kitchen*

Loos promoted the use of gas ovens in the kitchen, as they allowed for a better and faster preparation quickly cooked meals. Again, Loos saw this as an economic advantage.

"Every English stove with its fittings for roasting and frying meat over the open flame is one more victory for the Germanic spirit. This revolution is making itself felt even on the Viennese menus."[27]

The vertical connection to the kitchen, which was typically located below the living area in his houses, was solved by utilizing a dumb waiter that allowed the delivery of meals to the living area above and frequently even to the upper floors.

**American Culture**

Loos admired the close cultural bond that the urban and rural population shared in the American culture. He pointed out that according to his own experience both the rural and the urban population were educated according to their times and that they were familiar with contemporary manners and technical innovations unlike in Austria, where Loos found the population to be living in different centuries within close geographical proximity.

He adored the American mentality and development throughout his life, influencing students of his like R. M. Schindler and Richard Neutra to emigrate at an early age.

1 Bed
2 Basin
3 Dressing table
4 Desk
5 Table
6 Sofa
7 Wardrobe
8 Wall-closet
9 Nightstand
10 Chair

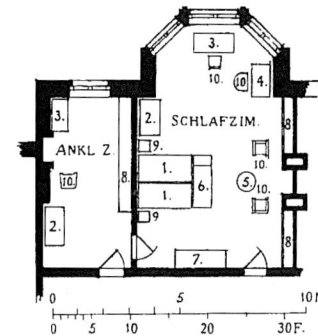

Otherwise, Loos typically preferred to choose examples from the English culture in his writings and works to emphasize its significance as pace setter and a measure of cultural development in Austria.

## Bathroom and Hygiene

Adolf Loos alluded to the backwardness of the German culture in regards to hygiene as compared to the English and American cultures. The promotion of higher residential sanitary standards was one of the primary concerns that he hoped to achieve through his struggle for a higher culture in Austria.

"We are behind the times. When, a few years ago, I asked an American lady what she thought was the most noticeable difference between Austria and America, she answered, 'The plumbing!' – heating, lighting, and water pipes. Our faucets, sinks, water closets, washstands, etc. are still way, way behind English and American fittings. [...]

"An apartment without its own bathroom! In America an impossibility. The idea that at the end of the 19th Century there is a country with a population of millions whose inhabitants do not have the opportunity of taking a bath every day would seem outrageous to Americans. [...]"[28]

## Japanese Culture

Loos mentioned Japanese culture only a few times in his writings, though it appeared to have made a large impact on his later work. Witness to this bares the fact that he designed the summer dining room with view of the roof terrace on the second floor of the Müller Villa in Prague as a Japanese room. The little salon in the Tzara House was also influenced by Japanese design, with African graphic inlays between black lacquered slats. Also in the Moller Villa we find important references to and elements from the traditional Japanese house. It was probably his friend Peter Altenberg, who started studying Japanese culture very early, to wake Loos' interest.

Japanese influences were already present in his earlier works, as Heinrich Kulka explains in his monograph in regards to the Villa Karma: "House on Lake Geneva (Villa Karma, 1904). This house was not completed by Loos, but rather by the architect Hugo Ehrlich. The grating on the one side of the house [veranda to the lakeside; remark by the author] was not as Loos intended. He wanted to put windows there as well, as can be seen in figure 20."[29]

Figure 20 shows translucent glazing subdivided in small horizontal rectangles framed in fine and dark profiles. This window clearly related to the traditional Japanese architecture and culture. The shielding of the exterior world, and the focusing on the interior. Generating a dematerialized lightness by using opaque light walls, while diffusing the light and creating an uniformly illuminated space. The windows in the traditional Japanese house, consisted of a layering of elements to control daylight and transparency, while maintaining the possibility of providing a direct contact with nature.

The traditional Japanese country house of the aristocracy spread across a wide artificial landscape. The path to the innermost, small room of the tea house was laid out to cover the longest distance possible, as it was supposed to cleanse and facilitate concentration on the imminent ceremony. Each step was determined by individual stepping stones. The tea garden, called *roji*, was intended to mark the threshold between the outer world with its demands and difficulties and the inner world. Whereas the "inner world" was not supposed to signify the interior of the tea room but rather the inner world of the tea guest himself. The *roji* was to enable the guests of the tea ceremony to sense the harmony and calmness in its entirety by contemplating on the plants, the stepping stones and all the other elements, and thus enter the tea room purified. The tea house was placed deep within the garden. Its appearance was typically oriented on a hermit's hut in the *sôan no cha* tradition. More than anything, such a tea house was supposed to be unassuming, leading the attention away from appearance to introspection and truth. A central aspect in this was certainly the aim for harmony, which meant focusing on the inner being rather than an outer splendor. Every view was controlled by the architect of the ensemble. The construction of the houses was in wood, and the other building materials were also natural local elements.

The rooms were laid out with tatami mats, and in the center of the room was a fireplace for preparing the tea. In the development of the tea house this room continuously shrank, accommodating an increasingly smaller number of people. Subsequently even the tea master was omitted and the patron himself served the tea. While the intimate interac-

Villa Karma, 1903-06: entrance hall (figure 20) (ALA 3154)

Veranda of a traditional Japanese house as Loos planned for Villa Karma (From B. Taut, *Das japanische Haus*, 1936)

Traditional Japanese house: living room of an estate owner (From B. Taut, *Das japanische Haus*, 1936)

Traditional Japanese house: the tokonoma in the living room with verandas
(From B. Taut, *Das japanische Haus*, 1936)

Traditional Japanese house: wall structure in the interior
(From B. Taut, *Das japanische Haus*, 1936)

Moller Villa, 1927-28: view from dining room to music salon
Photo by M. Gerlach Jr., ca 1930
(ALA 3194)

tion and spiritual connection with the guest became more immediate, the ritual remained in the same formal stringency.

The Japanese summer dining room in the Müller Villa had a view over the roof terrace looking out towards the horizon. It was placed to be the highest elevated room in the house and could only be reached by traversing the entire house. There was no door from this room out onto the roof terrace. One would expect that Loos guided the visitors up onto a fabulous roof terrace, but instead he lead them to a Japanese room from where they could look out over the broad horizon and the sky. The actual access to the roof terrace was narrow with a low ceiling and only accessible from the stair case. The roof terrace was reserved for family members and was meant to provide a space for exercise and short recreation. There was no seating, only a shower. The Japanese room had details in black lacquer, original Japanese wallpaper and calligraphies on the walls. The floor was made of the material tatami mats were made of. The room was furnished with upholstered wicker chairs from Prag-Rudniker.

There is an archive photograph of the Moller Villa that shows, instead of the dining table, only a tea pot and cups placed on a rug on the floor. There is no other furniture in the room except for the wall built-ins. The view leads into the music room, which had also no furniture other than the grand piano, towards the far side of the room where daylight enters through a translucent upper window. Sitting on the floor in the middle of the room one had a view into the garden through the glass wall which could be fully opened by folding. The garden was long and planted around its perimeter were tall trees and hedges that, in principle, established the outer spatial definition of the exterior. Loos did not build the terrace parapet out of brick for this reason but instead used thin, vertical, metal bars. The garden path, which led in a straight line deep into the garden, ran parallel to a rose bed with a small wall laid in natural stone. The path was made of single stepping stones.

Back to the interior. The connection between dining area, with a raised floor level of about 70 cm, to the music room was only possible by a very narrow set of stairs that could be folded out. This meant that every step had to be taken quite carefully and precisely, and the threshold to the dining area had to

be crossed deliberately and with concentration; it was not a random connection between two rooms. The walls were made of plain but precisely detailed sheets of plywood. Between the areas were sliding elements in the full height of the room that could disappear into the walls.

The proportioning of the walls in the central hall of the Moller Villa can also be traced back to the traditional Japanese house. Its vertical wooden posts were lacquered and projected out of an otherwise light colored plain and thin wall, a motive that Loos repeated later in the bedrooms of the Khuner Country House.

I would like to add three quotations that show just how much Loos was occupied with Japanese culture: "In the first place, then, 'Japanese' means giving up symmetry. Next, it means the dematerialization of the object being represented. The Japanese represent flowers, but they are pressed flowers. [...][30]; "Loos explains the frequent appearance of the corner bench in his apartments, as well as other furniture positioned along the wall, in this way: 'These days the floor plan has become centrifugal due to the influence of the Japanese. The furniture sits in the corners of the room (but straight, rather than diagonal). The middle is empty (space to move freely in). Artificial light belongs where it is needed. The center of the room is not emphasized"[31]; "[...] In front of a photograph of the Khuner Country House, Loos begins to speak. He pulls a matchbox from his pocket: 'Look,' he exclaims, 'this is modern architecture! The houses of the future will not be made of steel and concrete that one has to blow up with dynamite in order to do away with them – as was the case in the last exhibition in Paris... *the house of the future is made of wood! Like the little Japanese houses! They have sliding walls! Modern architecture is: Japanese culture plus European tradition!*"[32]

## Classical Antiquity

*The level of culture that mankind attained in classical antiquity can no longer simply be eradicated from man's mind. Classical antiquity was and is the mother of all subsequent periods of culture.* (Adolf Loos)[33]

This quote defined Loos' roots and gave voice to a preference for classical antiquity he shared with Semper. Loos was impressed by Semper's argument of tracing the form of the Greek amphora back to utility. Semper was able to show that there was not a single formal artistic idea in this specific form, but rather a progressively optimized usefulness, which we today regard as a pure and beautiful form. Semper had started to approach classical art not under formal aspects but to understand its forms under consideration of its functional qualities. This engineer-like attitude was even more pronounced with the Romans, and for this reason Loos liked to refer to Roman antiquity of Greek origin. Following this line of thought, Loos regarded the English of his time as the direct descendants of the Greeks: "If the Greeks had wanted to build a bicycle, it would have been exactly the same as ours. [...]

"But it is not Greek to want to express one's individuality in the objects with which one surrounds oneself and which are meant for daily use. [...] The Englishman, however, has only *one* outfit for a particular occasion, *one* bed, *one* bicycle. To him the best is the most beautiful. Thus, like the Greek, he chooses the best suit, the best bed, and the best bicycle. Modifications in form arise not from a desire for novelty, but rather from the wish to make the good more perfect yet. It is the business of our age to produce not a new chair, but the best chair."[34]

Thus, Loos managed to directly link antiquity and English culture.

He repeatedly used forthright copies of elements belonging to classical architecture, such as the marble columns that can be found in the facade of the House on Michaelerplatz and in the Strasser Villa. In both cases they were non-structural, which, however, could not easily be recognized.

Another classical citation widely used by Loos was the figurative frieze with juveniles. Supposedly, this was an accurate plaster replica of a relief found in a Greek temple. He used it for instance in the music room of the Duschnitz Villa and in the dining room of the Strasser Villa. He also used this frieze in his apartment interiors on various occasions.

In designing the Rufer House Loos wanted to avoid windows on the first floor towards the street in order to maintain the intimacy of the room. However, he felt that the facade was not well-balanced, so instead of a window he used a replica of a relief frieze of the Parthenon temple. It is unknown if this casting was in the possession of his client or if it was commissioned or bought by Loos.

The preference for a symmetrical layout, which can be found throughout antiquity, was always the point of departure for Loos to order things. Only after he had established this order would he occasionally and deliberately reintroduce some distortions. The open plan layout and the economy of form and volume did not allow him to think in overall symmetries. However, single rooms or walls were symmetrical in their design, so that one could speak of an additive approach of partial symmetries, which could lead to designs like the entrance area in the Duschnitz Villa, where Loos integrated blind doors behind which were merely walls. Or as in the Müller Villa, where the corner towards the street had to be set back a few centimeters in order to allow the entrance motif and the staircase behind it to be centered on the facade. These are examples of some rare exceptions where Loos could not resolve the situation by any means other than a purely formal solution to satisfy his preference for symmetry.

Loos also knew the locations of antique quarries, to which he traveled on various occasions in order to purchase particular stone blocks. The marble at the facade of the House on Michaelerplatz is from one of those quarries.

**Archaic Motives**
*That was the order in which mankind learned to build. In the beginning we sought to clad ourselves, to protect ourselves from the elements, to keep ourselves safe and warm while sleeping. We sought to cover ourselves. Originally consisting of animal furs or textiles, this covering is the earliest architectural feature. This meaning is still recognizable in the German languages. It had to be fixed somewhere if it was to provide sufficient protection for the whole family. Soon walls were added, to provide protection at the side.* (Adolf Loos)[35]

It was in this sense that Loos realized the bedroom for his wife Lina in 1904. A bedroom that was so direct and immediate in addressing an archaic drive and instinctive needs was certainly not repeatable.

The basic human need for safety and intimacy became a guiding principle for Loos' interior designs. Part of this was the archaic element of the fireplace at a central location within the living area, where people could gather.

Another basic human need was to be able to exercise control. Loos supported the inhabitants of his houses in that he gave them the opportunity to observe their guests without them being aware of it. Even though he established a very precise path through the house to be followed by the guests, he nonetheless disoriented them at the same time through multiple directional changes and spatial impressions. This allowed the host to assume a slight leading position in his house as he could observe the situation.

## Idea of Man, Ethics

Recapitulating, I would like to quote an essay by the architect and philosopher Paul Engelmann (student of the Loos Building School, friend of Ludwig Wittgenstein and Karl Kraus), which he published in memory of his mentor Adolf Loos after his emigration to Palestine in 1946. For me, this is the most poignant and lucid description of Loos' accomplishments within his context, and shows his timeliness, despite the fact that the text was written in 1946: "[...] If Loos desires, in short, simplicity from our time, this apparently simple demand is actually difficult to understand and even more difficult to act on. The individual, even though he might handle himself well in his day-to-day existence, often missteps when he takes aim at something special. How beautiful that girl was in her work clothes! When you see her on a holiday, you are appalled. And just as animals always build properly, as a matter-of-course and 'beautifully', one could say that people only build beautifully as long as they haven't enough money to build something ugly. How beautiful, how human the old Kibbuz X seems! As it was constructed, its builders had other concerns and little time to bother with appearances. What about the newly constructed buildings, that cost so much money and whose erection created so much aesthetic debate?? – In order to attain the special as well as the everyday, one must have culture, either the primitive community culture of the agrarian classes or that of highly-cultivated individuals. But we have lost our culture as a community. How many of us possess it as individuals? Loos is convinced, however, that we (at least potentially) possess culture today: especially where the 'architect' has not bungled it; one must merely 'poison the architects' in order for culture to make its appearance again. It is in this way that his demand for a complete lack of ornamentation is almost never understood in its deeper sense. From this standpoint Loos also had to do battle on two fronts: against the old and the new, the battle against error in both its manifestations. It is the battle against established conservative architecture with style imitations and against the 'modern'. [...] Today we are in a new epoch of style imitations. These are not such complete imitations as those in the 19th Century, but rather in opposition to soulless modernity, they are a search for the purely traditional; an altogether directionless search that regularly overlooks that which is living and galvanizes that which is dead. This is the difference between complete, finished forms and a living tradition that Loos has created from true meaning. Contemporary forms can never capture historical forms through adaptation. The true traditionalism is that which commits to the spirit from which the old forms once emerged and that which brings forth new forms from that spirit. That is to say, true traditionalism creates things in the way that the old spirit would, if it existed today, that is, if it were contemporary. This concept underlies the realization that form is always that which arises from the clash of the spiritual realm and reality. [...] The reaction of the same spirit at a different moment in time must appear differently! Loos and his friend Karl Kraus are the first fighters in an actual, in a cultural revolution: *the revolution against the revolutionaries. This has nothing to do with counter-revolution*: that is based upon purging, not upon the struggle against the revolution. Until now, counter-revolutions were as poorly built as the revolutions themselves and suffered from the same drastic problems that appear here in seemingly opposite signs. The same struggle is necessary for them as well; the struggle of the real against the apparent values. The particular danger of the revolutionary class is its lack of time, by which it is especially afflicted: 'Adolf Loos and I, he by the spoken word, I by the written word, have done nothing more than demonstrate the difference between an urn and a chamberpot and that culture plays a part in this difference. The others, the positivists, however, divide themselves into those who use the urn as a chamberpot and those who use the chamberpot as an urn.' (Karl Kraus) The inability to properly differentiate between the higher and lower order of things is identified here as the fundamental evil of our culture. The first misuse is the delusion of idealizing daily necessities, the second is the degradation of higher values into agents of basic needs ('art in the service of the businessman'). [...] In the current state of affairs all 'higher things' are contaminated by 'rhetoric'. The actual culture of our epoch cannot be deciphered from its works of art or from its philosophical and political systems because it is prohibited from this order of 'higher things'. Culture is recognizable only in the small things of everyday life, which appear too unworthy to be included in this realm of lofty rhetoric – in the everyday, human things, habits, basic commodities, methods of speech. Loos attempted, in his realm, to reconstruct forms from these ignored, inconspicuous, and unintentional cultural refuges, which fittingly express our hidden cultural condition as those useless official systems. With this method, he took a position against the rhetoric of forms, against the antiquated as well as the modernized and is in that way deeply misunderstood. This is because someone who combats modern rhetoric is a fascist in the eyes of modernism; and someone who combats the traditional is a Bolshevik in the eyes of the conservatives; but he who combats both is a *fool in the eyes of everyone*. The clamor of the struggle between both fills the world and drowns out every sound of the spirit. Will a state ever be reached where we hunt down both and begin the search for forms of existence less riddled with rhetoric? There is little hope that that will happen. The white ravens, who would like to help bring it about, should "direct their attention to Adolf Loos as an authoritative guidepost."[36]

[1] Hermann Muthesius, *Landhaus und Garten*, Verlagsanstalt F. Bruckmann, München, 1907 (Eng. trans. L.S.).

[2] Leberecht Migge, *Der soziale Garten*, Gebr. Mann Verlag, Berlin, 1999, new edition, chapter "Deutsche Binnenkolonisation - Sachgrundlagen des Siedlungswesens", 1926 (Engl. trans. L.S.).

[3] Valentin Otto, "Zeitgemäße Wohngärten", München, 1932, in *Die Gartenkunst*, issue 2, 1995; Barbara Bacher, *Auf der Suche nach dem neuem Garten*, Wernersche Verlagsanstalt, Worms, 1995 (Engl. trans. L.S.).

[4] A.L., "Wiener Architekturfragen" (1910), in *Trotzdem*, p. 113 (Engl. trans. L.S.).

[5] A.L., "Ornament and Crime" (1908), in *Ornament and Crime*, Ariadne Press, Riverside, 1998, p. 175, emphasis mine; original text "Ornament u. Verbrechen", 1908, in *Trotzdem*.

[6] A.L., "Heimatkunst" (1914), in *Trotzdem* (Engl. trans. L.S.).

[7] A.L., "Heimatkunst" (1914), in *On Architecture*, Ariadne Press, Riverside, 2002, p. 116; original text "Heimatkunst" (1914), in *Trotzdem*.

[8] A.L., "Architecture" (1909), in *On Architecture*, cit., p. 82; original text "Architektur", 1909, in *Trotzdem*, p. 101.

[9] Ibid., pp. 80-1.

[10] Paul Engelmann, *Dem Andenken an Karl Kraus*, Tel Aviv, 1949 (Engl. trans. L.S.).

[11] A.L., "Rules to Building in the Mountains" (1913), in *On Architecture*, cit., pp. 122-3.

[12] Heinrich Kulka, in *Frankfurter Zeitung*, 30 September 1933 (Engl. trans. L.S.).

[13] A.L., "The Principle of Cladding" (4 September 1898), in *On Architecture*, cit., p. 42; original text "Prinzip der Bekleidung", in *N.F.P.*, 4 September 1898, in *Ins Leere gesprochen*.

[14] Ibid.

[15] A.L., "My School of Building" (1913), in *On Architecture*, cit., p. 121; original text "Meine Bauschule" (1907), in *Trotzdem*.

[16] Heinrich Kulka, *Adolf Loos*, Verlag Anton Schroll, Wien, 1930, pp. 13ff. (Engl. trans. L.S.).

[17] Ibid.

[18] Cit. in Beatriz Colomina, *Privacy and Publicity*, The MIT Press, Cambridge (Massachusetts), 1994.

[19] Claire Loos, *Adolf Loos - privat*, Verlag der Johannes Presse, Wien, 1936, chapter "Marmor, Haus Müller" (Engl. trans. L.S.).

[20] Ibid., chapter "Leuchtende Fische, Haus Müller".

[21] A.L., "The Principle of Cladding", cit., p. 42.

[22] Claire Loos, *Adolf Loos - privat*, cit., chapter "Haus Müller", p. 45.

[23] A.L., "Glass and Clay" (26 June 1898), in *Ornament and Crime*, cit., p. 68, original text "Glas u. Ton", in *N.F.P.*, 26 June 1898, in *Ins Leere gesprochen*.

[24] A.L., "Kulturentartung" (1908), in *Trotzdem*, Brenner Verlag, Innsbruck, 1931, p. 74: "Mr. Muthesius, whom we thanks for a series of instructive books on English living and inhabiting..." (Engl. trans. L.S.).

[25] Dietrich Worbs, *Der Raumplan im Wohnungsbau von Adolf Loos*, Akademie der Künste Berlin, 1983 (Engl. trans. L.S.).

[26] A.L., "Chairs" (19 June 1898), in *Ornament and Crime*, cit., pp. 64-5; original text "Das Sitzmöbel", in *N.F.P.*, 19 June 1898, in *Ins Leere gesprochen*.

[27] A.L., "Plumbers" (1898), in *Ornament and Crime*, cit., p. 86; original text "Die Plumber", in *N.F.P.*, 1898, in *Ins Leere gesprochen*.

[28] Ibid., p. 84.

[29] Heinrich Kulka, *Adolf Loos*, cit., p. 28 (Engl. trans. L.S.).

[30] A.L., "Review of the Arts and Crafts" (1 October 1898), in *Spoken into the Void*, Institute for Architecture and Urban Studies and M.I.T., 1982, p. 105; original text "Kunstgewerbliche Rundschau I", in *Die Wage*, 1 October 1898, in *Ins Leere gesprochen*.

[31] Heinrich Kulka, *Adolf Loos*, cit., p. 28 (Engl. trans. L.S.).

[32] Claire Loos, *Adolf Loos - privat*, cit., chapter "Abreise", p. 104 (Engl. trans. L.S.).

[33] A.L., "Review of the Arts and Crafts", cit., p. 105.

[34] Ibid. p. 104.

[35] A.L., "The Principle of Cladding", cit., p. 42.

[36] Paul Engelmann, *Adolf Loos*, ed. by Paul Engelmann, Tel Aviv, 1946, pp. 5 ff. (Engl. trans. L.S.).

# Settlements

## General

After the First World War, the settlement and garden city movement began to organize itself in Vienna. In 1919, the movement found a strong mentor in Gustav Scheu, a city council member and a member of the socialist party who was in charge of housing. As part of his political functions, he helped further the causes of the garden city and settler movement. The housing shortage and the poverty in Vienna after the war were severe and, among other things, the city had to provide housing for the soldiers returning from the war or facilitate self-building efforts coordinated by the state and by the city itself.

Within the socialist party there were two camps, however: one which tended towards consolidated mass housing, a procedure in which apartments were assigned to families and families became pure consumers; the other camp actively supported the settler movement in garden cities in order to enable citizens to purchase a piece of property, allow them to partially build their own affordable house and use the surrounding garden for self-sufficiency.

Unfortunately, in 1924, city council member Scheu gave up his office after the internal fights within the socialist party had tired him. As an outcome, the ideas of the settler movement were no longer supported from within the city administration and the mass housing movement with its monumental architectural language of the empowered working class became generally accepted.

In 1919, immediately after he took up his office, Scheu appointed Loos as his assistant. After a two-year period of engaged work as his advisor, he procured him a job as chief architect of the settler movement, which he gave up in 1924 when Scheu resigned. Loos emigrated to Paris, where he hoped to find more favorable work conditions for himself.

It was during these years that Loos had been extremely engaged in the settler movement for reaching his personal goals and educational approaches (i.e. the education of the Austrian citizens towards higher culture). In his view, the settler movement offered a unique possibility for the realization of this task. He frequently reflected on the social and cultural advantages of this style of construction and removed architecture from the foreground. He emphasized instead the use of fruit and vegetable gardens and the economical advantages of the houses under self-building guidelines in the focus of his idea of urban development.

Loos' conception of the garden structure and its use in settlement construction, as well as its social significance, are strongly rooted in the work of Leberecht Migge. Loos and Migge knew each other, and Loos often invited Migge to lectures in Vienna. His student, Leopold Fischer, together with Migge, constructed a large settlement as a prototype project near Braunschweig in 1926.

## Leberecht Migge (1881-1935)

Leberecht Migge was born in 1881 in Danzig, and from 1904 to 1913 he served as the artistic director for the Ochs garden construction company in Hamburg. From 1913 to 1920 he worked independently as a garden architect for public works in Hamburg. From 1920 he lived in Worpswede in his own estate, "Sonnenhof", while working on a specific settlement concept of intensive garden construction. From 1926, his branch office in Berlin was busy with numerous settlement projects of the "Neues Bauen". From 1913 onwards, he published many articles and works on the reformation of the garden culture and the settlement.

He formulated his theoretical approaches and goals in 1918 in the so-called *Grünes Manifest* (*Green Manifesto*), whose practical implementation would be tested in numerous projects over the following years. In the manifesto, it was said, among other things: "The old German city of the old German society is dead, dead, dead! [...]

"The old idea was called City. The new is now alive. The general idea of the 20th Century: 'LAND'! [...]

"Who will save the city? The land will save the city.

"It will create 'city-land'!

"The cities should embrace their own land. A hundred-thousand hectares lie idle: land for building, land for barracks, land for streets, wasteland. [...]

"Let us plant: public gardens – for the city-bound youth

"Let us plant: leased gardens – for the city-bound cottagers

"Let us plant: settlements – for the city-bound workers

"And plant: prototype properties – for the under privileged.

"Let us plant!

"The public gardens (exactly 6 square meters per person) should not be a lazy-romantic, ornamental green, but rather an industrious, abundant green: sports parks and baths (youth parks).

"The fruit and vegetable gardens should not be fleeting, leased discards, but rather "proper gardens", certified precursors of settlements. These should be self-suffcent gardens (80 square meters per person) with all the tricks. Settlers, leasers and sharecroppers should all have self-determination. [...]

"In the future: new settlements to be seconded only by self-suffcent gardens – which themselves process all domestic wastes. [...]

"We only give up city-barracks, quickly erected, for mass-accommodation. A poorly administered pile of stones is what we leave behind, from which we cannot exist, and which we cannot love. And which now – without global economy – is completely without hope."[1]

Leberecht Migge was also an advocate of agrarian reform and the improvement of agriculture through irrigation, fertilization, and the use of machines. He suggested, for example, that organic refuse be composted, and that judicious consumption could minimize waste production.

But of particular interest to him was the garden development of small farm industries. He developed garden prototypes that could support an entire family on only 400 square meters through increases in productivity and harvests per year. He aimed for ten harvests annually. Soil quality could always be improved through proper analysis and appropriate action. Even climatic improvements could be effected through skilful plantings and placement of architectural structures. He tested such natural improvements of planting conditions on his "Sonnenhof" in Worpswede and gained experience on a larger scale on many settlement projects. He was a social reformer who did not just theorize, but who made constant efforts to improve practical applications of his theses. Consequently he developed extensive practical knowledge and was much in demand in all of Germany as a consultant for housing settlements from 1926. Unfortunately, his theories and assessments have fallen into oblivion even though they still remain highly relevant.[2]

## Comprehensive Architectural Plan for Vienna

In 1920 the Austrian Settlement and Allotment Society commissioned its members Peter Behrens, Josef Frank, Josef Hoffmann, Adolf Loos, and Oskar Strnad with the development of a comprehensive architectural plan for the City of Vienna.

This plan, based on the city's existing regulatory plan was to encompass the entire municipal area of Vienna and assign garden and settlement areas in the outer boroughs according to the society's guidelines. The plan defined a "high-rise section" and six settlement communities. It was essentially the basis for the important settlement developments in the following years.[3]

## Settler Requirements

In a number of essays, Loos expressed his beliefs and views of settlement construction in writing. Here, we begin with Loos' conception of the settler: "The new movement for housing developments with gardens, which has stricken all the inhabitants of this city like a fever, demands new people. People who, as that great gardener, Leberecht Migge, so rightly says, have modern nerves.

"It is easy to describe a person with modern nerves. It makes no great demands on our imagination, since they already exist, though not in Austria but a little farther to the west. The nerves the Americans have today will be those our descendants have tomorrow.

"In America there is not such a sharp division between town and country folk as here. Every countryman is half a city-dweller, every city-dweller is half a countryman. American townspeople have not moved as far away from nature as their European counterparts or, to be more precise, their continental counterparts. The Englishman is also a real countryman.

"Both, the American and the English, find sharing a roof with others a disagreeable situation. Everyone, rich or poor, endeavors to get their own home. [...]

"Anyone who wants to join the house-and-garden project will have to relearn. We must forget the inhabitant of the city tenement. If we want to go out into the country we must learn from the country folk and see how they do things. We will have to learn a new way of living."[4]

Loos saw man's primal urge to carry out destructive work as a motif of the settlement movement, providing the following example of the farmer who tilled the earth, centrifuged the seeds, mowed the grass and the grains, and harvested everything that nature produced. In his essay, "The Day of the Settler", he described this as follows: "The Father saw the free, uncultivated ground and although he had worked all day in the factory until he was weary, he took up his spade and began to dig over the land. It became arable farm-land. This is how the "Schrebergarten" came into being. It is the new self-made fatherland, the real land of the Siedler. It is the product of a revolution of the workers against the barracks-like constraint of the factory system, the product of a revolution that was bloodless and therefore had a humane outcome, in contrast to the bloody revolution forced on us by the inhumane tape measure.

"Do not think that these allotments are a momentary craze. For all time to come the patch of ground people can cultivate for themselves will remain what it is today, their refuge with Mother Nature, their true happiness and supreme bliss."[5]

We also read: "The food of a nation is determined by the produce of its land under cultivation. Every nation, therefore, has its own type of food, its own cuisine."[6]

And in a 1926 lecture, Loos affirmed: "Now it is completely natural for the allotment holder to have the possibility of living adjacent to his garden, to build his house there. This brings me to a curious postulation. Not every worker has the right to own a house and a garden, but only he who has the urge to cultivate a garden. Perhaps you will argue that this is no reason to be so strict as to forbid a worker from owning a small luxury garden of lawns and roses. I would be betraying the spirit of modernity if I were not so strict. [...]

"Now I say that only those who wish to cultivate a garden should be allowed to own one, namely the allotment holder. He is happy to have something to compensate his horrendous, grueling job. He will once again become a human being, both mentally and spiritually.

"Not everyone can own and cultivate an allotment garden. There are many professions that exclude people from the garden city. A precision mechanic must not wield a spade, as he would ruin his hands. Many intellectual professions are not suitable for allotment gardens. As chief architect of the settlement foundation of the City of Vienna, I have postulated that only he who has demonstrated through the years that he is capable of cultivating a garden shall possess a house.

"Outwardly everyone agrees, but then only a few stick to their guns. He who, of his own free will, after an eight-hour day feels compelled to grow food shall have the possibility of owning a home. He should not receive the house through public means, as freeloaders are not permitted in a humane society. I believe that the gardener should, however, if he receives help with the financial matters, receive a plot of land with the help of public funds, but that he must build the house himself. In this way I will place myself in conflict with the Social Democratic Party, which does not wish to breed homeowners; but that is of no concern to me, as I am not a partisan.

"Regarding this, I feel that if there are two people from the working class, one who has allocated a bit of his weekly salary for buying vegetables at the market, and one who, with the help of his work in his garden, which gave him desire and pleasure, has saved this money, then the situation equals out in that the people of the second group will build and pay for their own house and commit themselves to spending their savings on the care of their garden."[7]

The Garden

"We want to focus on the garden. The garden comes first; the house comes second. Of course, the garden is going to be the most modern garden. It has to be as small as possible; 200 square meters is the largest space a settler can farm. It would be even better if the garden were only 150 square meters, because the larger the garden the more inefficient and backward will be the methods of cultivation. The smaller the garden, the more efficient and modern will be the means of cultivation. The huge garden is the enemy of any horticultural improvement. There cannot be any objections by the settlers such as, 'Yes, but I need grass for my goat,' or 'I need potatoes.' Everyone has to buy grass for himself. Potatoes must also be bought, since potatoes require a whole year before harvesting, and subsequently there cannot be the necessary, frequent harvests in the settler's garden within one year. The more effective the farming the more frequent the harvests. In our climate we have to produce ten to fourteen harvests a year, and you can imagine the immense work this requires. The settler does not depend on the climate, the earth and his plot of land alone. In a remarkable statement, the reformer of horticulture, Leberecht Migge from Bremen says, 'The gardener provides climate and soil for himself.' This is a strangely paradoxical saying. But, regarding the soil, it is clear that the soil at hand cannot be used without some intervention and that only after continuous fertilization and the introduction of new soil and humus can the ground be made useful. [...]

"But the climate! We know that the sun is the garden's worst enemy. The sun has already caused great damage. The most beautiful and paradisiacal areas in the world, between the Tigris and the Euphrates through Syria, Egypt and the whole of northern Africa have been sacrificed to the sun. They have become a barren land. But the Arabs knew how to overcome this. Everywhere there is garden culture, thousands of years of garden culture in the Orient, there are walls around the gardens to provide protection from the wind and the sun.

"How can our settler do this? He will build such a wall around his plot of land and around his garden.

"Every housewife knows that the laundry dries quickly in the wind. But this quick drying is exactly what the gardener must avoid. We want moist warmth in the garden. If the ground dries out quickly, the gardener's work multiplies. The ground must

always be moist so that the micro-organisms may continue to live there, as they are constantly at work breaking up the soil. [...] And now Migge prescribes that the sun's rays bathe the garden at noon, so that no garden may have shade at this hour. In this way, everyone will have the same sunlight. It thus follows that the gardens must all be oriented from north to south!

"At twelve noon, there will only be sunny gardens. There is a wall to the left and one to the right. [...] These walls will be planted with espalier fruit. There will be no trees whatsoever in the garden. The tree is not a social creature. He does not give his shadows to those who want him, but rather, quite often to the neighbors. A tree in the garden is not a good thing. [...] and therefore, no trees may be planted – only espalier fruit."[8]

### The Settler's House

"The settlement house must be planned beginning with the garden – let us not forget that the garden comes first, the house second.

"Let us first ask ourselves which rooms a house must have.

"Above all, a toilet with waste composting. There may be no water closet in the settlement house, as the waste of the entire house, including human excrements, is necessary for preparing the soil. For this, it is important that there be a system of barrels or tubs. In no case should there be a large manure dump. That must not exist, as it is anti-social. If such a dump were only emptied out every six months, you can imagine the powerful stench that would result [...]. No, the tub must be emptied into the youngest compost pile daily and then shovelled over. This leaves the entire settlement odor-free."[9]

Thus, in his lecture in 1926, Loos began describing the settlement house, making it very clear that functional themes and an overall view of the uses of the gardens and settlement facilities should take precedence over any artistic elements. There is no more impressive way to begin a description of the settlement houses' design in order to clarify their general cohesion than with his description of the toilets and their meaning for the general economy of the settlement families. Let us hear how Loos further described his settler house: "The compost pile should stay there an entire year in order to completely ferment. The compost must never be placed directly

Prototype for a self-sufficient garden with a small settler house. Garden-size: 360 sq m. Drawing by Leberecht Migge, published in *Deutsche Binnenkolonisation*, 1926

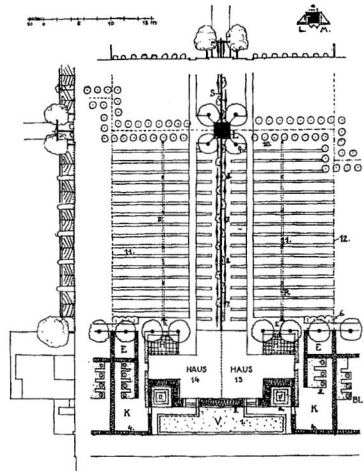

Staaken Settlement by Leberecht Migge. Sketch of two houses with self-sufficient gardens. Garden size: each 720 sq m. Drawing by Leberecht Migge, published in *Deutsche Binnenkolonisation*, 1926

over the vegetables. This creates a strong odor, especially with cauliflower.

"The toilet must not be located within the house. [...] It may lie within the floor plan of the house, but the door must open to the outside. [...] We must catch up to the Japanese, who return the favor of an invitation to dinner by using their host's toilet.

"Next, in the yard there will be an open shed for tools and machines. I need a stall for some animals, rabbits – which every settler should have, as they are economical and consume a great deal of vegetable waste, which would otherwise be wasted – and hens. Hens must have the largest possible, fenced-in area to range in.

"Therefore, one may not pass from the house directly into the garden, but must first traverse a farmyard where the shed and the stall are situated on either side. The actual garden begins with a work area, where the compost piles are situated against the wall. A workbench and various soil containers for the different types of vegetables complete the work area.

"Against the house, elevated by two steps, the farmyard is completed by a partially covered work area for the housewife. This veranda must be accessible from the scullery, which is a strangely modern thing. As the name implies, it is not a place for cooking, but rather for all the work of preparation and cleaning up that relate to cooking and domestic economy. Now I pose the big question: *kitchen* or *eat-in kitchen*? I must say upfront that I am for the eat-in kitchen from a purely evolutionary, modern perspective.

"The first objection to the eat-in kitchen is always: we want to have a room that does not stink. The answer I get when I ask where the stink comes from, 'from cooking.' But for the nourishment of people, it would be very well if food were cooked in such a way that it did not stink. [...] In an increasing number of households, food is more frequently prepared at the table. The entire breakfast is prepared there, with the help of a spirit stove or an electric cooker. [...] More and more often in restaurants, cooking is done in the dining rooms. [...] People enjoy watching it, and one day, in every middle-class home, the kitchen will also serve as a dining room. [...] As I mentioned before, the finer the cuisine, the more food will be prepared at the table. I wonder why the bourgeoisie

wish to exclude themselves from these beautiful things? A thousand years ago, every German ate in the kitchen. [...] Fire is a beautiful thing. The fire's warmth pervades the room and the house and is not lost. The kitchen warms the entire house and the fire is what it should be: the center of the house. [...]

"For all of these reasons, I build eat-in kitchens, which disburden the housewife and give her a stronger role in the apartment than when she has to spend all her time cooking in the kitchen. [...] The scullery must not be oriented towards the south so that it blocks the light from entering the eat-in kitchen. That is why it would be best to build a house on the north side of the street, where the eat-in kitchen is facing south and the scullery towards the garden, on the north side of the house.

"But the other side of the street is also for building. Here, wider houses are necessary because the street lies to the north and the garden to the south. Light and sun must enter the living room and the scullery must open to the garden. Therefore, both rooms must occupy the south side of the house and the following must be taken into account by the building planner: the parcels on the north side of the street need only be five meters wide, whereas those on the south side of the street must be wide enough for the scullery and the living room to be positioned next to each other. [...]

"So, first we have the toilet, then the shed and the stall. We have a living room and, not to forget, as large a pantry as possible for storing fruits and vegetables. In addition, we have an entrance from the street. This completes the ground floor. A basement is not necessary – it is actually completely superfluous and significantly raises the cost of the house. [...]

"When I think about the bedrooms, I find it first of all necessary to say that sleeping and living must be separated from one another. There must not be any mixture between the two. Sleeping should be subordinated as much as possible and take place in the smallest and humblest rooms. The bedroom must never become a living space. In the bedroom I change, lie down, sleep, wake up and get dressed again. This is it for the bedroom, and it is not used again during the course of the day. The mixture of living and sleeping is common in Germany and Austria. In America no one lives so basely, so miserably, so sordidly that his bedroom door opens directly to the living room. [...]

"In England the children have their own bedrooms. [...]

"There must be three rooms on the upper floor, serving as separate bedrooms for the parents, for the boys and for the girls. [...]

"Dividing walls do not have to be built initially. The bedroom will simply be larger at first, but when the children reach a certain age, the parents might consider creating a dividing wall. For this reason, the rooms on this upper floor must be divided so that the walls have nothing to do with those of the lower floor. The division may also be made through the use of armoires.

"It is also not necessary to install doors initially. Perhaps a curtain is sufficient at the beginning, so that the house may develop gradually. It is very wrong to place a settler in a pre-packaged house with furniture designed by an architect. On the contrary, the settler must be given the opportunity to select his furniture gradually. The house is never finished; there should always be room for development. [...]

"How do I arrive in these rooms? And yet another question: should the upper floor be accessible from the street or should it be reached through the living room? I have decided upon the entrance from the interior. I think it is wrong that one can reach the bedroom through an anteroom directly from the street, as is common in Germany. The danger of the ensnarement of renting the upper rooms is too great. However, if a tenant has to traverse the common living room, the decision of the rental is free from doubt. No one wants a stranger in his room. And furthermore, if I place the staircase in the living room, along the lines of the staircase in a hall, I gain a great airspace. The bedrooms will be heated by opening the doors to the upper floor just before going to bed so that the warmth is drawn in. [...]

"Above all, the ceilings must not be too thick. It is not necessary to fill the wooden beams with a layer of rubble; the heat rising through the floor could be beneficial for the family. [...] If the ceiling is simply made from wooden beams with boards nailed over them, perhaps three centimeters thick, and someone can be heard walking above, no one will be upset; rather, one happily says, 'There is father going to bed, or getting up.'

"These small observations that I have shared with you today will perhaps lighten the work of some architects who are not aggressive defenders of another opinion. It is not my intention to do more than this."[10]

It was in the discussion following his lecture that Loos for the first time discussed the theme of the "bathroom": "I believe that the bathroom is to expensive. Bathing should be done in the scullery. There should be a washing trough with a cover there, in which the family members can bathe. The cover can be used as a cooking surface. In this way, every house can offer a cheap means of bathing. It would also be quite possible to install a tank on the upper floor for bathing with cold and warm water there."[11]

With these indications regarding the settlement house, Loos wished to build a two-story house for one family on a very small building area of approximately 40-45 square meters, thus maximizing the size of the garden.

### The House with One Wall

On 11 September 1921, Loos submitted his plans for a "House with one wall" to the patent office. It was a two-story settlement row-house, built off of the wall which divided it from the neighboring house; it was only 5 meters wide, so that the wood-beamed roof could freely span the distance between the dividing walls of contiguous houses. The remaining two facades, towards the street and the garden, were to be built in a lightweight construction of wood and fastened with hangers to the floor and roof, avoiding the need for a foundation.

The motive for this plan was the housing shortage in Vienna after the First World War, which he was aware of and involved in, through his occupation with the Settlement Bureau and through his daily interaction with settlers. For this reason, he also knew that the urgently required living space had to be extremely cost-effective and quick and easy to build, and it should be suitable for self-assembly so that the interior construction, less urgent, could be left to the tenants.

In the following passage, Loos describes the advantages of his system: "Openings for doors and windows can be sawn out.

"A second layer of vertical boards is nailed to the window frames.

"The pipes are run inside the hollow walls, which are then plastered over on the interior. On the exterior they are clad with the weatherboarding. Now the hollow hanging walls are protected against wind and weather.

"The houses the Americans live in from Florida to Alaska consist of such walls, which must not be filled in.

"They are warm and durable. Washington's birthplace has been standing for two hundred years.

"Why are my walls left hovering above the ground?

"You save half the foundations.

"In the interior any change (enlargement) of the rooms can easily be carried out.

"The house can be repeatedly extended on the garden side by lengthening the party walls.

"If there are houses there already, one can erect a new house with just one wall.

"That is why it is called the *House with one wall*."[12]

By making such statements Loos clearly admitted that he found inspiration and influences for his construction in the United States and that he now merely developed this construction method further to meet Austrian demands.

## Alternatives in the Construction of Multi-level Apartments

As we learn from Loos' written commentary, he drafted a strict catalogue of criteria for the settlers. Loos felt that not everyone looking for an apartment was appropriate for the settlement development; therefore, he designed his alternative to Vienna's single-floor apartment construction of the time. Loos designed the so called "terrace houses", where two-story units were stacked on top of each other. Loos confronted this type of apartment with the single-floor design, thereby choosing to use elements from the settlement house in this mass-housing construction. The City of Vienna decided not to pursue his project, which thus never evolved beyond the planning stages.

Loos on his plans: "[...] I have only provided for two-story apartments. This is not my own invention. The English and the Americans have rental apartments that are composed of two stories within a ten- or 20-story building. People place great value on having their living rooms well separated from their bedrooms, preferring them to be separated by stairs. In this way, they can imagine that they had their own house. This raises their feeling of worth. [...]

Patent by Loos of the House with one wall

"So, I envision these apartments of two stories with an entrance from the street. The realization of my plans must therefore resemble a terraced house with an open stairway leading up to the various terraces. These terraces can also be considered an overpass, each with its own entrance, with its own arbor, where one may sit and linger on the overpass in the open air of the evening. The children can play on the terrace without the danger of being run over by an automobile or the like. [...] The safe and peaceful terrace-street will provide them the opportunity of spending the entire day outside, near the house and under the protection of the neighbors. This is how I have thought of taking care of the children."[13]

## Werkbund Settlements

Architecture was the focal point of the model Werkbund Settlements in Stuttgart (Weissenhof Settlement) and Vienna (Werkbund Settlement). There were various types of architecturally designed, small residential houses, arranged either in a row or free-standing. The garden, the do-it-yourself part for the house – the settlers' social connection – only had a secondary function in these settlements. This is why Loos called them "beautiful bourgeois houses" in a lecture on the modern settlement (1926), contrasting his idea of workers homes. Loos did a great deal for them in his Vienna settlements. In his terms these were two separate worlds.

He was nevertheless very upset when he was not asked to be the architect of the Weissenhof Settlement despite the fact that he had been so involved with it. "[...] I have kept well away from this vanity fair. People will say it is just sour grapes, which is true. When I tried to exhibit a house in Stuttgart it was refused point blank. I had something that would have been worth showing, namely a solution for the organization of living rooms in three dimensions, not two, from one story to the next, as has been the case up to now. This invention of mine would have saved humanity much time and labor in its development."[14]

In the construction of the Werkbund Settlement in Vienna, Loos was invited from the very beginning by Arch. Josef Frank. Loos was commissioned to begin the construction of two duplex houses; however, it came to changes in the plot and extensive alterations of the original project. Loos wanted to build a cost-efficient settlement house with only one supporting wall, with a produce garden, without basement, wooden-construction facades and wooden ceilings. He had Heinrich Kulka re-draft a type of house from the Heuberg Settlement. This was in exact correspondence to his standards for a settlement house.

The Werkbund Settlement was conceived largely as a urban, petit-bourgeoisie, single-family house, with the objective of contributing to the "white modern". As the land parcels were very small, the self-sufficient aspects, such as a produce garden, as Loos developed, were not made possible under these circumstances.

Thus arose a fundamental conflict, which was drawn out through the entire construction period and almost caused Loos to resign from his contract and to remove his name from the project, in that he could not justify such exuberant expenses in a social construction project. He fought for 5 cm, strong wooden floors and lower clearance in the side rooms, with steeper stairs, in order to gain more surface efficiency from a constructed volume of the same size. With this, Loos wanted to show that row-houses could be constructed at the same cost as single-floor rental units in apartment buildings, making them a better alternative for society, as the inhabitants, through their own resources and self-sufficiency, could gain a significantly greater independence from the state and from economic crises. Loos was interested in ethical and social concerns as opposed to the Werkbund's concept of form and lifestyle.

Kulka continued to arbitrate, re-drafting the object and trying to convince Loos to respond to the new conditions. Loos, on the other hand, had Kurt Unger draft a new project according to his notions, which Kulka took very personally.

In the end, all parties agreed upon a solution, based on Kulka's arbitration, and the plans were accepted by everyone.

A full basement was built. All outer supporting walls were built with bricks and the ceilings were finished with cement. The first floor had a corridor, toilet, storage room, kitchen, and living room. The living room was built 4 meters high, wrapped by a double-sided, L-shaped gallery at about 2.05 meters. A two-story window illuminated the room from the street-side. The dining room was situated under the gallery. An open stairwell reached from the living room to the gallery. In addition, an open fireplace was built into the apartment's dividing wall.

Loos furnished the gallery with an office space and low-hanging shelves. The back area would receive a small storage room.

A steep stairway reached from the gallery to the upper floor, where three bedrooms and a bathroom could be found. Both rooms facing the street were also connected by a narrow balcony.

With modest building costs and a minimal surface area and volume, Loos realized a two to three floor solution through the insertion of the galleries. With the four meter high living room, the fire place, the gallery and the open development, Loos transferred the fit-out and furnishing elements from his urban villa concept to the social housing construction standard.

## Conception of Man, Ethics

In order to clarify Loos' concerns tied to his work in settlement construction, the chronicles of Max Emers, the director of the Vienna's Settlement Foundation at the time and a co-worker of Loos, represent an exceptional source. He wrote these personal memoirs on the occasion of Loos' 60th birthday, appearing on the day of his death in articles about Loos, briefly and precisely summarizing his motivations in this settlement construction engagement: "[...] Above all, however, he taught his students to respect great art, in that he defined the occupation of an architect as a true and selfless work of a craftsman for people and their real needs. His architecture was education.

"What Loos accomplished in these 'Settlement Years' finally deserves to be extensively presented. He was truly the servant of the absolute poorest settlers, who, through homesteads, he wished to 'de-proletarianize' – to make gentlemen out of them. [...] A building population has never had such a true, helpful and knowledgeable friend. Inner wealth, lightness of being, good living, frugality in all things were the guidelines of his building concept. He would reject the title of Socialist Builder, but that is what he was. [...]

"*Building and designing is always the last consequence of eating, dressing, relaxing, moving, living healthily and humanly – and not a pseudo-artistic whim. From this consequence, his buildings and furnishings have the quality of eternal youth. They do not grow old.*"[15]

And also: "In his involvement with settlements, which he had the opportunity and also the obligation to carry out in part with the administration and in part against the administration in the beginning of the 1920's, his housing reform, urban building, cultural and nourishment ideas found their most coherent synthesis. Here, Loos achieved for himself and for all of us the vision of a new existence. [...]

"Utterly deplorable that the municipality of Vienna's lack of judgment and the sabotage files of city-hall bureaucracy frustrated his ideal drive. A powerful energy, which would have been capable of connecting the entire, momentous city building activity in splendid and noble ways. Vienna surrounded by a wreath of blooming fruit garden cities, instead of the 60,000 multi-story building blocks with apartments for rent – a hundred-thousand single-family houses with their own gardens were thus lost to the City of Vienna. [...]

"In the period of conflict between 1918 and 1919, Loos had just drawn out his *Guidelines for a Ministry of Arts* – eternally memorable guidelines – as Gustav Scheu, City Councilor at the time, had commissioned me with the foundation and direction of a Settlement Office for the City of Vienna. Loos immediately made himself available for the building consultation and for more than a year, he temporarily served the ministry with his daily service as an unpaid – as an enthusiast and an expert. We located the plots, inspected them for their practical building capacity, prepared small house prototypes and blueprints, and we prepared the settlers who, in masses, flooded our office in Prinz-Eugen-Palais on the Parkring. As we then expanded our office, City Councilor Scheu proceeded in appointing Loos as Chief Architect. The bureaucrats in city hall were naturally not very pleased with us Non-Officials and tried to make things difficult for us whenever they could. But it worked nonetheless. We created the settlement funds and later made the proposal for the house construction tax: those with homes should help those without.

"Settlement after settlement was created by our hands – more than a dozen. Despite a thousand stoppages, the blessing of intimate Loosian guidance and a perfect intuition were bestowed upon you.

"*Through the form and means of construction of the home and of the garden, he wished – an old ideal of his – to transform the worker into a gentleman, to educate. The blueprints and the form of the house were completely dictated by the produce garden, which was located at the center of every settlement area and supplied numerous harvests annually.*

"His guidelines were the successive finishing of the house (*author's note*: construction of the basic house with subsequent finishing by the tenant's own initiative), southern orientation and maximum window sizes to the garden, an eat-in kitchen, sun walls, the absence of a basement, separate children's bedrooms and intervention of the settler on the climate and the soil.

"The settlement should create new people, new happiness for family and children, sensible use of free time and healthy nutritional reform. It seemed to him 'the result of a bloodless movement of the people, and with it a human outcome'.

"In those years, Loos was just a settler; nothing but a settler. [...] His entire heart was with the workers and their new living culture, with the settlers and allotment holders, who were not always overly willing to comply with his new ideas. But he never tired of convincing them. When it got difficult, he called Germany's greatest garden reformer, Leberecht Migge, to Vienna to help.

"In 1922, we then went as a delegation to the Garden City Congress in London where Loos' ideas found their first success. The Viennese settlement movement thus gained its first recognition – in England."[16]

## Conclusion

In conclusion, Loos' vision, written by his third wife, Claire Beck, who thus repeats his words: "[...] I am against all parties, against all factionalism. The social multi-story residential blocks have been built to breed factionalism. People are penned up together so that they will vote for the party. "Every person should have his own house and his own garden. Buildings for rent should only exist for commercial purposes. In England, there are commercial districts, and the people live in cottages outside the city. [...] Only then will humanity truly be happy, when people may live like this. Poor and rich, the little worker has a house just as the rich businessman, but every man is his own master. So must it be!"[17]

[1] Leberecht Migge, *Der soziale Garten, das grüne Manifest*, Gebr. Mann Verlag, Berlin 1999 (Engl. trans. L.S.).
[2] Ibid.
[3] R+S, *Adolf Loos*, Residenz Verlag, Salzburg 1987, p. 533 (Engl. trans. L.S.).
[4] A.L., "Learning a New Way of Living" (1921), in *On Architecture*, Ariadne Press, Riverside 2002, pp. 164-7; original text "Wohnen lernen!" (1921), in *Trotzdem*.
[5] A.L., "Social Housing Development Day" (1921), in *On Architecture*, cit., pp. 160-1; original text *Der Tag der Siedler*, 1921, in *Trotzdem*.
[6] Ibid., p. 159.
[7] A.L., "Die moderne Siedlung, ein Vortrag" (1926), in *Trotzdem*, Brenner Verlag, Innsbruck (Engl. trans. L.S.).
[8] Ibid.
[9] Ibid.
[10] Ibid.
[11] Ibid.
[12] A.L., "The House with One Wall" (1921), in *On Architecture*, cit., p. 144; original text "Das Haus mit einer Mauer, Patentbeschreibung" (11 February 1921), in *Die Potemkinsche Stadt*, ed. by Adolf Opel, Georg Prachner Verlag, Wien 1983, p. 180.
[13] A.L., "Die moderne Siedlung" (1926), cit.
[14] A.L., "Josef Veillich" (1929), in *On Architecture*, cit., p. 185; original text "Josef Veillich" (1929), in *Trotzdem*.

[15] Max Emers, Director of the Settlement Federation of Vienna, who worked with Loos for a number of years; published in "Generationsführer, Zum 60. Geburtstag des Architekten und Lebensreformers", in *Der Wiener Tag*, 10 December 1934 (Engl. trans. L.S.).
[16] Max Emers, published in "Adolf Loos' Siedlerzeit Einige persönliche Erinnerungen zum ersten Todestag des Lebensreformers", in *Die Zeit*, September 1934 (Engl. trans. L.S.).
[17] Cit. in Claire Loos, *Adolf Loos - privat*, Verlag der Johannes Presse, Wien 1936, chapter "Jeder sein eigener Herr", p. 69 (Engl. trans. L.S.).

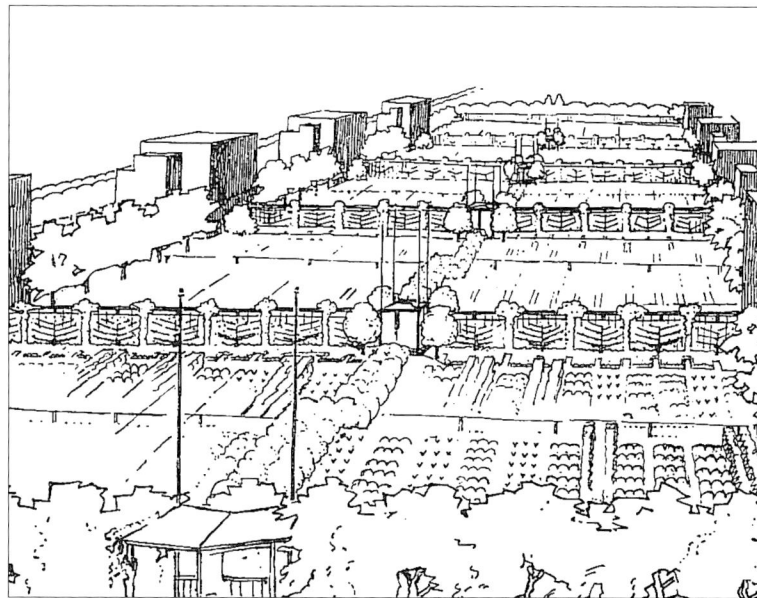

Staaken Settlement by Leberecht Migge.
Sketch for the self-sufficient garden structure.
Drawing by Leberecht Migge, published in
*Deutsche Binnenkolonisation*, 1926

**Note to the works' entries**

The biographical information on the individuals
who commissioned the projects are as follows:
*First and last name*
*Place and date of birth and death*
*Profession*
*Circle of friends*
*Other projects with Loos*
If any information is missing, it is because
it is unknown.

The catalog number is comprised as follows:
the letter indicates the type of construction
(W=Wohnung/apartment; H=Haus/house, villa;
L=Läden und Lokale/shops, cafés and bars);
the first number refers to the chronological list
of works published by Burkhardt Rukschcio
and Robert Schachel in *Adolf Loos - Leben
und Werk*, Residenzverlag, Wien-Salzburg
1987 (2nd ed.), pp. 675-76 (reproduced in this
volume on pages 297-99);
the second number is the year the project
began.

If not mentioned otherwise, the drawings
of the objects try to be as close as possible
to the as built drawings. To reach this aim,
we used building permit drawings, if available;
drawings belonging to the present owners;
historic pictures from Albertina Archive.

*Legend for the drawings*
Wall hatches: dark gray: existing before
                middle gray: load bearing
                light gray: partition wall
Plants: green
Wall mirror: purple
Fireplace: orange
Walkway through the house: sky blue
Axis: green dashed

**Works**

# Café Museum

Operngasse/Friedrichstraße
1010 Vienna

Ferdinand Rainer
Owner of the café
Ferdinand Rainer Apartment
(1040 Wien, Schwindgasse 13),
1903, work cat. no. W.24.03

**Class**
Café; reconstruction of ground floor with interior fit out.
**Type of construction / Construction design**
Existing structure in solid brick.
Column-free interior from facade to middle support wall through slightly arched ceiling, span ca 5.4 m.
**Dimensions**
Two-winged guest room: 30 x 5.4 m and 19 x 5.4 m.

**Materials**
*Double-winged great room*
Floor: oak parquet floor.
Walls: wood paneling in red-brown mahogany veneer to above table height, over which green English velour wallpaper with wide vertical longitudinal stripes bordered above with polished brass band.
Ceiling: smooth plaster, painted yellowish-white.
Lighting: polished brass bands for cable ducts on the ceiling hanging cables and exposed light bulbs.

**Description**
See Chapter 3 "Shops, Cafés and Bars".
**Work catalog no.**
L.06.99

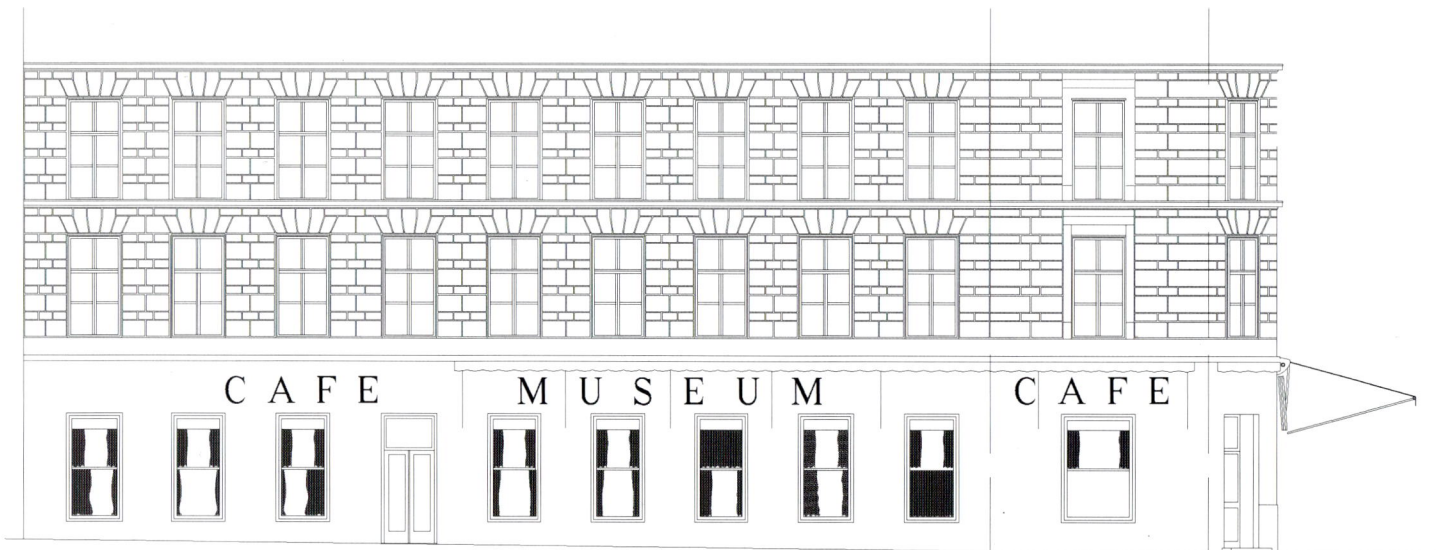

C A F E    M U S E U M    C A F E

0    1            5

Modification of ground floor facades of an existing building in typical Vienniese style built towards the end of 19th Century. Simple window openings flush with facade, interior short blinds and a canopy by continuous retractable awnings

Present situation after reconstruction in 2003

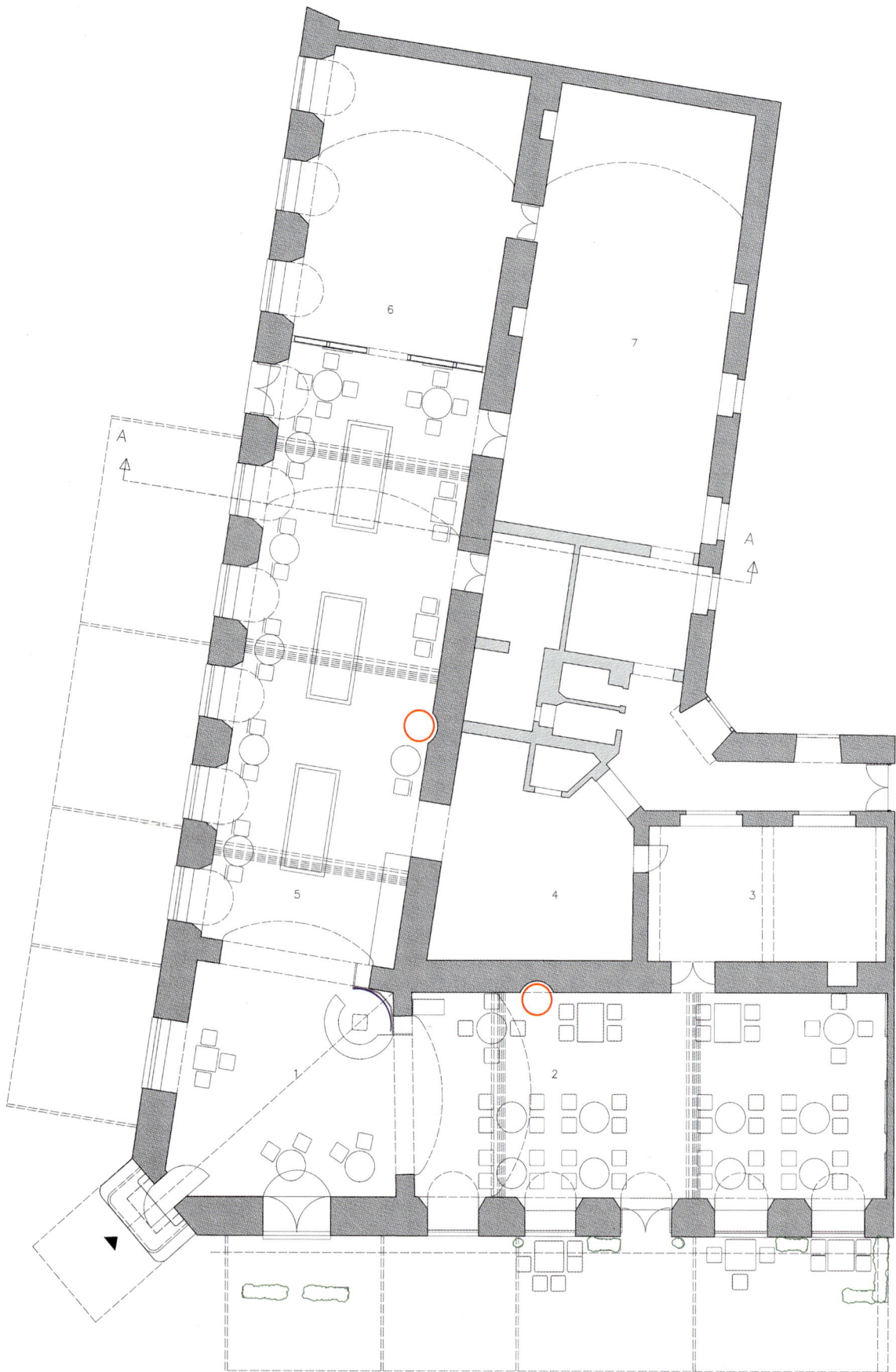

Ground floor
1 Entrance
2 Café, reading, communication
3 Gibson room
4 Preparation
5 Billiard
6 Gambling room
7 Room

Cash desk opposite from entrance as central
control point. Small "stage" for the guests
after entrance. Important is the zoning
of different activities inside the café

6

7

A

A

A

A

5

4

3

1

2

N

0    1                                    5

View into the right wing after reconstruction
in 2003

View from entrance to cash desk after
reconstruction in 2003

# Villa Karma

Clarens
Montreux (Switzerland)

Theodor Beer
Vienna 27.3.1866 - 27.9.1919
Physiology Professor at University
of Vienna

Laura Beer, born Eisler
Vienna 3.9.1883 - Clarens 23.3.1906

**Class**
Villa; reconstruction and extension with
interior fit out.

**Type of construction / Construction
design**
The existing three-floor country house with
a base area of 14.5 x 11.5 m is kept and
a new top floor built. Additional floor area
was created by a ca 3.5 m extension on
all four sides around the house, which on
the top floor forms an ample roof-terrace
and on the north side a loggia in the raised
ground floor level.
Load-bearing solid brick walls of the original
construction surrounded by a new exterior
wall, formed by load-bearing columns and
horizontal beams, generating large window
areas for the loggia and veranda.
The new building corners are constructured
as solid towers.

**Dimensions**
Base area: ca 22 x 18 m.
Levels: 4.
Stories: 4.
Living area, without basement:
ca 700 sq m.

**Materials**
*Entrance*
Floor: black and white, chessboard patterned
marble fitted to the basic oval shape.
Walls: white-red Skyros marble.
Ceiling: cupola-like vault on the ceiling above
the ground floor, decorated with gold mosaic,
covered with backlit, frosted glass ceiling.
*Hall*
Floor: white marble floor.
Walls: wall paneling in dark oak.
Ceiling: oak-beamed ceiling with white
plaster panels.
*Dining room*
Floor: black and white marble, chessboard
pattern.

Walls: white marble with a five-section
window in stained glass mosaic.
Ceiling: bronze coffered ceiling.
*Smoking room*
Walls: the room is dominated by the color
of the ceramic tiling of the fireplace. Walls
covered in "straw-colored" grass-cloth
wallpaper to the height of the doors with
wood molding and built-in furniture in
natural oak and mirrors. Above, painted
with a pale-blue coating.
Ceiling: pale-blue coating.
*Library*
Floor: oak parquet floor covered with
Persian rugs.
Walls: bookshelves in black marble
with mahogany wood surfaces. Mirrors
on opposite wall surfaces between
the windows.
Ceiling: coffered mahogany panels.
**Work catalog no.**
H.16.03

West facade
Green facade. Corners massive as little towers,
between these big window openings, in
original idea glazed translucent to achieve a
Japanese effect to the veranda behind (raised
ground floor + first floor)

View from south with park

View to north facade with park
Photo by Jean Schlemmer

The existing villa is wrapped by a structure
from Loos. Remarkable staging by Loos for the
way through the house

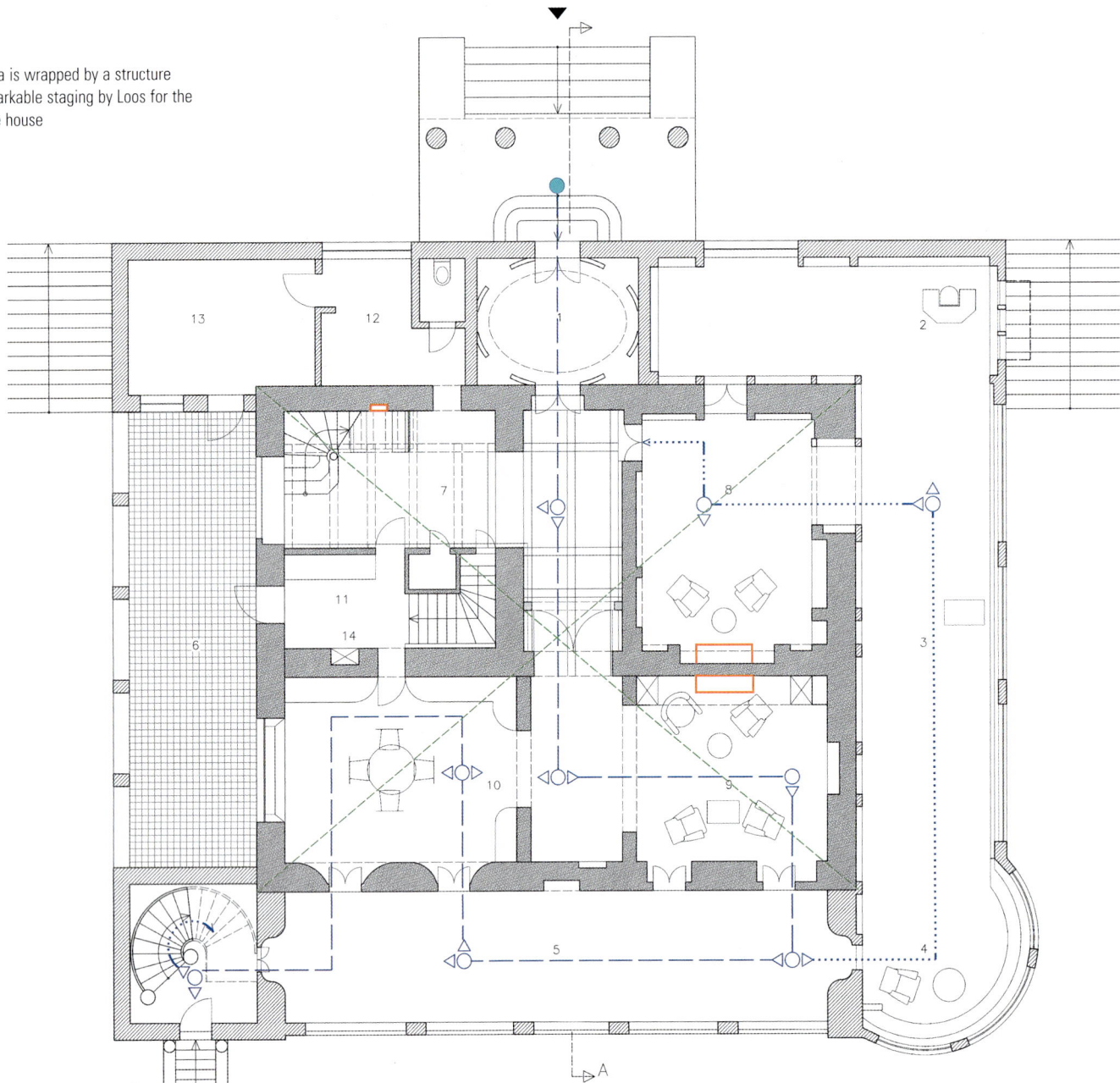

Raised ground floor
1 Vestibule
2 Study
3 Library, owner's working desk
4 Sitting area, view over lake
5 Veranda
6 Terrace
7 Hall
8 Gentlemen room
9 Fireplace, smoking salon
10 Dining room
11 Stair to kitchen in basement,
food preparation
12 Wardrobe
13 Servant (Butler)
14 Dumb waiter

Section AA
1 "Sala terrena", summer
  dining room
2 Vestibule
3 Fireplace smoking salon
4 Veranda
5 Veranda
6 Music salon
7 Gallery
8 Terrace

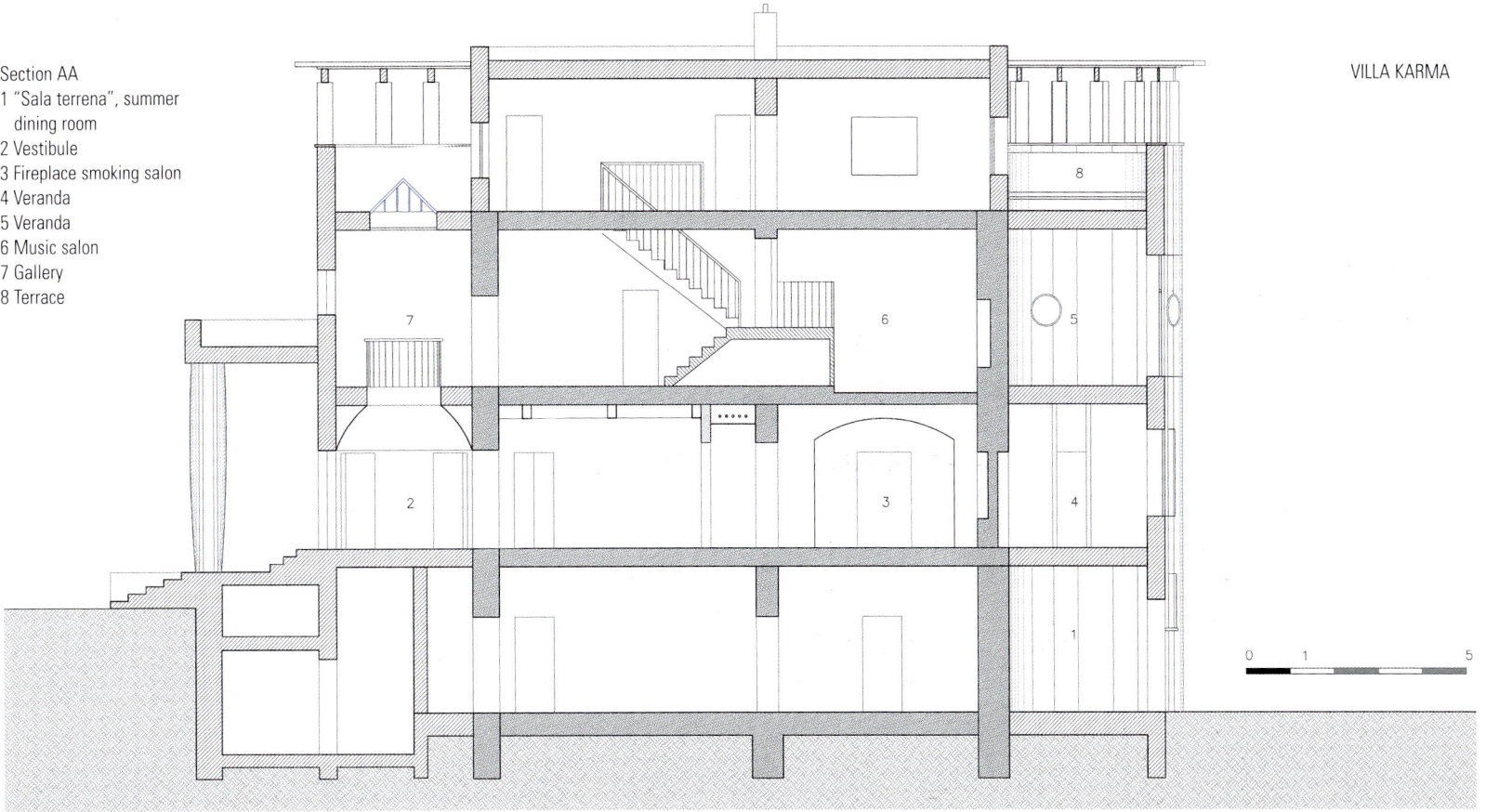

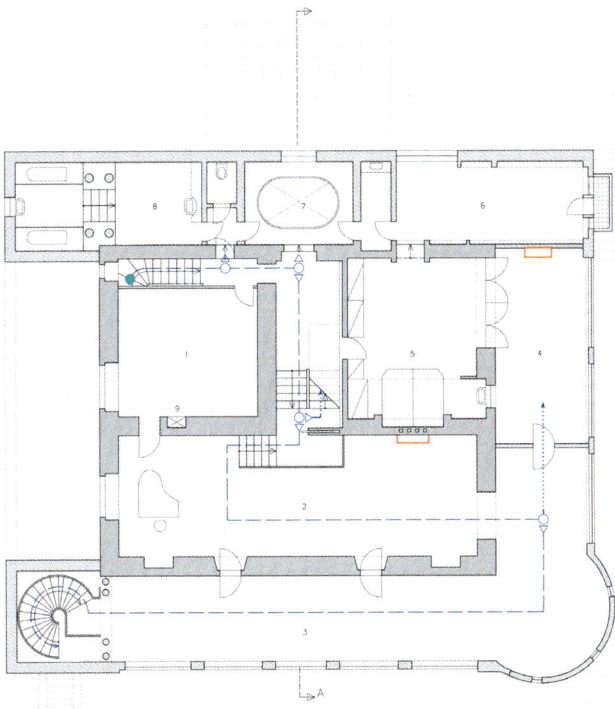

First floor
1 Bedroom
2 Music salon
3 Veranda
4 Annex to bedroom with fireplace
5 Master bedroom
6 Balcony room
7 Gallery
8 Bathroom
9 Dumb waiter

Music salon is centrally located and the end
point of the public way through the house.
Connection for the owner directly from his
private rooms to the music salon

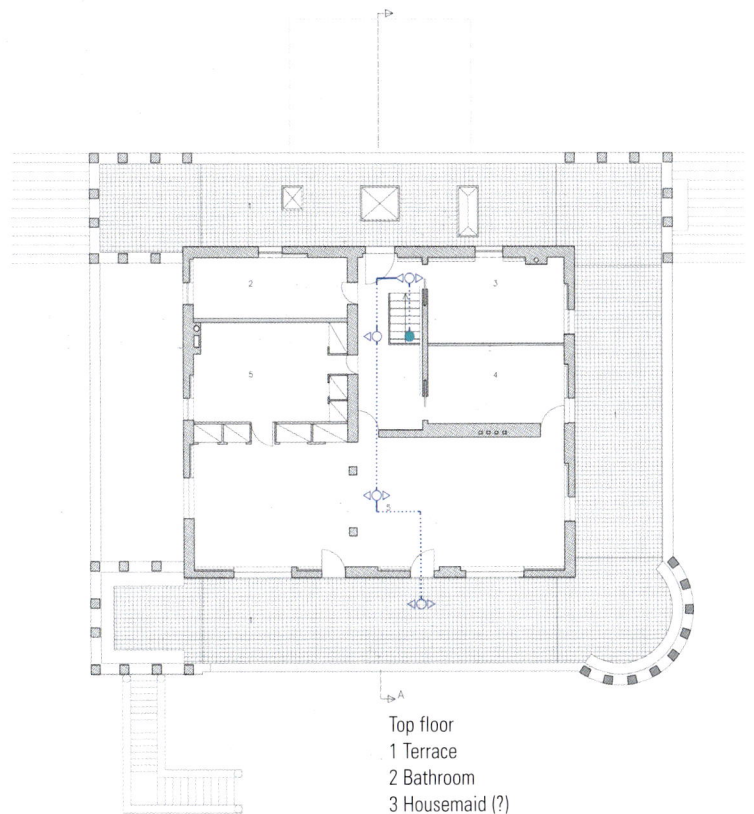

Top floor
1 Terrace
2 Bathroom
3 Housemaid (?)
4 Wardrobe (?)
5 Guest apartment (?)

Upper floor interior design unfinished by Loos.
Large terrace with impressive panoramic view
surrounds this floor of private and service
personnel rooms

Entrance hall with translucent glazing; on the right side inglenook and stair to first floor (ALA 3154)

Dining room with colored glass window and indirected light through glazed doors from veranda
Photo by M. Gerlach Jr., ca 1930
(ALA 3157)

Library with owner's working desk in the back and on left side access to inner fireplace room (ALA 2251)

Music salon on first floor. Access from above, from the landing on the right side. Mixture of different furniture styles and types, typical of Loos in the living area
(ALA 2244)

Library in raised groundfloor. View to the working desk of the owner
(ALA 2249)

Bathroom on first floor. View from the higher
level to the lower area with the two marble
bathtubs. References to classical Roman
antiquity style
(ALA 2240)

# Adolf Loos Apartment

Giselastraße 3 (today: Bösendorferstraße)
1010 Vienna
today: Wien Museum
Karlsplatz
1040 Vienna

Lina, Loos' first wife. Her parents paid
for the interior fit out of this apartment,
which was the home for Loos till the end
of his life

Adolf Loos
Brünn 10.12.1870 - Vienna 23.8.1933
Architect
Karl Kraus, Peter Altenberg, Arnold Schönberg,
Oskar Kokoschka, Genia Schwarzwald

Lina Loos, born Obertimpfler
Vienna 9.10.1882 - 6.6.1950
Actress, poet
Peter Altenberg, Egon Friedell, Theodor Csokor,
Dr. Rudolf Beer, Grete Wiesenthal,
Strindberg Kerstin

**Class**
Apartment; reconstruction with interior fit out.
**Type of construction / Construction
design**
Load-bearing solid brick walls of
the existing house.
Loos does not make any significant
constructive intervention, except for a large
opening of the living area into the closet,
which becomes the inglenook. In the
inglenook, a new, suspended ceiling was
added, thus lowering the existing room-
height. The suspended ceiling was made of
visible wooden beams, between which are
panels spanned by white linen. The visible
wood beams in the inglenook and in the
living area beneath the ceiling were added
by Loos; they are not necessary to the
structure and are purely elements of the
interior decoration.
**Dimensions**
Flat in residential building: ca 95-100 sq m
living area (living-dining room; inglenook,
bedroom; vestibule, kitchen, bathroom).

**Materials**
*Living area*
Floor: oak parquet floor covered with
Persian rugs.
Walls: the lower half are covered with
darkly stained oak wainscoting; above:
smoothly plastered wall surface, painted
white. The seating corner is integrated into
the wall covering. Likewise, there are two
small storage areas which Loos had finished
with red Skyros marble, they can only be
seen when the timber wall covering in this
area is folded down.
Ceiling: dark wood beams with white ceiling
panels.
*Bedroom*
Floor: parquet floor with pale blue wall-to-
wall carpet above which a large Angora
rabbit fur rug lies, pulled up over the bed.
Walls: covered to door-height all around,
including the window area, with white
curtains in "Batist rayée". The softwood
wardrobes lie under the curtain material
and are integrated into the wall covering.

Ceiling: smooth plaster, painted white.
*Inglenook*
Floor: oak parquet floor covered with
Persian rugs as in living area.
Walls: large, open fireplace in brick
masonry, covered with a fireplace hood
in sheet copper. Otherwise covered all
around with bookshelves and benches.
The window fanlight is paned with colored
cullet from Murano.
Ceiling: darkly stained oak wood beams
ceiling, panels spanned by linen.
*Vestibule*
Floor: covered with a coco fiber rug.
Walls: finished with white lacquered
softwood.
Ceiling: painted white.
Furniture: bench and armchair in cane work
with a small, green table (R+S, pp. 430-31).
**Description**
See Chapter 4 "Apartments".
**Work catalog no.**
W.18.03

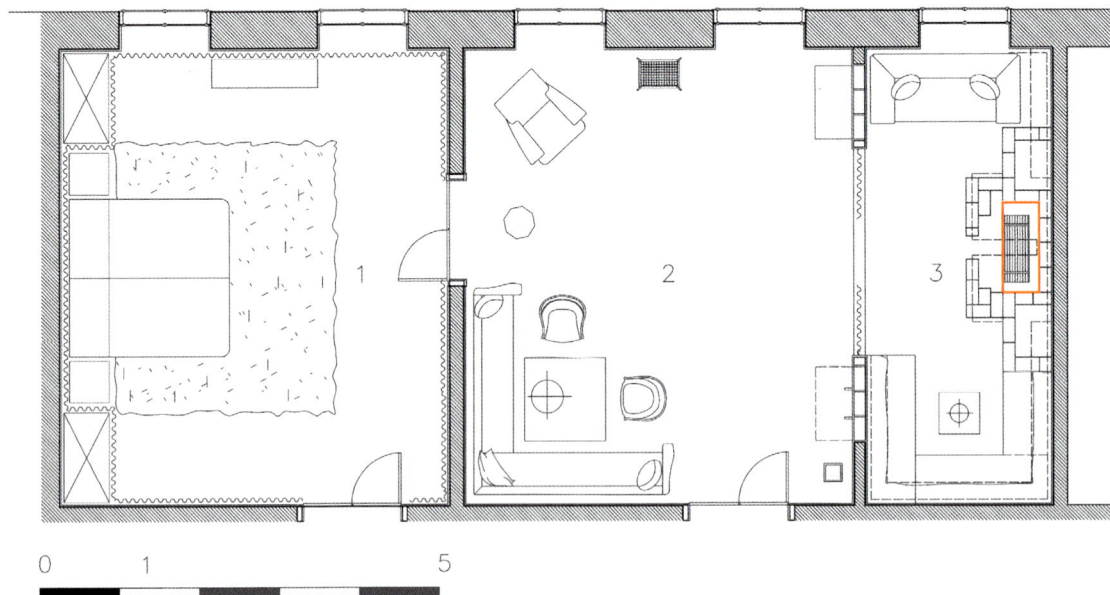

Ground floor
1 Bedroom
2 Living room, dining room
3 Inglenook, library

0     1                    5

View to the inglenook with library and sitting
bench

View to the inglenook from living/dining room

View to the dining area and door to the
bedroom

Impression from inglenook; window-fanlight
of Murano glass

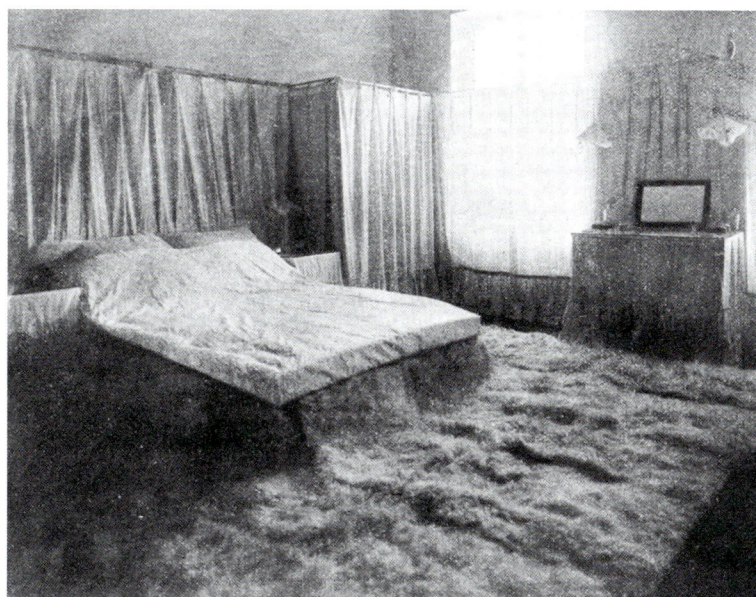

The bedroom, the ultimate intimate space;
a fur used as a bed cover. Room impression:
soft and white with archaic references

# Kärntner Bar

Kärntner Durchgang
1010 Vienna

**Class**
Bar; reconstruction with interior fit out.
**Type of construction / Construction design**
Load-bearing solid brick walls of the existing house.
No significant structural modifications made.
**Dimensions**
Base area: 4.45 x 6.15 m.
**Materials**
*Interior*
Floor: black and white, checker-board, marble squares.
Walls: division into three case bays of equal dimensions. Pilaster in dark green marble (tinos green); panels: semi-gloss mahogany wainscoting

and above head-height large wall mirrors.
Interior entrance facade: mahogany wood with glass fillings, covered to eye-height with "short blinds". Above: translucent, backlit onyx marble.
Ceiling: beams in dark green marble (tinos green) with rectangular coffers made of marble with darker veins (rosso antico). Every coffer is made from only a single, thinly cut marble-slab, the gaps are backlaid with brass.
*Entrance*
Exterior: four superimposed, Skyros marble pillars, brass door frames with glass panels, covered with "short blinds".
Above doors: fanlights composed of dark blue cullet, illuminated from the interior.
Over the wall pillars is a backlit construction

of stained glass, in the design of the American flag "popping out" of the facade, displaying the words "Kärntner Bar". Above this is the writing, "American Bar" in single letters, with a background again in pieces of dark, broken glass on a wavy surface.
*Facilities*
Bar counter: mahogany wood with polished brass fittings.
Benches: originally designed of green automobile leather; actually completed in English floral pattern fabric.
**Description**
See Chapter 3 "Shops, Cafés and Bars".
**Work catalog no.**
L.62.08

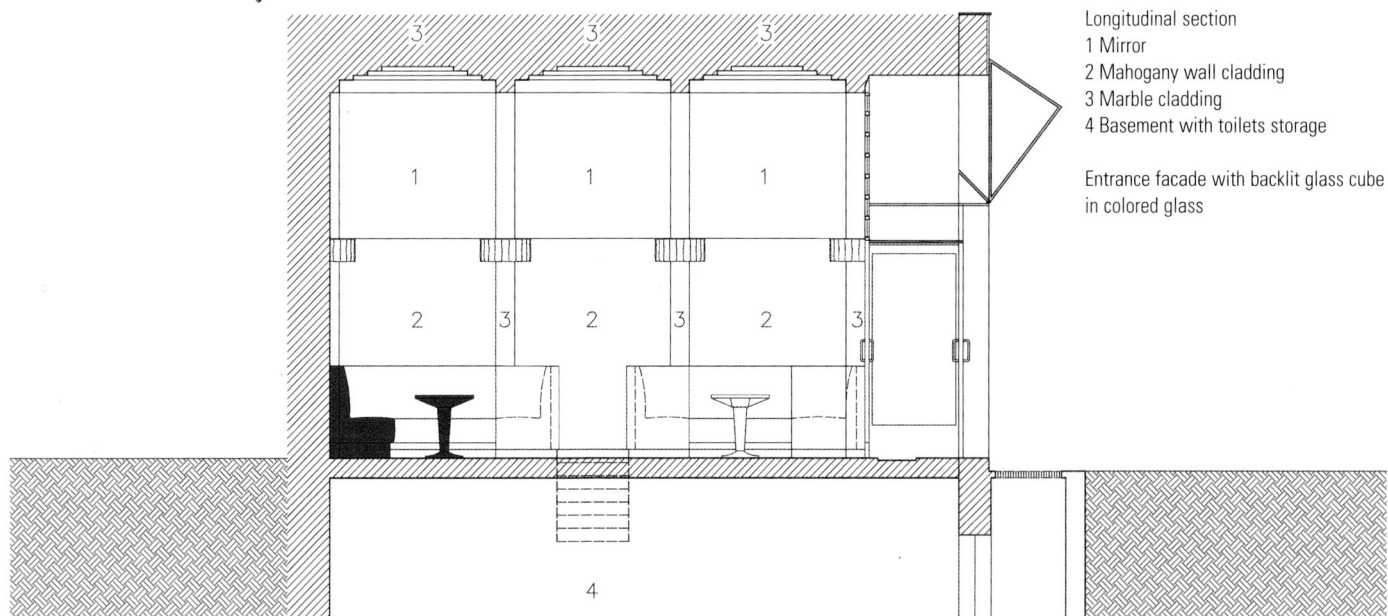

Longitudinal section
1 Mirror
2 Mahogany wall cladding
3 Marble cladding
4 Basement with toilets storage

Entrance facade with backlit glass cube in colored glass

View to entrance facade with backlit onyx wall

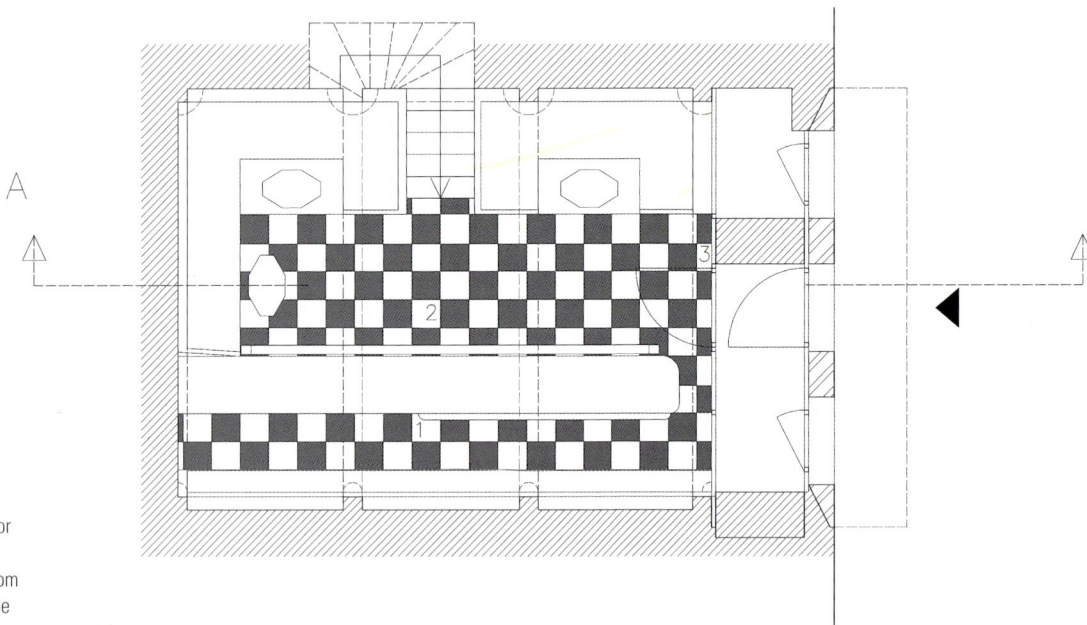

Ground floor
1 Bar
2 Guest room
3 Garderobe

Bar takes one third of the narrow total
space, coming from the original concept
of a standing bar

0    1              5

View from entrance with Peter Altenberg
portrait; to be noted the great illusion of space
extension

# House on Michaelerplatz

Michaelerplatz
1010 Vienna

Leopold Goldman
Vienna 27.9.1875 - dead in Nazi-concentration
camp Maly Trostinec 15.6.1942
Tailor and outfitter for men, merchant
Goldman & Salatsch Men's Tailor Salon
(1010 Vienna, Graben 20), 1898-1903, project for
Leopold's father and company founder Michael
Goldman, work cat. no. L.2.98
Leopold Goldman House (1190 Wien, Hardtgasse
27-29), 1909-1911, work cat. no. H.68.09
Leopold Goldman Apartment (1190 Wien
Hardtgasse 27-29), 1911, work cat. no. W.84.11

Emanuel Aufricht
(husband of Leopold Goldman's sister Berta)
Vienna 14.12.1871 - dead in Nazi-concentration
camp in December 1941
Partner of Goldman & Salatsch
Emanuel and Berta Aufricht Apartment
(1010 Wien; Graben 20/ Naglergasse 1), 1904,
work cat. no. W.30.04

## Class

Multifunctional building; new construction
with interior fit out of the men's tailor and
outfitters salon Goldman & Salatsch.

## Type of construction / Construction design

Exterior walls: reinforced concrete
framework infilled with brick masonry.
Interior: reinforced concrete supports.
Ceilings: reinforced concrete.
Roof: constructed in reinforced concrete
and clad with copper sheeting (R+S, p. 465).

*Facade*

The facade on Michaelerplatz was built as
a five-story high frame or beam, so that
the four marble columns in the portal zone
did not have to take on any load from the
building.

*Interior*

A nearly squared grid of 16 interior columns
with beams in the center of the tailor salon
gave Loos the opportunity to design his first
*Raumplan*-space. The only load bearing wall
is around the staircase, which functions
as core for the shearing forces. On the
living/office floors the first row of interior
columns behind the facade eliminated
creating a support-free room spanning
of ca 6.5 m.

In general, the construction of concrete
columns and beams is designed for
a flexible layout of the living and office
floors. The ceilings in the upper levels are
slab-beamed ceilings (slab thickness 5 cm,
distance between beams 71 cm), in the
lower floors there are mostly coffered
ceilings between length and width-wise
perpendicular beams (slab thickness
6-7 cm).

First time *Raumplan*-principe by Loos in the
mezzanine area of the Goldman & Salatsch
Men's Tailor Salon.

## Dimensions

Street facade length: Herrengasse:
ca 28.35 m; Michaelerplatz:
ca 14.2 m; Kohlmarkt: ca 10.5 m.
Building depth: Herrengasse:
ca 8.5 m; Michaelerplatz: ca 13 m.
*Goldman & Salatsch Men's Tailor
and Outfitter Salon*
Levels: 7.
Stories: 3 (basement, ground floor,
mezzanine).
*Apartments/Offices*
Levels: 4 + roof.
Stories: 4 + roof.

## Materials

See Chapter 3 "Shops, Cafés, and Bars".

## Work catalog no.

H.67.09

Impression of Cipollino marble cladding in the
base zone, with bay windows in mezzanine;
the choice of marble is a citation of the
classical ancient world, because exactly this
stone was used by the Romans

"Dialogue" of the House on Michaelerplatz
with Michaeler church

Loos integration of the House on
Michaelerplatz into the square shows the
strong relation to the oldest buildings on the
right side. Refusal of the art-historic revival
style fashion from end of 19th and beginning
20th Centuries, but Loos demonstrates his
understanding of a direct link to the ancient
culture of the Romans and the Viennese
tradition by using classical antiquity citations
in his facades, such as cornices, columns,
special corners details and natural stone,
which was already used by the Romans

Column behind entrance with glass vitrine

View from stair to ground floor shop

Ground floor
1 Men's outfit and accessories shop
2 Separate small shops for rent
3 Court with glass brick floor

Main entrance on the line of symmetry.
Regular column grid in shop area.
Men-outfit-shop on the ground floor, access
to sport fashion shop in basement and tailor
shop in mezzanine. Cash-desks at the
beginning of main stair in central control
position

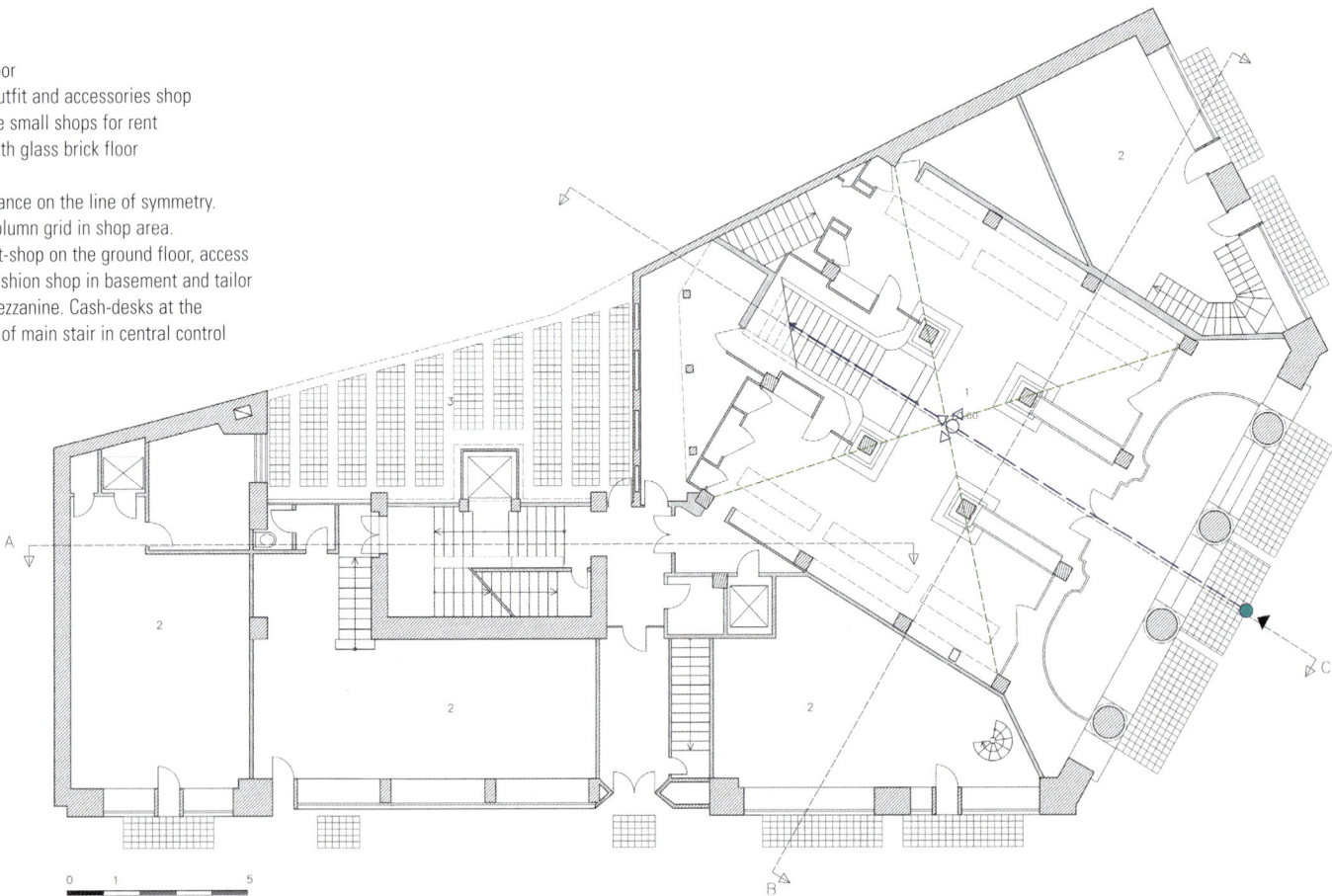

Lower mezzanine floor
1 Reception tailor shop
2 Accounting
3 Office
4 Drapery store
5 Sewery
6 Ironing

Multilevel situation as first *Raumplan* by Loos.
Control of customers coming up the stair from
accounting by wall mirror

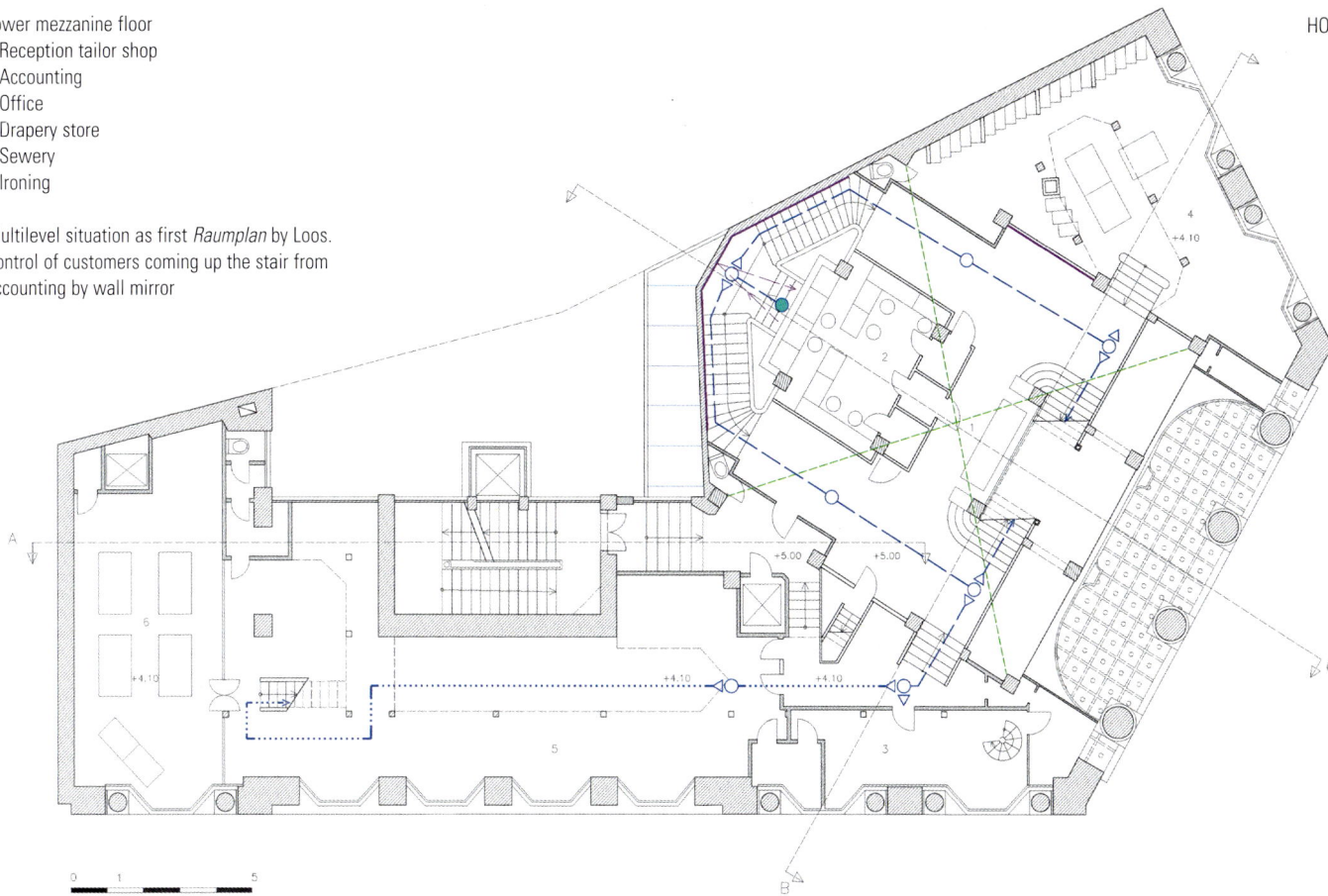

Upper mezzanine floor
1 Waiting (Lounge)
2 Dressing room
3 Drapery store
4 Tailor cutting
5 Void (Ironing)
6 Void

Central area as customer area for tailor salon,
left side tailor workshop on two levels

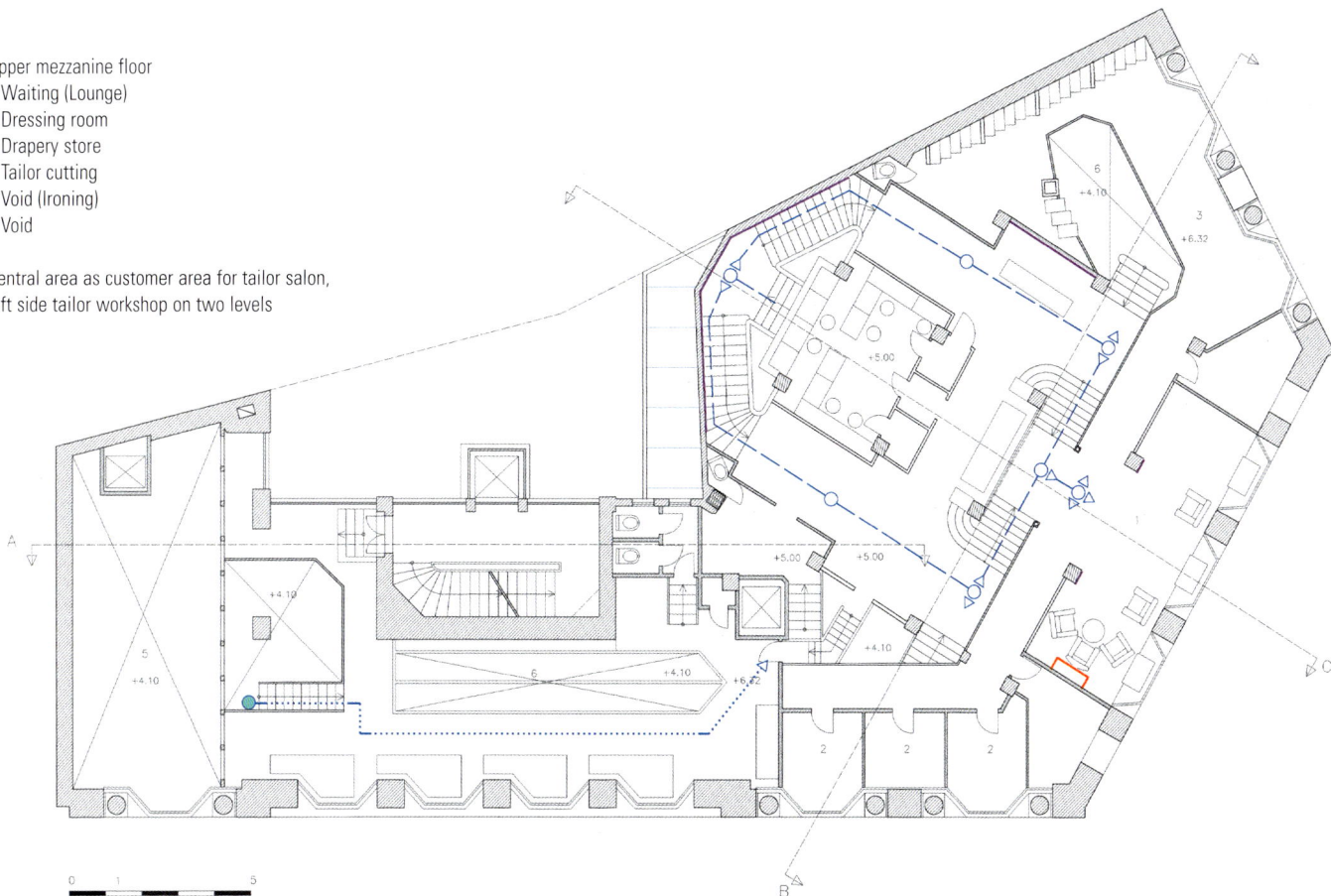

Two views of the office and dressing rooms
area on mezzanine level

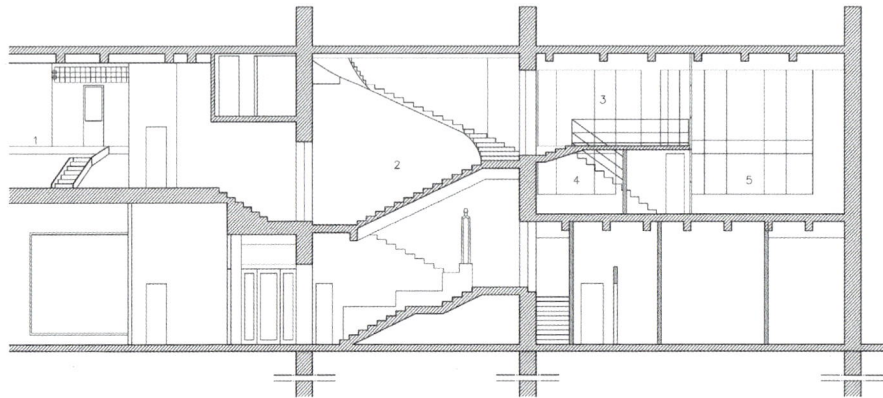

Section AA
1 Shop upper mezzanine
2 Staircase residential
3 Tailor cutting
4 Sewery
5 Ironing

View from gallery in front of the dressing
rooms on upper mezzanine level to the former
drapery store

View to stair arrival in mezzanine, with the
complete size of the small skylight

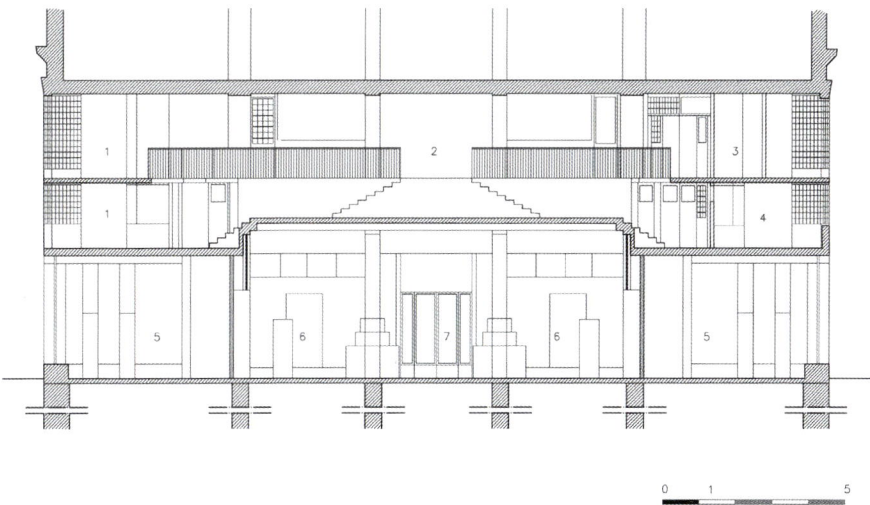

Section BB
1 Drapery store
2 Waiting (Lounge)
3 Dressing rooms
4 Office
5 Separate shops for rent
6 Men's outfit and accessories shop
7 Entrance

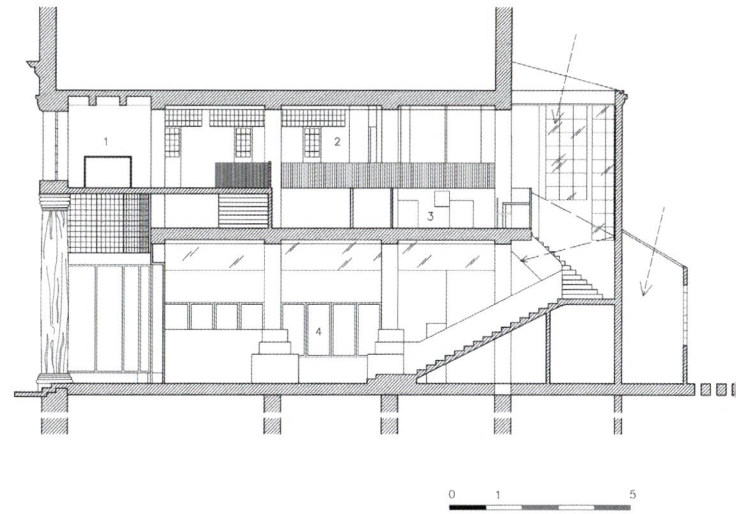

Section CC
1 Waiting (Lounge)
2 Dressing rooms/Upper mezzanine
3 Accounting
4 Men's outfit and accessories shop

Stair landing to mezzanine; illusion of space
extension with skylight in glassbricks, wall
mirrors and polished mahogany cladding

Stair landing to mezzanine; view from account
department, control point for shop owner
by using wall mirrors; great space illusion

Impression of comfortable waiting area with
fireplace; bay windows to Michaelerplatz

Public staircase in Carrara marble to office and apartment floors above

Workshop area (mostly white); view to connection door with the customer area

Entrance vestibule for office and apartment floors in Skyros marble with endless space effect through opposite mirrors

# Steiner House

St.Veitgasse 10
1130 Vienna

Hugo Steiner
1874 - Paris 1947
Manufacturer, since 1927 manager of Kniže Paris
Karl Kraus, Ludwig Wittgenstein, Adolf Loos
Hugo and Lilly Steiner Apartment (1060 Wien,
Gumpendorferstr. 22), 1900, work cat. no. W.11.00

Lilly Steiner, born Hofmann
Vienna 7.4.1884 - Paris 1961
Painter, graphic artist
Arnold Schönberg, Alban Berg, Arturo Toscanini,
Aristide Maillol, Adolf Loos

**Class**
Villa; new construction with interior fit out.

**Type of construction / Construction design**
Outer walls and middle wall are load-bearing, made from brick masonry. Prefabricated slightly arched brick ceiling over basement. Ceiling over raised ground floor and first floor: wood beam ceiling. Roof trusses in wood with timberboard linings and clad in copper sheeting. Flat roof area: wood-cement roof. Continuous ceilings without height differences.

**Dimensions**
Base area: 13.50 x 14.50 m.
Clear room heights: raised ground floor: 2.85 m; first floor: 3.00 m; top floor: 2.10 m.
Levels: 4.
Stories: 4 (basement, raised ground floor, first floor, top floor).
Living area without basement: ca 410 sq m.

**Materials**
*Living/dining area, hall, corridor*
Floor: oak parquet floor covered with Persian rugs.

Walls: covered to door-height with dark stained oak, matt-finished. Above: smooth plaster, painted white.
Ceiling: visible ceiling beams also in dark stained oak, matt-finished; with smooth plaster, painted white, ceiling panels.
*Bedroom*
Walls: white lacquered, matt-finished softwood to door-height; above: colorful floral wallpaper.

**Work catalog no.**
H.75.10

Elevation with original green facade

Present view from street, entrance has been
modified by the Steiner family from original
idea of Loos with a niche (see floors plans)

View from street showing the shape of the roof

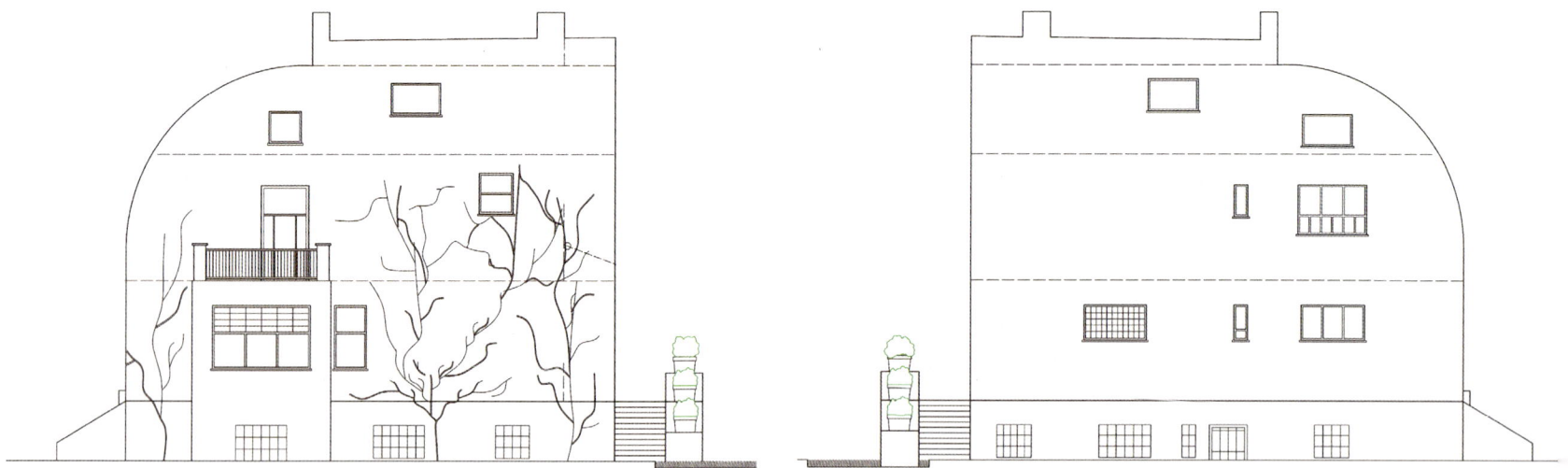

Side elevations
Irregular window openings on side elevations;
almost symmetrical design for street and
garden elevation

Present view from garden with three-story
facade. Water basin under terrace. Access
to terrace by a small and low door to the right
of the middle window. Access to garden by
lateral stair; closed wall as parapet to garden

View to original garden facade
(ALA 3236)

Garden elevation, original green balustrade;
terrace canopy by retractable large awning

139

Raised ground floor
1 Kitchen
2 Pantry
3 Cloakroom
4 Hall
5 Library niche, reading bay
6 Working
7 Corridor
8 Salon
9 Dining room
10 Winter garden
11 Water basin
12 Terrace

Original entrance situation
with the walk-through concept
by Loos. Living/dining area with
dividing possibilities using heavy
curtains

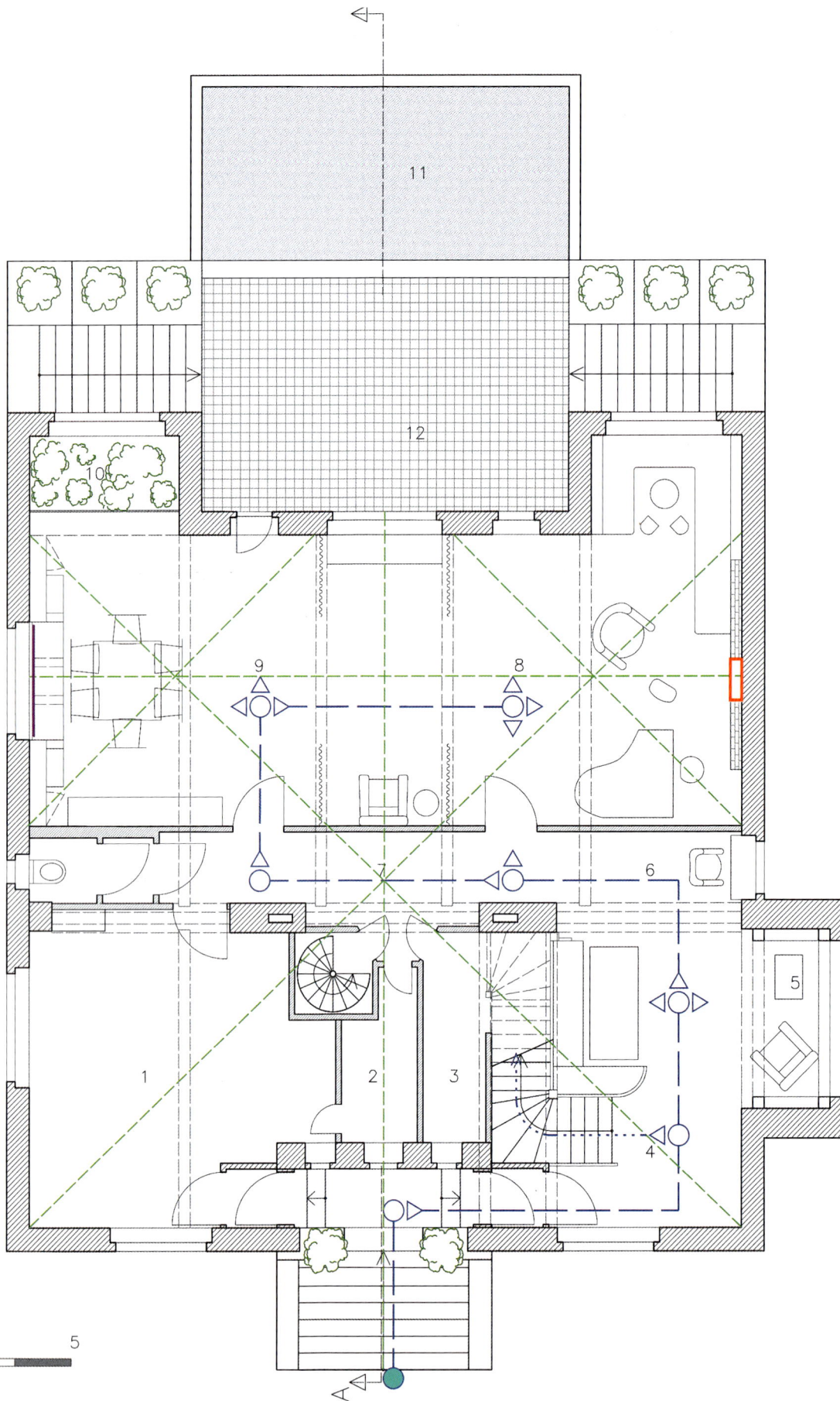

11

12

10

9

8

7

6

5

1

2

3

4

0    1            5

A

First floor
1 Atelier
2 Butler
3 Children room
4 Corridor
5 Children room
6 Bathroom
7 Master bedroom

Private rooms with white softwood
cladding, big window with
translucent glass between
bathroom and corridor

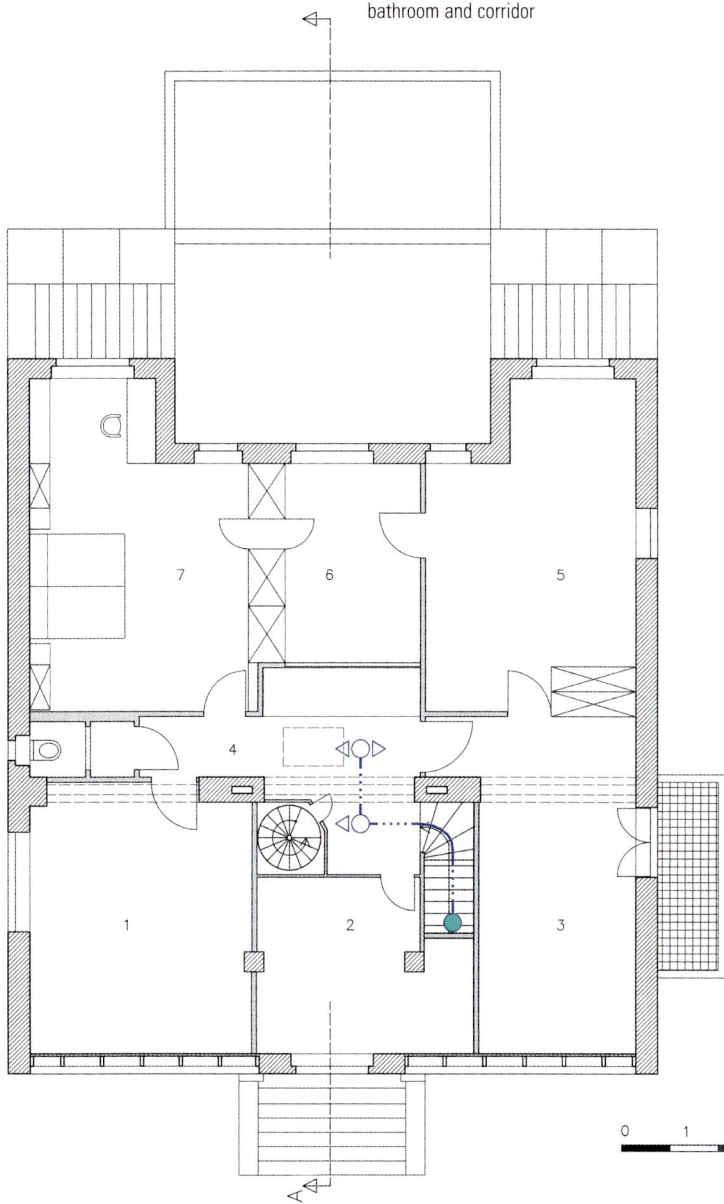

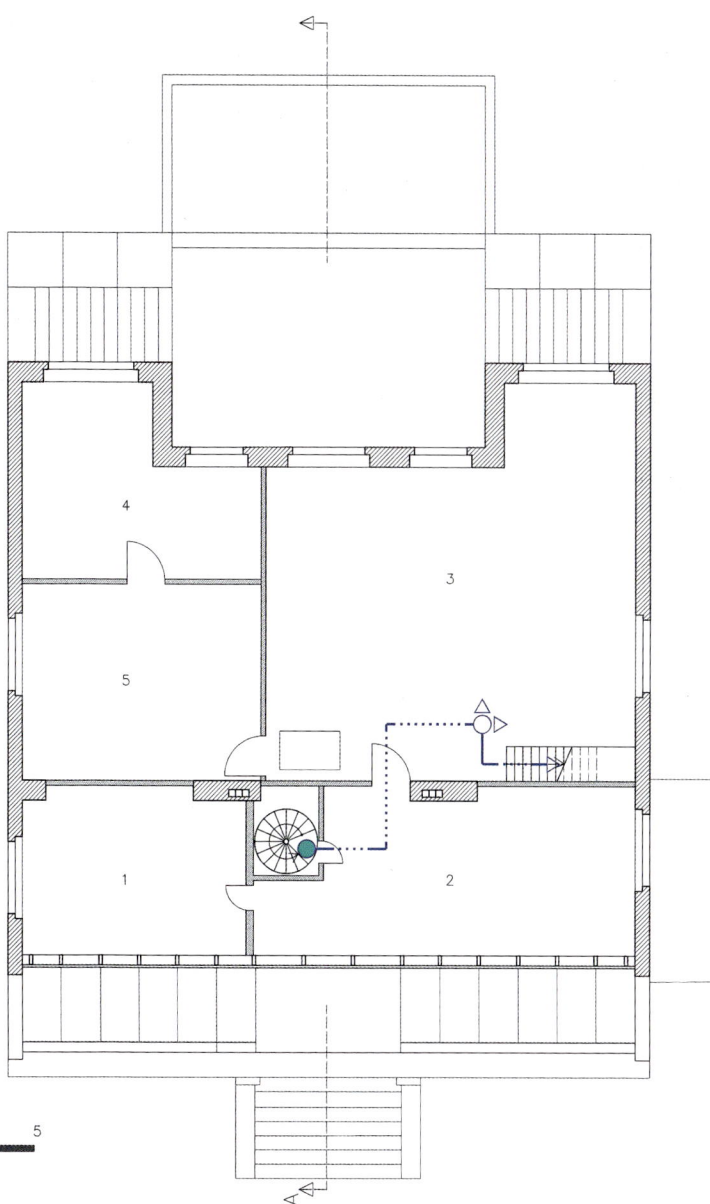

Top floor
1 Reserve
2 Reserve
3 Drying room
4 Ironing room
5 Laundry

Only utility and service rooms on this level,
stair to roof terrace above

View of entrance and stair to private rooms

View of entrance hall with library niche
and sitting corner

Section AA
1 Storage (Cellar)
2 Water basin
3 Terrace
4 Dining room
5 Corridor
6 Pantry
7 Butler
8 Corridor
9 Bathroom
10 Drying room
11 Reserve
12 Roof terrace

Raised ground floor, continous floor levels,
protected terrace by canopy and lateral wings

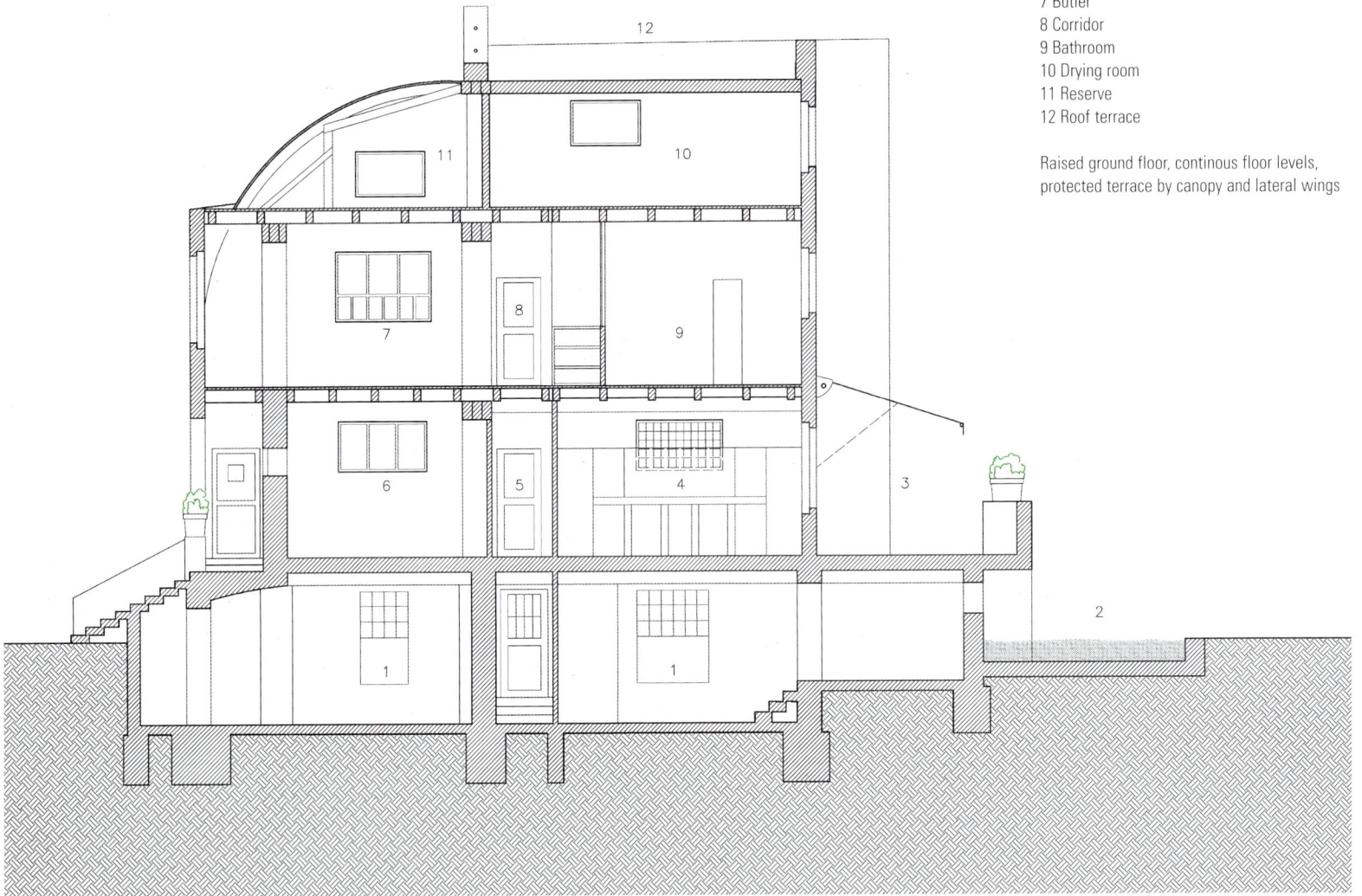

Master bedroom with white softwood cladding
and textile wallpaper

View to dining area. The window is partly
covered by interior mirror; niche to garden
designed as winter garden
Photo by M. Gerlach Jr., 1930
(ALA 3240)

View from dining room to salon. Curtains as
flexible room deviders. Fireplace in central
axis; on the right, the piano

# Kniže Tailor Salon

Am Graben
1010 Vienna

Gisela Steiner (sister of Hugo Steiner)
1867-1942
Business woman
Arnold Schönberg and Adolf Loos were clients
of Kniže
Kniže Tailor Salon Berlin (Berlin NW 7, Neue
Wilhelmstr. 9-11), 1924, work cat. no. L.172.24
Kniže Tailor Salon Paris (Paris VIII, 146, Avenue
des Champs-Elysees), 1927-1928, work cat.
no. L.189.27

Fritz Wolff-Kniže (son of Gisela Steiner)
Vienna 25.7.1890 - New York 31.10.1949
Tailor and merchant
Oskar Kokoschka, Jungnickl, Marc Chagall,
Georges Braque, Adolf Loos
Fritz and Annie Wolff-Kniže Apartment
(1010 Vienna, Bräunerstraße 7; source:
Markus Kristan, *Adolf Loos - Läden u. Lokale*,
Album Verlag Wien, 2001, p. 82)
Fritz and Annie Wolff-Kniže Apartment II,
(1040 Vienna, Wohllebengasse 8; interior
fit out by H. Kulka), 1936 (source: Peter A. Kniže,
January 2006)

## Class

Tailor salon; reconstruction with interior
fit out.

## Type of construction / Construction design

Existing house with solid brick walls
and wood-beamed ceilings (Viennese
standard in the late 19th Century).
Installed mezzanine level with galleries on
first floor; suspended ceiling over showroom
on first floor, stairway connections.

## Dimensions

Sales area: ca 150 sq m; workshop
area/back office: ca 240 sq m.
Levels: 3.
Stories: 2 (ground floor, first floor).

## Materials

*Entrance facade*
Black Swedish granite, with display
windows in narrow cherry wood frames
with curved glass. On top of the granite
cladding the writing in Roman type
and emblem in gold-plated brass.
*Showroom on the ground floor, stairway*
Walls: high gloss cherry wood, glass
display cases, strong cornice in cherry
wood to the ceiling.
Ceiling: smooth plaster, painted white.
Stairway: green linoleum, covered with red
carpet and in the center, a narrow white
fabric rug held with polished brass rods.

*Showroom on the first floor*
Floor: green wall-to-wall felt covered
with Persian rugs.
Walls: high gloss cherry wood with built-ins
and display cases to the height of the
gallery; above: white painted wall surface.
Ceiling: in both high salons: white painted.
In the lower reception area: high gloss
cherry wood coffered ceiling.
*Work and side rooms*
Walls: white lacquered, matt-finished
softwood; above: white painted smooth
plaster.
Ceiling: smooth plaster, painted white.

## Work catalog no.

L.77.10

Shop facade to street level

View from first tailor salon on first floor
backwards to the men's outfit salon with
lower timber ceiling

Ground floor
1 Cashier
2 Shop (shirts, outfits and accessories)
3 Dressing rooms

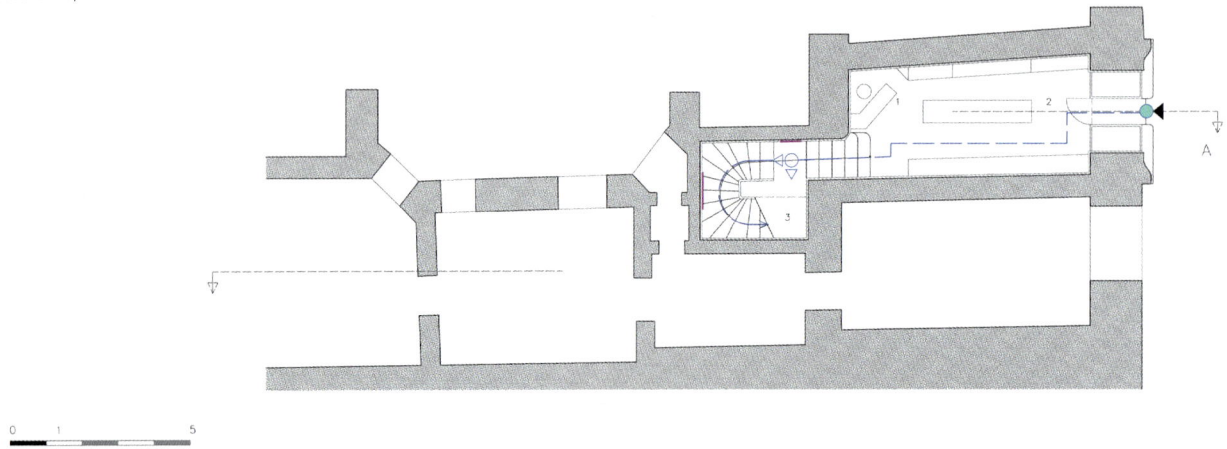

First floor
1 Men's outfit salon
2 Waiting area of men's outfit salon
3 Sewery
4 Dressing rooms
5 Salon - Drapery store/Waiting area
6 Salon taylor - Suits and shirts
7 Cashier
8 Office manager

Room and cash point controlled by manager
from his office through special mirror in vitrine

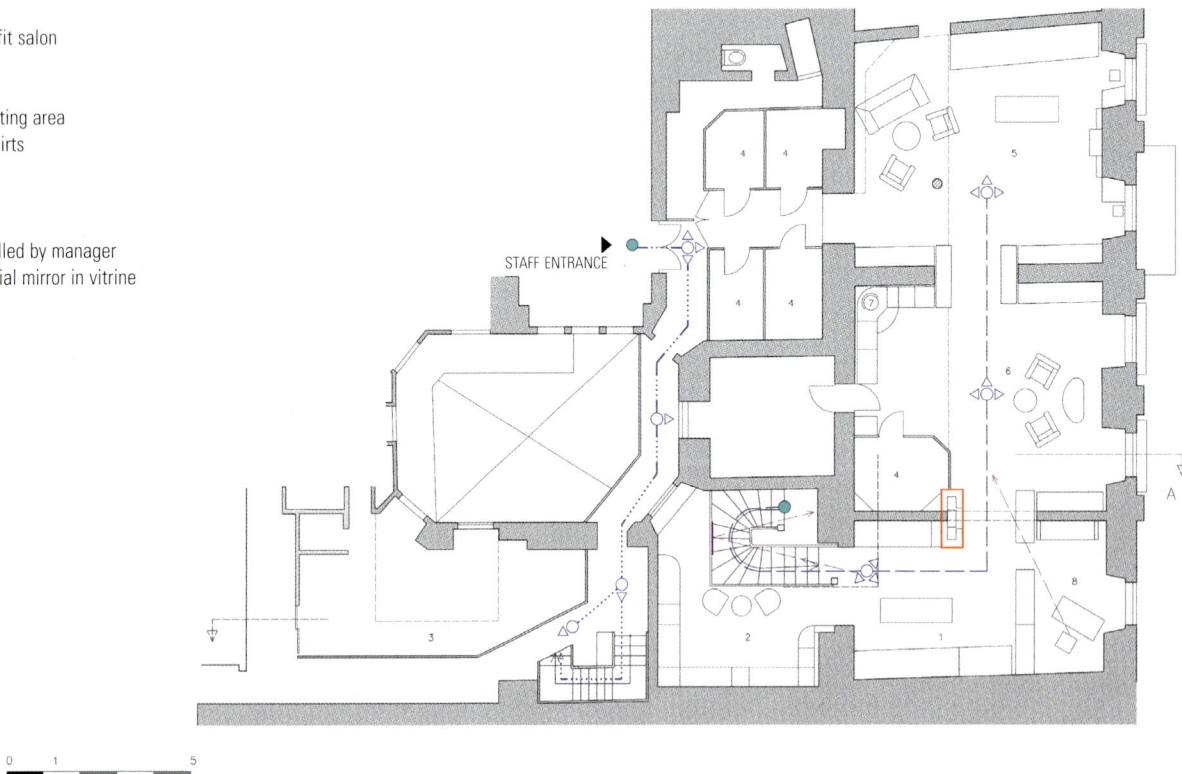

STAFF ENTRANCE

Section AA
1 Shop window
2 Men shirts and accessories
3 Dressing room
4 Shirt sewery
5 Tailor cutting
6 Tailor workshop
7 Gallery accounting
8 Staff room (behind)
9 Salon

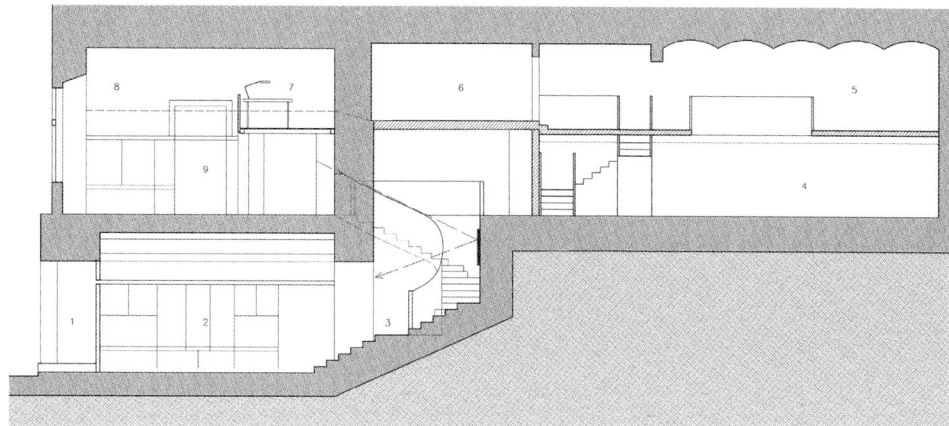

Mezzanine level
1 Tailor workshop
2 Staff room
3 Void salon
4 Void salon
5 Gallery - Correspondence
6 Tailor workshop
7 Gallery - Accounting
8 Tailor cutting

Tailor workshop and the accounting
department on the gallery

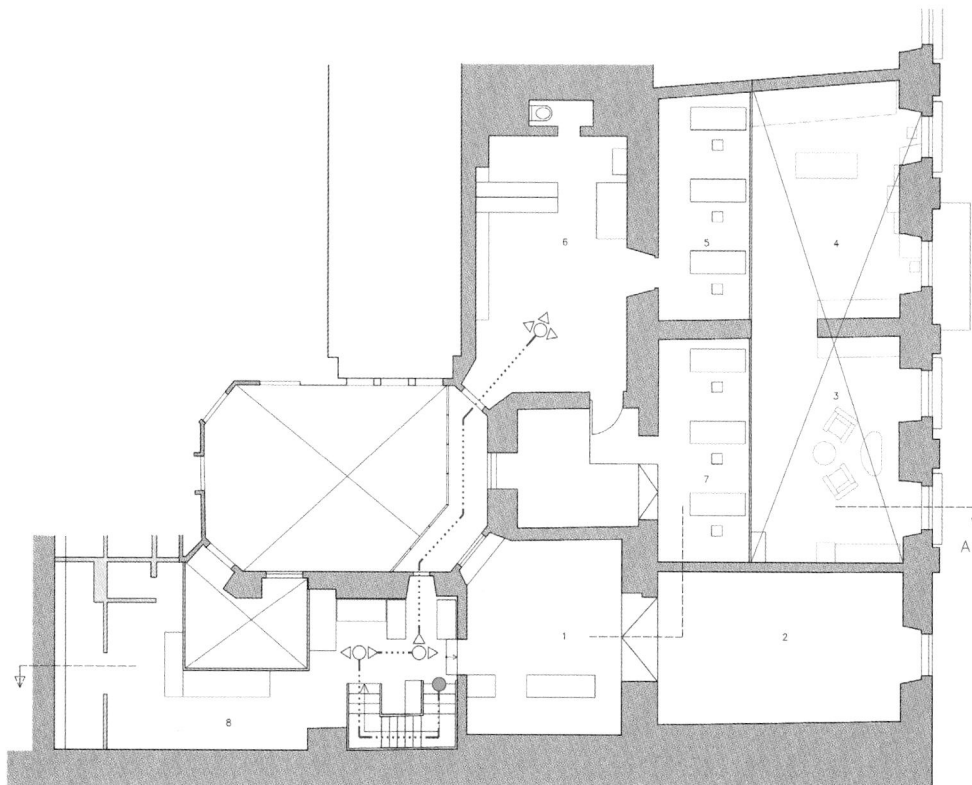

**149**

View of men's outfit salon through wall mirror, with staircase from ground floor

Waiting area of men's outfit salon with staircase from ground floor

Stair to first floor, with wall mirror for access control from first floor

# Friedrich Boskovits Apartment I

Frankgasse 1
1090 Vienna

Friedrich Boskovits
Merchant
Friedrich Boskovits Apartment II (1010 Vienna,
Bartensteingasse 9), 1913

**Class**
Apartment; reconstruction with interior
fit out.

**Type of construction / Construction
design**
Walls solid brick, ceilings in wood,
traditional Viennese type of construction
in late 19th Century.
No significant structural modifications
by Loos.

**Dimensions**
Flat in residential building: ca 170 sq m
living area.

**Work catalog no.**
W.79.10

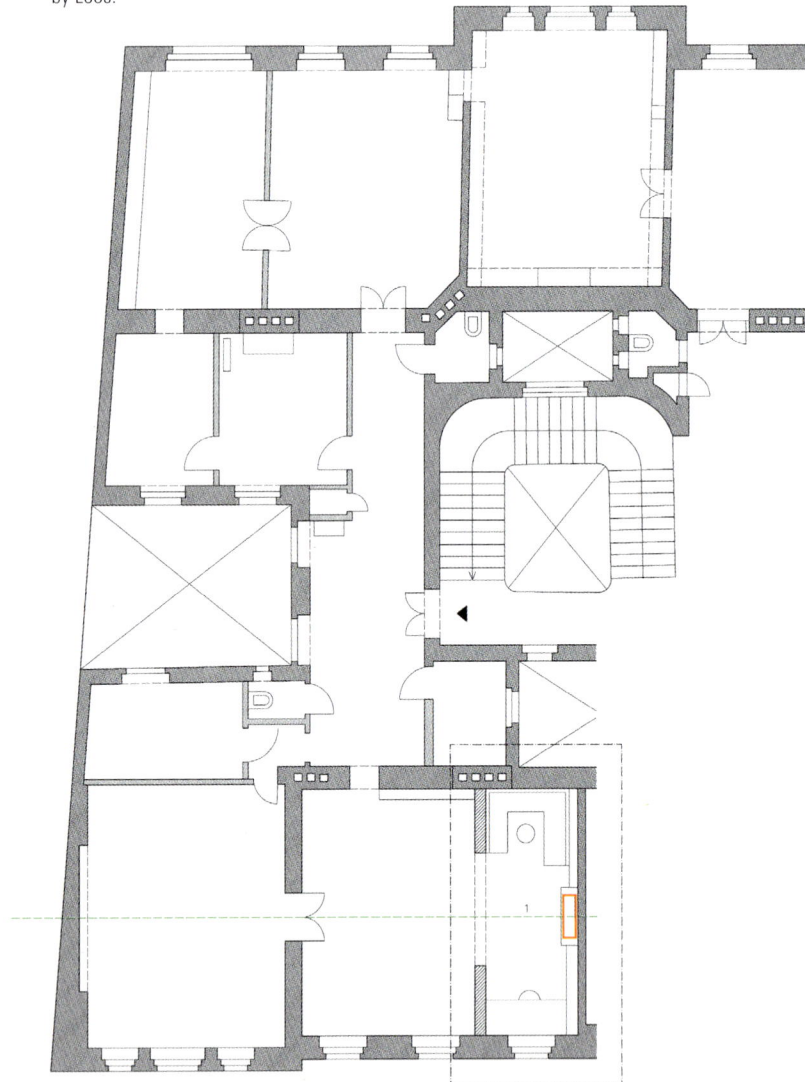

Ground floor
1 Annex to salon (inglenook)

Original floor plan of the first flat for Friedrich
Boskovits. Boskovits moved from this flat
to Bartensteingasse 9 (see p. 180), that too
outfitted by Loos. Loos integrated most of the
furniture in the new flat, only the original
inglenook remained in this one

Views to the inglenook with central fireplace
and wall mirror; library to the right side with
working desk at window and the sitting niche
for conversation on the left side

0    1                    5

# Stoessl House

Matrasgasse 20
1130 Vienna

Otto Stoessl
Vienna 2.5.1875 - 15.9.1936
Clerk of railway society, author, literary
and theatre critic
Karl Kraus, Robert Scheu, Samuel Lublinski,
Paul Ernst, Adolf Loos
Furnishings for Dr. Otto and Auguste Stoessl
Apartment (1130 Wien, Auhofstr. 235), 1900,
work cat. no. W.10.00

Auguste Stoessl
Vienna 1872 - after 1948
Teacher

**Class**

Villa; new construction with interior fit out.

**Type of construction / Construction design**

Nearly square layout with outer walls
and middle wall load-bearing in brickwork.
Prefabricated slightly arched brick ceiling
over basement, other floors have
wood-beamed ceilings. The first villa
by Loos in which he begins to work with
lower floor heights for the side rooms
in order to give the rooms above more
overhead. Ground floor and ceiling above
the first floor (+1) are respectively divided
into two different levels.
The wood roof trusses in the form of an hip
roof with a mansard are covered with brick.

**Dimensions**

Base area: 9.2 x 10.4 m.
Levels: 7.
Stories: 5 (basement, raised ground floor,
first floor, first and second attic floors).
Living area without basement:
ca 250 sq m.

**Furnishing**

The dining room furniture derives from
the apartment that Loos designed
for Mr. and Mrs. Stoessl in 1900.

**Materials**

*Living/dining area, hall*
Floor: oak parquet floor covered with
Persian rugs.
Walls: white painted; furniture and
bookshelves in natural oak.

Ceiling: smooth plaster; painted white.
*Library (work room)*
Floor: oak parquet floor.
Walls: bookshelves all around, upper walls
in dark laquered softwood.
Ceiling: smooth plaster, painted white.

**Work catalog no.**

H.82.11

Second attic floor

First attic floor

First floor

Ground floor

Section AA
1 Coal storage
2 Heating
3 Dining room
4 Entrance
5 Kitchen
6 Child room
7 Gallery
8 Office/Library
9 Veranda
10 Terrace

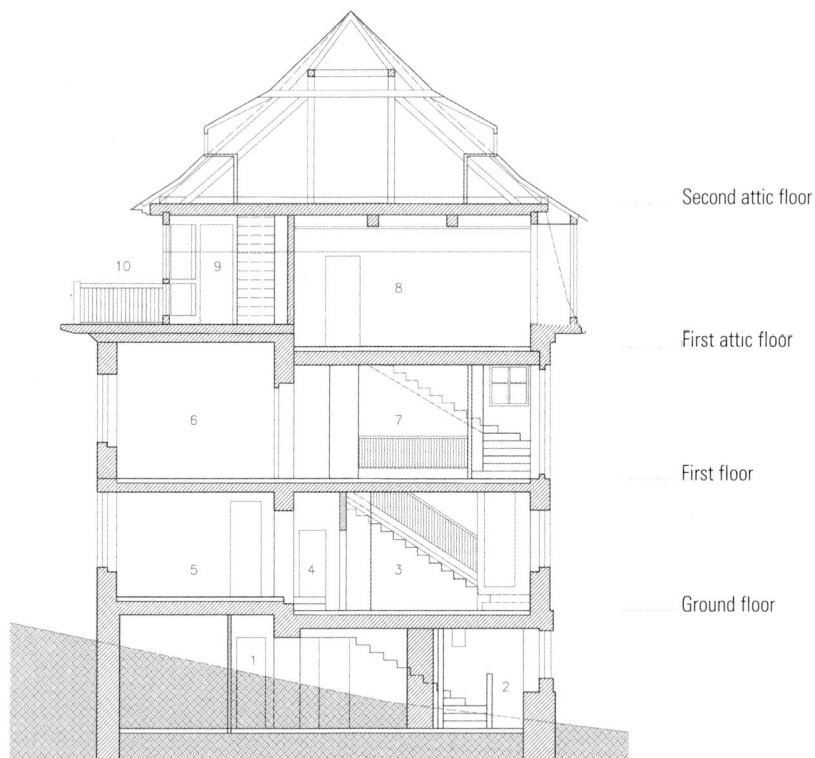

Kitchen floor level higher than living/dining
area. On first floor gallery, bathroom and
dressing room with lower ceiling height,
so the working room of Otto Stoessl above
has more clear height

0    1         5

View from garden to the south facade
with veranda on first attic floor

Raised ground floor
1 Entrance
2 Dining room
3 Wc
4 Laundry
5 Kitchen
6 Pantry
7 Cloakroom
8 Dumb waiter

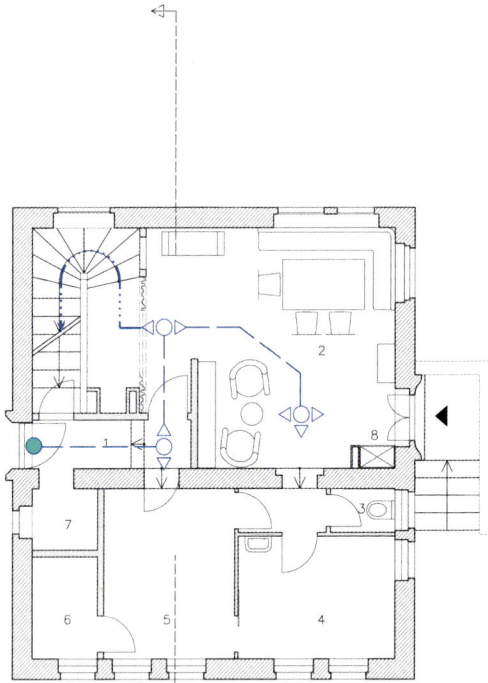

First floor
1 Gallery
2 Garderobe
3 Bathroom
4 Master bedroom
5 Child room
6 Dumb waiter

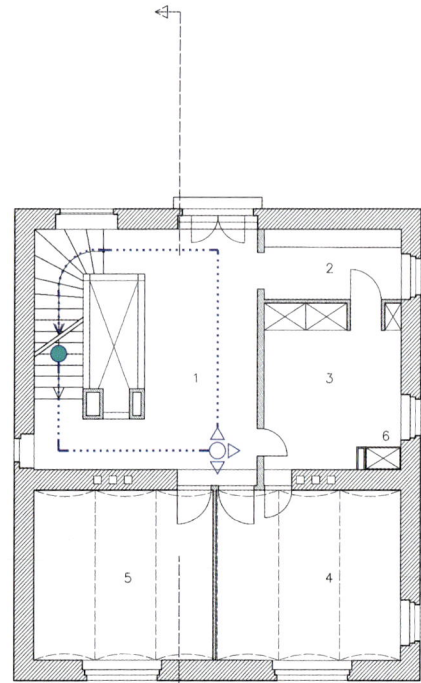

First attic floor
1 Office/Library
2 Veranda
3 Terrace
4 Dumb waiter

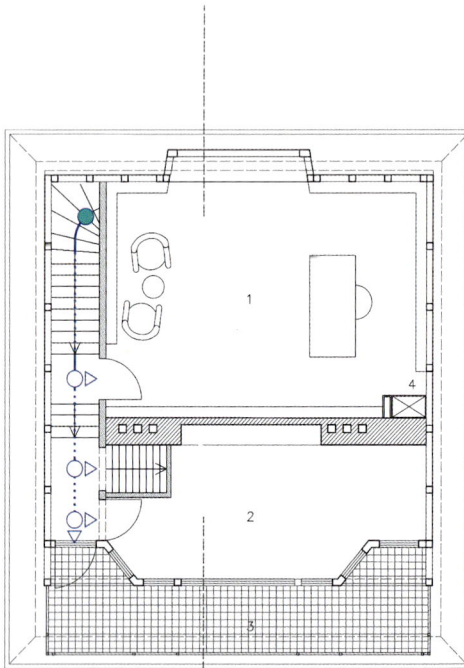

Second attic floor
1 Guest room
  (Original book storage)
2 Wc

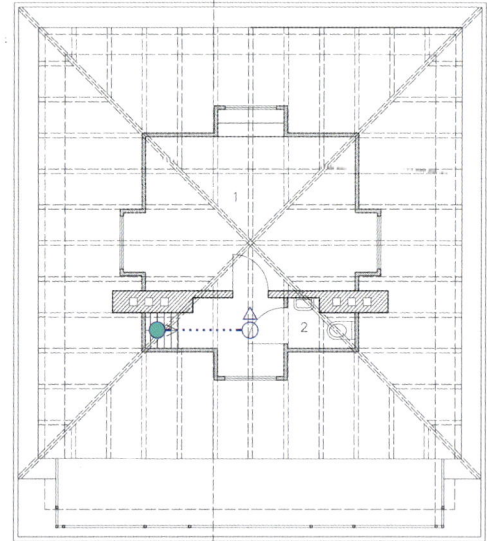

0  1          5

N

A

View to dining area

View to stair hall on first floor with gallery

# Horner House

Nothartgasse 7
1130 Vienna

Helene Horner

Andreas Horner
Concierge of Hotel Krantz in Vienna

**Class**
Villa; new construction.

**Type of construction / Construction design**
Nearly square layout with outer walls load-bearing in solid brickwork with one central column, in which two chimneys are incorporated.
Prefabricated slightly arched brick ceiling over basement, other floors have wood-beamed ceilings. Dividing walls in plaster and not load-bearing.

Loos takes advantage of the efficient span of the wood ceiling of ca 5 m and disperses the load to the interior through beams attached to a central column in brickwork, in which he also incorporates the chimneys. A principle that he would use ten years later as the constructive basis of the *Raumplan* in the Rufer House.
Roof trusses in wood with timberboard linings and clad in painted metal sheeting. Continuous ceilings without height differences.

**Dimensions**
Base area: 11 x 10 m.
Clear room heights: ground floor and first floor: 3.00 m.
Levels: 4.
Stories: 4 (basement, raised ground floor, first floor, first attic floor).
Living area without basement: ca 260 sq m (with first attic floor).

**Materials**
No significant interior fit out carried out.

**Work catalog no.**
H.86.12

Simple and quite cheap house with minor interior fit out by Loos

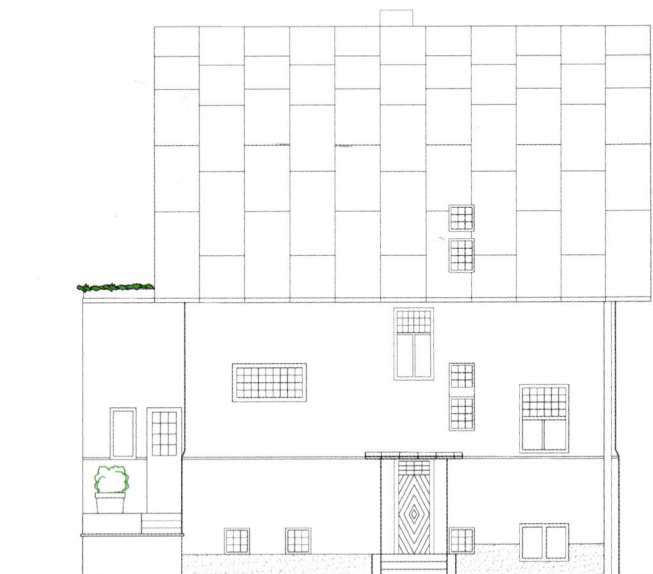

North-east facade

South-west facade

Present view from garden (south), with green
facade and greenhouse

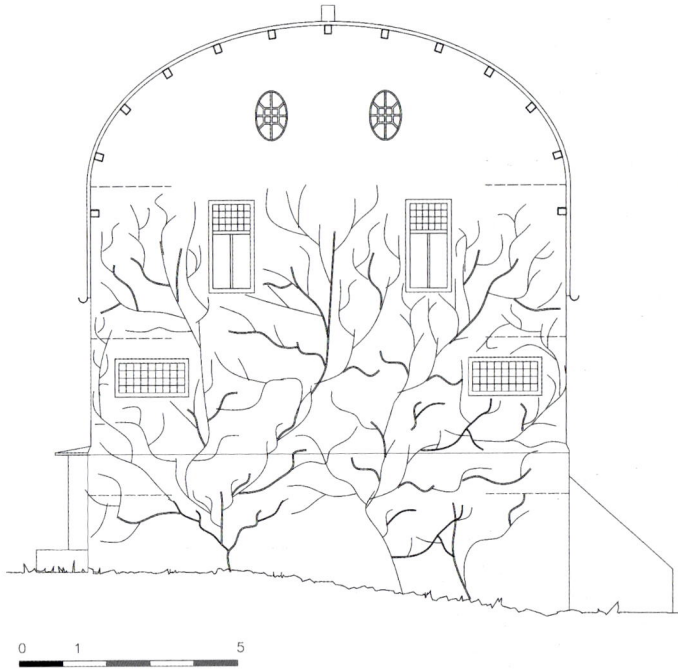

North-west facade
Facade with two "eyes"

Basement
1 Service personnel bedroom
2 Garage
3 Greenhouse
4 Laundry
5 Cellar
6 Heating
7 Coal cellar
8 Front room
9 Kitchen

Small apartment, garage and greenhouse

Ground floor
1 Vestibule
2 Kitchen
3 Salon
4 Dining room
5 Hall
6 Veranda
7 Glassroof

Open stair to first floor in hall; no terrace, only a glazed veranda with a stair into the garden. Only one central load bearing column

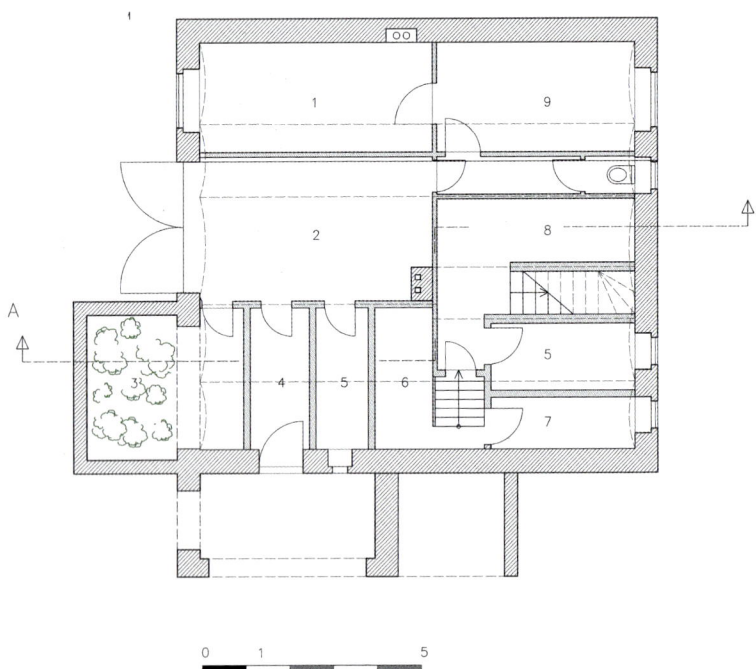

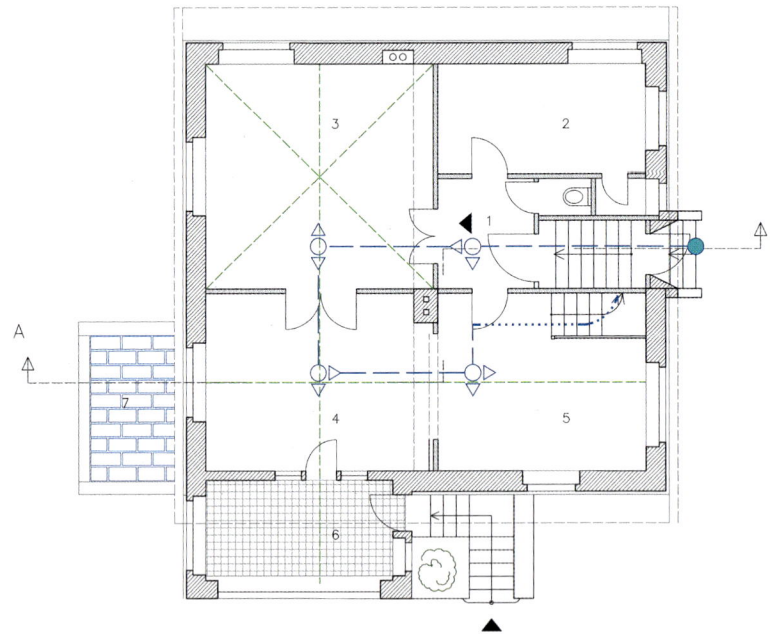

Section AA
1 Greenhouse
2 Laundry
3 Cellar
4 Heating
5 Cellar
6 Vestibule
7 Salon
8 Master bedroom
9 Corridor

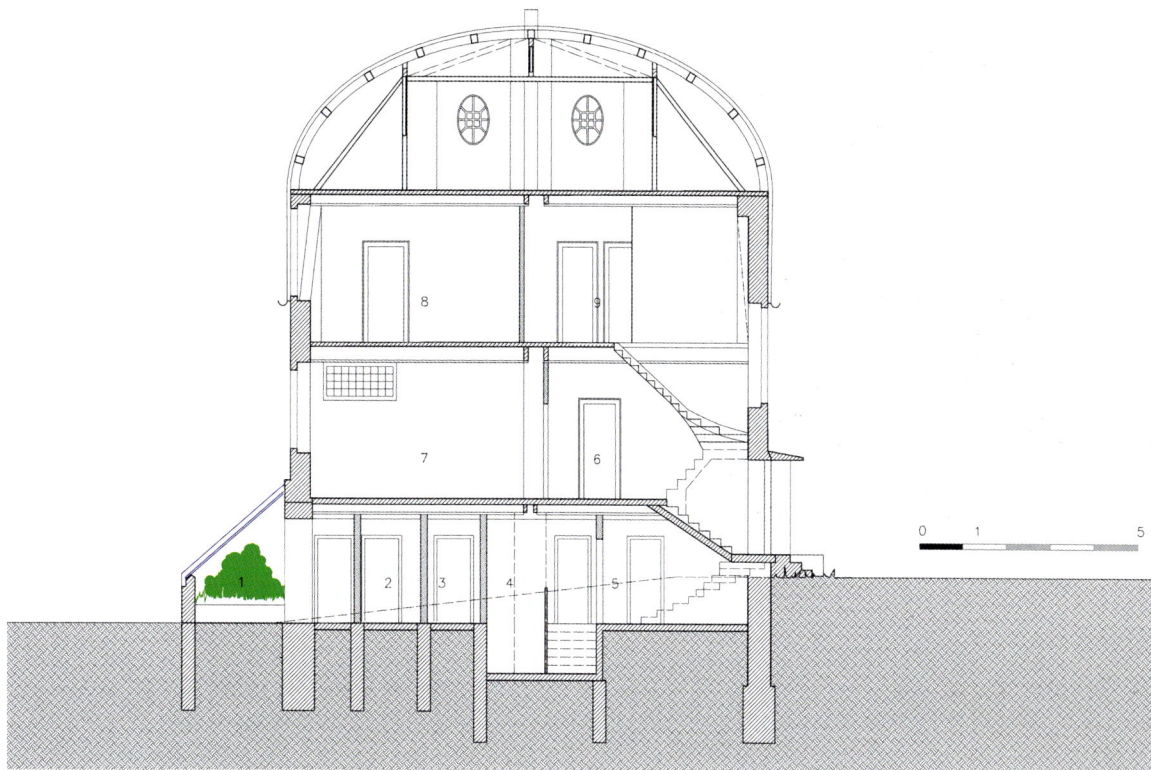

First floor
1 Master bedroom
2 Children room
3 Anteroom
4 Housemaid
5 Guest room
6 Bathroom

Private rooms in white softwood wall cladding.
Small steep stair behind door to first attic level

First attic floor
1 Room
2 Storage
3 Drying room

Utility and service rooms; space reserved
for a possible extension

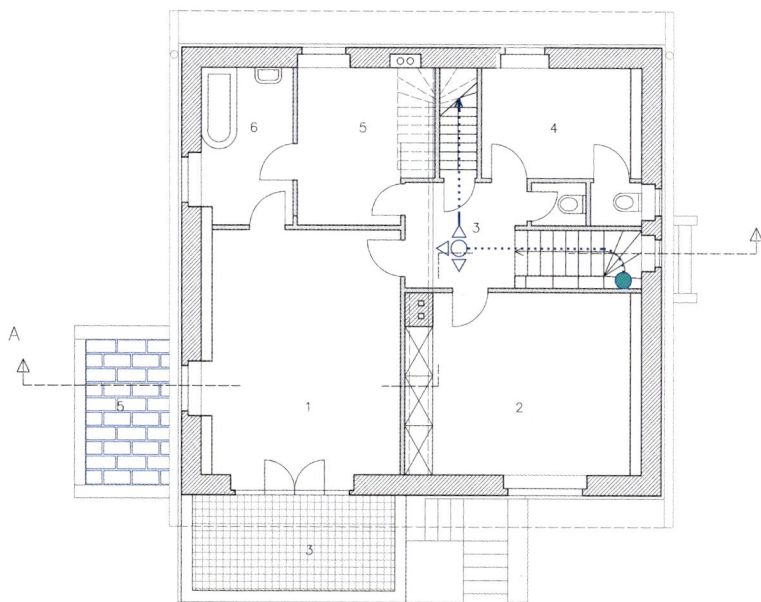

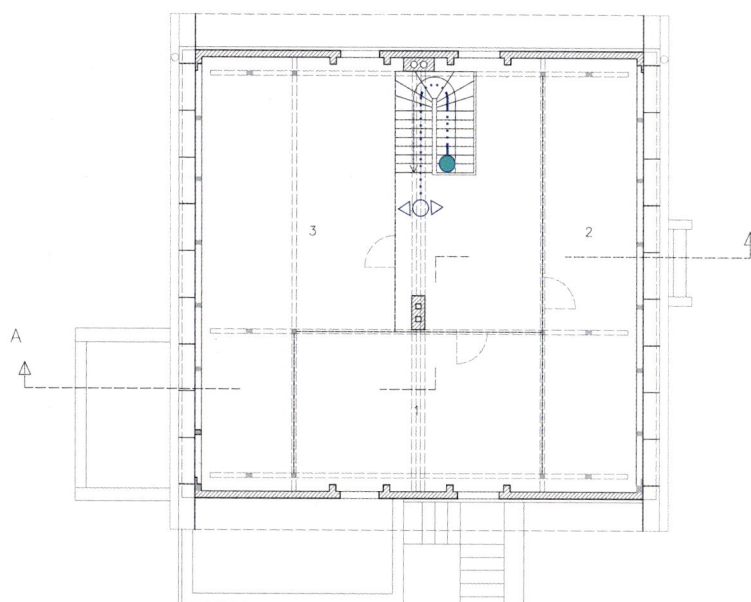

163

View from street with irregular window openings

Present view from south-east to veranda and stair to garden level

Archive picture from south
Photo by B. Reiffenstein
(ALA 2528)

# Scheu House

Larochegasse 3
1130 Vienna

Gustav Scheu
Vienna 7.10.1875 - 9.3.1935
Lawyer and politician of socialdemocratic party,
city councilor
Alban Berg, Eugenie Schwarzwald, Adolf Loos
"Friedensstadt" Lainz Settlement
(1130 Vienna, Hermesstrasse 1-77, 85-99), 1921,
work cat. no. H.128.21
Heuberg Settlement (1170 Vienna, Röntgenstrasse
138, Plachygasse 1, 3, 5, 7, 9, 11, 13), 1921,
work cat. no. H.129.21
Laaerberg Settlement (1100 Vienna, Oberlaa,
Unteres Feld), 1921, work cat. no. G.136.21
All contracted as city councilor

Helene Scheu-Riesz
Olmütz 18.9.1880 - Vienna 8.1.1970
Author, translator and editor
Adolf Loos, Eugenie Schwarzwald,
Oskar Kokoschka, Arnold Schönberg

**Class**
Villa; new construction with interior fit out.

**Type of construction / Construction design**
Load-bearing outer walls and two
load-bearing middle walls in brickwork.
Prefabricated slightly arched brick ceiling
over basement, other floors have
wood-beamed ceilings. Flat roof and roof
terraces as wood-cement roof.
The outer walls to the terrace are sustained
by beams that bear on the street and garden
facades and on the middle wall or on columns
around chimneys.
Continuous ceilings without height
differences.

**Dimensions**
Base area: 11 x 16 m on ground floor.
Room heights (gross): raised ground floor:
3.45 m; first floor: 3.45 m; top floor:
3.45 m.
Levels: 4.
Stories: 4 (basement, raised ground floor,
first floor, top floor).
Living area without basement: ca 310 sq m.

**Materials**
*Living area*
Floor: oak parquet floor covered
with Persian rugs.
Walls: natural oak wall covering to
door-height, matt-finished; above: white
smooth plaster, painted white.
Ceiling: smooth plaster, painted white;
only above the inglenook: suspended
lower ceiling with visible ceiling beams
in natural oak cladding, matt-finished,
with smooth, white painted ceiling
panels.
*Dining area*
Floor: oak parquet floor covered with
Persian rugs.
Walls: covered with natural oak to
door-height, matt-finished; above:
white plaster areas.
Ceiling: visible ceiling beams in natural
oak cladding, matt-finished, with white
painted ceiling areas.
*Hall*
Floor: Oak parquet floor covered with
Persian rugs.

Walls: longitudinally striped English
wallpaper.
Stairs in natural oak.
Ceiling: visible ceiling beams in natural oak,
matt-finished, with white painted ceiling
panels.
*Bedroom*
Floor: softwood floor boards covered
with wall-to-wall carpet.
Walls: white lacquered softwood
to door-height.
Ceiling: smooth plaster, painted white.
**Work catalog no.**
H.87.12

East facade
Kulka called this the first terrace-house in
Europe, with a significant influence in
architecture development of the 20th Century.
Green facades by building permit order

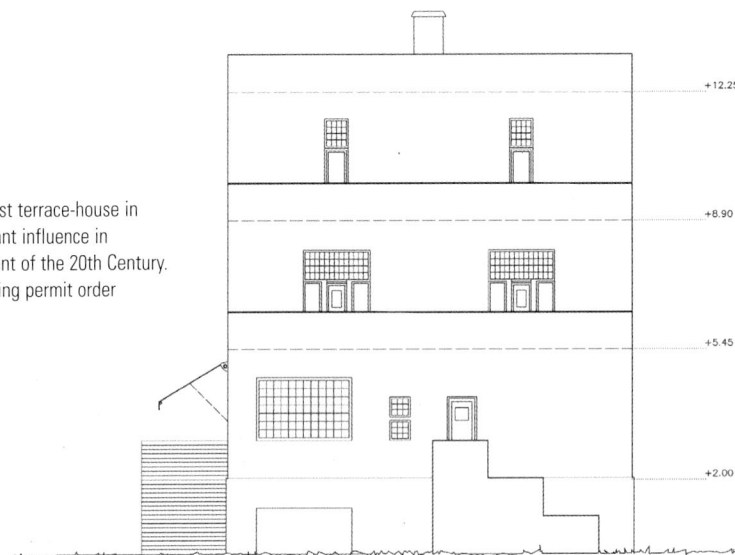

+12.25

+8.90

+5.45

+2.00

Present view on garden facade. Glazed
veranda, small terrace with closed wall as
parapet and lateral stair in garden level

South facade towards the garden

+12.25

+8.90

+5.45

+2.00

SCHEU HOUSE

+12.25

+8.90

+5.45

+2.00

Section AA
1 Library + Music salon
2 Hall
3 Veranda
4 Terrace
5 Child bedroom
6 Passage
7 Bathroom
8 Housemaid
9 Bathroom
10 Garden salon

0   1           5

Raised ground floor
1 Library + Music salon
2 Hall
3 Terrace
4 Veranda
5 Vestibule
6 Dining room
7 Study
8 Fireplace (inglenook)

Kitchen in basement, English hall,
music salon with library; inglenook,
access to garden only over veranda

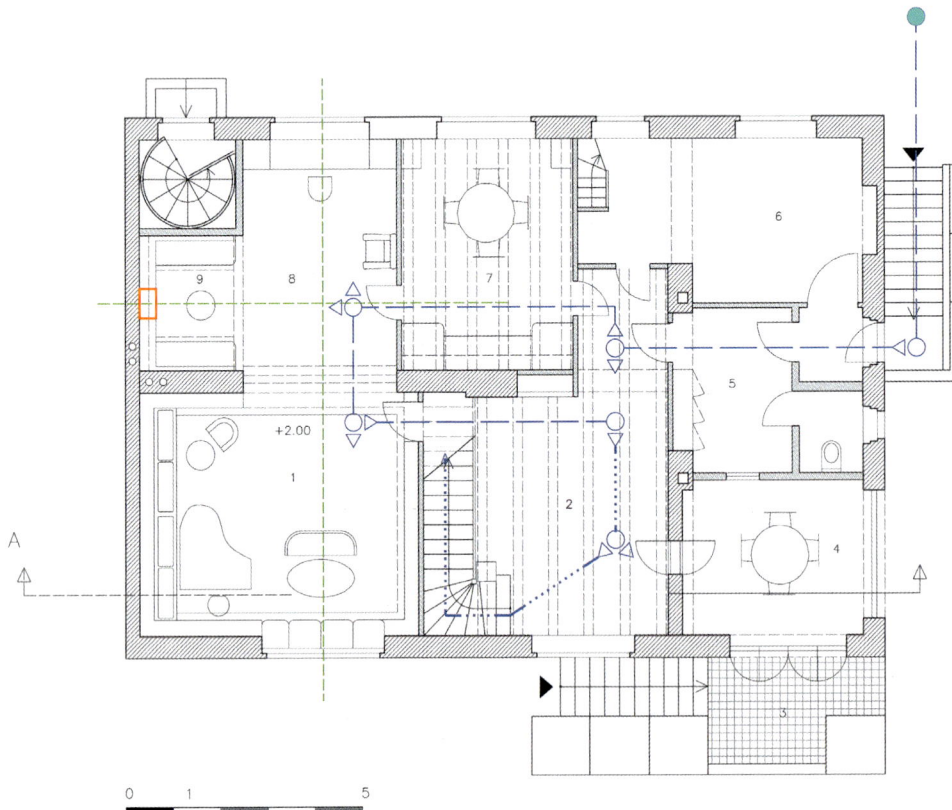

A

0   1           5

**168**

First floor
1 Bedroom
2 Housemaid
3 Bathroom
4 Passage
5 Child bedroom
6 Terrace
7 Master bedroom

Private rooms with terrace in front of master
bedroom and children's room. Hidden small
stair to top floor

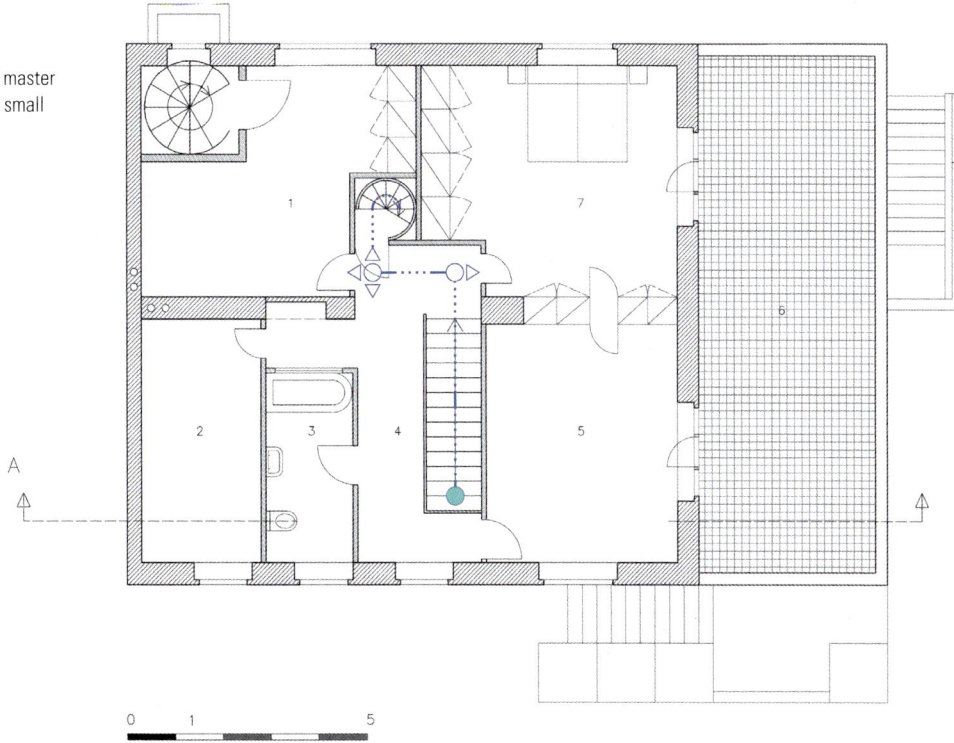

Top floor
1 Service personnel bedroom
2 Vestibule
3 Bathroom
4 Terrace
5 Garden salon

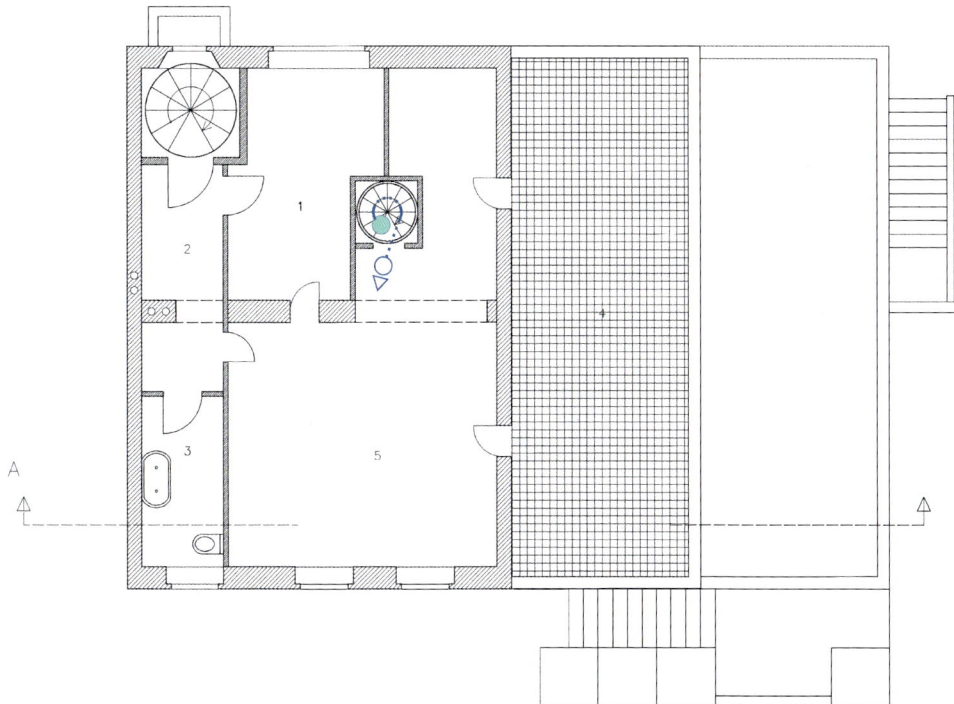

View to inglenook with lower ceiling and music salon with library. Loos motif: upholsterd leather bench in front of bookshelves

Helene Scheu-Riesz for Loos' 60th birthday, 1930: "Anyone who has ever come into contact with this creator of modern life knows that he is one of the great teachers of his time, one of those who, like Socrates, grabs people in the marketplace and curses them for not thinking about the essential goodness of existence, about great, inspired art, about material authenticity, about what endures, what emerges from the present and harkens to a future transformation. Like Socrates, he is misunderstood, and he bears it as Socrates did, smiling and happy, in the sure knowledge that he is truly serving time and the future. He plants trees in whose shade he knows he himself will never sit.

"Adolf Loos, who has promoted the art of his time like a true patron, is also as modest in his needs as Socrates and as free of possessions as he was. [...] The establishment of a Loos school would be the most beautiful gift that he could give to the world for his sixtieth birthday. And because he is only happy when he can give – like every truly creative person – it would also be the gift that would make him the most happy. Anyone who adds a stone to this school is laying the foundation for a modern building system, in which space, light, sun and order, peace of mind and strength of mind are a fundamental principle for all."

Hall in raised ground floor with stair to private
rooms

View from dining room to inglenook. Loos
motif: dining table exactly in center of room;
mirror over cupboard at headheight by sitting

View to veranda with translucent glazing
to neighboring villa

View from street

View to terrace on first floor

Stair to top floor, with separate entrance from street

Master bedroom in white with soft materials, representing ultimate intimacy

# Manz Bookshop

Kohlmarkt 16
1010 Vienna

Markus Stein
Gabrielsdorf near Kamenitz 1845 - Vienna
29.5.1935
Booktrader and owner of Manz Bookshop
and k.uk. Hof-Verlags- und Universitätsdruckerei
Vienna

Richard Stein (son of Markus Stein)
Vienna 20.8.1871 - 6.10.1932
Partner and manager of Manz Bookshop and k.uk.
Hof-Verlags- und Universitätsdruckerei Vienna
Adolf Loos, Oskar Kokoschka, Arnold Schönberg
Dr. Richard Stein Apartment (1030 Vienna,
Pfarrhofgasse 16), 1913, work cat. no. W.101.13

Original situation with plant pots on top of
shop facade and in front of the personal office
of Richard Stein

Present view of shop facade on the adjacent
building to the House on Michaelerplatz. Loos
realized the shop front for Markus Stein and
his son in the same period as he built the
House on Michaelerplatz. About 25 years
before Markus Stein had erected the building
Kohlmarkt 15 in historicism style (see picture
on p. 127)

**Class**

Shop; reconstruction shop facade; interior fit
out of clients personal office.

**Type of construction / Construction design**

Entrance facade design and office furnishing
of the work rooms of Richard Stein
above the shop entrance. No structural
modifications made by Loos.

**Dimensions**

Width: 8.2 m; depth: 6 m.

**Materials**

Existing facade columns covered with black
marble, display windows and entrance
construction in mahogany frames. Glass
panes in the upper part translucent
and backlit; in the display area transparent.
On top of the marble cladding the writing
in Roman types and emblem in gold-plated
brass.

**Work catalog no.**

L.88.12

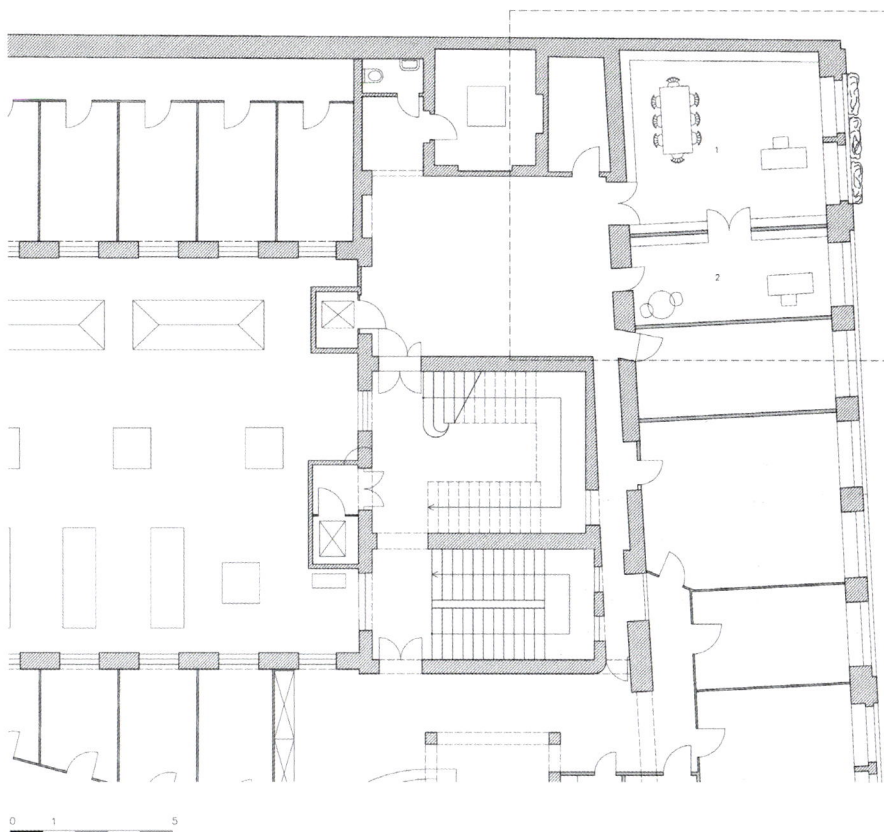

Mezzanine floor
1 Client office (Original by Loos)
2 Secretary office

Area of the personal office of Richard Stein
with interior fit out by Loos

View to the smaller office in polished
mahogany cladding

# Rosenfeld House

Wattmanngasse 11
1130 Vienna

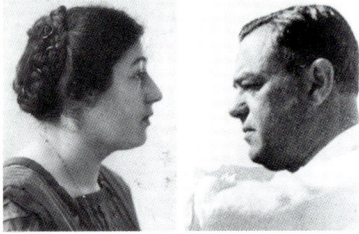

Valentin Rosenfeld
Vienna 2.3.1886 - London 1970
Lawyer
Valentin and Eva Rosenfeld Apartment
(address unknown), 1912, work cat.
no. W.-.12 (missing in the list published
by Rukschcio/Schachel)

Eva Rosenfeld
Berlin 1892-1977
School founder, educationist
Anna and Sigmund Freud, Melanie Klein,
Siegfried Bernfeld

**Class**
Villa; reconstruction with interior fit out.

**Type of construction / Construction design**
Solid brick walls with wood-beamed ceilings.
Existing two-story Biedermeier house with load-bearing outer walls and load-bearing middle wall. Courtyard wing structure with load-bearing outer walls and wood veranda. Loos carries out only small constructive interventions, in the area of the semi-circular stairway, in which he distances the load-bearing wall in the wellhole and opens the stairway to the dining area. In the living room he distances a partition wall and creates a room along nearly the entire house width. The necessary interception of the ceiling by beams is concealed through a wooden beam covering. Loos added a glazed veranda at the garden facade, which is also the covered entrance to the house.

**Dimensions**
Base area: main area 10.3 x 12.5 m + wing 3.85 x 12 m.
Levels: 2 + basement.
Stories: 2 + basement.
Living area without basement: ca 240 sq m.

**Materials**
*Living area*
Floor: oak parquet floor covered with Persian rugs.
Walls: covering to door-height with dark oak, matt-finished; above: longitudinally striped English wallpaper with ornaments. The inside of the facade wall is completely covered with bookshelves.
Ceiling: visible ceiling beams in dark oak, matt-finished, with white painted ceiling panels.
*Dining room*
Floor: oak parquet floor.
Walls: white lacquered softwood

to door-height; above: plaster, painted strongly (maybe red or ochre).
Ceiling: smooth plaster, painted white.

**Work catalog no.**
W.89.17

Ground floor
1 Corridor
2 Salon
3 Dining room
4 Garderobe
5 Kitchen
6 Summer veranda
7 Garden
8 Courtyard
9 Veranda

Loos' interior fit out in an original Biedermeier house with sensitive modifications to the structure of the house

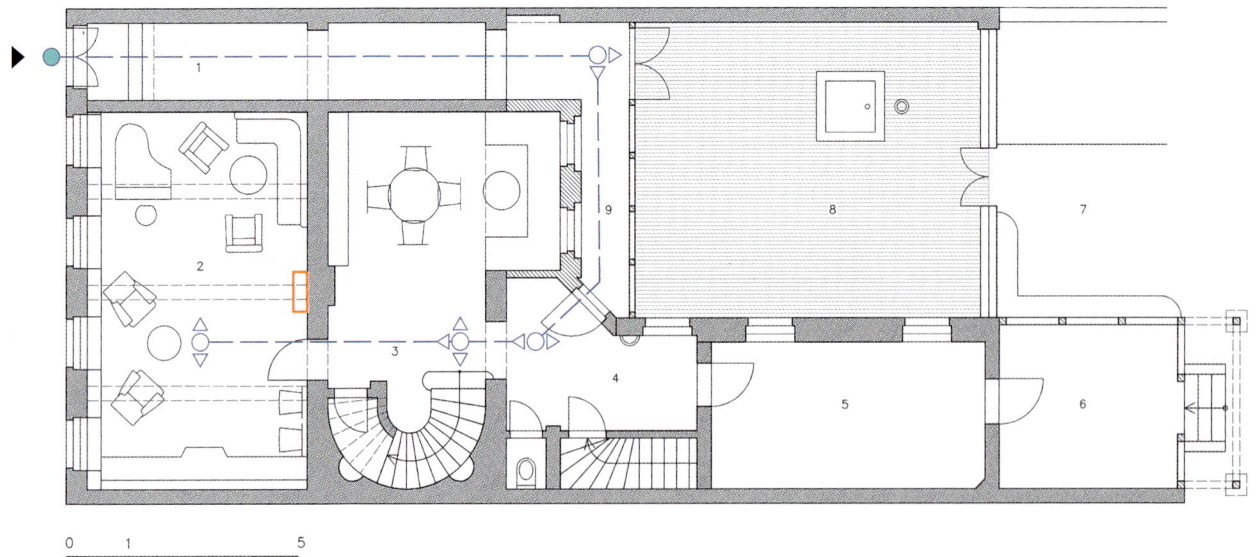

0    1         5

Present view from street

Original facade, which Loos did not change.
An example of a traditional facade trying
to hide the steep roof behind the attic

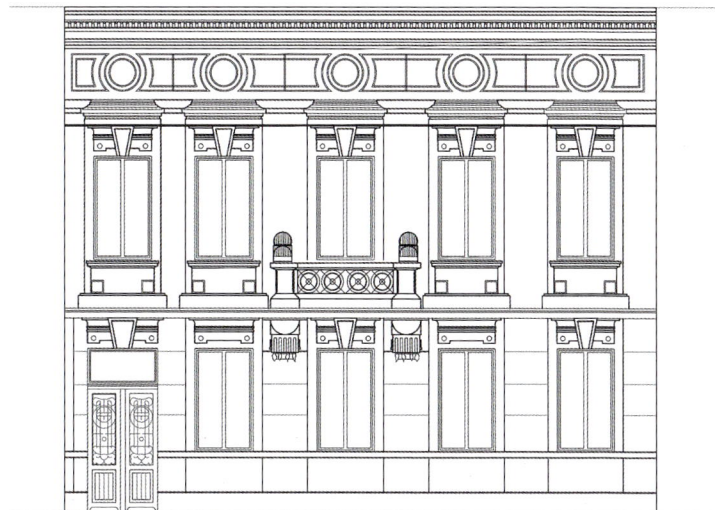

177

View to veranda added by Loos with the relocated entrance

Modified existing staircase by Loos, now open and integrated in the dining area

Present view to living area with piano
and sitting corner. Window wall cladded
entirely with bookshelves

Original living area
Photo by M. Gerlach Jr., ca 1930
(ALA 3135)

Original dining room
Photo by M. Gerlach Jr., ca 1930
(ALA 3136)

# Friedrich Boskovits Apartment II

Bartensteingasse 9
1010 Vienna

Friedrich Boskovits
Merchant
Friedrich Boskovits Apartment I
(1090 Vienna, Frankgasse 1), 1910,
work cat. no. W.79.10

**Class**
Apartment; reconstruction and interior fit out.
**Type of construction / Construction design**
Walls solid brick, ceilings in wood, traditional Viennese type of construction in late 19th Century.
No structural modifications made by Loos.
**Dimensions**
Living area: 380 sq m.

**Materials**
*Dining room*
Floor: red wall to wall carpet covered with Persian rug.
Walls: coffered wall covering in polished mahogany cladding; above: bas-relief frieze in plasterwork with a motif of the classical antiquity era, painted white.
Ceiling: lowered suspended ceiling in smooth plaster, painted white, by Loos.

*Baroque salon*
Floor: red wall to wall carpet covered with Persian rugs.
Walls: stretch fabric on the walls (red brocat). Window niches in laquered white softwood.
Ceiling: existing plasterworks, painted white.
*Music salon*
Floor: red wall to wall carpet covered with Persian rugs.
Walls: plaster painted. Window niches in laquered white softwood, fireplace in marble.
Ceiling: existing plasterworks painted in gold.
**Work catalog no.**
Not listed in the catalog of Ruckschcio/Schachel in 1983, it was discovered later and restored by Ruckschcio.

Ground floor
1 Anteroom
2 Child bedroom
3 Baroque salon
4 Music salon
5 Salon
6 Dining room
7 Bedroom
8 Bathroom
9 Kitchen
10 Housemaid
11 Garderobe
12 Court

A typical huge Viennese flat in historicism style of 1895 is divided in two. Loos re-organized and fitted out one half for Friedrich Boskovits and his family

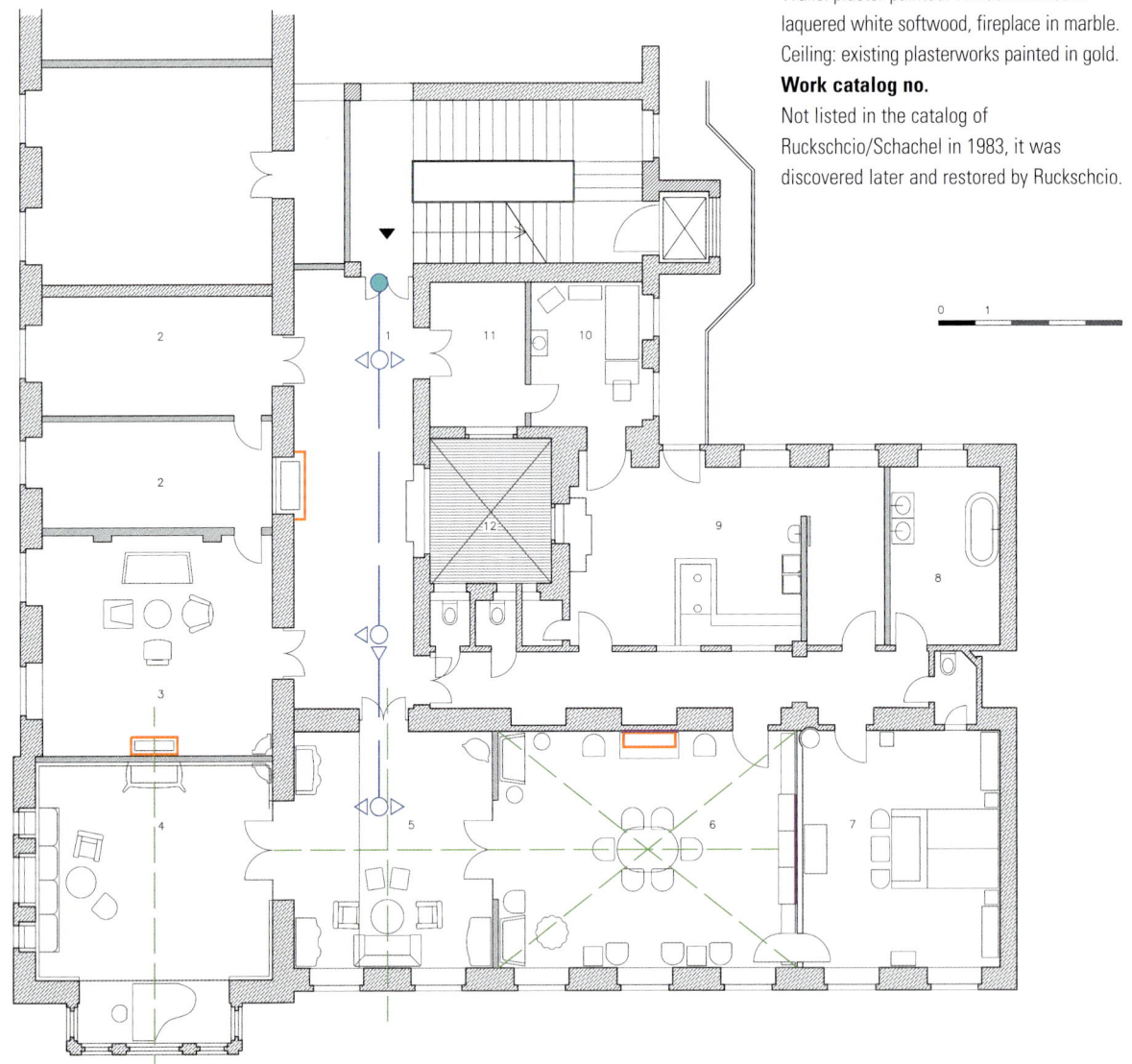

Present view into the restored dining room designed by Loos, with Chippendale chairs and a continuous bas-relief frieze with a classical antiquity motif

Fireplace in dining room cladded in marble

Wall mirror on the back for the illusion of continous space

# Anglo-Österreichische Bank II

Mariahilferstraße 70
1070 Vienna

Hermann (Hemme) Schwarzwald
1871-1939
Lawyer, mathematician, diplomat, State
secretary of ministry of finance; director
of Anglo-Österreichische Bank, vice-director
of Österreichisches Handelsmuseum
Robert Scheu
Hermann and Eugenie Schwarzwald Apartment
(1080 Vienna, Josefstädterstr. 68), 1905,
work cat. no. W.41.05
Anglo-Österreichische Bank I (1060 Vienna,
Mariahilferstraße 13), 1913, work cat. no. L.96.13

Eugenie Schwarzwald, born Nußbaum
Polupanokowa 4.7.1872 - Zürich 7.8.1940
Schoolfounder (first high school for girls in
Austria), reform educationist and founder of many
private social organizations and activities
Karin Michaelis, Helene Scheu-Riesz, Peter
Altenberg, Egon Friedell, Oskar Kokoschka, Robert
Musil, Adolf Loos, Grete and Else Wiesenthal
Schwarzwaldschule I (Semmering, Gemeinde
Breitenstein, NÖ), 1911-1912, work cat.
no. H.85.11.P
Bauleitungshütte for the Schwarzwaldschule I
(Semmering, Gemeinde Breitenstein, NÖ),
1912-1913, work cat. no. H.90.12.P
Schwarzwaldschule II (Vienna), 1912-1914,
work cat. no. H.93.12.P
Schwarzwaldschule III (1010 Vienna,
Johannesgasse 3), 1912-1914, work cat.
no. H.94.12.P
Schwarzwaldschule IV (1010 Vienna, Herrengasse
6-8/heute 10), 1913-1914, work cat. no. L.97.13
Schwarzwald community kitchen (1130 Vienna,
Siedlung Friedenstadt), 1921, work cat.
no. L.131.21

## Class

Bank; reconstruction and part new
construction with interior fit out.

## Type of construction / Construction design

Transformation of the interior courtyard into
a column-free main teller hall under a large
skylight and creation of a monumental
and imposing granite entrance.
Triangular steel beams span from wall
to wall over the courtyard. Outside cladding
in glass as skylight. Inside the horizontal

lower beam is cladded in natural stone,
panels between translucent horizontal glass
panes.

## Dimensions

Entrance: width: 5.00 m, height: 9.00 m.
Base area ground floor: ca 360 sq m.

## Materials

*Entrance facade*
Walls: black Swedish granite. On top of the
granite cladding the writing in Roman type.
*Teller hall*
Floor: white marble.

Walls: ceiling-high covering with white
marble (Carrara bianco), divided by vertical
pilaster in a medium gray marble (Carrara
bardiglio). Door frames are also in this gray
marble. Teller desks in dark granite with
white marble deskplate.
Ceiling: white cornice in plasterworks all
around; horizontal suspended translucent
glass ceiling areas between white cladded
beams with a glass skylight above it.

## Work catalog no.

L.103.14

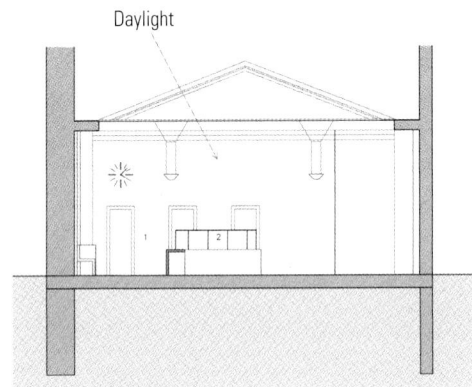

Daylight

Cross section
1 Customer area
2 Teller area

Horizontal translucent glass ceiling under
skylight

Longitudinal section
1 Entrance
2 Vestibule
3 Lobby
4 Customer area
5 Customer office
6 Mezzanine floor

A column-free main teller hall in the court
under a large skylight

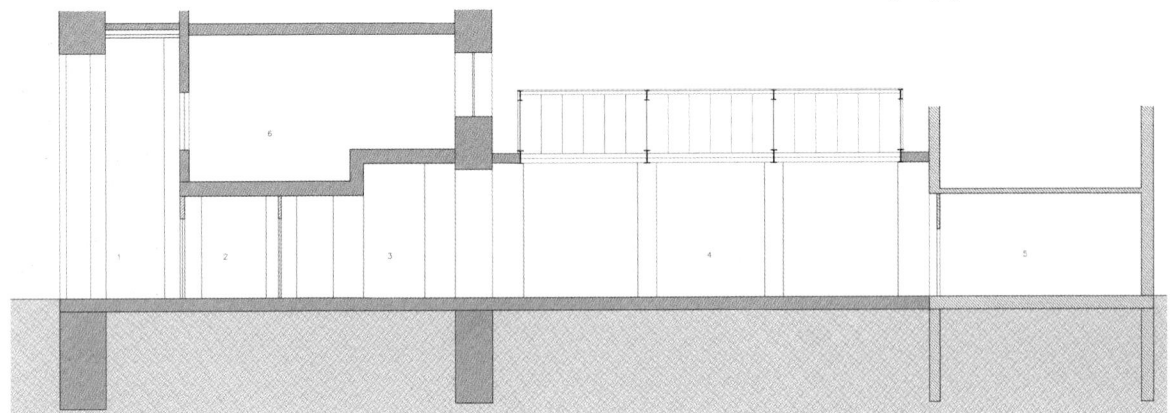

Ground floor
1 Entrance
2 Vestibule
3 Lobby
4 Customer area
5 Teller area
6 Treasure
7 Customer office
8 Back office

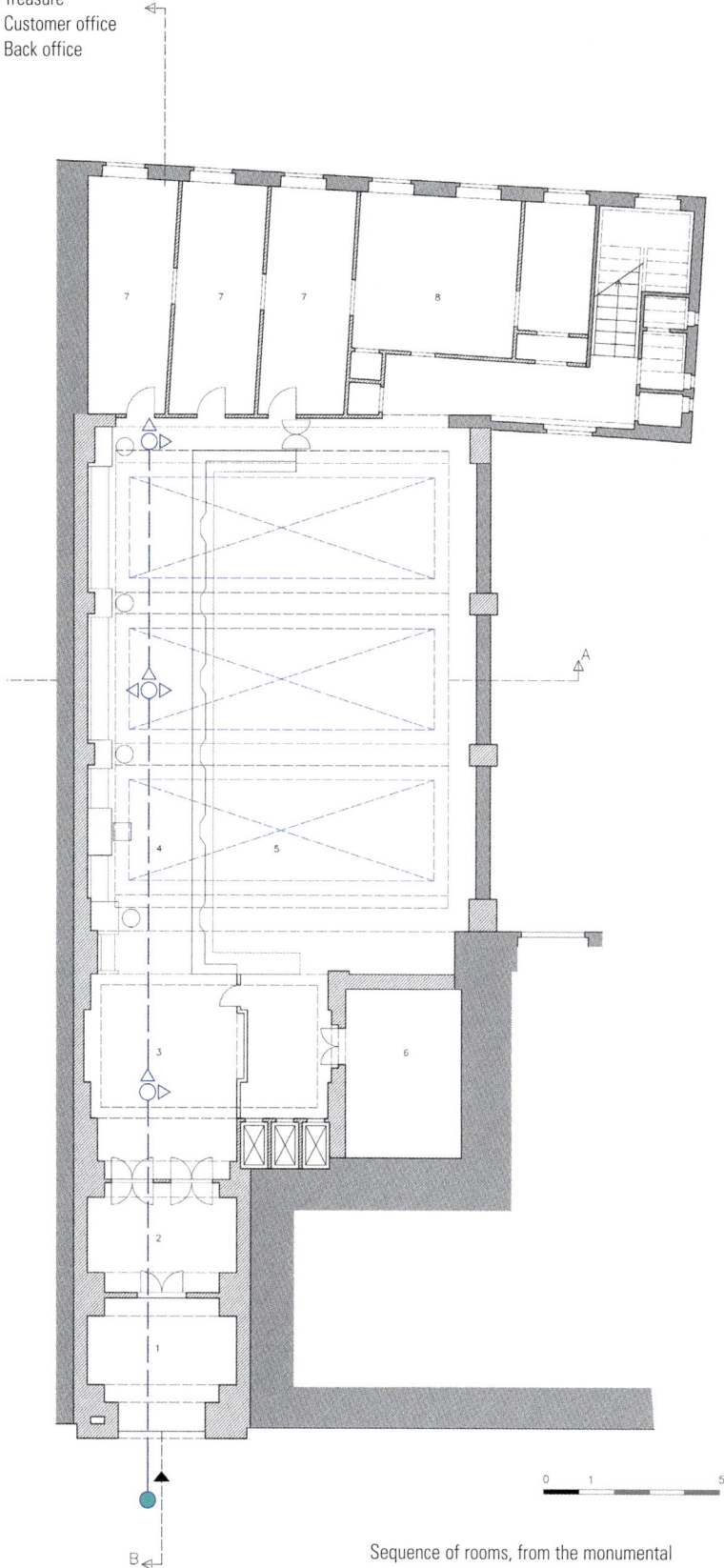

Present view to the entrance. "The bankhouse
must tell you: Here is your money kept safe
in the hands of honest people." (A. Loos,
"Architektur", 1909, in *Trotzdem*, 1931)

Sequence of rooms, from the monumental
entrance to a low and narrow vestibule zone
to the bright and large teller hall

The teller hall with the translucent glass
ceiling

# Duschnitz Villa

Weimarer Straße 81
1190 Vienna

Willibald Duschnitz
Vienna 1884 - Teresopolis,
near Rio de Janeiro 1976
Manufacturer, art collector
Wilhelm von Bode, Gustav Glück,
Jacques Goudstikker, Max Friedländer,
Julius Böhler

Jenka Duschnitz, born Loeff
Holleschau 1886 - Geneva 1967
Pianist

**Class**

Villa; reconstruction and interior fit out.

**Type of construction / Construction design**

Load-bearing solid brick walls with wood-beamed ceilings. Prefabricated, arched brick ceiling over the basement. Roof trusses in wood with timberboard linings and clad in metal sheeting.

Flat roof area and terraces: wood-cement roof.

Existing load-bearing walls taken over from existing structure; newly added structural elements with load-bearing external walls made in brick masonry.

Continuous ceilings with two small height differences on the sleeping floor, which result from a height difference of ca 40 cm firstly, between the addition of the music room and the existing height of the first floor and secondly, by gaining the necessary headroom above the newly located stairway on the ground floor by raising the bathroom above.

**Dimensions**

Base area: 12.8 x 17.2 m on ground floor.
Clear room heights: Music salon:
ca 4.2 m; existing raised ground floor:
ca 3.8 m; first floor: ca 2.8 m.
Levels: 6.
Stories: 4.
Living area without basement: ca 400 sq m.

**Materials**

*Music salon*

Floor: luxurious parquet floor of square panels with inlaid designs.

Walls: pilaster in green Cipollino marble from Euböa; between: smooth plaster, painted wall surfaces for hanging paintings. Circumferential figured frieze in plasterworks under the ceiling.

Ceiling: strongly profiled coffered ceiling in stucco.

*Dining area*

Floor: oak parquet floor covered with Persian rug.

Walls: white marble with strong, gray-violet veins (Pavonazzetto marble)

Ceiling: smooth plaster, painted white.

*Inglenook with bar*

Floor: oak parquet floor covered with Persian rug.

Walls: white painted, with vertical dark stained oak wood mullions.

Ceiling: dark stained oak wood beams with white painted panels between.

Copy of an aristocratic Renaissance fireplace from France; other copies are in F.O. Schmidt shop in Vienna and in Brummel House in Pilsen (see pp. 252-57).

*Renaissance room*

Floor: parquet.

Walls: natural stone (lacustrine limestone) cladding, from floor about 80 cm high;

above dark colored stretch fabric.

Ceiling: wood ceiling from a renaissance palace, bought by Duschnitz integrated by Loos.

*Entrance hall*

Floor: white marble slabs (Carrara bianco) inside a narrow black marble grid.

Walls: lower part in white marble (Carrara bianco), upper part painted smooth plaster, openings framed with porous, light limestone. There were originally two glass walls in the vestibule which were framed and profiled with limestone.

Ceiling: smooth plaster, painted white.

*Wardrobe, stair to first floor*

Walls: coffered, darkly stained oak wall covering.

Ceiling: smooth plaster, painted white.

Floor cloakroom: luxurious square paneled parquet floor.

**Work catalog no.**

H.105.15

Present view from garden. Garden level was original one floor lower (see drawings). Clear cubic volumes added by Loos to the existing house. The balustrades are extraordinary by the design of Loos

Present view from street, showing the shape of the original house

185

Basement
1 Treasure depot for art
and paintings
2 White room
3 Laundry
4 Pantry
5 Kitchen
6 Housemaid
7 Storage
8 Garage

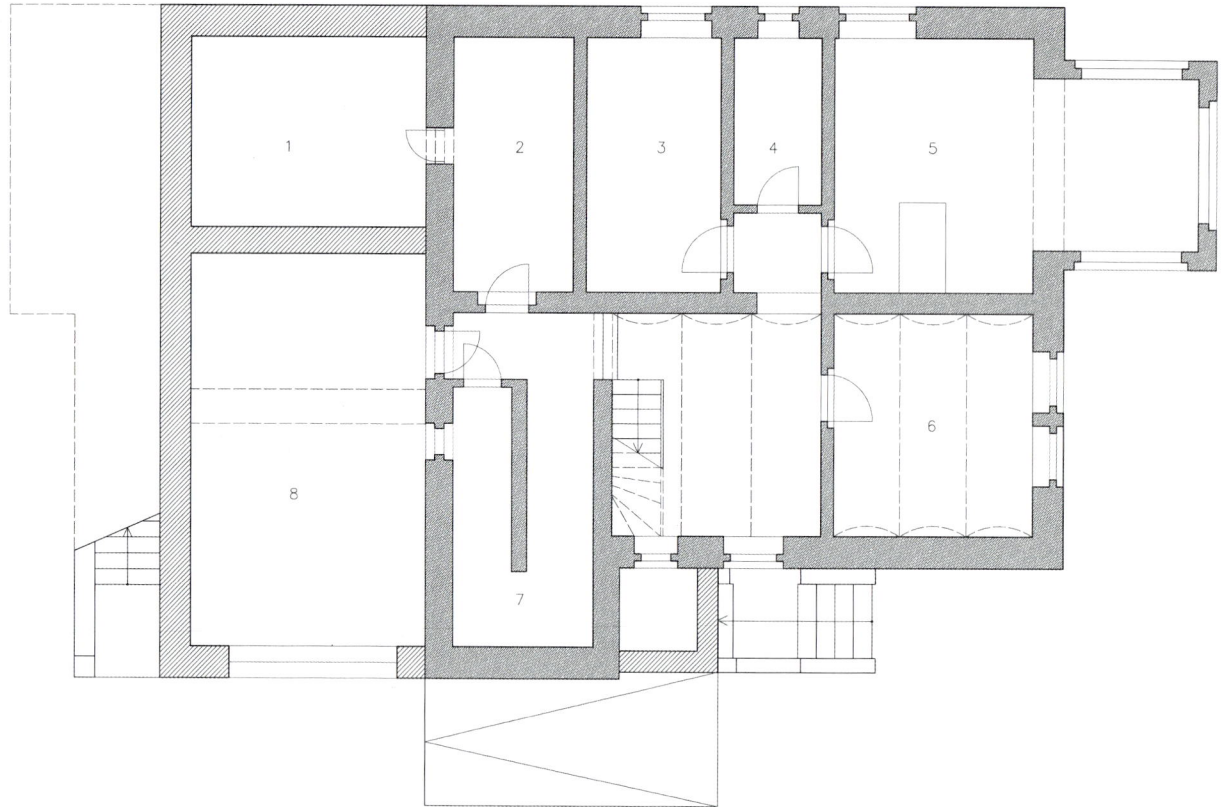

Raised ground floor
1 Music salon
2 Terrace
3 Organ
4 Fireplace
5 Hall
6 Bar
7 Dining room
8 Cloakroom
9 Renaissance room
10 Winter garden

New entrance situation and additional
building volume for the music salon
by Loos. Complete transformation
of the former interior design

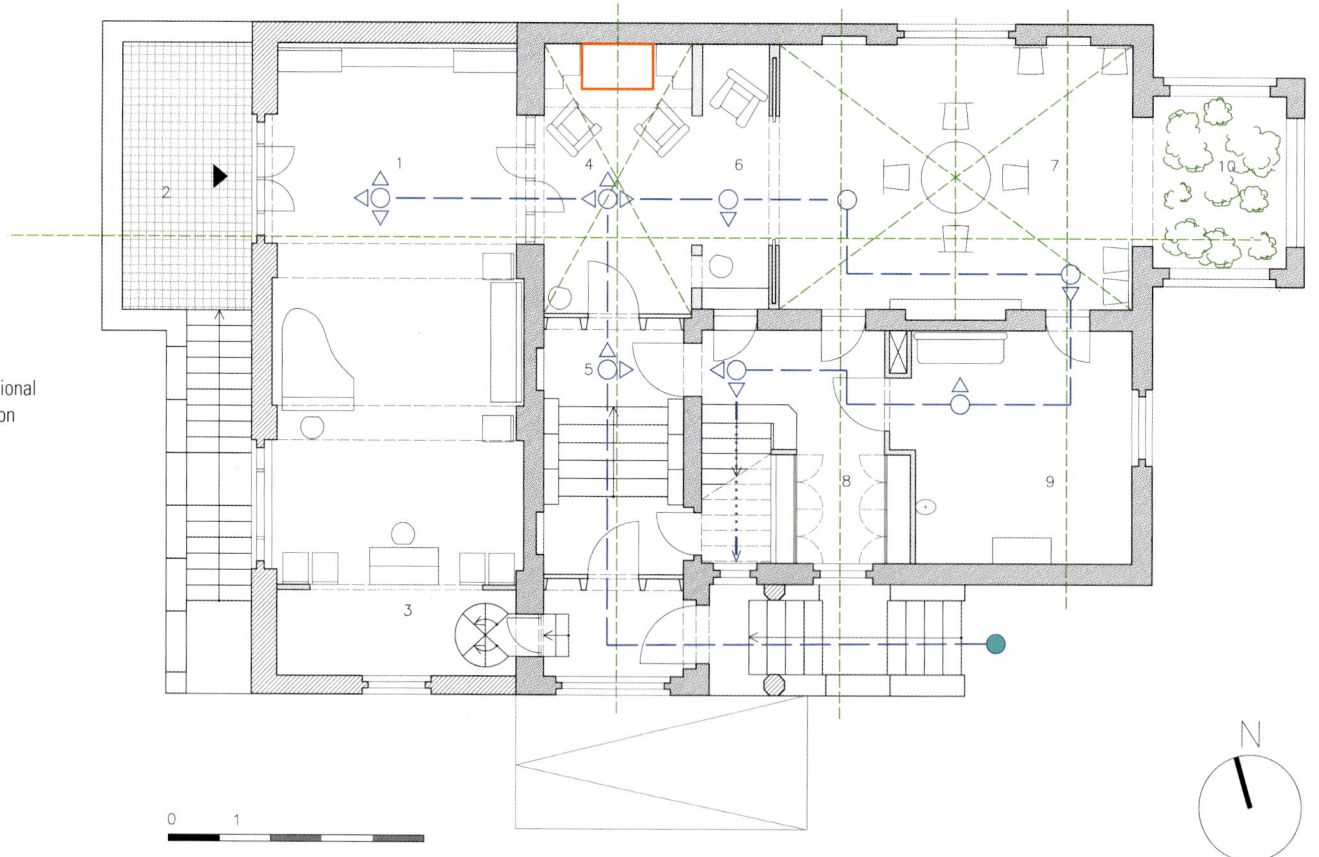

First floor
1 Gentlemen's room
2 Space for organ
3 Bathroom
4 Gentleman bedroom
5 Lady bedroom
6 Bathroom
7 Lady salon
8 Terrace

Private rooms; increased building
volume by Loos for the gentlemen's
room and organ pipes

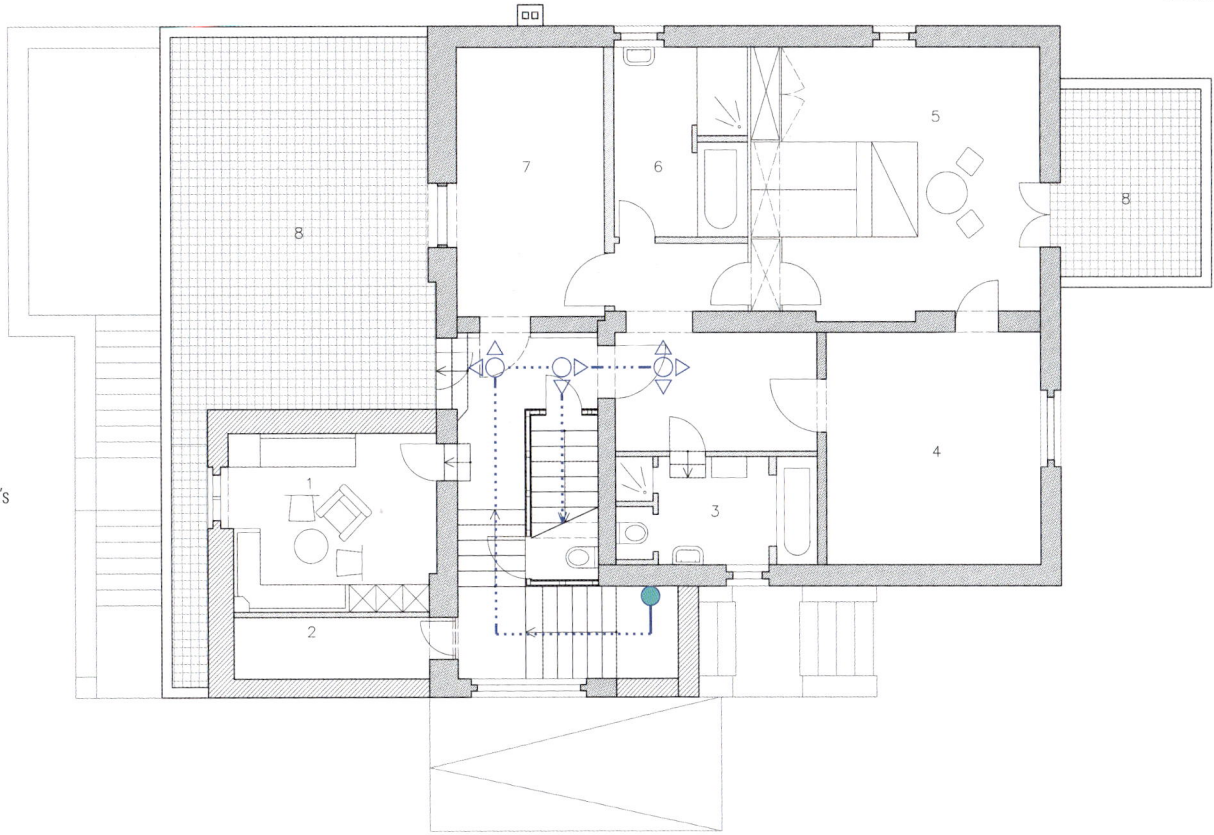

Attic floor
1 Housemaid
2 Bathroom
3 Guest room
4 Child room
5 Storage
6 Terrace

Private rooms and service
personnel rooms with stairway
to the small tower room

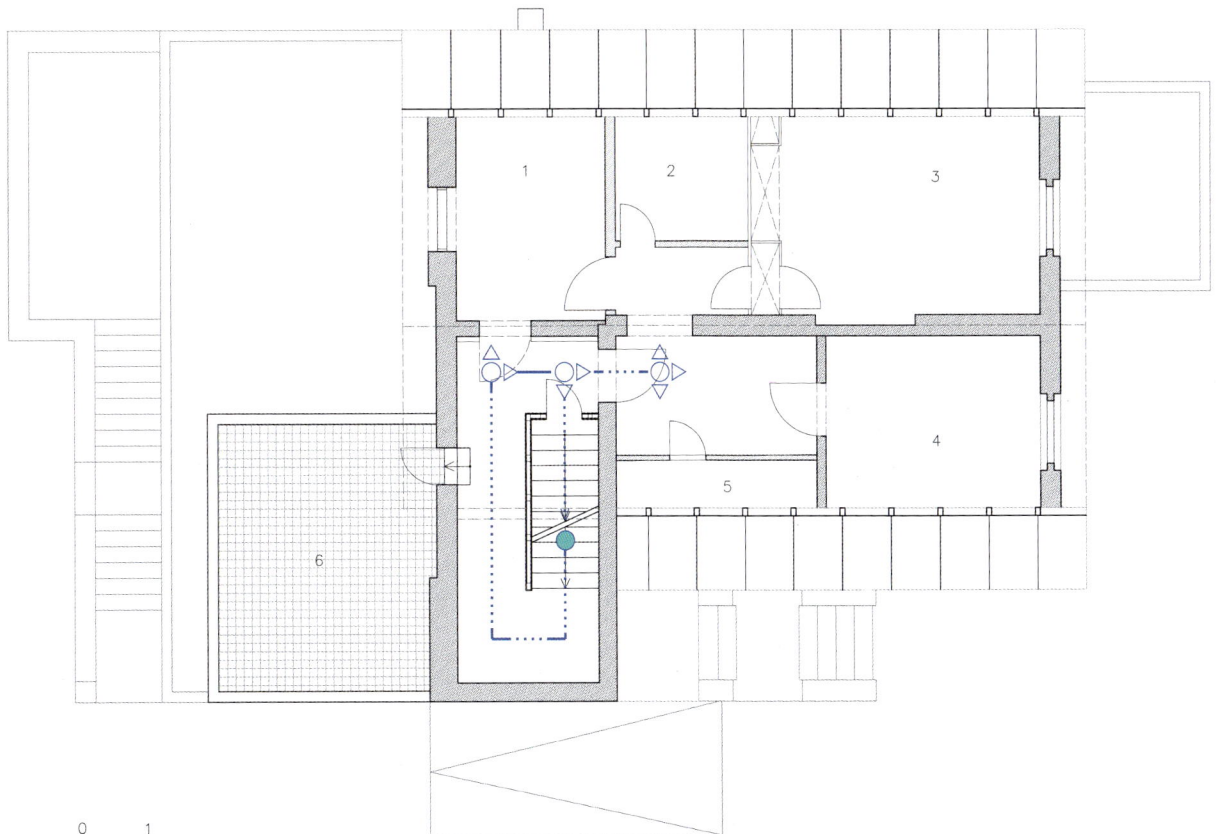

0   1

View from vestibule to inglenook and bar;
blind door on the left, only for symmetry

View from music salon to dining room. The
winter garden at the end is designed by Loos
as a filter to the street

Private pictures from the family archive
with the interior of "Renaissance room"
on raised ground floor
(Courtesy Dr. Harold Chipman, Zürich)

Music salon today with door to the inglenook

Dining room with a view to the winter garden.
The table and chairs are not original

Detailed view of the connection between
dining room and bar with integrated sliding
door in partition wall. Straight ahead, service
door with access to dumb waiter

# Mandl Villa

Blaasstraße 8
1190 Vienna

Erich Mandl
Merchant and men's outfitter
Erich Mandl Men's Fashion Salon
(1010 Vienna, Stephansplatz, Rotenturmstraße
2, 4), 1923, work cat. no. L.159.23

Anna Mandl

**Class**

Villa; reconstruction and interior fit out.

**Type of construction / Construction design**

Load-bearing solid brick walls with wood-beamed ceilings. Prefabricated, arched, brick, ceiling over the basement. New building volumes with load-bearing outer walls are added to the construction design of the existing villa (load-bearing outer walls + middle wall). On the south side the largest addition was integrated over the full length and height of the facade. On the west side a roofed loggia with a stairway down to the garden and a bay to the living area is added. The roofs of the additions are used as terraces. Ceiling: wood-beamed ceilings; the existing ceilings were partly strongly modified by Loos new space concept.

In the hall area, which is completely redesigned by Loos, he did his first *Raumplan* approach in a villa. A mezzanine floor with an elevated writing gallery is placed as a visible connection to the newly located entrance vestibule. Loos also integrated a new stair connection to the upper floors.

**Dimensions**

Base area: 12.9 x 14.35 m
Clear room heights: living area, hall raised ground floor: ca 3.7 m; gallery: ca 1.8 m; first floor: ca 3.4 m.
Levels: 7.
Stories: 4.
Living area without basement: ca 440 sq m.

**Materials**

*Hall*
Floor: oak parquet covered with Persian rugs.
Walls: coffered wall covering in oak to two-thirds of the ceiling-height; above: smooth plaster, painted white
Ceiling: visible oak beams with white, smooth plaster panels.
*Music salon*
Floor: oak parquet covered with Persian rugs.
Walls: plastered, articulate by pilaster with stucco meander relief.
Ceiling: coffered stucco ceiling with a light bulb in the middle of every coffer.
*Dining area*
Floor: oak parquet covered with Persian rug.
Walls: pilaster in green Cipollino marble with wall sections in smooth, dark oak panels.
Ceiling: smooth, white.

**Work catalog no.**

H.106.16

Section AA
1 Terrace
2 Hall
3 Wardrobe
4 Room
5 Gallery
6 Bedroom

First *Raumplan*-design for a villa by Loos

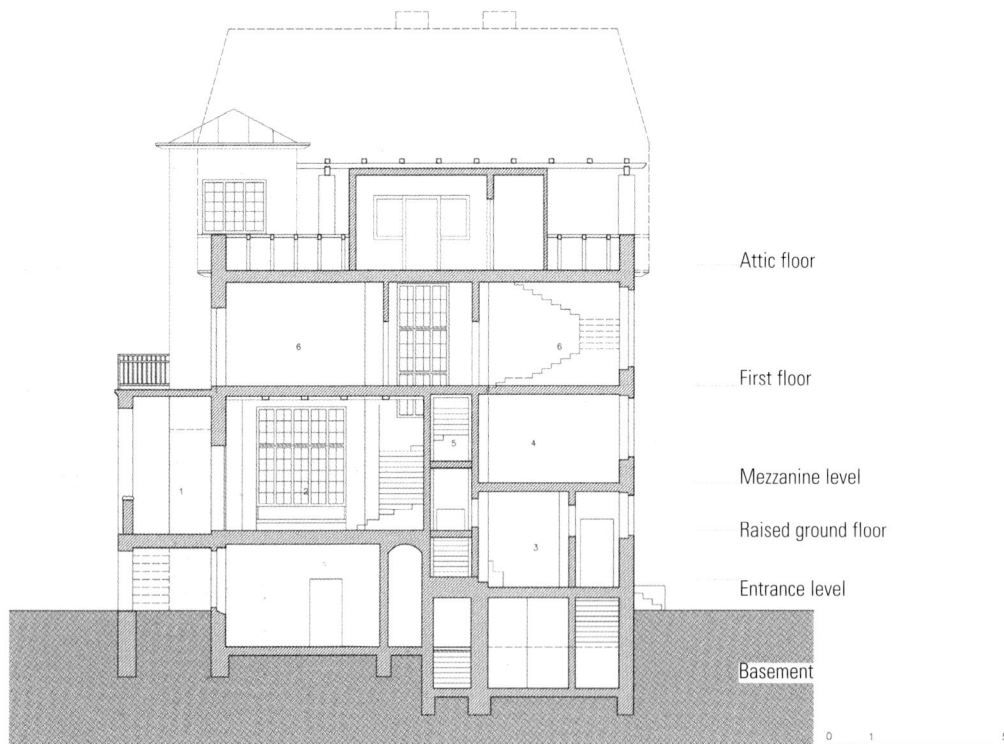

Attic floor

First floor

Mezzanine level

Raised ground floor

Entrance level

Basement

Section BB
1 Dining room
2 Gallery
3 Bathroom
4 Housemaid

Complex composition between new design and existing structure. Basement level with garage, kitchen, service personnel rooms and utility rooms under the raised ground floor

Second floor

First floor

Mezzanine level

Raised ground floor

Entrance level

Raised ground floor
1 Entrance (porch)
2 Hall
3 Music salon
4 Dining room
5 Preparation kitchen
6 Wardrobe/Vestibule
7 Terrace

Concept of living space: hall with sitting
facilities for relax and communication, music
salon and dining room

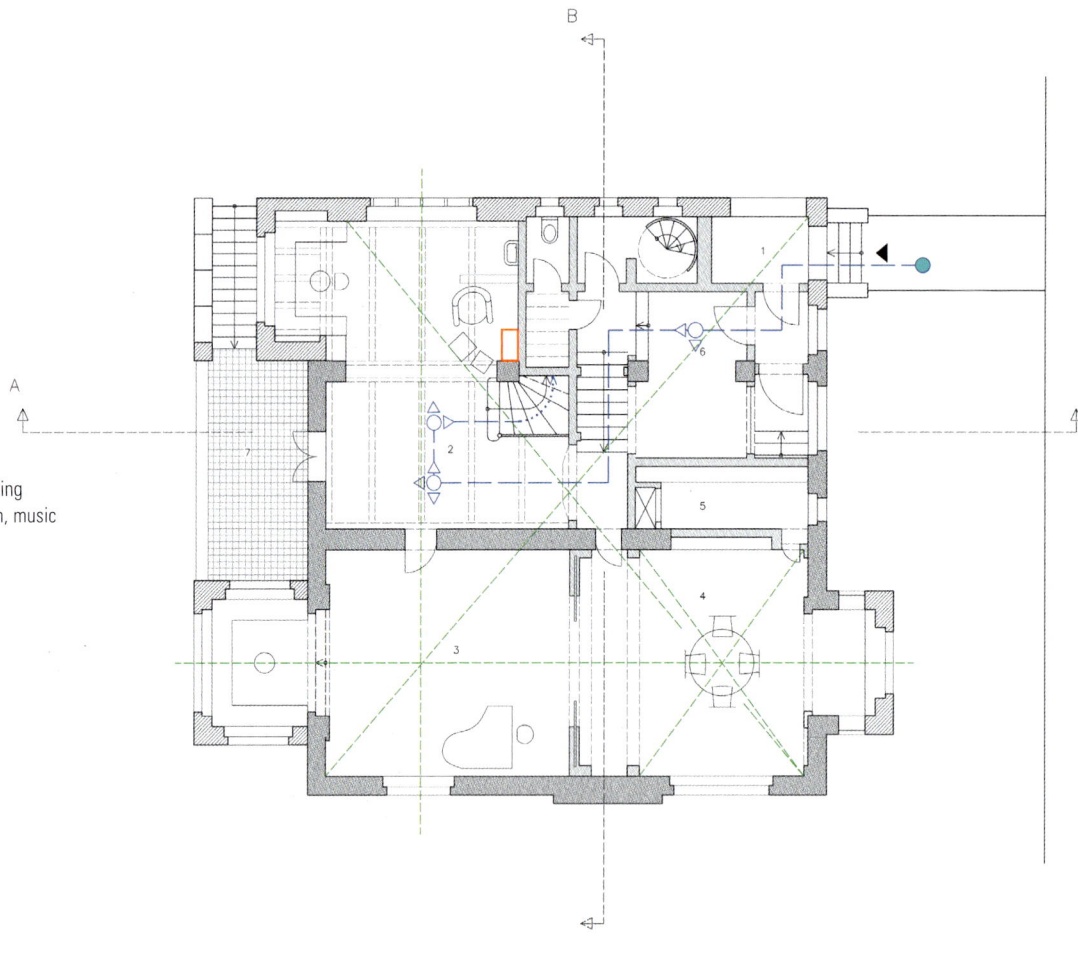

Mezzanine floor
1 Gallery
2 Room

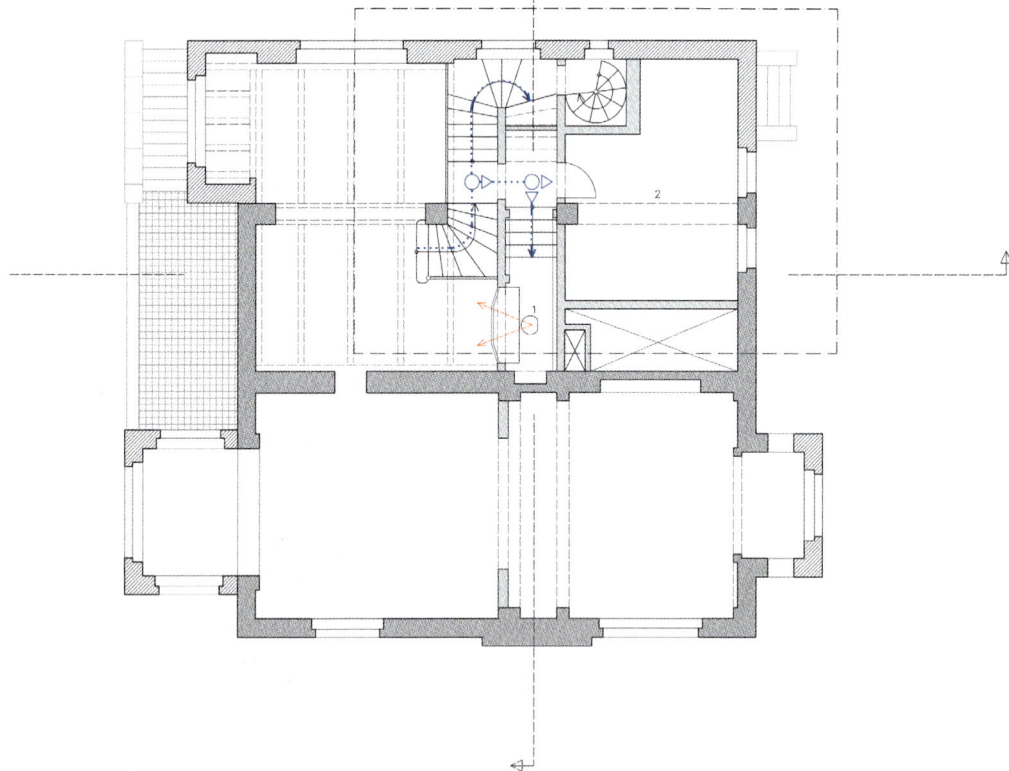

First floor
1 Master bedroom
2 Bathroom
3 Bedroom
4 Terrace

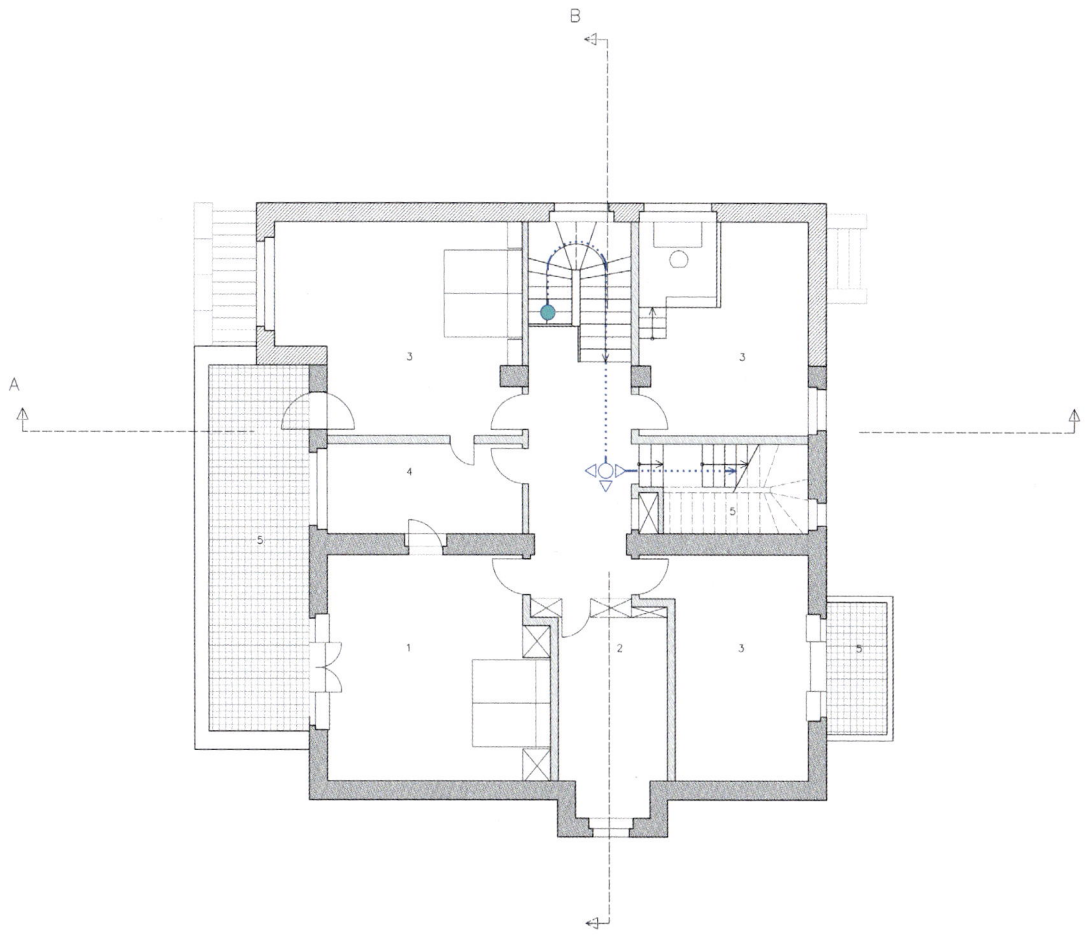

Private rooms

Attic floor
1 Servant housemaid
2 Housemaid
3 Terrace
4 Tower room
5 Bathroom

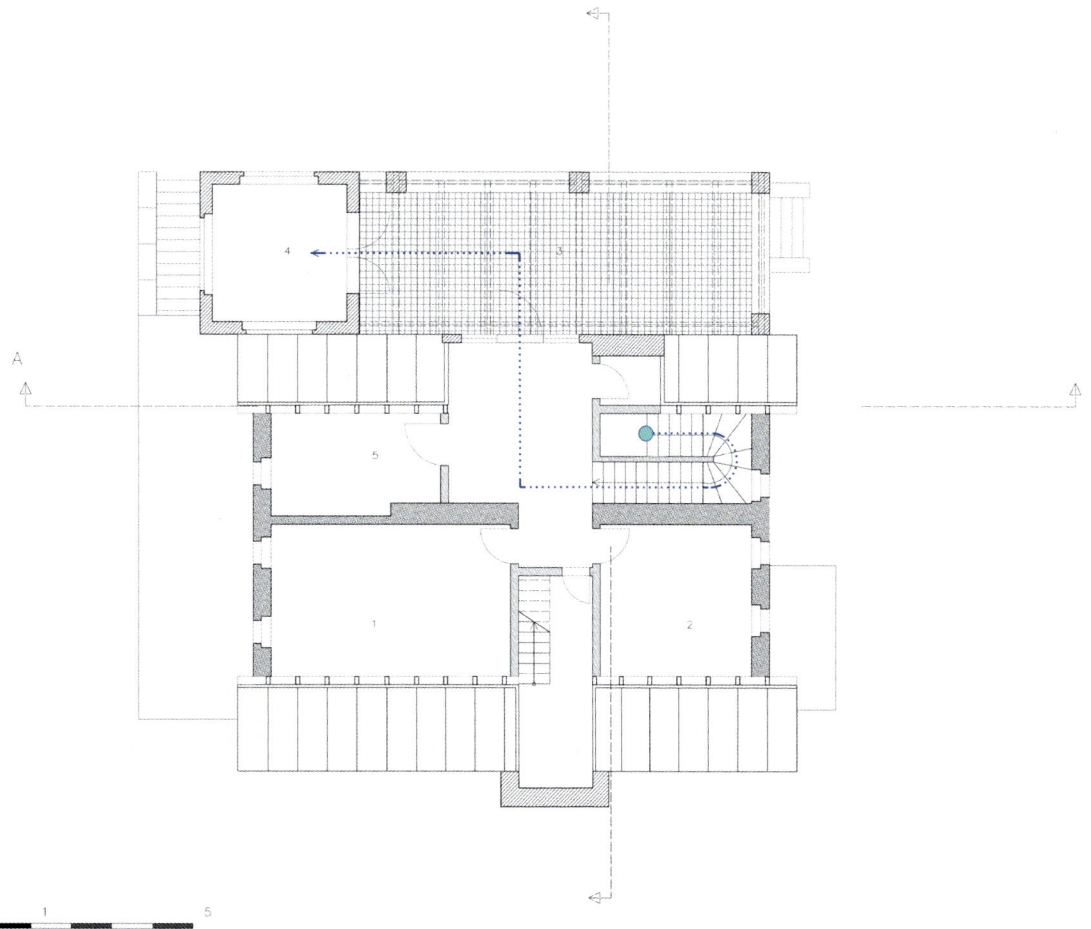

Central hall as living space with gallery
and open staircase
Photo by M. Gerlach Jr., 1930
(ALA 3187)

Erich Mandl: "I am convinced that my house is the most beautiful; in the end it was just as we both had imagined it. Loos was not my architect, I was not his client – we built it together."

View into central hall with sitting facilities. Translucent glazing in the big window to the adjacent villa
(ALA 2401)

Dining room with a transition zone to music salon and on the other side the bay to the street, used as a buffer space to the public
(ALA 2400)

# Bauer Villa (Factory Director's Villa)

Rohrbach (Hrusovany)
near Brno (Czech Republic)

Victor Ritter von Bauer
Brünn 2.4.1876 - 3.8.1939
Director of Rohrbacher Sugar Factory AG;
manager of a huge family empire of industrial and
agricoltural production; pilot, art collector, author
Rohrbacher Sugar Factory (Hrusovany near
Brno/CZ), 1916, work cat. no. H.108.16.Z
Victor Ritter von Bauer Castle (Brünn/CZ,
Vystaviste 1), 1925, work cat. no. H.181.25
Dr. Victor Ritter von Bauer Apartment (Brünn/CZ,
Alte Lehmstätte 39-41), 1930, work cat.
no. W.211.30

Margarethe Druschba
1886-1963

View to the small village in the landscape
dominated by the sugar factory

**Class**
Villa; new construction.

**Type of construction / Construction design**
Load-bearing outer walls and two
load-bearing middle walls in brick
work with wood-beamed ceilings.
Prefabricated, arched, brick ceiling
over the basement.
Flat roof area and terraces: wood-cement
roof.

Continuous ceilings without height
differences.

**Dimensions**
Base area: 29 x 15 m on raised ground floor;
19 x 15 m on first floor.
Clear room heights: raised ground floor/first
floor: 3.30 m.
Levels: 3.
Stories: 3.
Living area without basement:
ca 540 sq m.

**Materials**
No more specific information available.

**Work catalog no.**
H.112.18

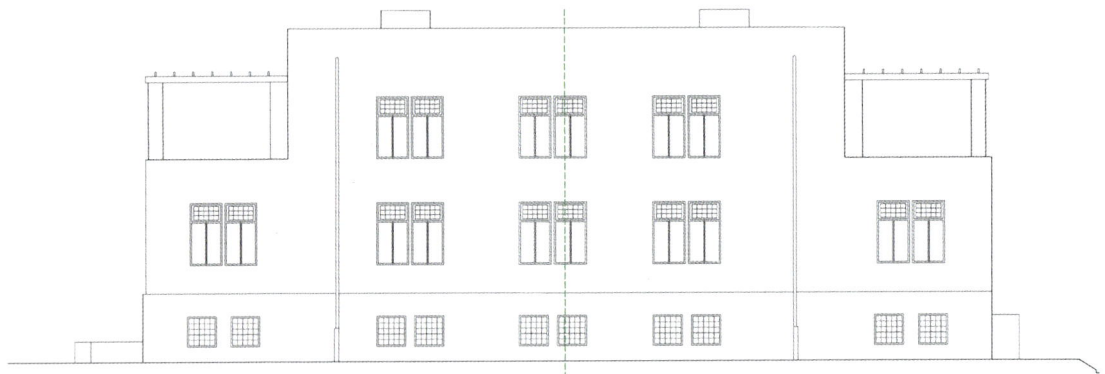

East facade
Street elevation facing on the east with
asymmetric window postions in the centre

West facade
Facade (covered with Japanese ivy) with
typical Loos motif for terrace. Sited on both
sides are the additional terraces on the first
floor level with pergola

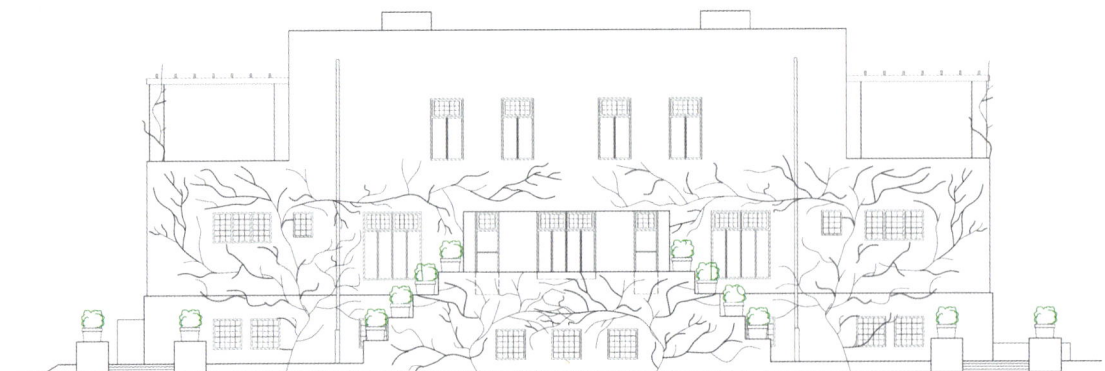

Sugar production hall adjacent to the villa
possibly designed by Loos

Present view from garden, former terraces
with pergolas on first floor are boxed in

Present view from street

Present view from production hall to main
entrance on north facade

South facade with terrace on first floor
in front of bedrooms

North facade with main entrance and
terrace above

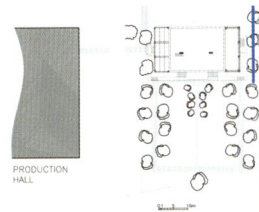

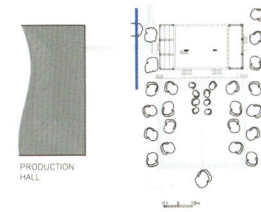

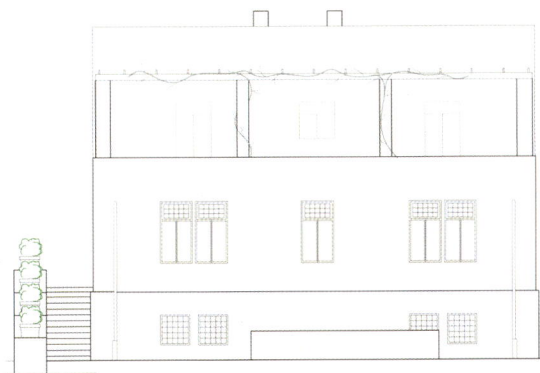

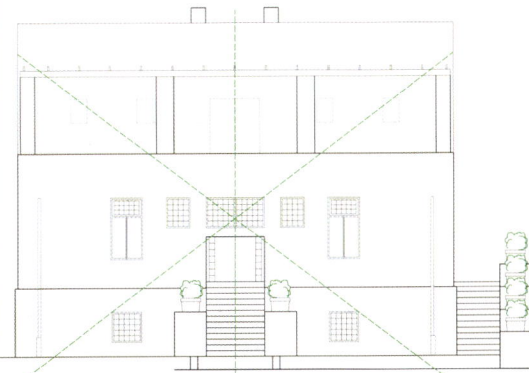

PRODUCTION
HALL

PRODUCTION
HALL

Raised ground floor
1 Entrance
2 Hall with stairs and wardrobe
3 Living room - Salons
4 Library
5 Gentlemen room
6 Hall
7 Terrace
8 Kitchen
9 Storage room
10 Servants room
11 Corridor

The original floor plans are not available; this floor plan is based on documentation produced after 1950. Some characteristics are not in compliance with other Loos' works, such as the simple middle corridor

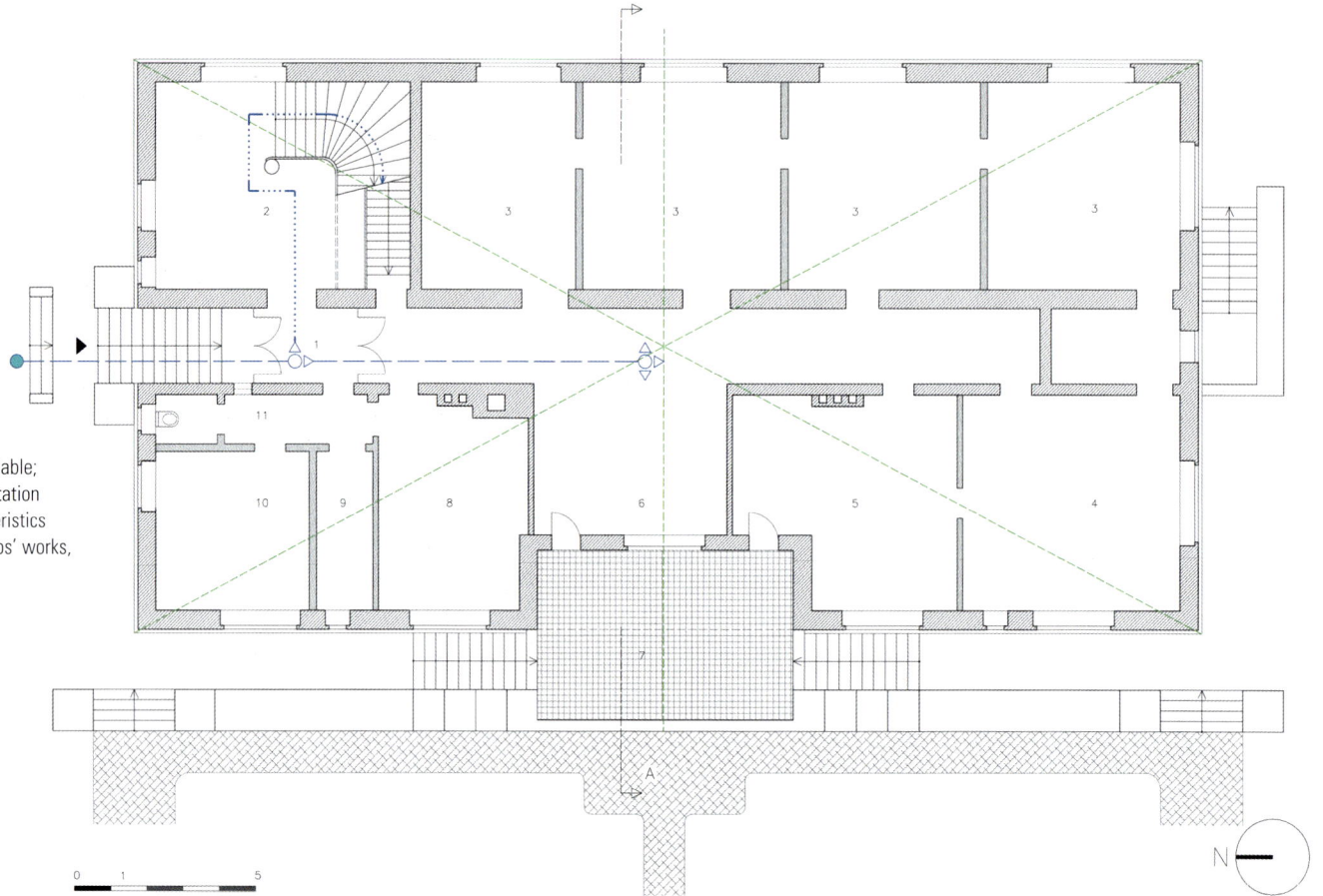

First floor
1 Corridor
2 Guest room
3 Parents bedroom
4 Terrace
5 Bathroom
6 Nanny room
7 Child room
8 Bathroom

Private family rooms and large terraces. The original floor plans are not available; this floor plan is based on documentation produced after 1950. The position of the stair to the roof terrace is an assumption of the author

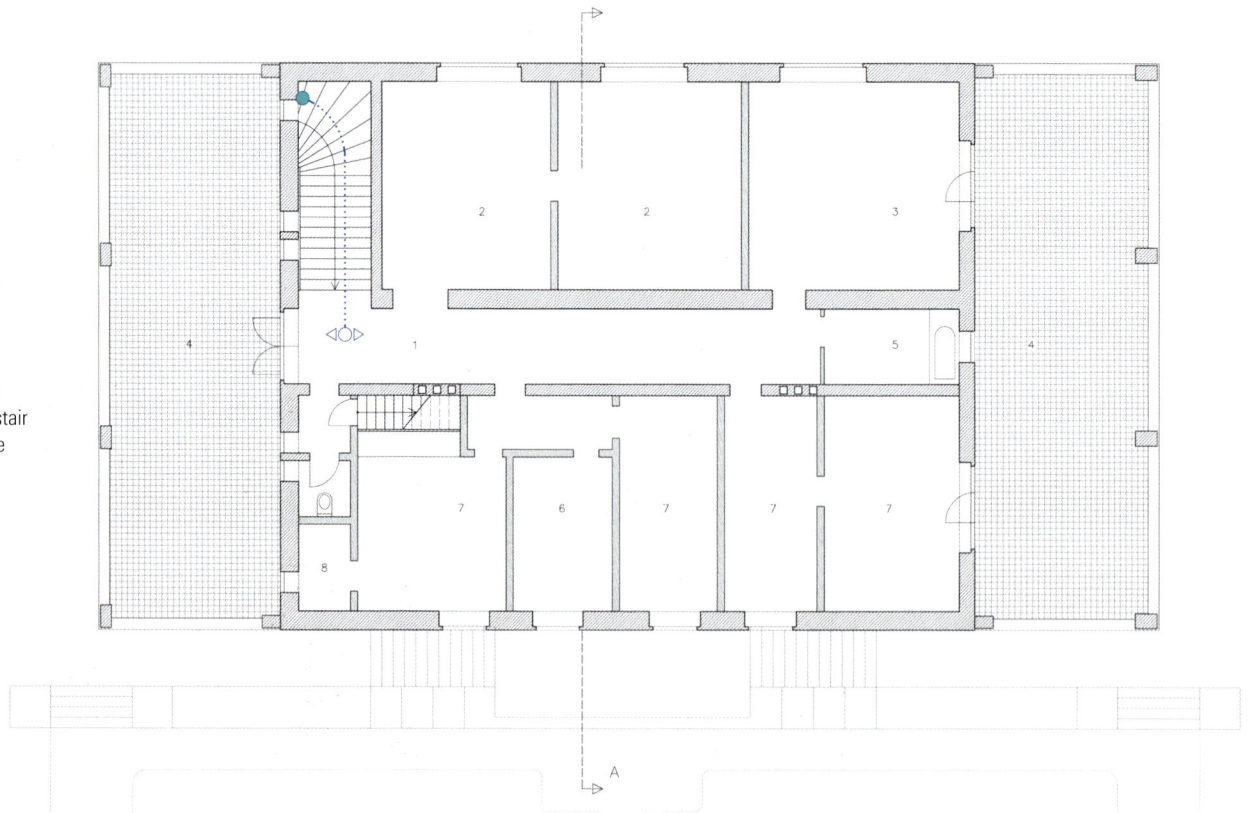

Section AA
1 Corridor
2 Guest room
3 Living room - Salon
4 Corridor
5 Hall
6 Terrace garden
7 Nanny room
8 Roof terrace

The terrace, half inside half outside, is clearly positioned higher than the garden level. The use of the huge roof terrace is not yet clearly documented

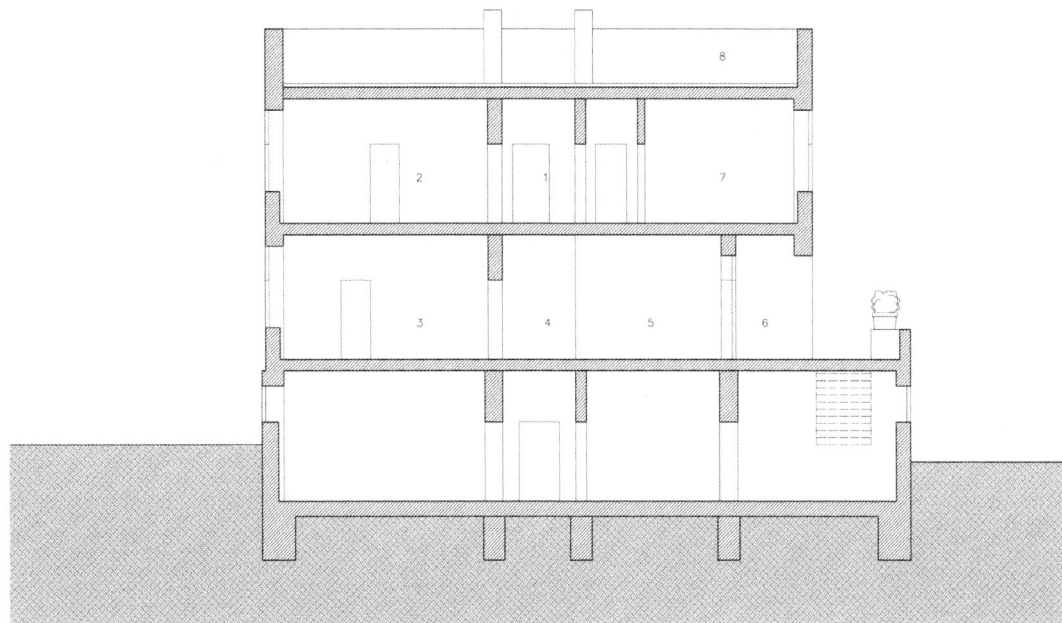

View from garden, with plant pots on the roof level and ground floor terrace
(ALA 2502)

# Strasser Villa

Kuppelwiesergasse 28
1130 Vienna

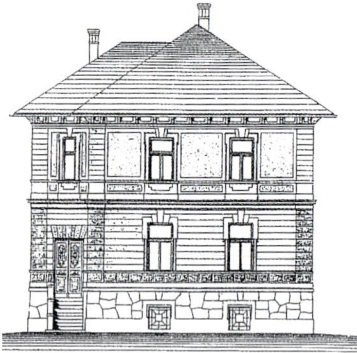

Original villa before transformation
by Loos

Karl Strasser
Died before 1941
Manufacturer, owner of Gebrüder Strasser
company (1140 Vienna, Diefenbachg. 33)

Hilda Strasser, born Fischer
15.7.1886 - died in Nazi concentration camp
Theresienstadt 25.5.1943

The large roof deck on top of the house
with a view over the public park

**Class**

Villa; reconstruction and interior fit out.

**Type of construction / Construction design**

Load-bearing solid brick walls with
wood-beamed ceilings. Prefabricated,
arched brick ceiling over the basement.
Existing construction partially modified
with a new static load concept: load-bearing
outer walls, transformation of the two
load-bearing middle walls in four central
columns and short wall sections
with chimneys around the service lift.
An additional support in the stairwell
to the first floor to bear the load from the
newly created hole in the ceiling.
*Raumplan.*

**Dimensions**

Base area: 13 m x 13.4 m.
Clear room heights: raised ground floor:
3.4 m; second floor: 3.5 m.
Levels: 8.
Stories: 4.
Living area without basement: ca 430 sq m.

**Materials**

*Entrance area*
Floor: red ceramic tiles.
Walls: coffered, white lacquered softwood,
matt-finished.
Ceiling: smooth plaster, painted white.
*Living area*
Floor: oak parquet floor covered
with Persian rugs.
Walls: coffered, white lacquered softwood,
matt-finished, above dark yellow paint
rough plaster (as in Rufer House).
Ceiling: white lacquered visible wood
beams with dark yellow paint rough plaster
ceiling areas.
*Library*
Floor: oak parquet floor covered with
Persian rugs.
Walls: coffered mahogany wood covering,
room height, with strong cornice at the
ceiling.
Ceiling: smooth, white plaster ceiling.
*Dining room*
Floor: luxurious parquet floor of square

panels with meander inlay, covered with
Persian rug.
Walls: wall covering in white-yellow
Egyptian onyx, whose porous openings are
darkly primed; above: figure frieze
with cornice at ceiling.
Cherry wood furniture.
Transition to music salon: division by heavy
tapestry (Gobelin).
Ceiling: smooth plaster, painted white.
*Music salon*
Floor: like dining room.
Walls: smooth, white walls with meander
frieze in stucco plaster as wall outline.
Free standing Skyros marble column
and brass-glass cabinets at transition
to music podium.
Ceiling: smooth plaster, painted white.

**Work catalog no.**

W.113.18

Present view from garden. Loos did not make the original and new parts of the building visibly separable. Protected terrace on raised ground floor

Vestibule after entrance at street level.
Left side opening to stair leading to raised
groundfloor

Section BB
1 Heating
2 Anteroom
3 Storage
4 Wardrobe
5 Drawing room
6 Library
7 Bedroom
8 Bathroom
9 Storage
10 Summer dining room

*Raumplan*-structure; complex composition
between new and existing structure

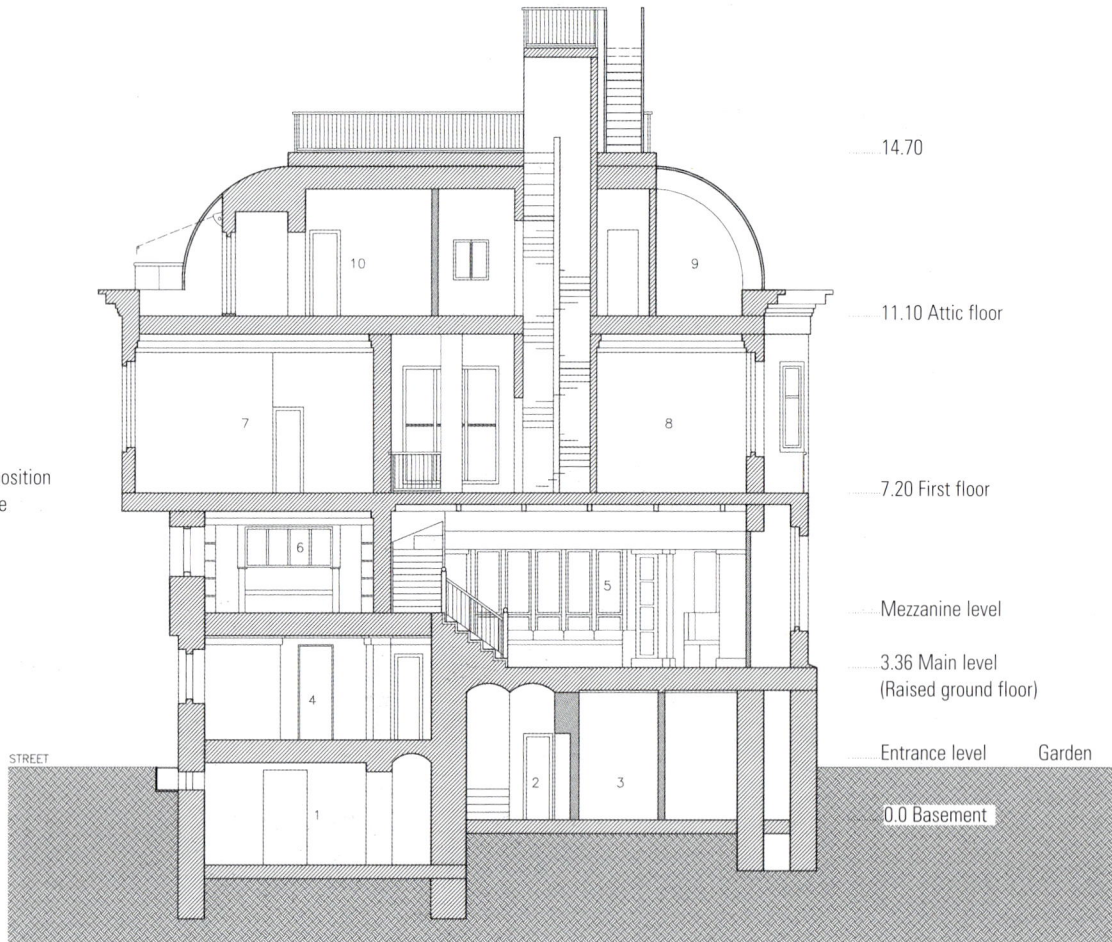

14.70

11.10 Attic floor

7.20 First floor

Mezzanine level

3.36 Main level
(Raised ground floor)

Entrance level        Garden

0.0 Basement

STREET

0    1              5

View from the central point of the house
to the stair from the vestibule and the piano
mezzanine above, from which the owner could
control the guests coming up by a wall mirror
behind the photographer's position

View from the piano podium on the mezzanine
to the wall mirror

Section AA
1 Coal room
2 Heating
3 Cook
4 Cloakroom
5 Vestibule
6 Music salon
7 Piano podium
8 Library
9 Bathroom
10 Bedroom
11 Drying/Sewing/Ironing room
12 Summer dining room
13 Housemaid
14 Dining room

Section through mezzanine level with
the library (gentlemen's room) and music
salon, below on street level, entrance
with garderobe

Section CC

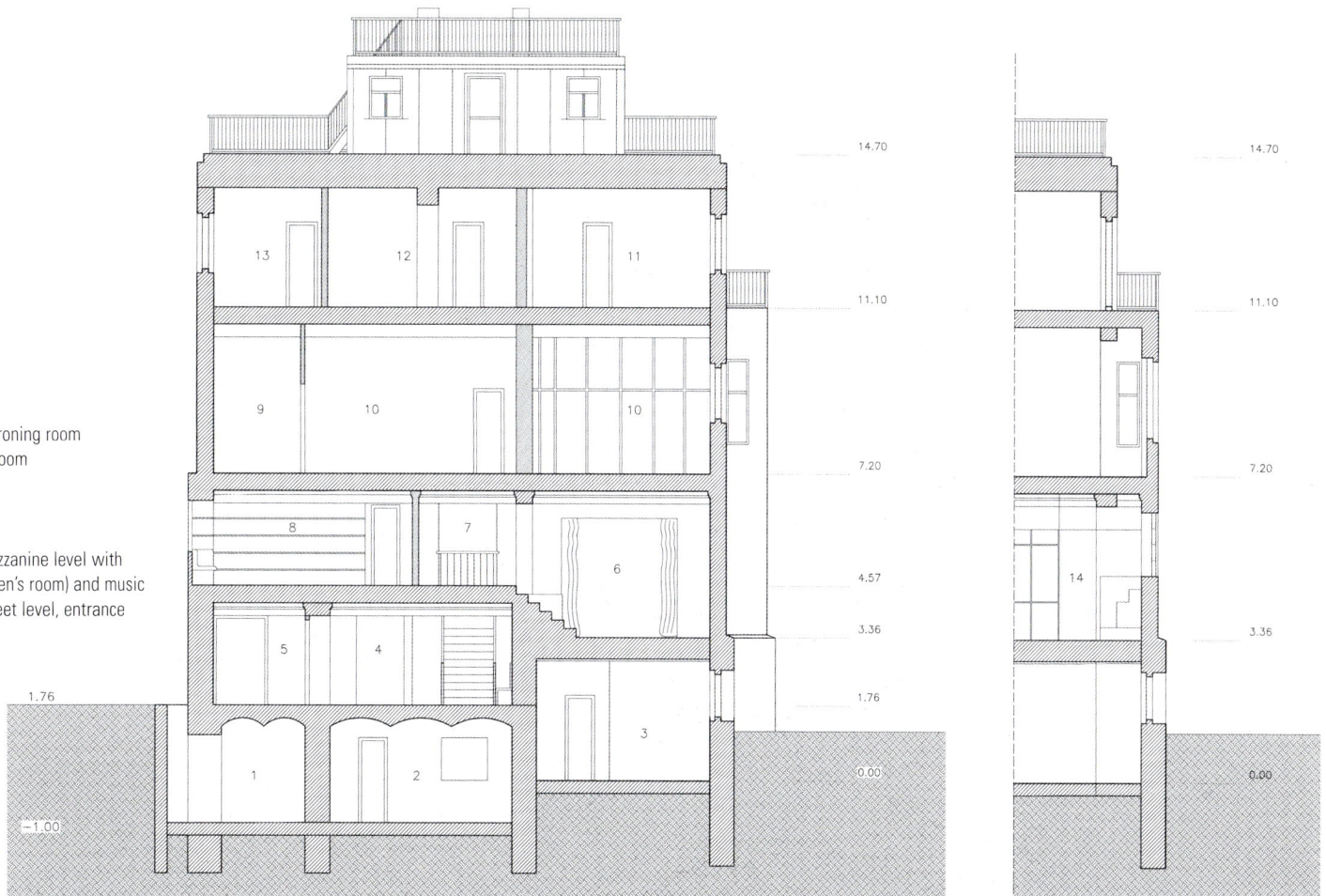

Raised ground floor / Mezzanine level
1 Dining room
2 Music room
3 Piano podium
4 Library (Gentlemen's room)
5 Salon
6 Lift
7 Präparation kitchen
8 Terrace

Concept of living space: hall with sitting
facilities for relaxing and communication,
music salon and dining room. Library
(gentlemen's room) separated

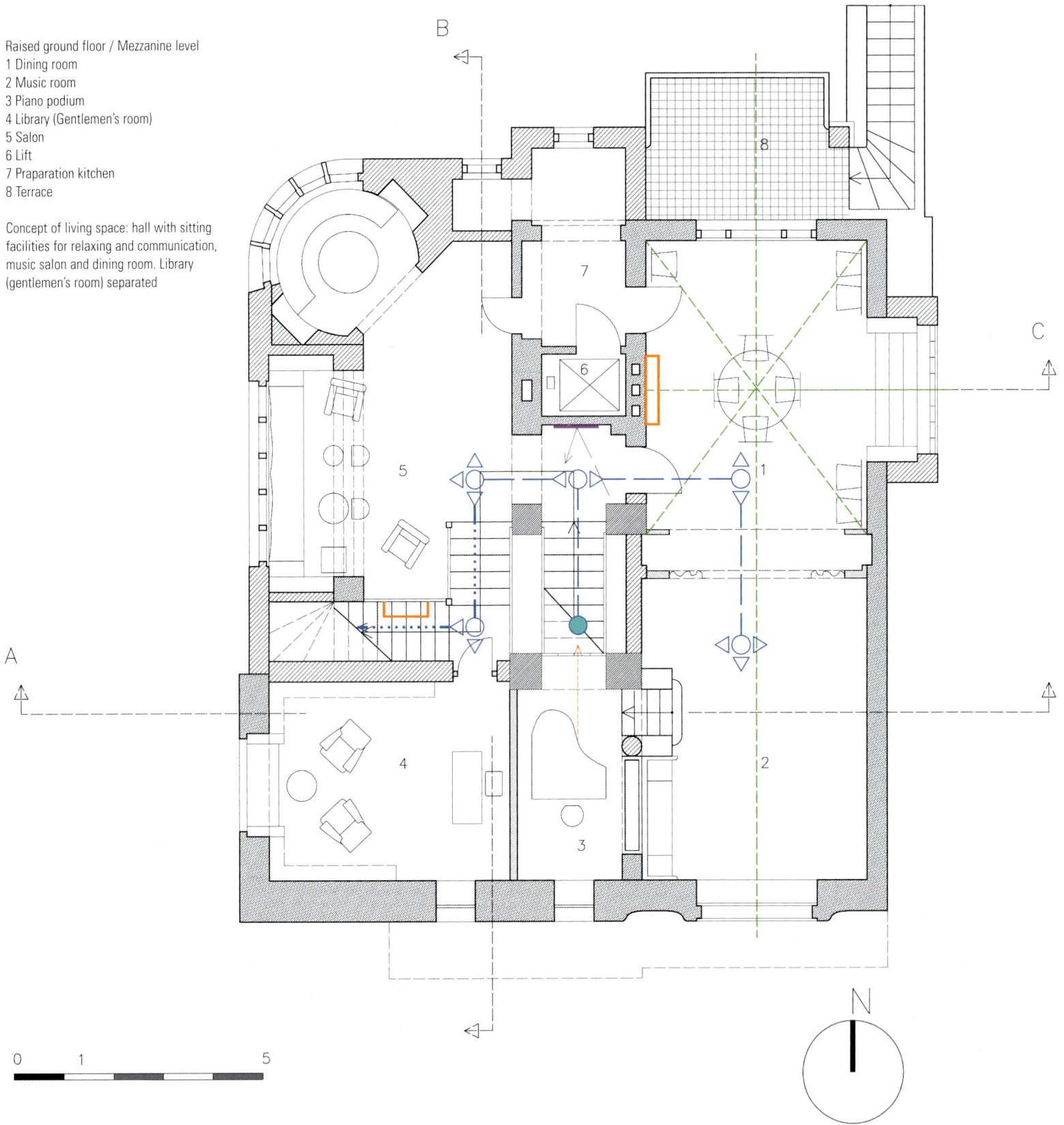

B

C

A

8

7

6

5

1

3

4

2

N

0    1         5

Entrance level
1 Vestibule
2 Cloakroom

Entrance from street. Kitchen with service
personnel rooms and utility rooms in the
basement

First floor
1 Bedroom
2 Bathroom
3 Guest room

Private rooms with small hidden stair
to top floor

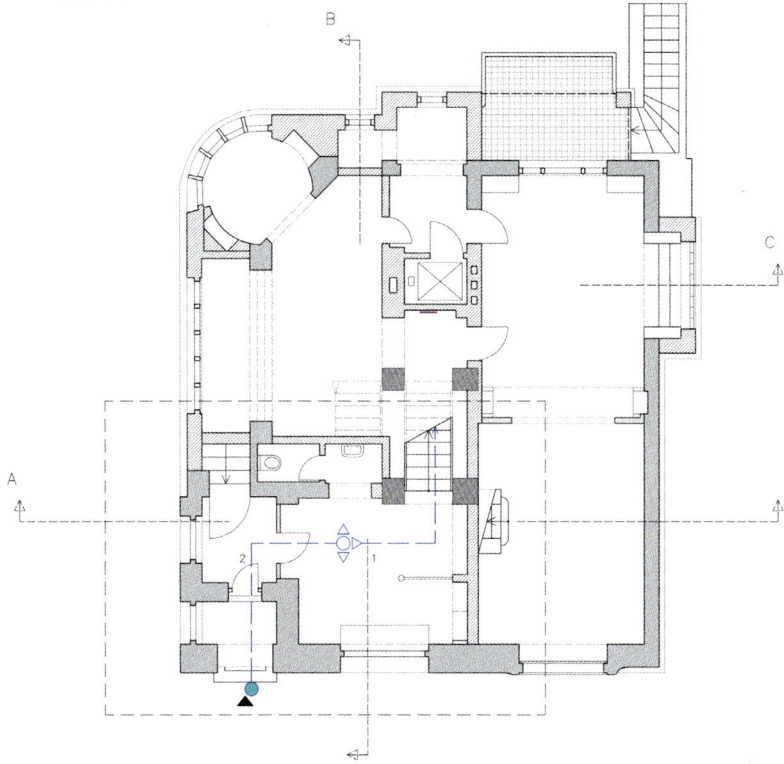

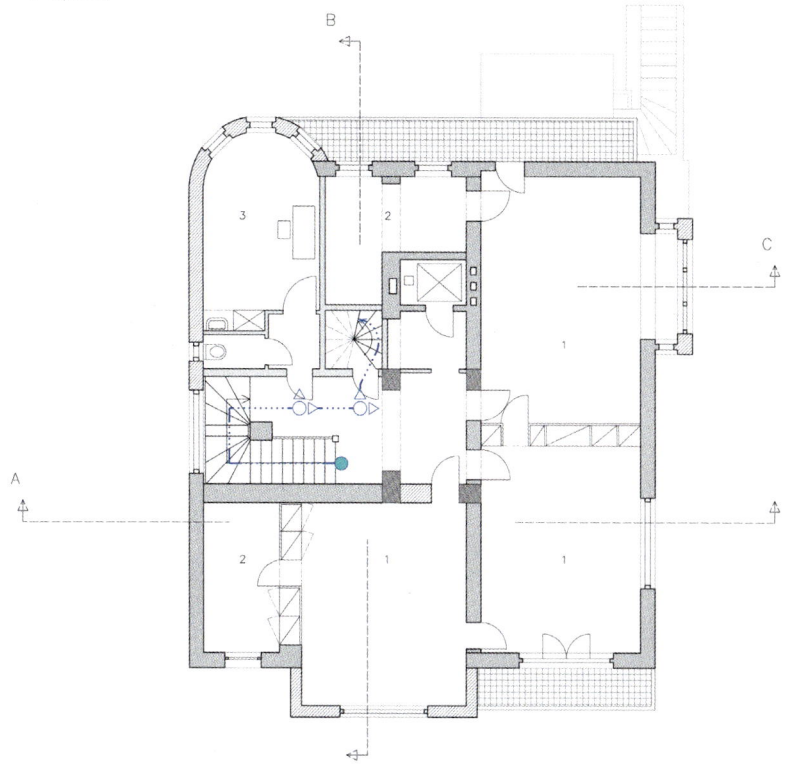

Attic floor
1 Laundry
2 Drying/Sewer/Ironing room
3 Summer dining room
4 Housemaid
5 Storage

Roof terrace
1 Terrace
2 Cabin

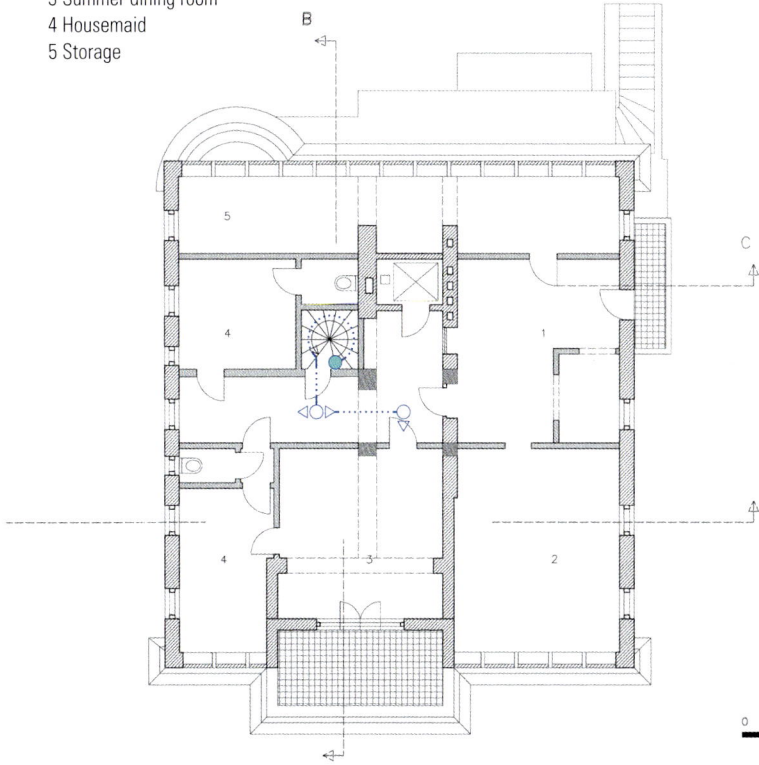

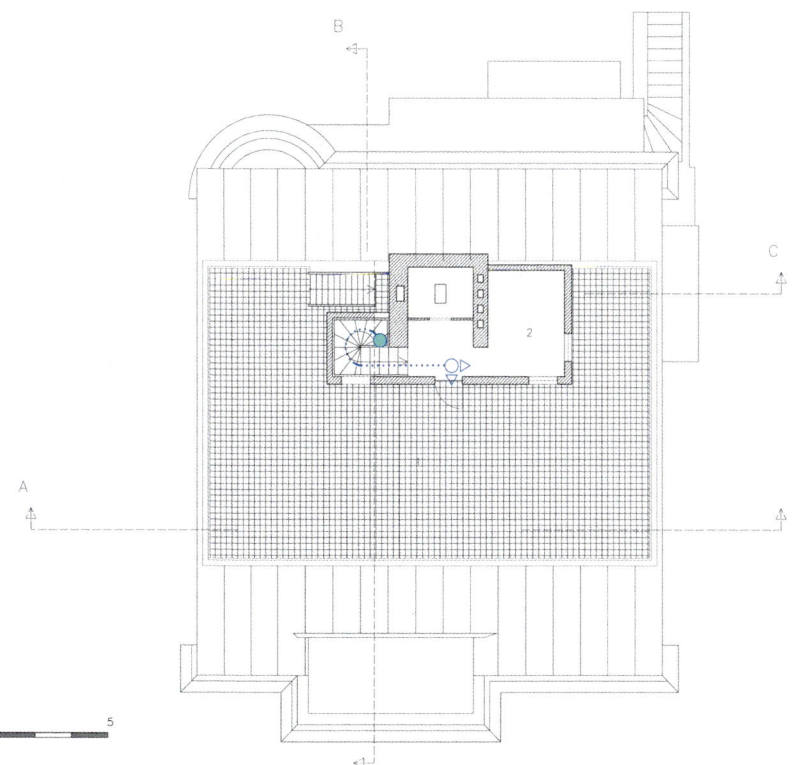

0  1      5

Stair to first floor with landing at mezzanine
level and access to library (gentlemen's room)

Salon with seating against the bay window,
open stair to first floor and fireplace

View to the hall with a second seating against
a bay window

View from music salon to dining room with wall cladding in onyx and bas-relief frieze under ceiling

Niche in dining room with translucent glazing to adjacent villa. Outside covered with Japanese ivy

View from music salon to piano gallery. Column in Skyros marble, which is used already by the Greeks and the Romans

# Settlement House in "Friedensstadt" Lainz

Hermesstraße 93
1130 Vienna

Lainzer Tiergarten - Friedensstadt
First non-profit settlement cooperative
in war-damaged Austria

**Class**

Settlement row house; new construction.

**Type of construction / Construction design**

Solid brick walls and visible wood-beamed ceilings with simple timberboard lining without a ballast layer for noise absorption. Only load-bearing outer walls, no load-bearing elements in interior. Continuous ceilings without height differences.

**Dimensions**

Base area: 7 x 6 m.
Clear room height: ca 2.3 m to underside of beams ground floor; ca 2.45 m to underside of beams first floor.
Levels: 3.
Stories: 3
Living area without basement: ca 65 sq m.

**Materials**

Construction and interior fit out by owner.

**Work catalog no.**

H.128.21

0    1         5

North facade

Building permit drawing with preparation for espalier fruits on facade

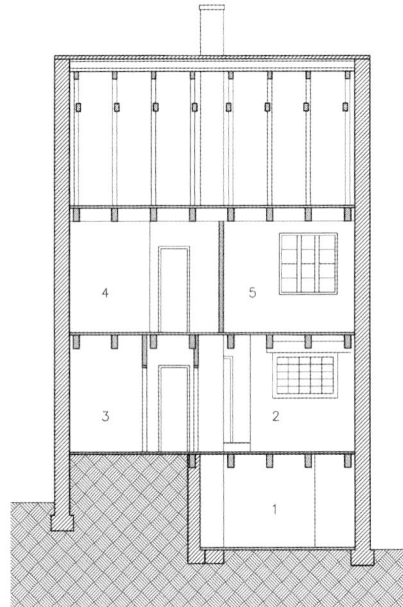

Section AA

Two-story house with basement. Only outer walls are load bearing. This is the building permit design by Loos that was never permitted, because stairs are too steep and ceilings without noise absorption

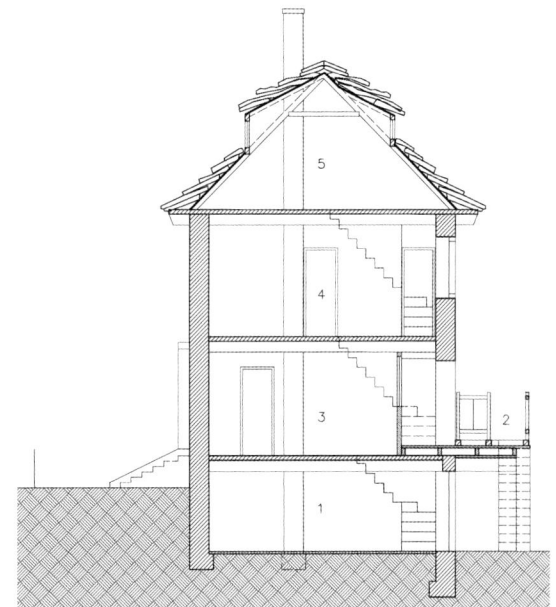

Section BB

The executed projects were changed by other architects according the building law in Vienna, which was made for multistory residential buildings. Loos was fighting for special rules for settlement houses according to the rules in England and the Netherlands, which have a long tradition of small private houses

Present view from street to the row houses.
Only one is still in reasonable original
conditions

Large fruit and vegetables garden

Present view from garden

Basement
1 Garden (fruit, vegetables)
2 Shelter
3 Stable
4 Cellar

Stable for keeping small animals connected
to garden level. Self-sufficient facilities
are the main criteria for the settlement house
and garden design of Loos

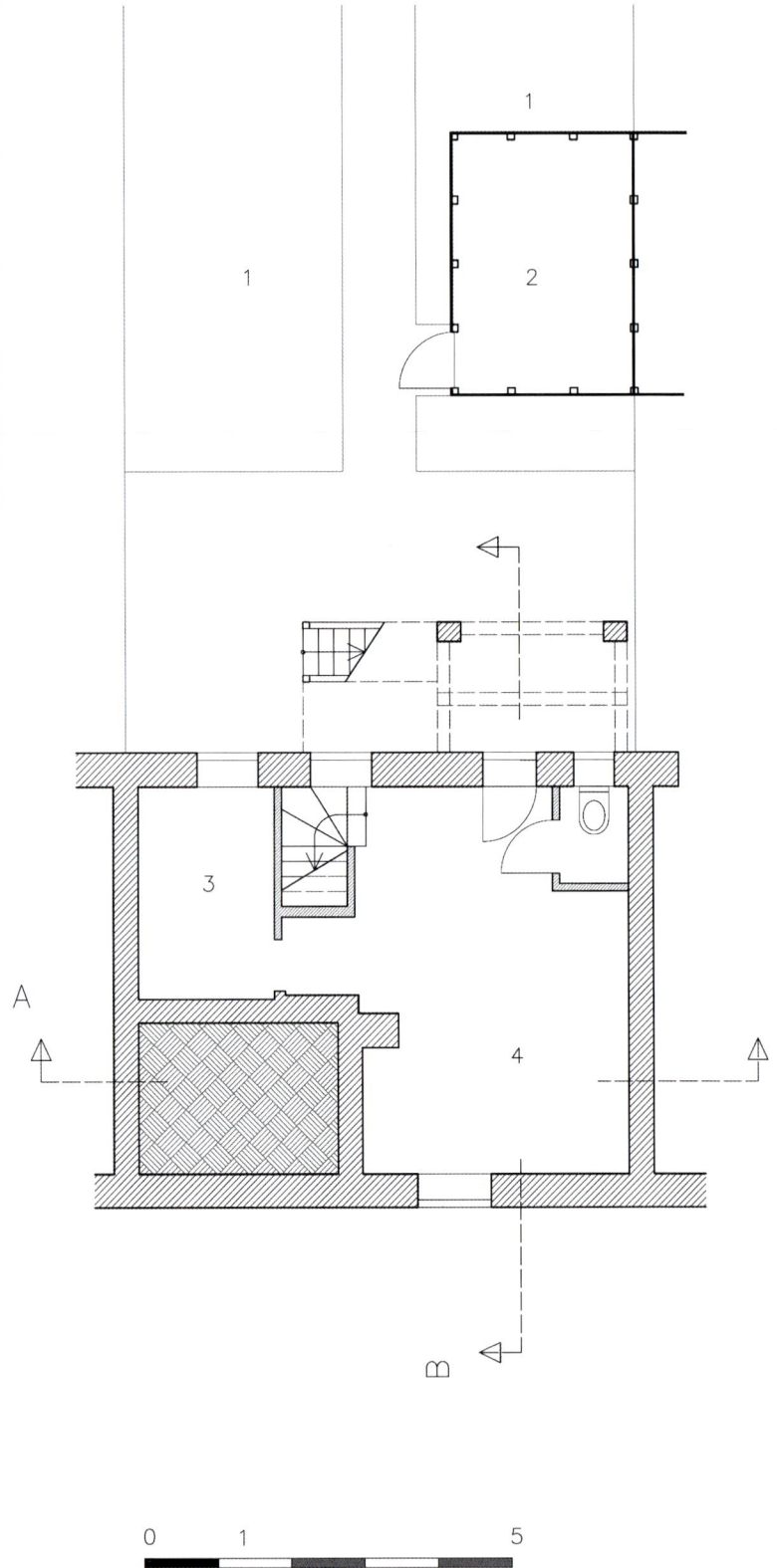

Raised ground floor
1 Small room
2 Veranda/Terrace
3 Living/Dining/Cooking
4 Sink

Cooking/dining/living combined in one central
room with an open stair to the first floor

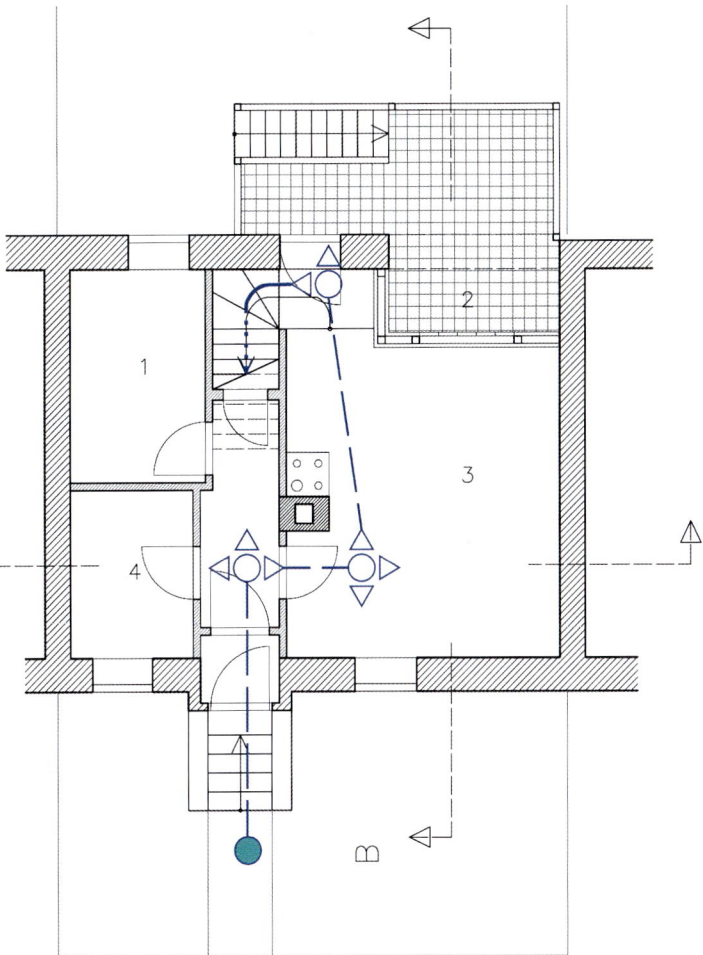

First floor
1 Child bedroom
2 Bedroom
3 Child bedroom

Private rooms, but without bathroom

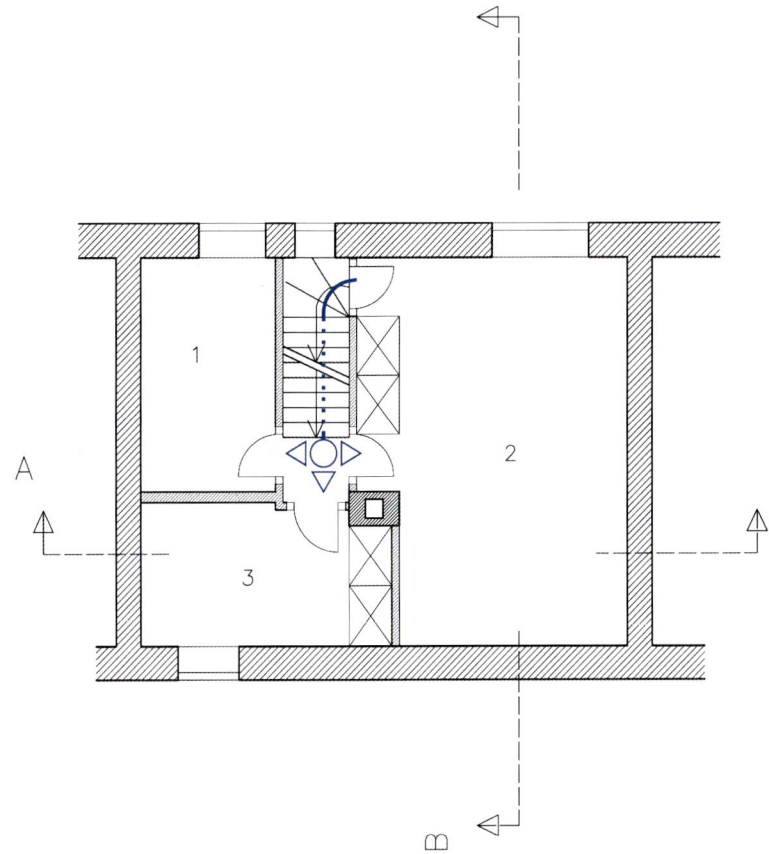

# Rufer House

Schliessmanngasse 11
1130 Vienna

Josef Rufer senior
Died before 1949
Merchant, sugar import
Arnold Schönberg

Maria Rufer senior
One of her three children, Josef Rufer jun.,
was the assistent of Arnold Schönberg at the
University of Berlin

**Class**

Villa; new construction with interior fit out.

**Type of construction / Construction design**

Square floor plan with load-bearing outer walls and only one load-bearing middle column. Wood-beamed ceilings.
All partition walls are non-load-bearing. Loos takes advantage of the maximum span width of the wood ceiling of ca 5 m and concentrates the load in the interior with beams to a central support.
A principle that he used ten years earlier in the Horner House. In the Rufer House, it also serves as a constructive aid, which facilitates his *Raumplan*. The individual areas of the house are oriented in a spiral around the central support in various levels up to the sleeping floor. The chimney is also integrated in the central support.
The roof trusses are very flat with the minimal slope for the sheet metal covering. In the publication by Heinrich Kulka (1931), which Loos himself influenced, the external view is retouched and the pitched roof with its small gable to the street is removed; in the building permit drawings, however, it is very clearly represented.

**Dimensions**

Base area: 10 x 10.4 m.
Levels: 7.
Stories: 4.
Living area without basement:
ca 280 sq m.

**Materials**

*Entrance area*
Floor: coco fiber carpet.
Walls: coffered, white, matt-finished lacquered softwood.
Ceiling: smooth plaster, painted white.
*Living area (music salon)*
Floor: oak parquet floor covered with Persian rugs.
Walls: coffered white lacquered, matt-finished softwood to door-height; above: dark paint on rough plaster.
Ceiling: white lacquered wood beams with dark paint (yellow-ochre or red) ceiling areas on rough plaster.
*Library*
Floor: oak parquet floor covered with Persian rugs.
Walls: smooth cherry wood covering to ceiling-height with recessed areas for graphics, which are integrated into the wall covering.

Ceiling: smooth plaster, white painted, with circumferential wood cornice profile.
*Dining area*
Like living area, but: integrated sideboard in wall covering, including the dumb waiter and a large wall mirror instead of a window, on the east side facing the neighboring property. Directly to the dining room there is only one window facing the garden, which was conceived of by Loos as a bay window for flowers and plants.

**Work catalog no.**

H.147.22

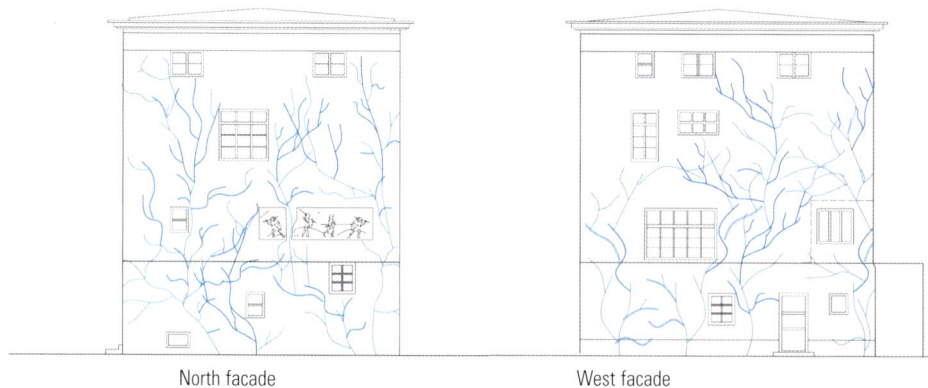

North facade

West facade

Street elevation (North facade)
Compostion of unregular window positions, balanced out by a frieze of a classical antiquity era motif; Loos do not want a window from music salon towards the street. Motif of a "mask" is partly recognizable, covered by Japanese ivy

Side elevation (West facade)
Entrance for service personnel and goods

The view from street with a copy of a piece from the bas-relief frieze of the Parthenon

Side elevation (South facade)
Simple entrance on street level

Garden elevation (East facade)
Terrace on raised ground floor level half inside and half outside of building, covered by roses and Japanese ivy, typical Loos' motif. Stairs lead along the house wall into the garden

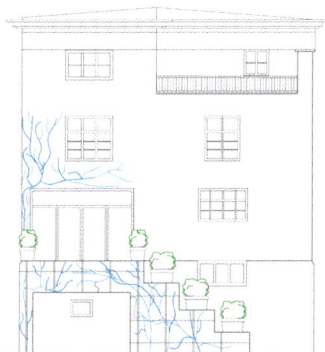

South facade

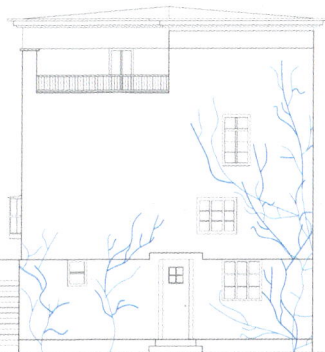

East facade

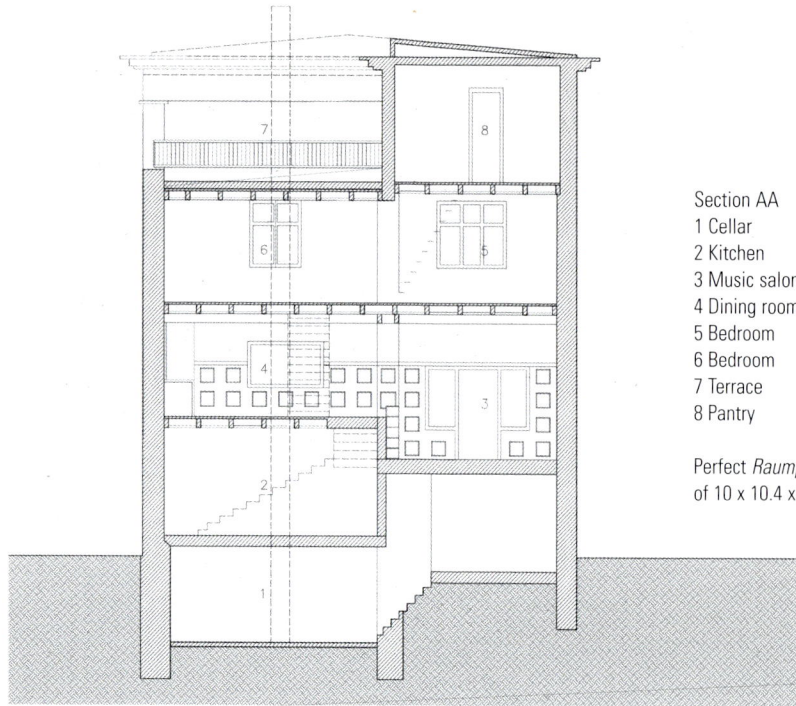

Section AA
1 Cellar
2 Kitchen
3 Music salon
4 Dining room
5 Bedroom
6 Bedroom
7 Terrace
8 Pantry

Perfect *Raumplan*-concept in a cube
of 10 x 10.4 x 11 m

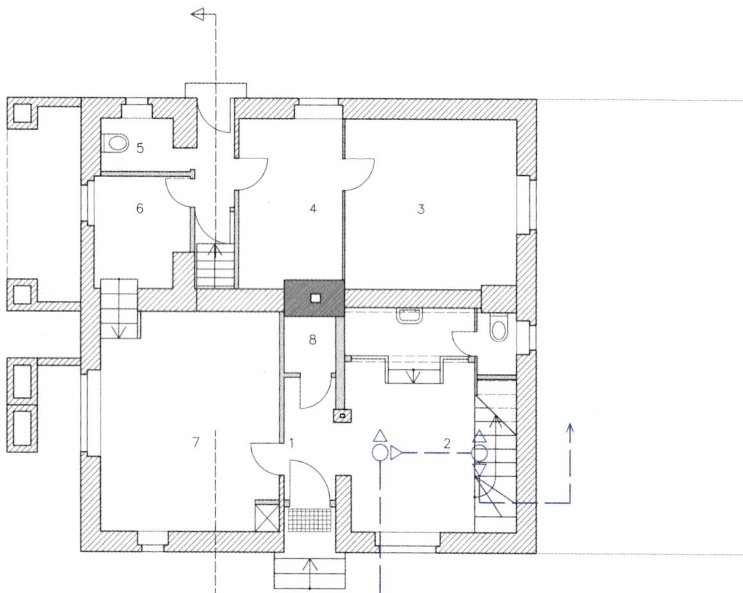

0    1                    5

Basement
1 Pantry
2 Hall
3 Housemaid/Service personnel room
4 Kitchen
5 Toilette room
6 Pre-cellar
7 Kitchen
8 Wardrobe

Entrance from street level leading to vestibule
with open stairs to raised ground floor level.
Further on basement level: kitchen and service
personnel rooms

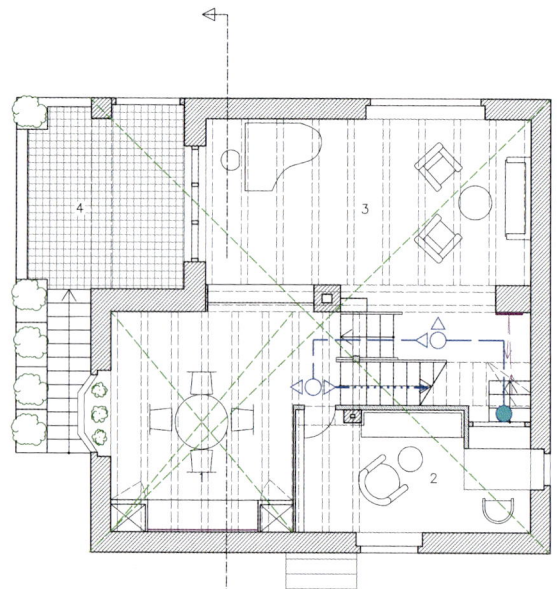

0    1                    5

Raised ground floor
1 Dining room
2 Library
3 Music salon
4 Terrace

Concept of living space: music salon
with sitting facilities for relaxing and
communication and dining room. Library
(gentlemen's room) separated. Owner has
control of arriving guests from his working
desk in library, by a small interior window
and a wall mirror reflecting the entrance stair

N

View to the entrance hall
Photo by M. Gerlach Jr., ca 1930
(ALA 3222)

Library (gentlemen's room) with working
desk over entrance stair
Photo by M. Gerlach Jr., 1930
(ALA 3225)

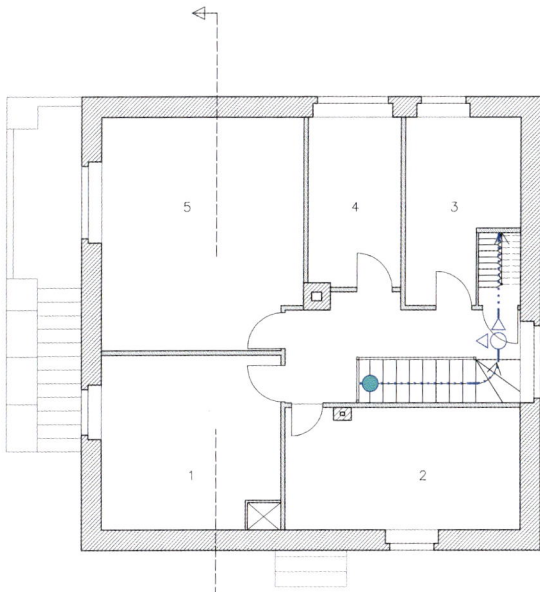

First floor
1 Bedroom
2 Bedroom
3 Bedroom
4 Bathroom
5 Bedroom

Private rooms with a hidden, small, steep
stair to the top floor

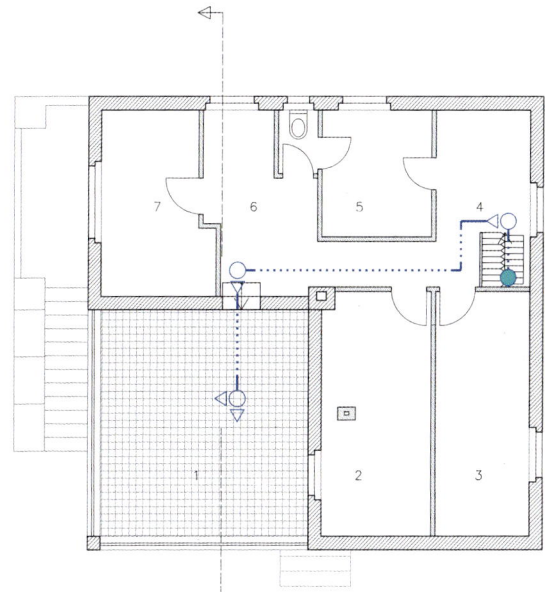

Top floor
1 Terrace
2 Bedroom
3 Housemaid
4 Corridor
5 Laundry
6 Pantry
7 Sewing room

Service personnel and utility rooms

View from dining area to lower hall level
with open stairs to first floor
Photo by B. Reiffenstein, 1930
(ALA 2522)

View from music salon to entrance stair
landing and open stair to first floor
Photo by M. Gerlach Jr., 1930
(ALA 3218)

View from dining area to music salon
Photo by M. Gerlach Jr., 1930
(ALA 2523)

View from music salon to dining area on higher
level. Mirror instead of window on the wall
facing the adjacent villa
Photo by M. Gerlach Jr., 1930
(ALA 3219)

# Spanner Country House

Rotes Mäuerl, 270
Gumpoldskirchen (Austria)

Position in landscape on the hill over the vineyards. Present situation with steep roof instead of original flat roof

Carla Spanner: biographical information unknown

**Class**

Country house; new construction on existing foundation walls.

**Type of construction / Construction design**

Load-bearing solid brick outer walls and load-bearing solid brick middle wall with a wood-beamed ceiling and a height difference on ground floor. On the upper floor, the middle wall is reduced to three supports. In these supports the chimney is also integrated.

**Dimensions**

Base area: 13.7 m x 9.4 m.
Levels: 4.
Stories: 3.
Living area without basement:
ca 200 sq m.

**Materials**

Interior finishing not conserved and inclomplete documentation.

**Collaborators**

Leopold Fischer.

**Work catalog no.**

H.171.24

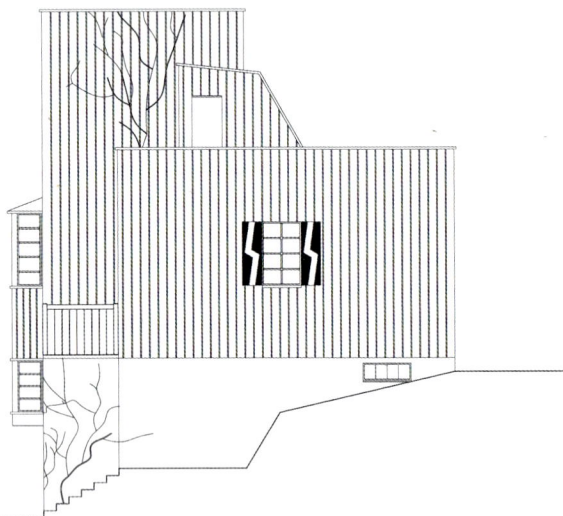

South facade

Facade covered by Japanese ivy on garden level and on terrace level. Tower with bay window

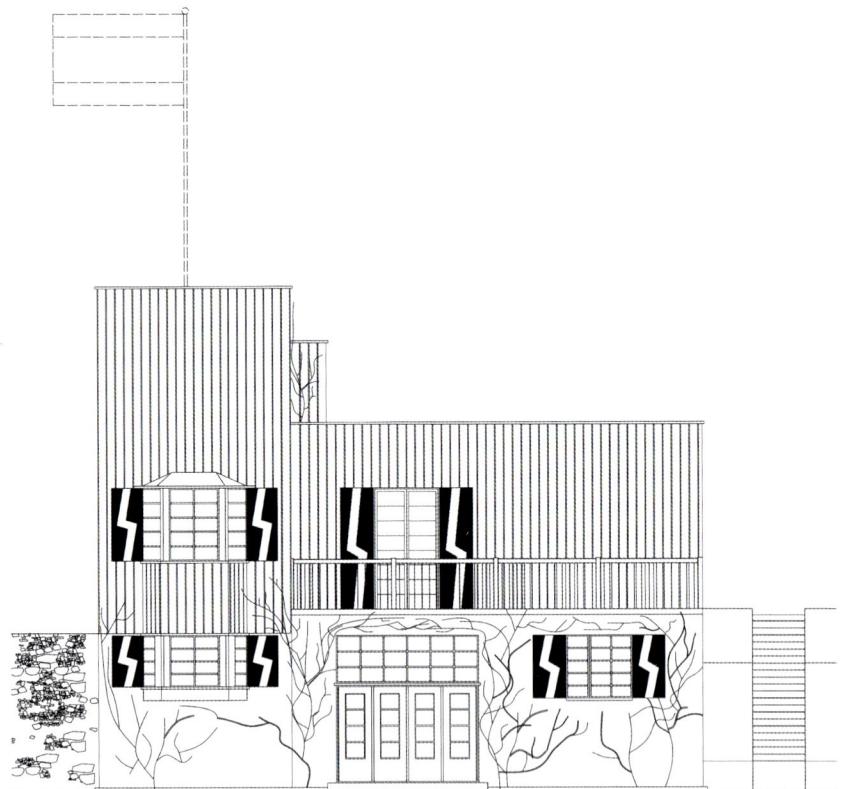

West facade

Big opening from living area to garden terrace with view over the vineyards

Present view of garden facade. Original timber cladding, painted green and white, has been replaced with a new material. A new roof over the terrace has been added

225

Top floor
1 Room in the tower
2 Terrace room

Tower room with large roof terrace
and plant pot for covering the facade
with Japanese ivy

Ground floor
1 Hall
2 Dining room
3 Kitchen
4 Pantry
5 Cellar
6 Salon

Hall with fireplace in central postion with
direct access to garden terrace and connection
to open stair to first floor and dining area.
This central room has a higher room height
by lowering the floor level

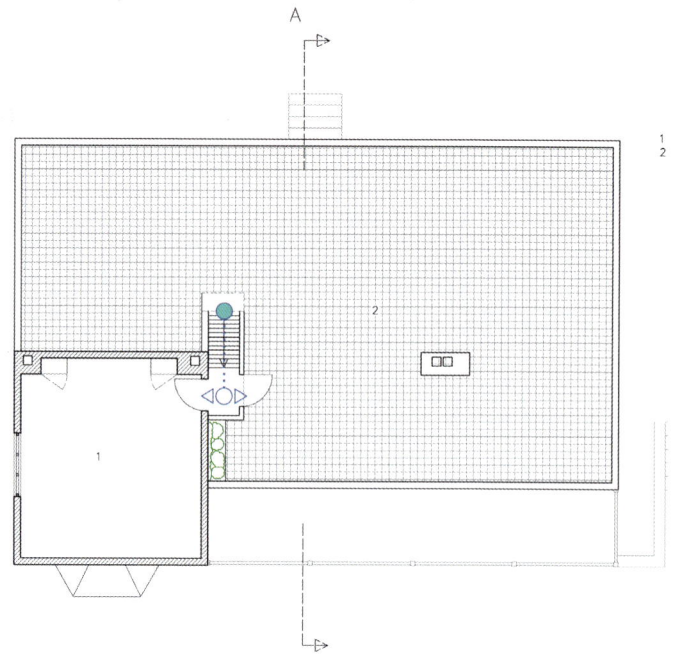

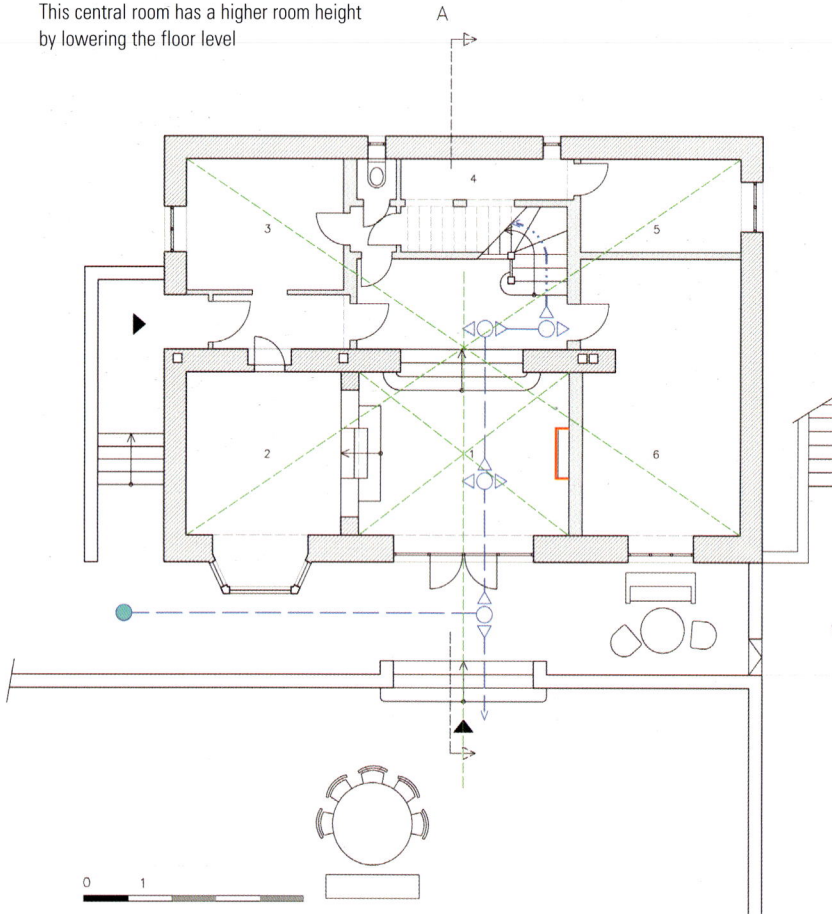

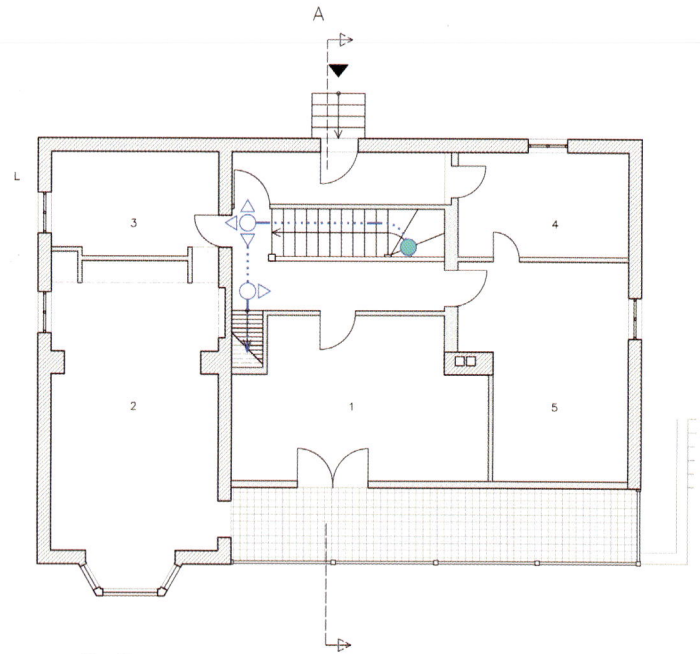

First floor
1 Bedroom
2 Bedroom
3 Bathroom
4 Service personnel
5 Bedroom

Private rooms with separate entrance from
street for service personnel. Access to master
bedroom through bathroom

Garden facade
Photo by M. Gerlach Jr., ca 1930
(ALA 3232)

Section AA
1 Hall
2 Bedroom
3 Terrace
4 Roof terrace
5 Vestibule
6 Garden terrace

Cross section through central hall, showing
also the four terrace levels of this project
in the vineyards landscape

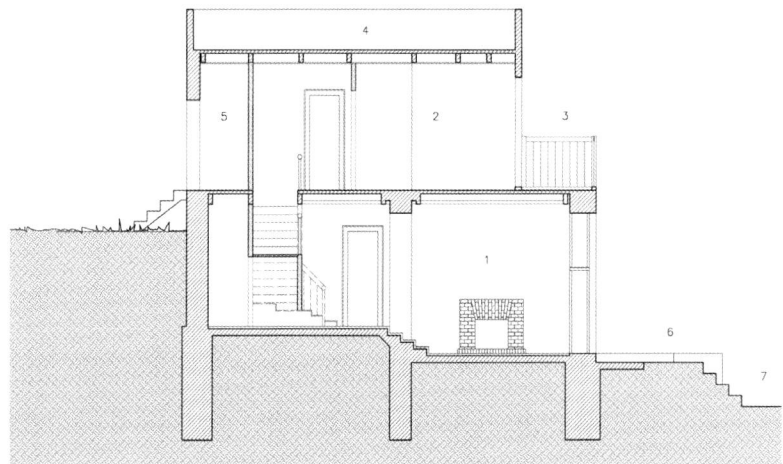

0    1

# Tristan Tzara House

15, Avenue Junot
Paris XVIII

Tristan Tzara (orig.: Samuel Rosenstock)
Moineti (Romania) 16.4.1896 - Paris 24.12.1963
Writer and poet, founder of Dada
Josephine Baker, Hans Arp, Hugo Ball,
André Breton, Man Ray and many other artists
and intellectuals

**Class**
Villa; new construction with interior fit out.
**Type of construction / Construction design**
Nearly square floor plan with load-bearing outer solid brick walls and only one load-bearing solid brick middle wall, which splits into two columns on the upper floors. The middle offset of the street facade is transferred to two additional columns below it. The higher positioned terrace with the studio of the artist is sustained by an additional wall and supports to the ground.
*Raumplan* in the area of the main living levels.

**Dimensions**
Base area: 10.6 x 17.6 m, on the lower floors completely overbuilt; standard floor: 10.6 x 12.6 m.
Levels: 8.
Stories: 5.
Living area (without rental unit): ca 320 sq m.
**Materials**
*Living area*
Floor: painted screed covered with Persian rugs.
Walls: pilaster strips and up to ca 1 m height and partly room height: smooth oak plywood panels visibly screwed in. Remaining surfaces smooth plaster painted. Marble fireplace.
Ceiling: painted smooth plaster.

*Dining room*
Floor: oak parquet floor.
Walls: oak plywood panels visibly screwed in.
Light painted doors.
Ceiling: smooth plaster, painted.
*Little salon*
Floor: oak parquet floor covered with rugs.
Walls: black lacquered strips of wood in which works of African art are hung.
Low benches with horse hair upholstery.
Ceiling: smooth, stretch fabric.
**Collaborators**
Zlatko Neumann.
**Work catalog no.**
H.180.25

North facade
Symmetric facade; main level for living in the third floor above ground with the access to main loggia

Present view of street facade after restoration

Section AA
1 Anteroom
2 Storage
3 Living/Dining room
4 Hall
5 Lowered and covered terrace
6 Cellar
7 Storage
8 Wc
9 Dining
10 Salon (Drawing room)
11 Terrace
12 Gentleman bedroom
13 Wc

*Raumplan*-structure; Loos' original intention
was to add another floor on top. Main terrace
with a balustrade designed for planting

View from garden, ca 1930
(ALA 3254)

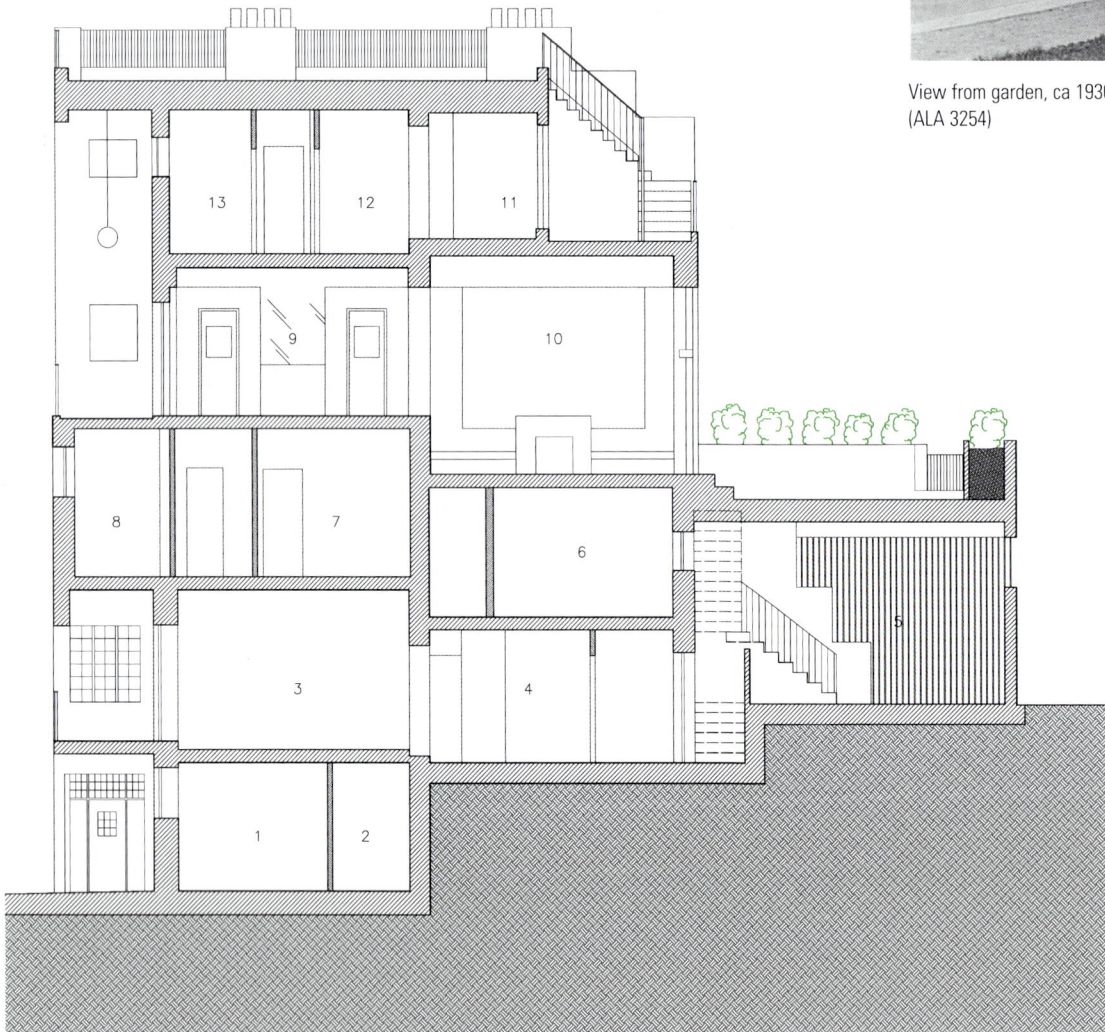

Ground floor
1 Garage
2 Storage
3 Entrance
4 Anteroom

Street entrance and garage level

First floor
*Apartment for rent*
1 Lowered and covered terrace
2 Kitchen/Pantry
3 Living/Dining room
4 Room
5 Bathroom
6 Hall

Apartment for rent with entrance from
the back under main terrace

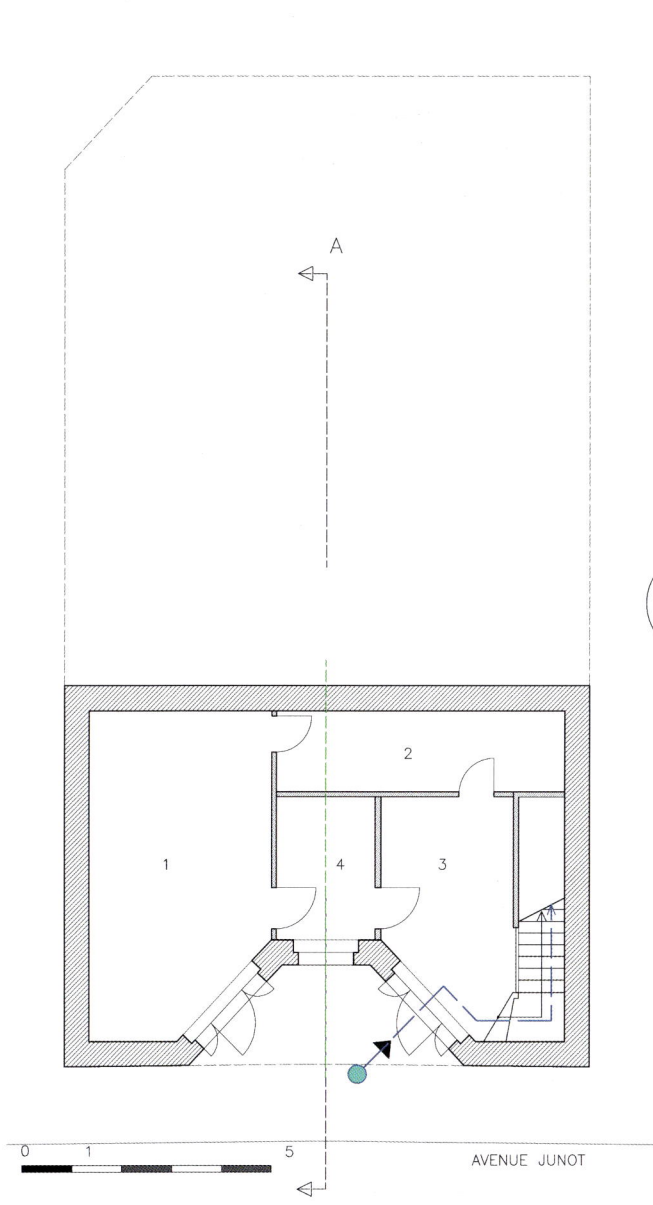

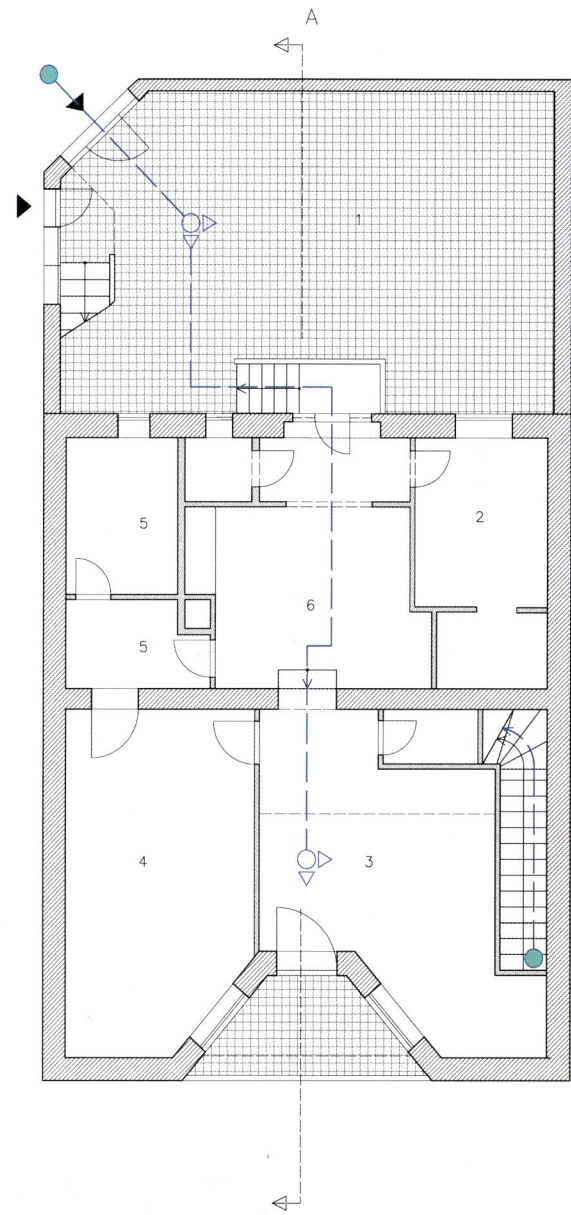

A

A

N

0   1        5

AVENUE JUNOT

TRISTAN TZARA HOUSE

Second floor
1 Storage
2 Cellar
3 Wine cellar
4 Cloakroom
5 Wc
6 Kitchen
7 Storage
8 Void

Level with kitchen, service personnel
and utility rooms

Third floor
1 Terrace
2 Atelier
3 Salon (Drawing room)
4 Dining room
5 Office/Library
6 Little salon
7 Connection to kitchen downstairs

Main level. Concept of living space: salon
with sitting facilities for relaxing and
communication, dining room on higher level.
Little salon, office and atelier are separated

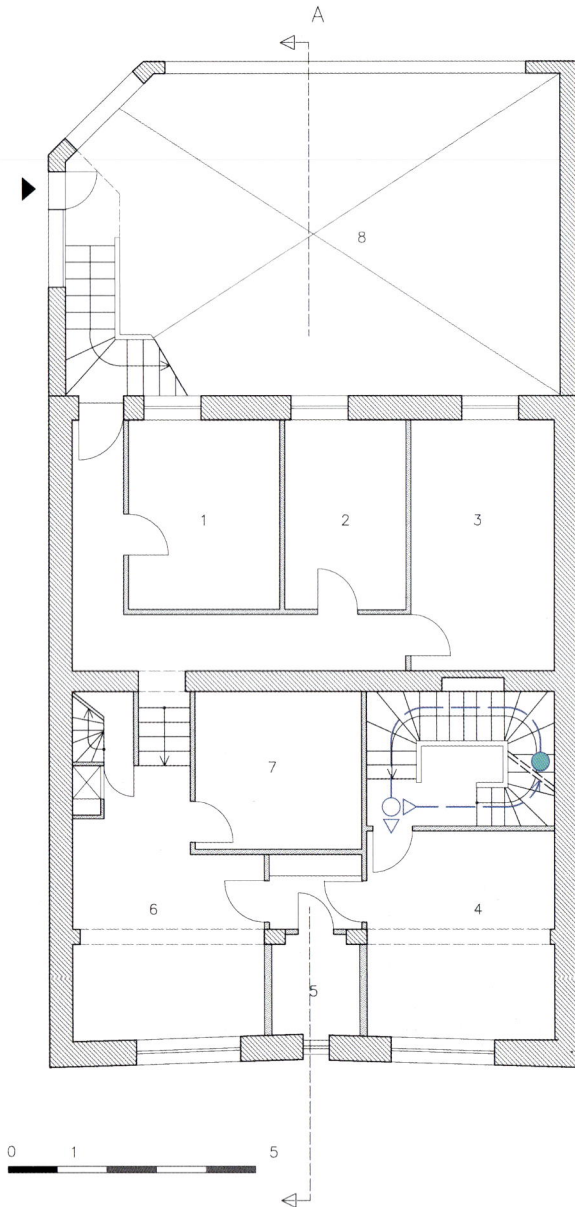

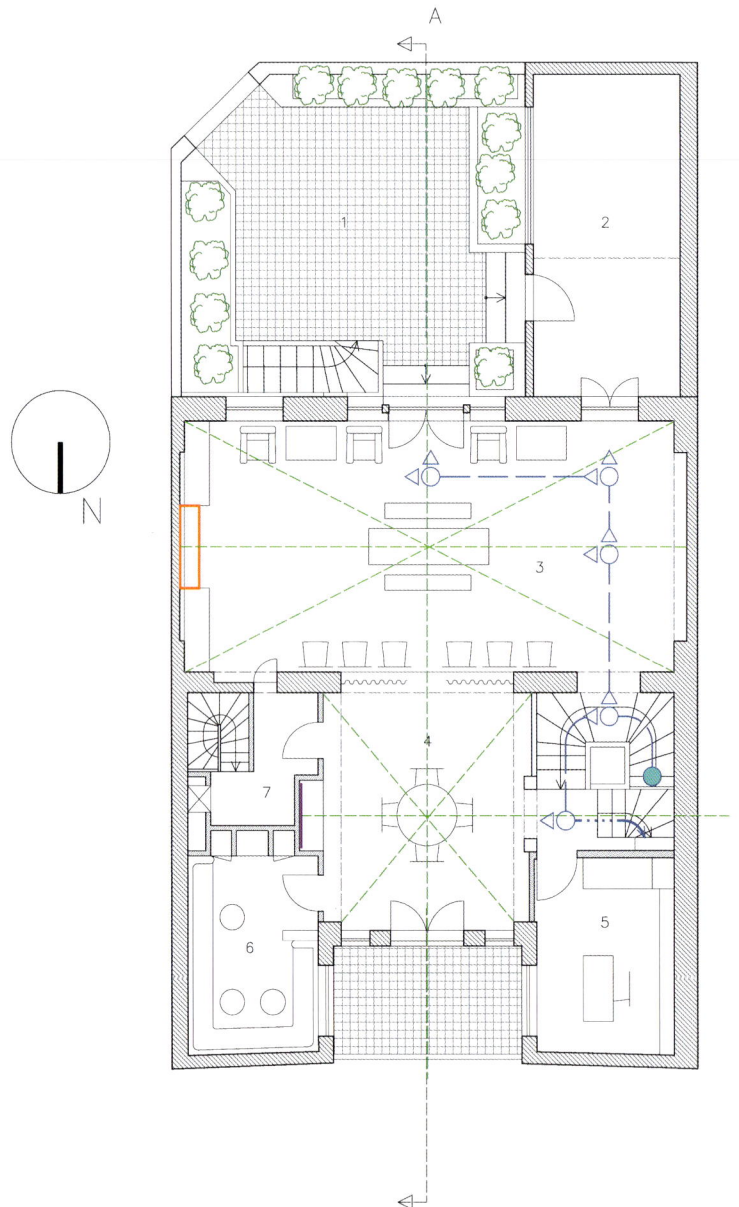

Fourth floor
1 Terrace
2 Gentleman bedroom
3 Working area
4 Anteroom
5 Bathroom
6 Wc
7 (Guest) room
8 Bedroom

Private rooms on different floor levels.
Outside stair from terrace to large roof
terrace above

Top floor
1 Roof terrace

Large roof terrace with access
by external stair

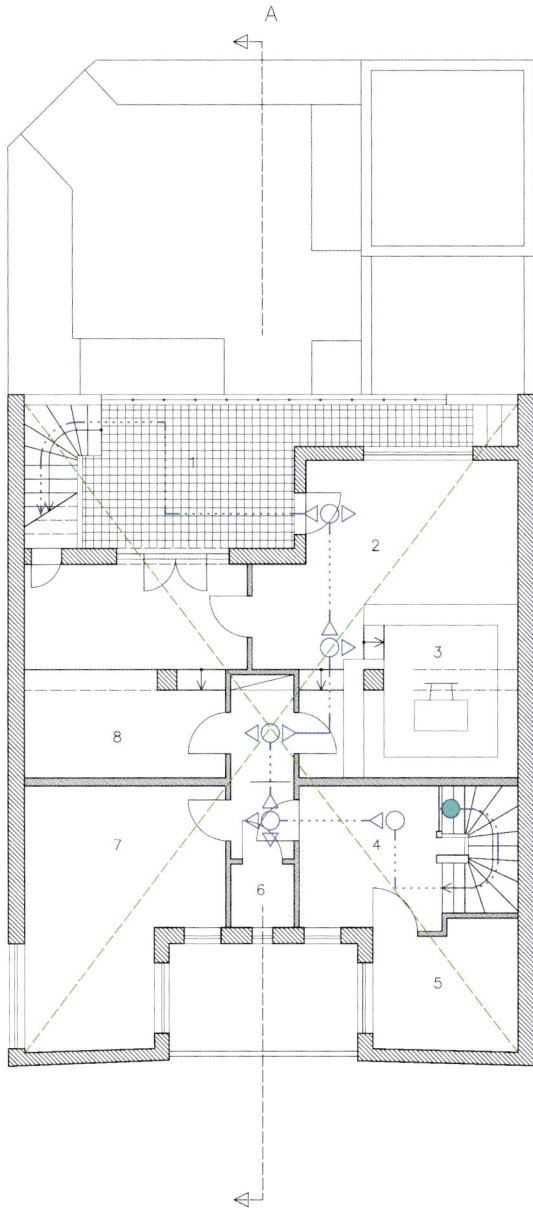

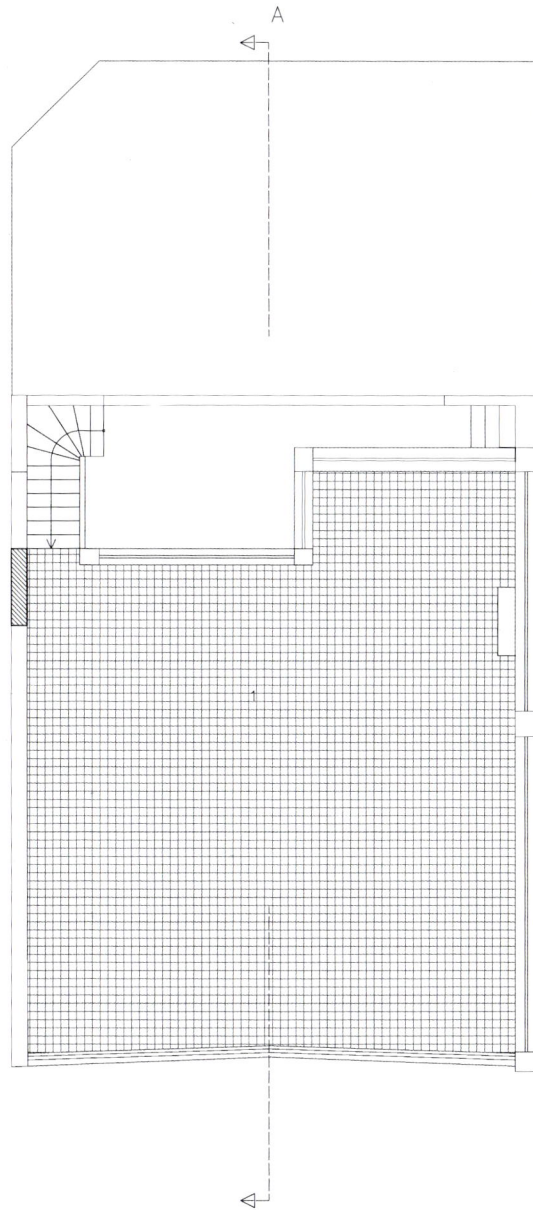

A

A

View from salon to dining area on higher level, there is only a direct visible connection, but there are not direct stairs between these two areas

View from dining area to salon on lower level. The two areas can be sperated by wall curtains. Door gives access to the dumb waiter

View into hall from staircase arrival.
Smooth wall covering with plywood panels.
Curtains before windows, ca 1930
(ALA 3256)

Working area of Tristan Tzara on fourth floor.
Tzara was an artist and art collector which
represent the interior objects in his house
Photo by M. Gravot, Paris, ca 1930
(ALA 2634)

# Moller Villa

Starkfriedgasse 19
1180 Vienna

Hans Moller
Vienna 12.7.1896 - Palestine 1.10.1962
Manufacturer, cottonspinnery in Babi,
near Nachod (CZ), founder and board chairman
of ATA Textil AG in Palestine
Arnold Schönberg, Karl Kraus, Helge Lindtbergh,
Eduard Steuermann
Workers Settlement (Babi, near Nachod/CZ),
1931, work cat. no. H.217.31

Anny Moller, born Wottitz
Budapest 17.05.1903 - Haifa Juli 1945
Artist with education at Bauhaus
Johannes Itten, Arnold Schönberg,
Max Bronstein alias Mordechai Ardon

**Class**
Villa; new construction with interior fit out.
**Type of construction / Construction design**
Nearly square floor plan with load-bearing
solid brick outer walls and only one
load-bearing solid brick middle column
with wood-beamed ceilings.
The middle column also incorporates
the chimney for the centralized heating.
*Raumplan.*
**Dimensions**
Base area: 12.75 x 10.4 m.
Levels: 8.
Stories: 4.
Living area (without utility rooms
in basement): ca 280 sq m.
**Collaborators**
Jacques Groag.
**Work catalog no.**
H.188.27

North facade on Starkfriedgasse
Symmetric facade, with a central bay
for the sitting corner in the hall

South facade
Top floor with atelier and guestroom without
any normal window towards the garden
and roof terrace, only a narrow door from
the common corridor provides access
to the roof terrace

0    1         5

Present view of northern street facade. References to an abstract "face" illustrate the citation of Loos in which he said that the outside of a house should recall a mask which protects the inner wealth and intimacy

Terrace still on raised groundfloor level, but
here completely in front of the building and
with a transparent balustrade to the garden;
stairs lead straight forward into the garden
and not lateral like in the other projects

Section AA
1 Storage
2 Laundry
3 Garage
4 Music salon
5 Hall
6 Living room
7 Sitting niche in a bay (loge)
8 Bedroom
9 Bedroom

*Raumplan*-structure, section through hall and music salon, showing also the different terrace levels

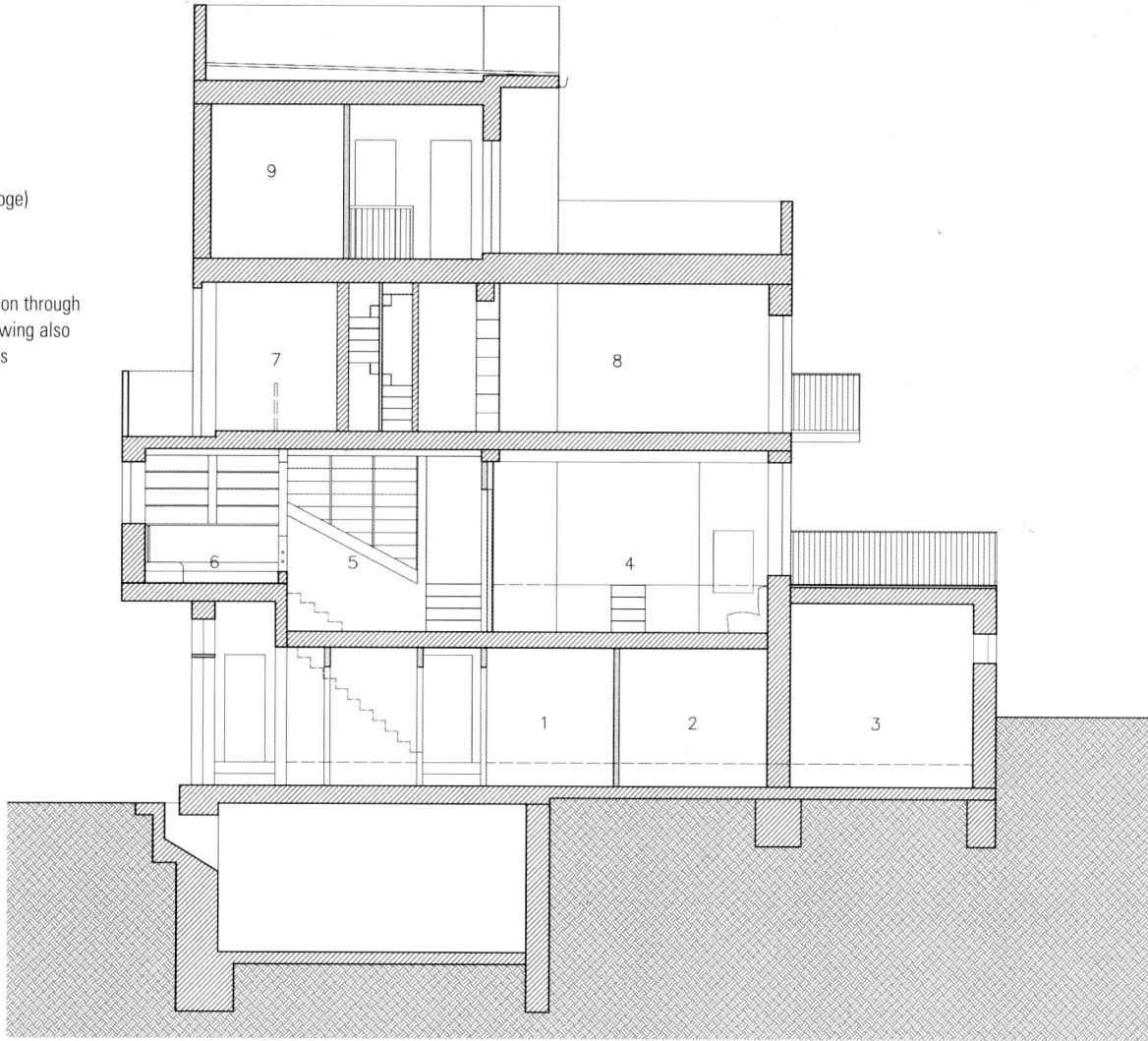

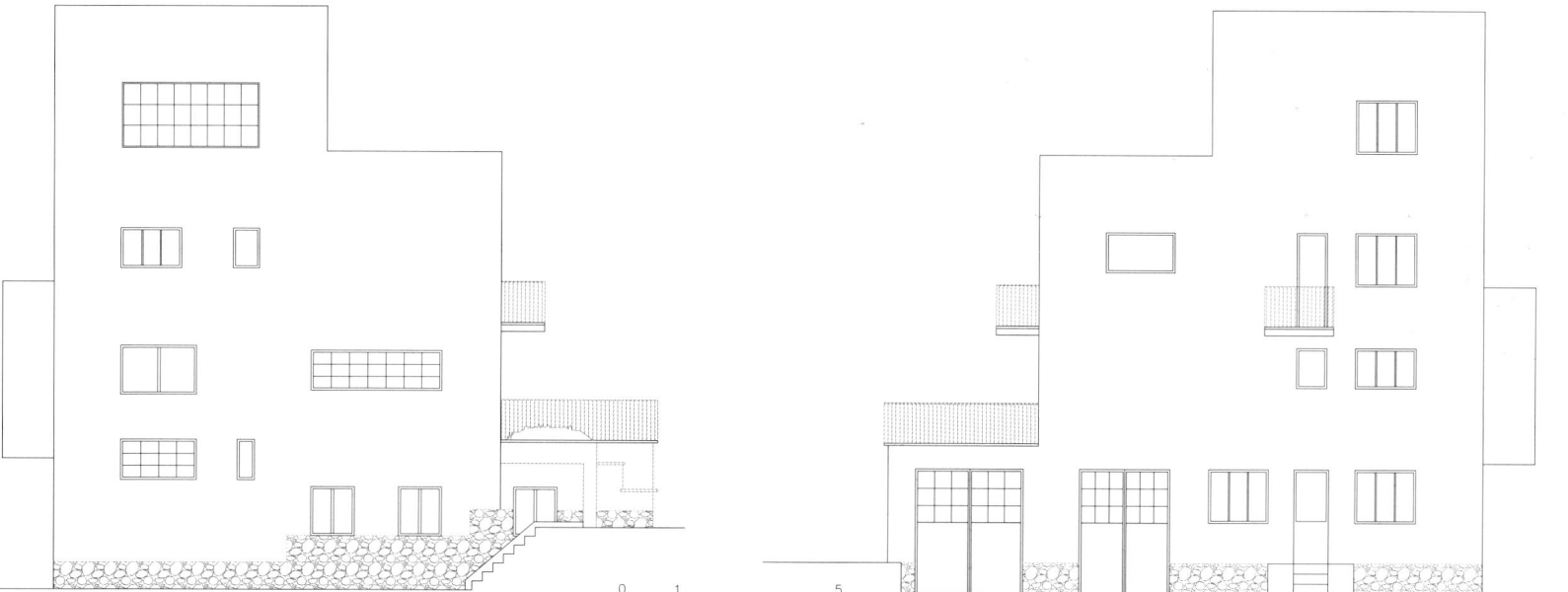

0  1        5

West facade

East facade

0  1      5

**239**

MOLLER VILLA

Basement
1 Housekeeper
2 Anteroom
3 Cloakroom
4 Pantry
5 Housemaid
6 Laundry
7 Garage
8 Kitchen housekeeper
9 Storage

Entrance from street level leading to vestibule with open stairs to raised ground floor level. Further in basement level: garage, service personnel and utility rooms

Raised ground floor
1 Kitchen
2 Living room
3 Library (gentlemen's room)
4 Hall
5 Music salon
6 Dining room
7 Terrace
8 Garden
9 Dumb waiter

Main level. Concept of living space: hall with sitting facilities for relaxing and communication, dining room on higher level and large music salon. Library (gentlemen's room) and kitchen are separated

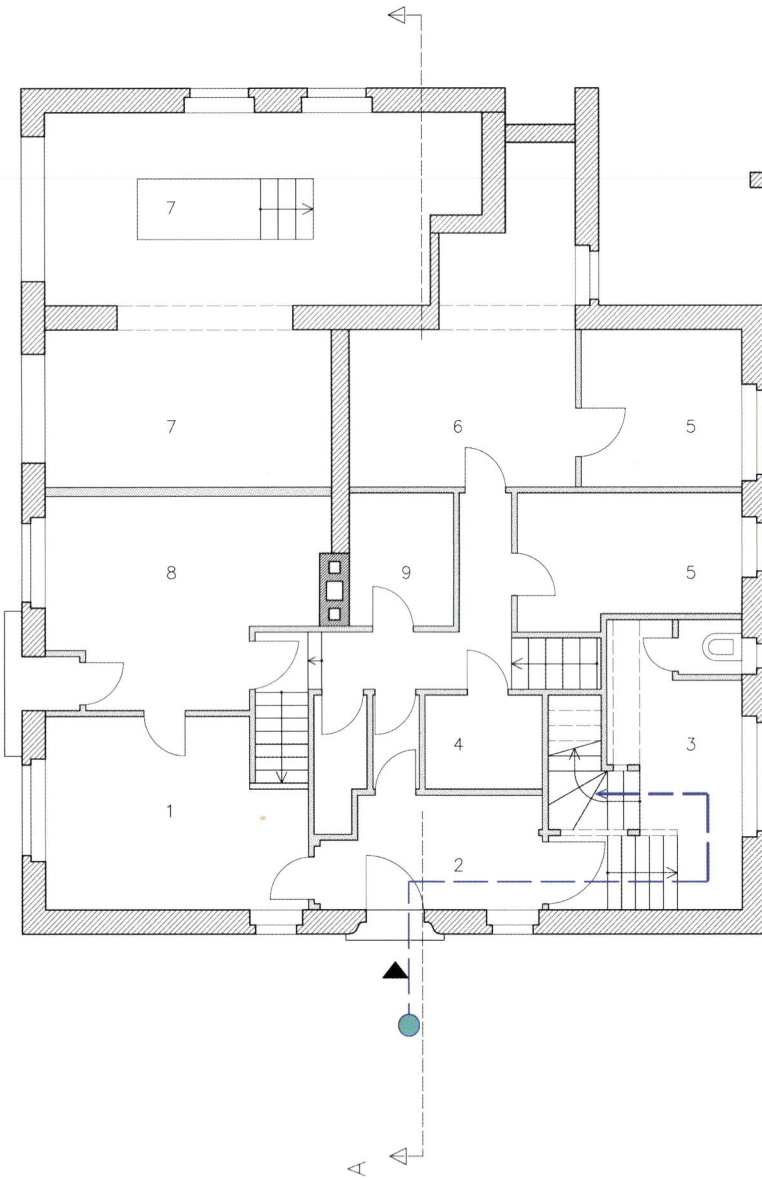

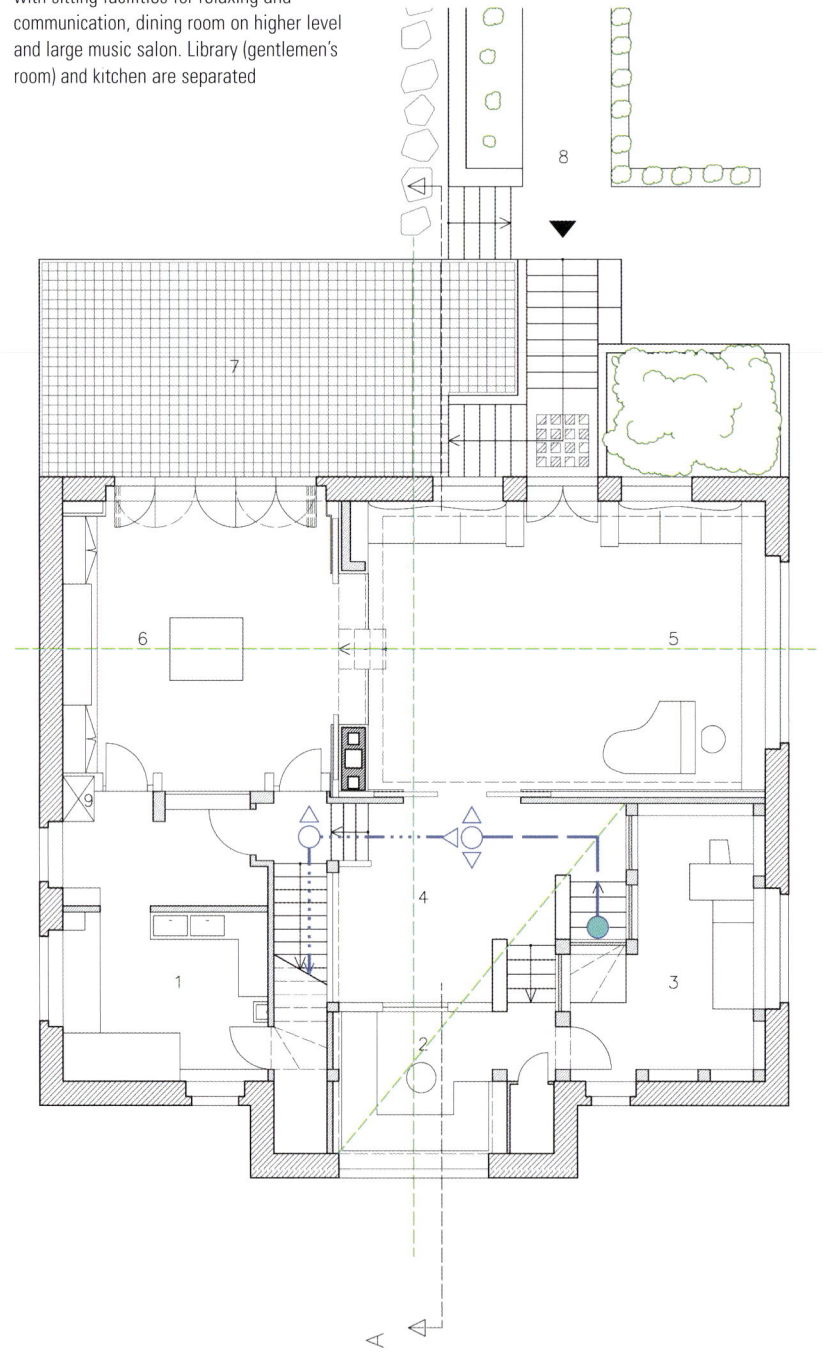

0   1        5

First floor
1 Room
2 Bath
3 Room
4 Bedroom
5 Dumb waiter
6 Balcony

Private rooms, partition walls as built-in
wardrobes. Hidden, narrow stair to top floor

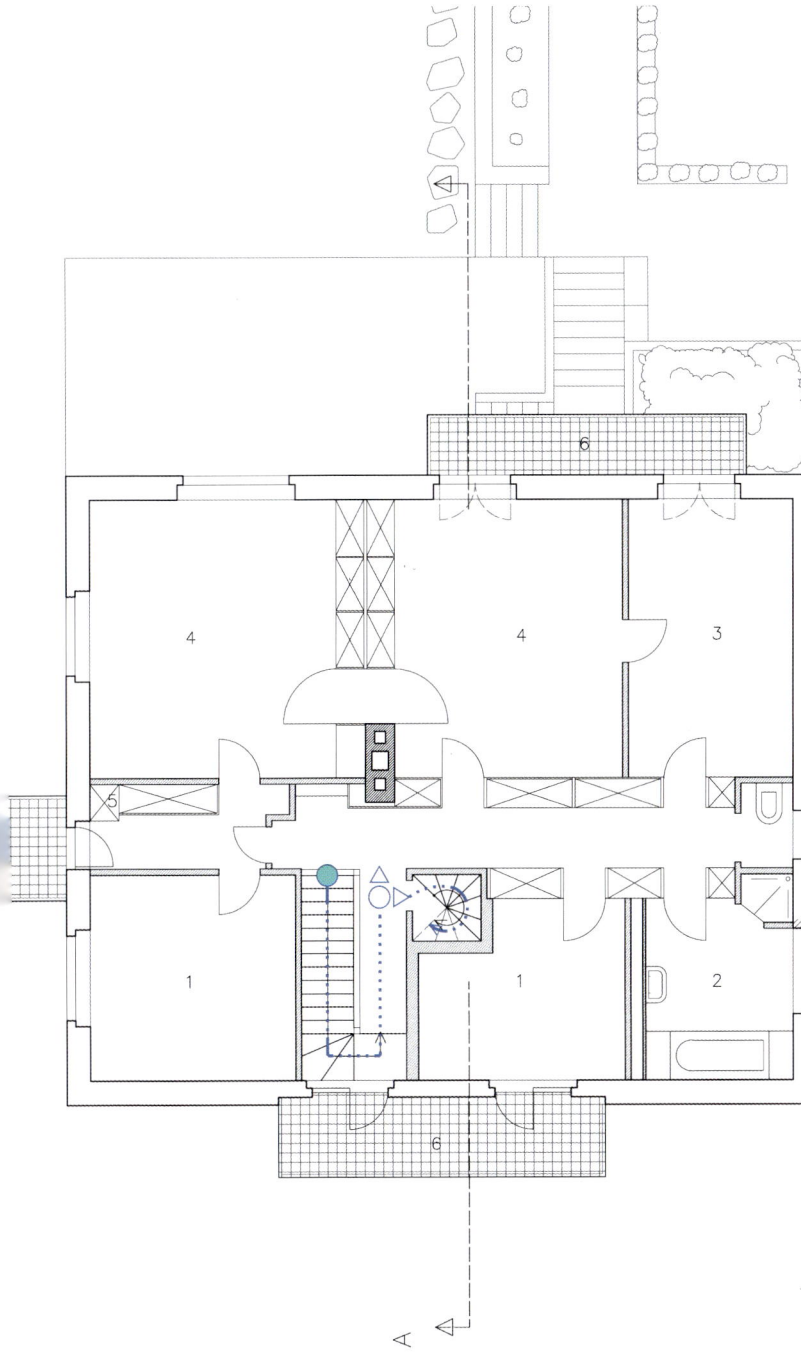

Top floor
1 Guest room
2 Atelier
3 Wc
4 Roof terrace
5 Dumb waiter

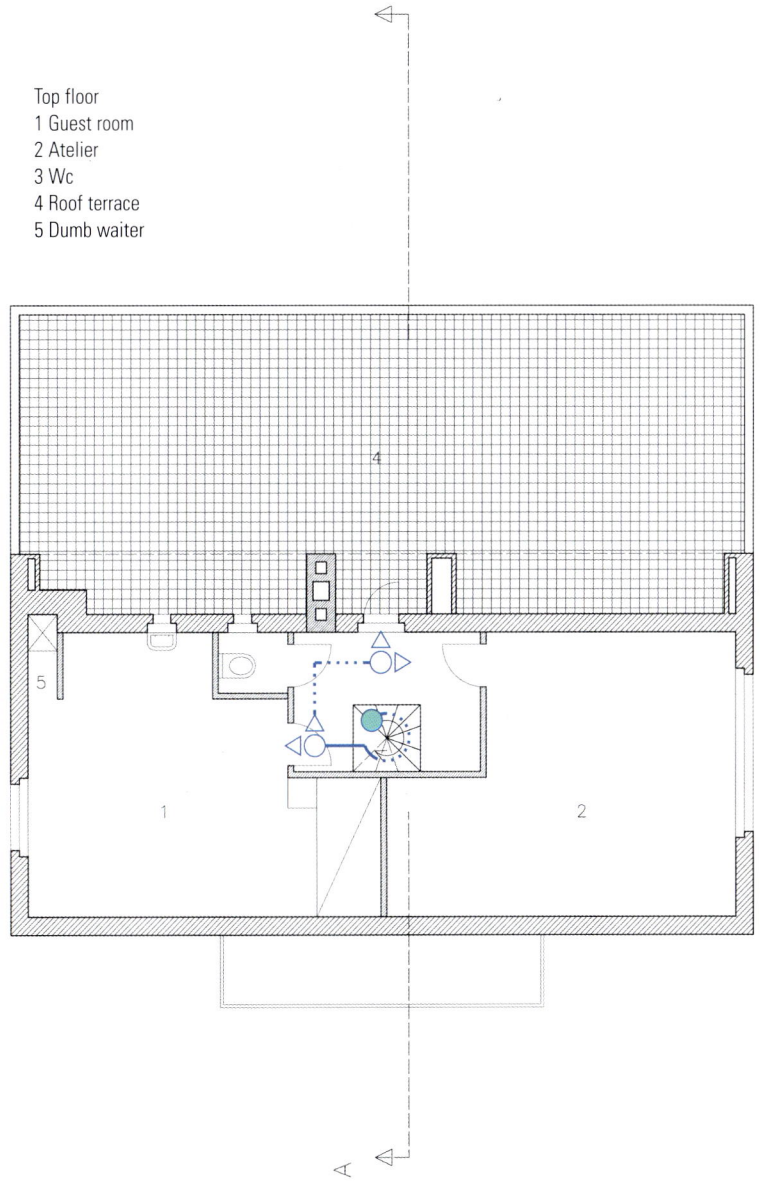

**241**

View from the landing in front of the dining
room towards the main hall. In the back the
loge and the entrance to the library

View from the loge in the bay towards the hall.
In the background, the music salon

View from hall to seating niche against the bay
window. Designed as a loge in a theatre with
the view of the inner landscape. On the right,
the open stair to first floor

Present view from dining room to the music
salon, which was originally without furniture

Present view from music salon to dining room,
the large stairs are not as originally designed.
Room separation facility with wall integrated
sliding doors

Detailed view to the sideboard with special
reflecting glass in the dining room

245

View from dining room to hall and stair to first floor. On the right side the horizontal sliding element as the direct connection to the kitchen

Present view in the library (gentlemen's room)

Archive picture of original situation. View from dining room to music salon. Strong influences of Japanese culture are visible in the interior design by Loos for this house. Some elements, like the wall cladding, are a direct design development from the Tzara House in Paris
Photo by M. Gerlach Jr., ca 1930
(ALA 3194)

The original connection between dining room
and music salon was with a very narrow stair
which can be folded out, an element strongly
influenced by Japanese culture
Photo by M. Gerlach Jr., ca 1930
(ALA 3191)

# Josephine Baker House

Paris

Josephine Baker
Saint Louis (Missouri) 3.6.1906 - Paris 12.4.1975
Dancer, singer, actress, civil-rights activist against
racism

**Class**
Villa; new construction project.
Not realized.
**Dimensions**
Base area: 26.5 x 12.55 m.
Room heights: vestibule: 7.8 m (from first
floor to skylight); grand salon: ca 4.3 m;
swimming pool corridor: 2.2 m.
Levels: 9.
Stories: 4.
Living area (without basement):
ca 840 sq m.

**Construction design**
Load-bearing outer walls with load-bearing
middle wall. Swimming pool is especially
supported.
*Raumplan*, with multiple height differences
on each floor.
**Materials**
Facade: natural stone covering; horizontal
stripes in black and white marble.
**Collaborators**
Zlatko Neumann and Kurt Unger.
**Work catalog no.**
H.191.27.P

Section DD
1 Bedroom
2 Swimming hall
3 Petit salon
4 Office
5 Kitchen
6 Housekeeper apartment
7 Room
8 Garage
9 Grand salon

Section through swimming pool which is at the
centre of the house. The water is illuminated
by strong daylight from above through a large
skylight and light through underwater
windows. The swimming Josephine Baker
would have been the performing attraction
of this house

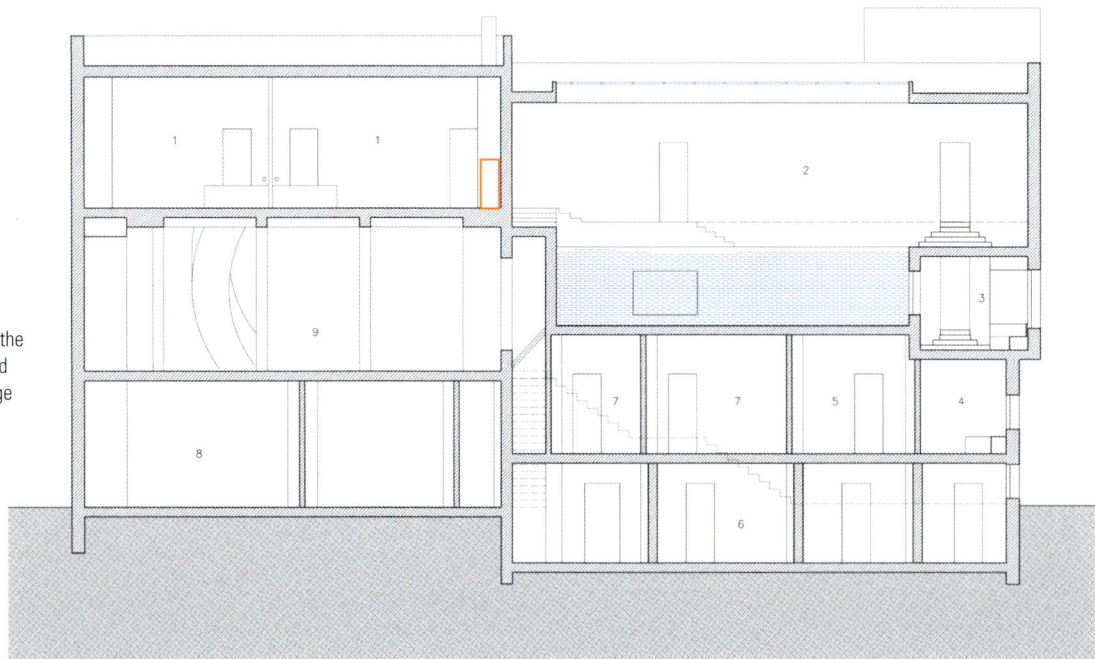

0   1   5

Original model from Loos' office. This is the
only unrealized project of Loos in this book,
because it is for me a fascinating project,
which shows impressively the staging effects
in the work of Loos
Photo by M. Gerlach Jr., ca 1930
(ALA 3145)

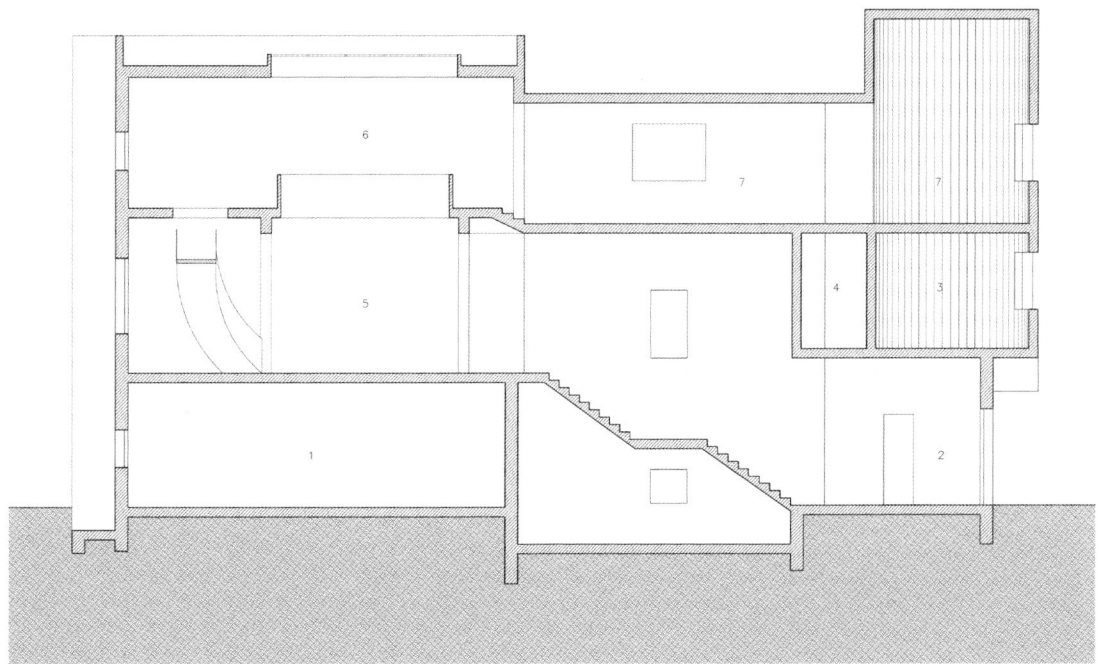

Section AA
1 Changing room
2 Entrance
3 Café
4 Office
5 Hall
6 Vestibule
7 Dining salon

Section through the entrance stairs
with the skylight over the hall

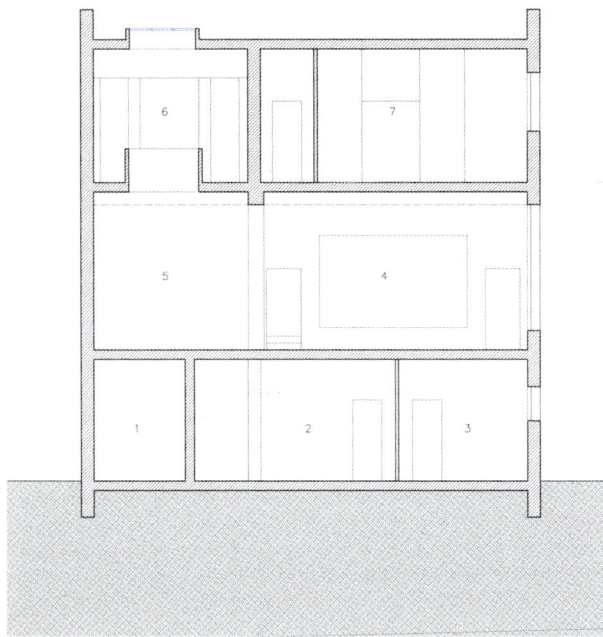

Level bedroom

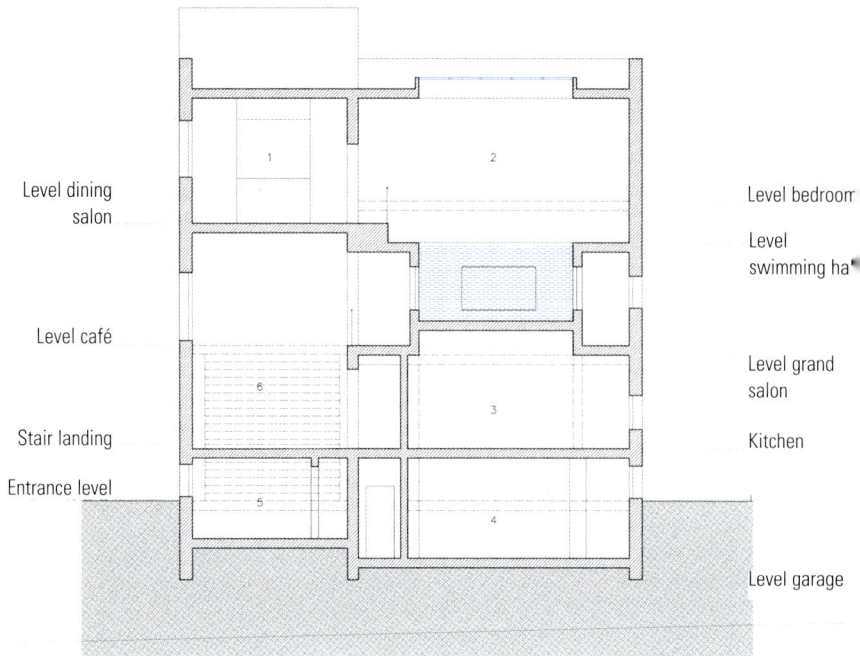

Level dining salon

Level grand salon

Level café

Level bedroom

Level swimming ha•

Stair landing

Level grand salon

Entrance level

Kitchen

Level garage

Level garage

Section BB
1 Changing room
2 Storage
3 Room
4 Salon
5 Hall
6 Vestibule
7 Bedroom

Section through hall and salon

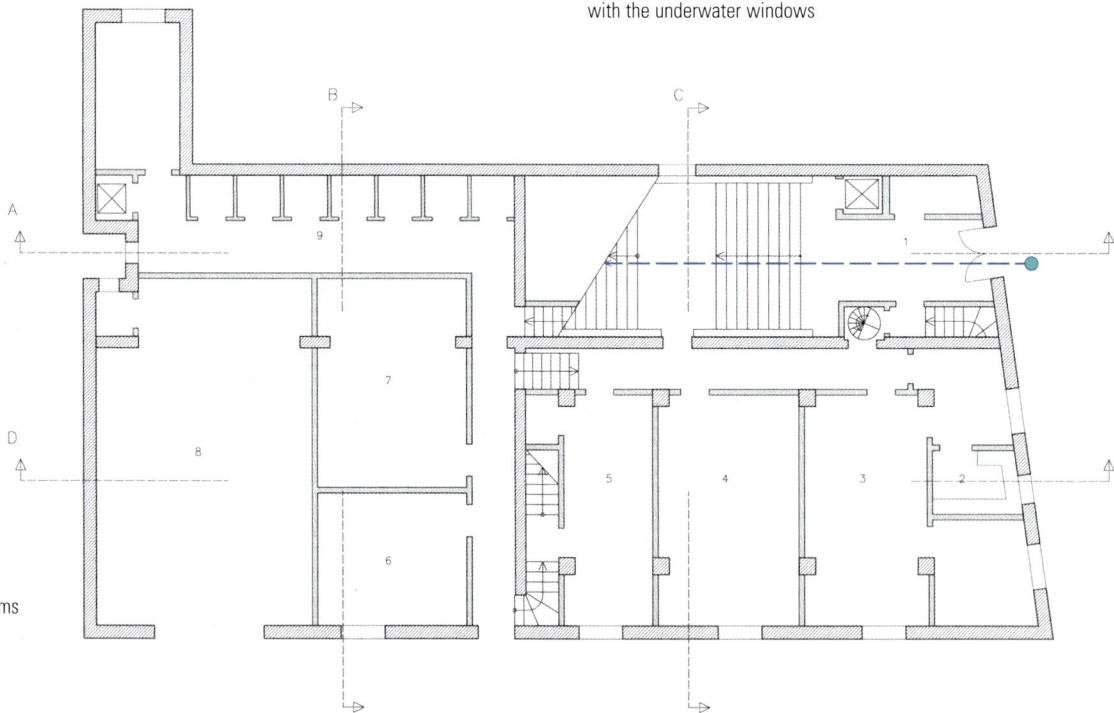

Section CC
1 Dining salon
2 Swimming hall
3 Kitchen
4 Housekeeper apartment
5 Cellar
6 Staircase vestibule

Cross section through swimming pool
showing the viewing gallery around the pool
with the underwater windows

0    1                    5

Ground floor
1 Entrance
2 Office
3 Kitchen
4 Room
5 Room
6 Room
7 Storage
8 Garage
9 Changing rooms

Entrance from street. Kitchen and
service rooms, but also dressing rooms
for showgirls and artists

0    1              5

First floor
1 Wardrobe
2 Hall
3 Office
4 Café
5 Petit salon
6 Swimming pool
   Underwater level
7 Grand salon

Representative floor with large hall and grand salon. No direct access to the swimming pool for guests is possible, the swimming objects can only be viewed from this underwater position by walking through the viewing gallery around the pool

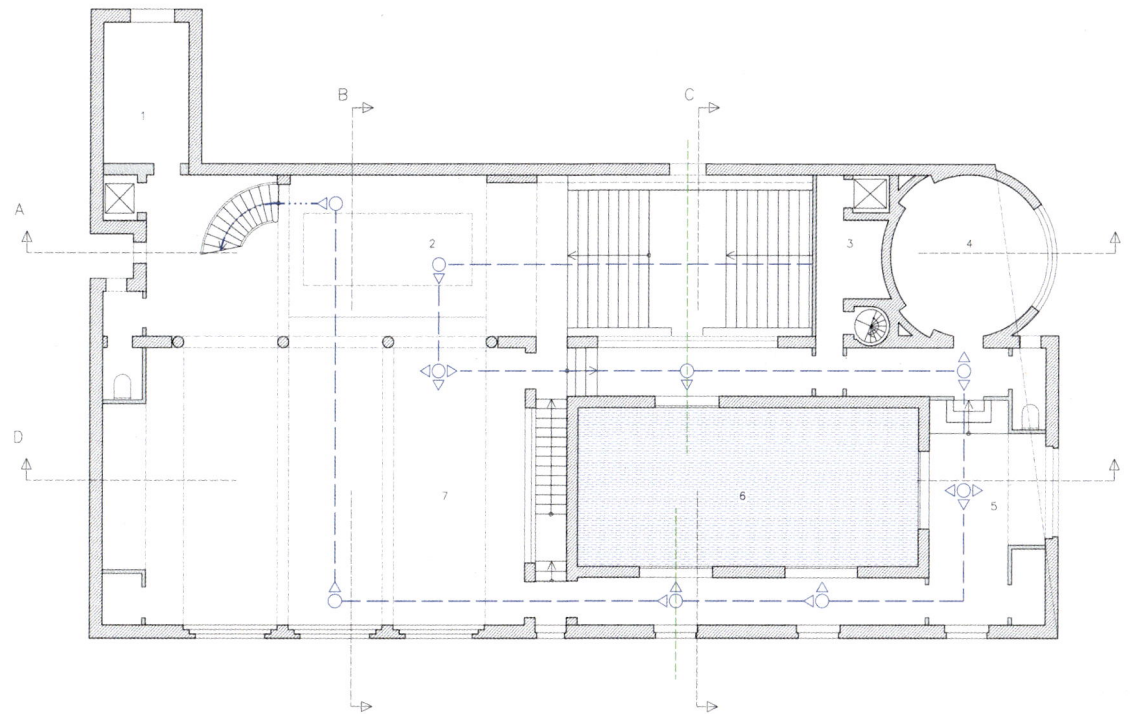

Second floor
1 Void + Skylight
2 Vestibule
3 Dining salon
4 Swimming hall
5 Swimming pool + Skylight
6 Bedroom
7 Bathroom

Private rooms with two bedrooms that are interconnected by sliding door elements. Direct access for Josephine Baker from her bed/dressing room to the swimming pool. Also a representative large dining salon on this level

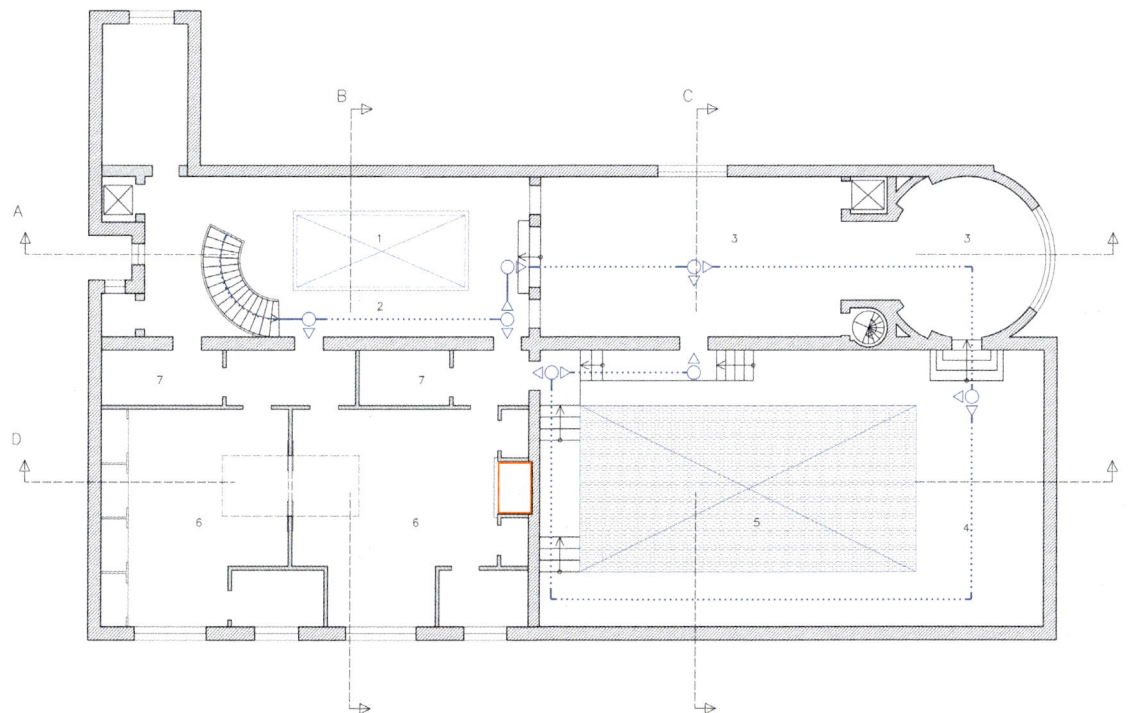

# Brummel House

Husgasse 52
Pilsen (Czech Republic)

Jan Brummel
Klatovy 21.12.1892 - Pilsen 13.9.1960
Merchant, timber trader, clerk
Otto Beck
Leo and Trude Brummel Apartment
(Pilsen/CZ, Fiedrichsplatz 26), 1929,
work cat. no. W.203.29
(Leo was Jan's brother and Trude was
Jana's sister)

Jana Brummel
1.07.1902 - Pilsen 25.02.1980
Nurse

## Class

Villa; reconstruction, and part new
construction with interior fit out.

## Type of construction / Construction design

Load-bearing solid brick outer walls with
a load-bearing solid brick middle wall with
wood-beamed ceilings and an arched brick
ceiling over the basement. New construction
with flat roof; existing gabled roof not
modified, the facade over the eaves
is merely elevated so that the pitched roof
could no longer be seen from the street.
Levels of the existing structure were
maintained in the extension. New building
part has one additional floor than existing
structure.
Continuos ceilings without height
differences.
Roof terrace on top of the new building part.

## Dimensions

Base area: 24.7 x 12.75 m.
Levels: 3.
Stories: 3.
Living area (without basement and ground
floor): ca 360 sq m.

## Materials

*Inglenook*
Floor: oak parquet covered with green felt
and on top Persian rugs.
Walls: dark oak paneling and cornices.
Yellow curtains hanging in front of
windows.
Ceiling: smooth plaster, painted white.
*Dining area with sideboard*
Floor: oak parquet covered with green felt
and on top Persian rugs.
Walls: smooth panels in poplar-root
plywood to door-height; above: dark green
English wallpaper; yellow curtains hanging
in front of the windows. Wall above
sideboard completely mirrored. In wall
cladding integrated painting opposite
window side.
Columns: smooth panels in poplar-root
plywood to room-height.
Ceiling: smooth plaster, white painted.
*Mother's living room*
Floor: parquet covered with green felt
and on top Persian rugs.
Walls: in primary colors, colorfully lacquered
softwood furniture (yellow bookshelves, red
lacquered hexagonal table with embedded
marble plate); vermilion lacquered radiators;
above the height of the benches, pale blue
smooth softwood paneling with a white
horizontal strip of wood on top. Above: dark
colored wallpaper with geometrical pattern.
Ceiling: smooth plaster, white painted;
extended down to the upper border of the
wallpaper strip.
Additional: open fireplace in brickwork,
free-standing in the room with no visible
chimney.
*Mother's bedroom*
Floor: oak parquet covered with green felt
and on top with Persian rugs.
Walls: light wall covering in ash wood.
All built-in furniture in light ash wood (wall
cabinets, work area in front of window).
Bed is imbedded as a pull-out element in
the wall, so that this room can also be used
during the day and for entertaining guests.
Yellow curtains hang in front of the
windows.
Ceiling: smooth plaster, painted white.

## Work catalog no.

H.193.28

Present view from street

Street facade showing the compostion
by Loos with the transformed existing house
and the new building volume

Section AA
*Jan and Jana Brummel residence*
1 Court
2 Garage
3 Salon
4 Dining room
5 Room
6 Roof Terrace

*Jana's mother apartment*
7 Living room
8 Ladies room

Section through existing building and new building volume by Loos, with the flat on the first floor for the Brummel family. From the newly erected building part leads a stair to the rooms on the second floor and to the roof terrace on top with a shower

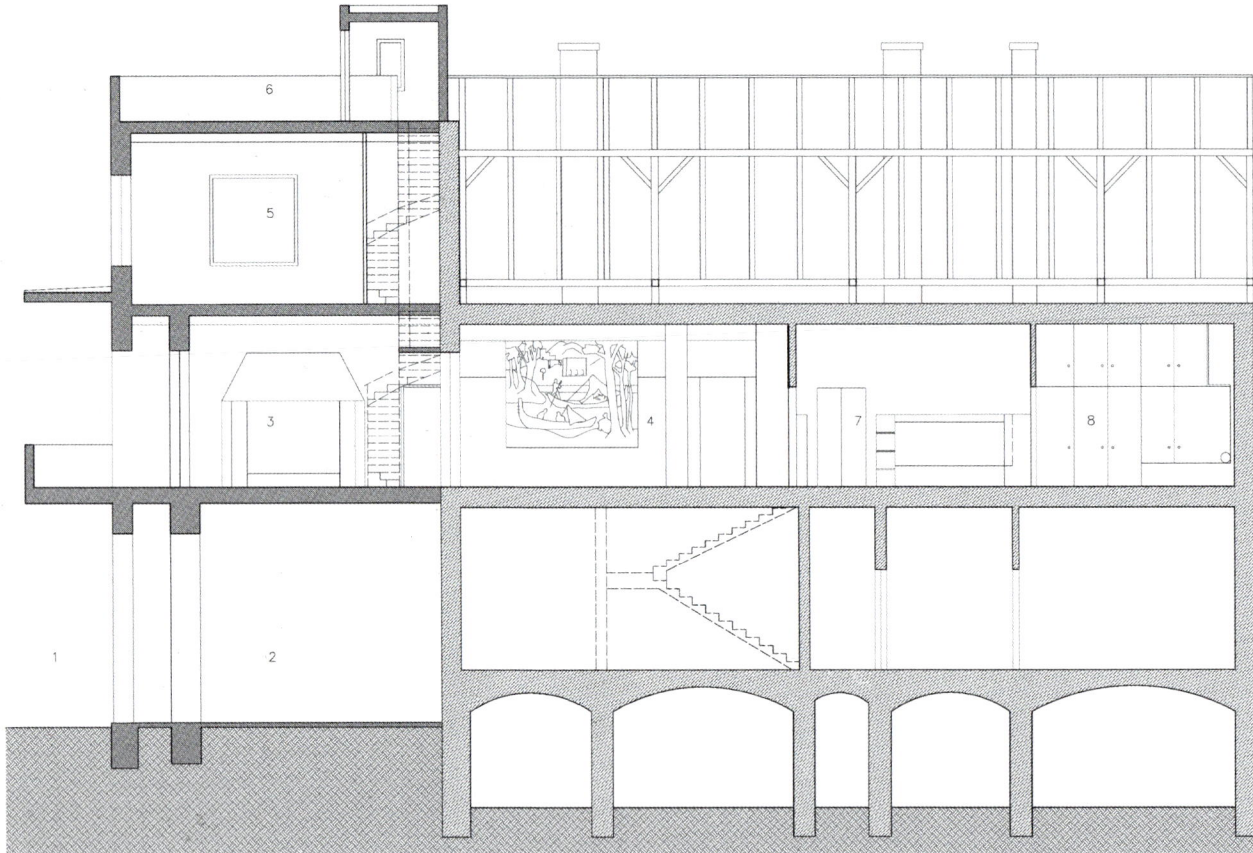

The fireplace, a copy of French original. Other copies exist in the shop of F.O. Schmidt, Vienna, and in the Duschnitz Villa (see pp. 184-93)

First floor
*Jan and Jana Brummel residence*
1 Master bedroom
2 Bathroom
3 Cloakroom
4 Salon
5 Dining room

*Jana's mother apartment*
6 Living room
7 Ladies room

*General*
8 Kitchen
9 Hall

Apartment of Jan and Jana Brummel and her
mother Hedvica Liebstein. Ms Liebstein resided
in rooms 6 and 7 (Floor plan based on
reconstruction drawings by Arch. Girsa)

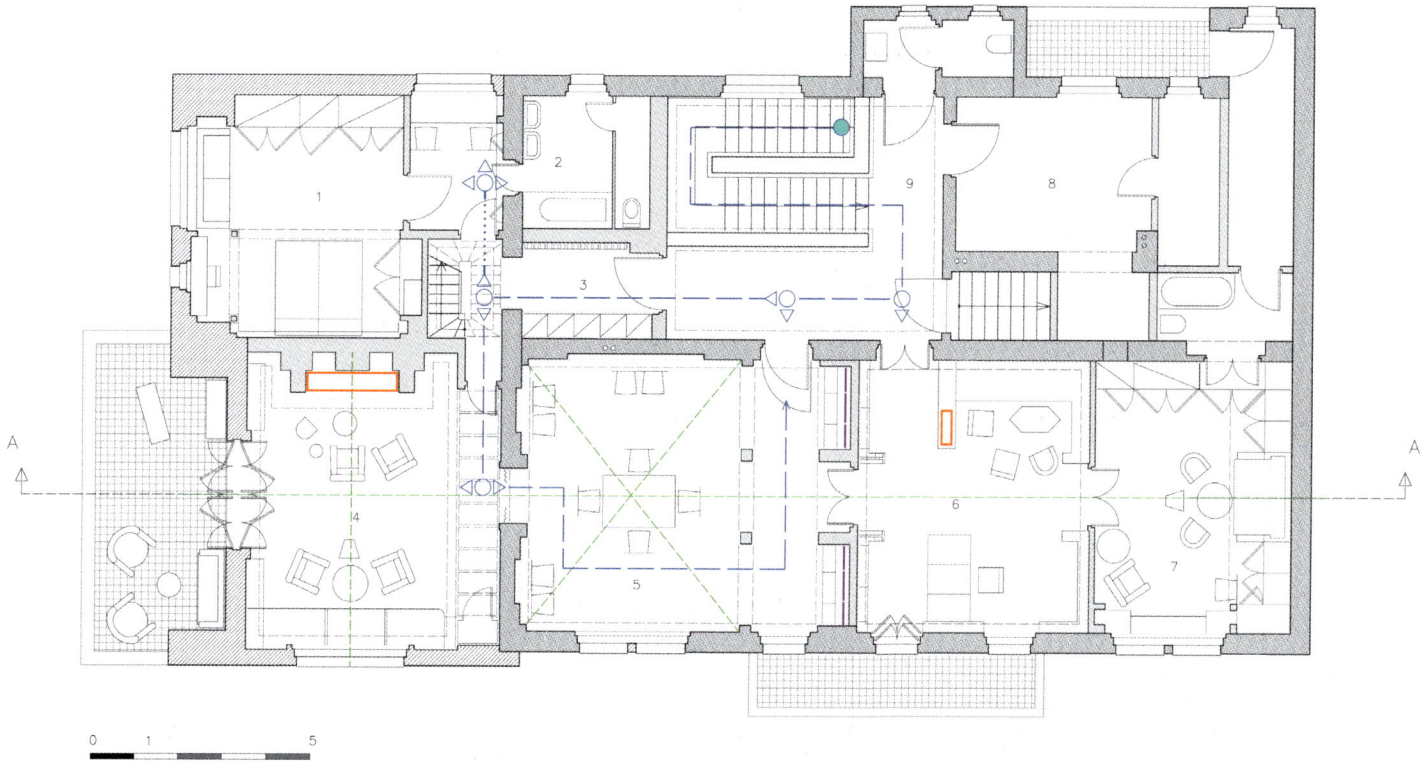

0    1         5

Master bedroom. Bed in a cove with lower
ceiling. Integrated desk for the woman in front
of a small window. Day-bed under large
window
Photo by M. Gerlach Jr., 1930
(ALA 3151)

Living room of Jana Brummel mother. Wall
claddings and fixed furniture in this room in
strong colors (yellow, blue, red). Free standing
fireplace without vertical connection
Photo by M. Gerlach Jr., 1930
(ALA 3148)

Dining room with view to the living room
of Jana's mother. Wall mirrors over sideboard
and door create the illusion of space
Photo by M. Gerlach Jr., ca 1930
(ALA 3150)

View from dining room to salon. Wall painting
by Aigner on recommendation of Loos. For Loos
this landscape painting must be strong enough
to substitute the outside view on the large
industry area opposite the house
Photo by M. Gerlach Jr., ca 1930
(ALA 3147)

Detailed view of dining room with interior
columns, which are reflected by wall mirrors
creating an effect of duplication
Photo by M. Gerlach Jr., ca 1930
(ALA 3149)

# Müller Villa

Stresovicka 842
XVIII Prague

Frantisek Müller
Pilsen 3.12.1889 - Prague 20.12.1951
Building contractor, co-owner of building company
Kapsa & Müller
Dr. Lumir Kapsa Villa (Prague VII, Dejvice
Na Presypu 7), 1929, work cat. no. H.200.29
"The last house", project for M. Müller, 1933,
work cat. no. H.237.33.P

Milada Müller, born Kratka
Died in Prague 8.9.1968

**Class**
Villa; new construction and interior fit out.
**Type of construction / Construction design**
Rectangular cube with load-bearing solid brick outer walls and four load-bearing middle supports in reinforced concrete.
Flat roofs designed as roof terraces, only flat roof over top floor is not for use.
Ceilings and stairways are in reinforced concrete.
*Raumplan.*
**Dimensions**
Base area: 12.40 x 18.25 m.
Levels: 11.
Stories: 5.
Living area (without basement): ca 440 sq m.
**Materials**
*Living-hall*
Floor: oak parquet covered with Persian rugs.
Walls: Cipollino de Saion, marble from the Rhone Valley green-white veined; other surfaces smooth plaster, white painted; yellow curtains.
Ceiling: smooth plaster, painted white.
Further: built-in sofa, violet upholstery; built-in fireplace in brickwork; built-in aquarium
*Dining area*
Floor: oak-parquet floor covered with Persian rugs.
Walls: mahogany, glossy lacquered.
Curtains: yellow.
Radiators: vermilion.
Ceiling: squared coffered mahogany panels, glossy lacquered.
*Boudoir (ladies room)*
Floor: oak-parquet floor covered with light wall-to-wall carpet and above Persian rugs.
Walls: polished lemon wood.
Curtains: yellow.
Ceiling: smooth plaster, painted white.
*Study and library (gentlemen's room)*
Floor: oak-parquet floor and Persian rugs above.

Walls: polished mahogany wall covering integrating bookshelves and wall cabinets.
Curtains: yellow.
Ceiling: white painted with polished mahogany beams.
Furniture: red-brown leather seat trimming.
Fireplace: Delft tiles.
*Japanese summer dining room*
Floor: wine red, arched woven rice mats.
Walls: Japanese pressed grass wallpaper silver painted, with emerald-green edge molding, Japanese color woodcuts.
Black and green lacquered built-in furniture.
Ceiling: smooth plaster, painted white.
Furniture: wicker chairs by Prag-Rudniker.
**Collaborators**
Karel Lhota.
**Work catalog no.**
H.194.28

Garden facade
Big windows of main hall with Japanese pattern in the fanlight

View from street of entrance and east facade.
East facade is covered by Japanese ivy,
according original garden design drawings
by Camillo Schneider

East facade
Basic order of side elevation starting from
a line of symmetry. Covered by Japanese ivy

Section AA
1 Garage
2 Salon
3 Bedroom
4 Pantry

*Raumplan*-structure, section through the salon,
open stairway and service staircase, showing
also the different terrace levels

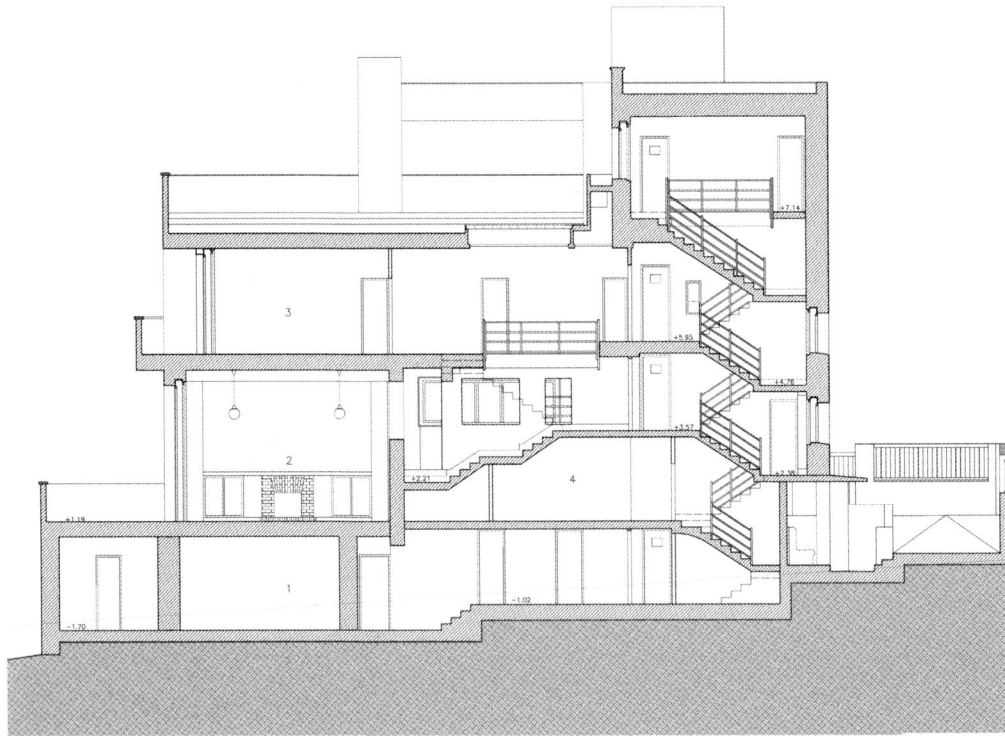

South facade
Entrance elevation with decorative set back at
the left corner to have the staircase windows
in the line of symmetry

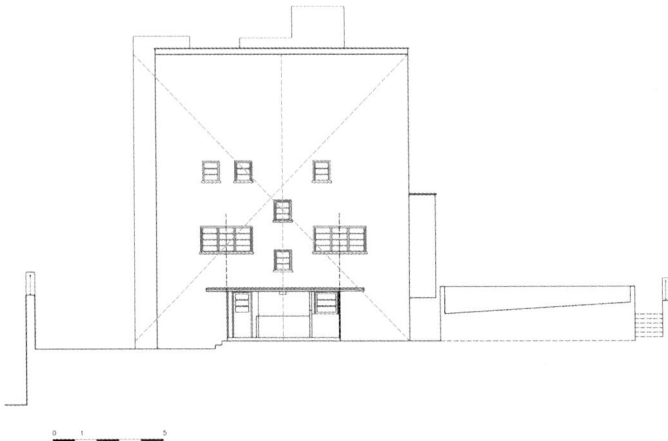

West facade
Side elevation with a basic order starting
from the line of symmetry

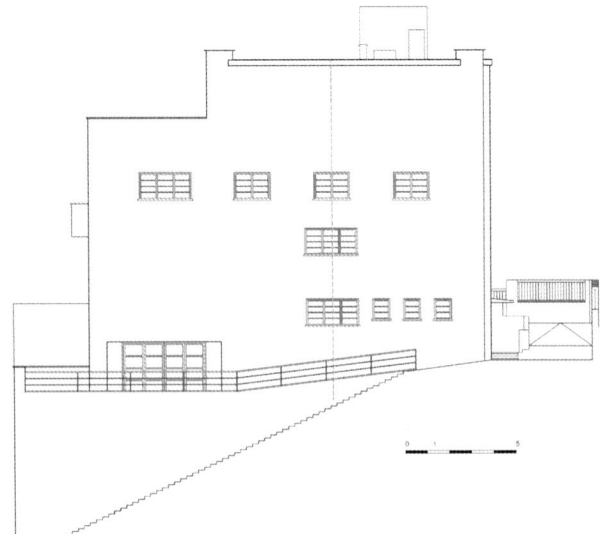

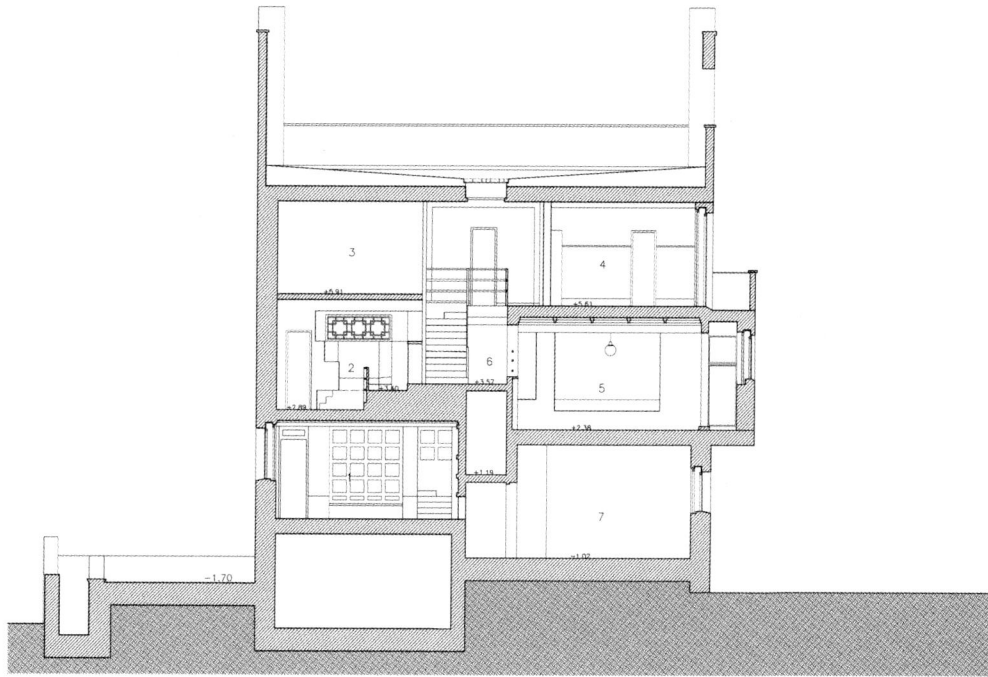

Section BB
1 Cloakroom/Vestibule
2 Boudoir
3 Guest room
4 Child bedroom
5 Dining room
6 Pantry
7 Washing/Drying room
8 Roof and terrace

Cross section through dining room and boudoir
(ladies' room) showing the low ceiling
vestibule below

North facade
Garden elevation

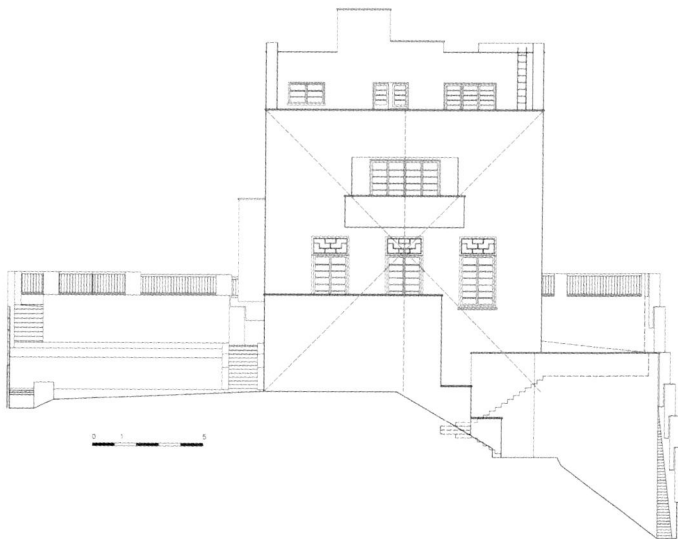

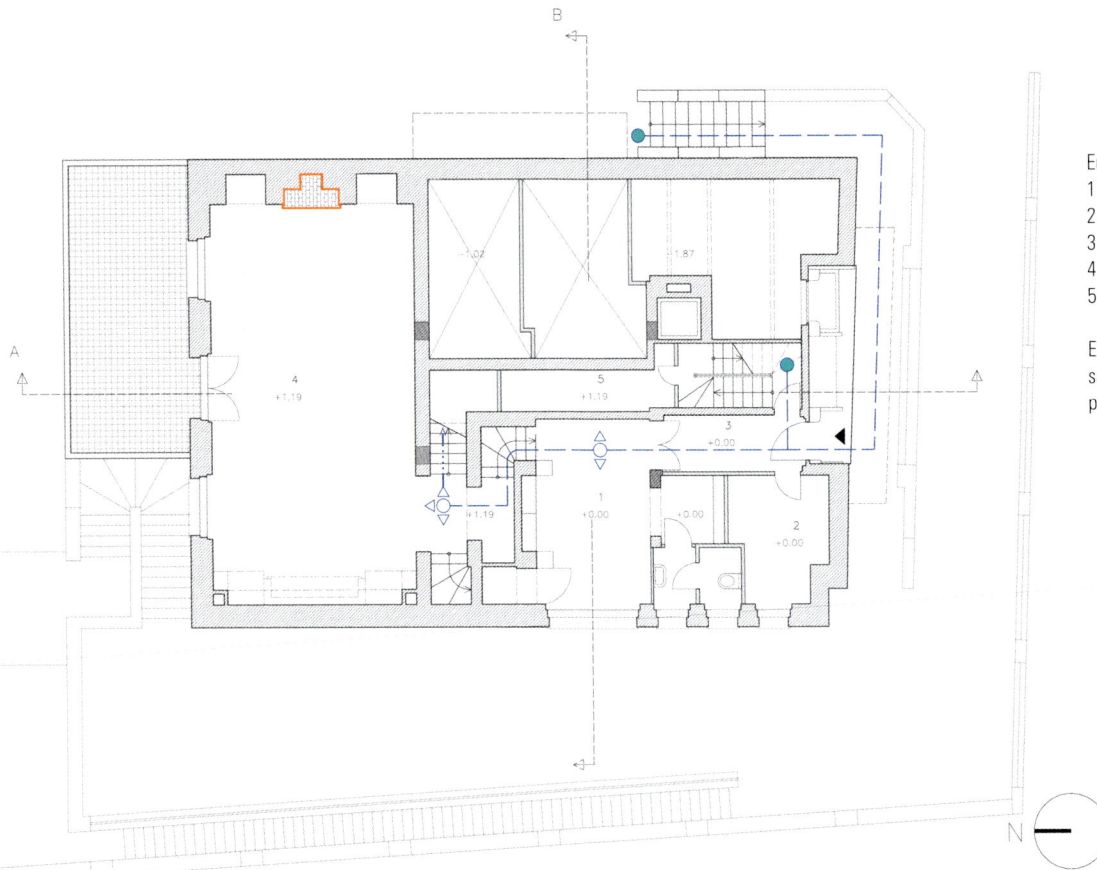

Entrance level
1 Vestibule
2 Cloakroom
3 Chauffeur
4 Salon
5 Pantry

Entrance with vestibule and steps up to the salon. Niche outside for sitting bench and plant pot beneath entrance

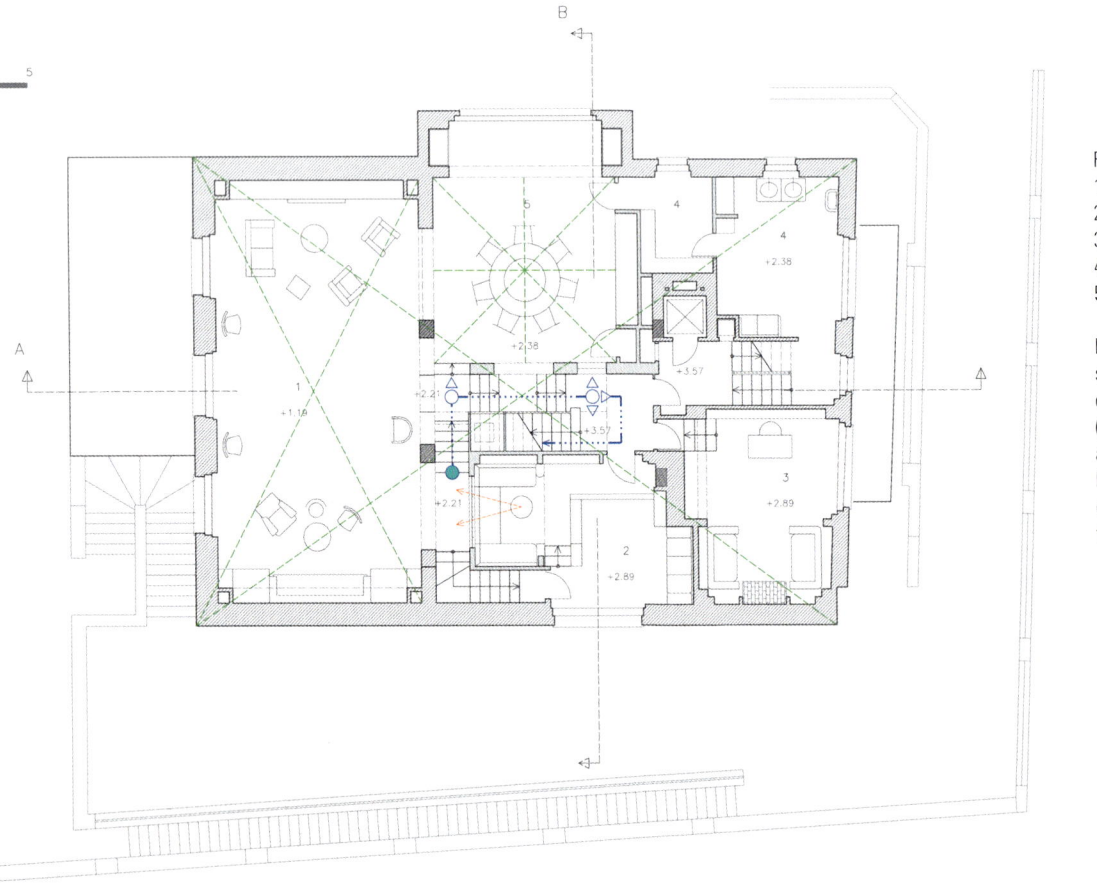

Raised ground floor
1 Salon
2 Ladies' room/Boudoir
3 Gentlemen's room/Library
4 Kitchen
5 Dining room

Main level. Concept of living space: salon with sitting facilities for relax and communication, dining room on higher level. Library (gentlemen's room), boudoir (ladies' room) and kitchen are separated. Control of the salon by the interior window in the boudoir. The lady of the house has from her room her own stairs for access to the salon

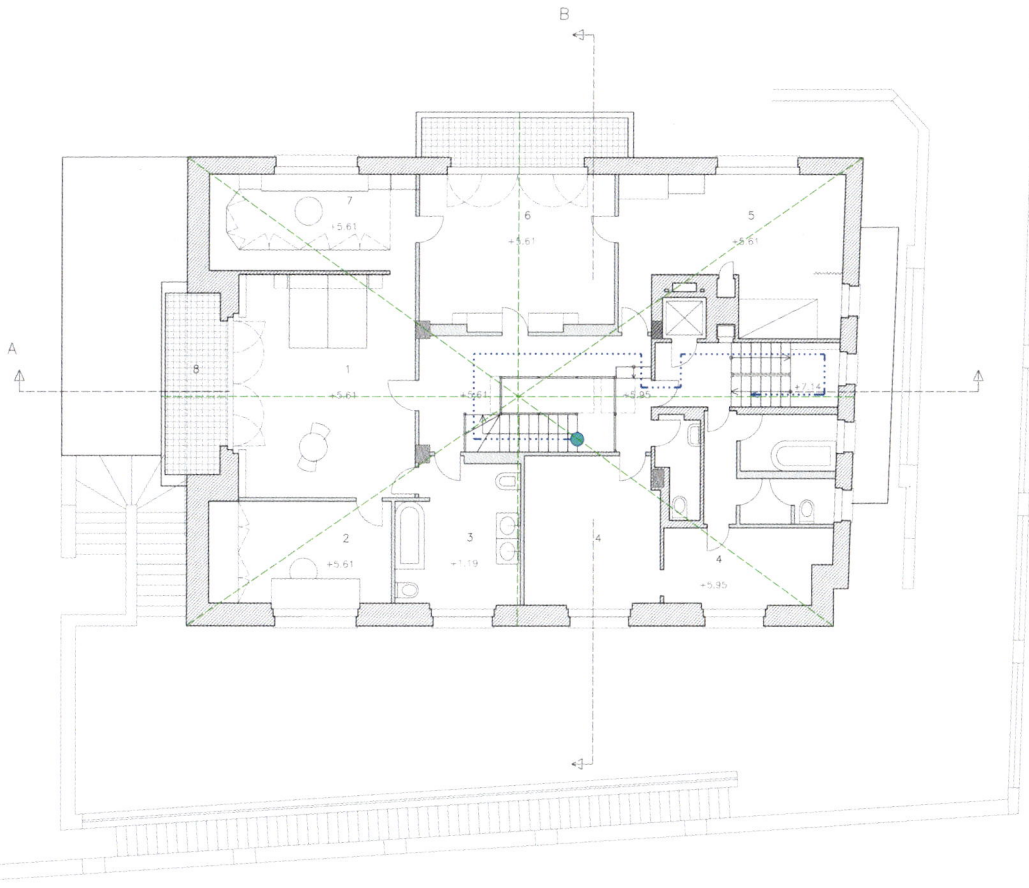

First floor
1 Master bedroom
2 Man's dressing room
3 Bathroom
4 Guest apartment
5 Child room
6 Child day room
7 Lady's dressing room
8 Balcony

Private rooms with separate guest apartment

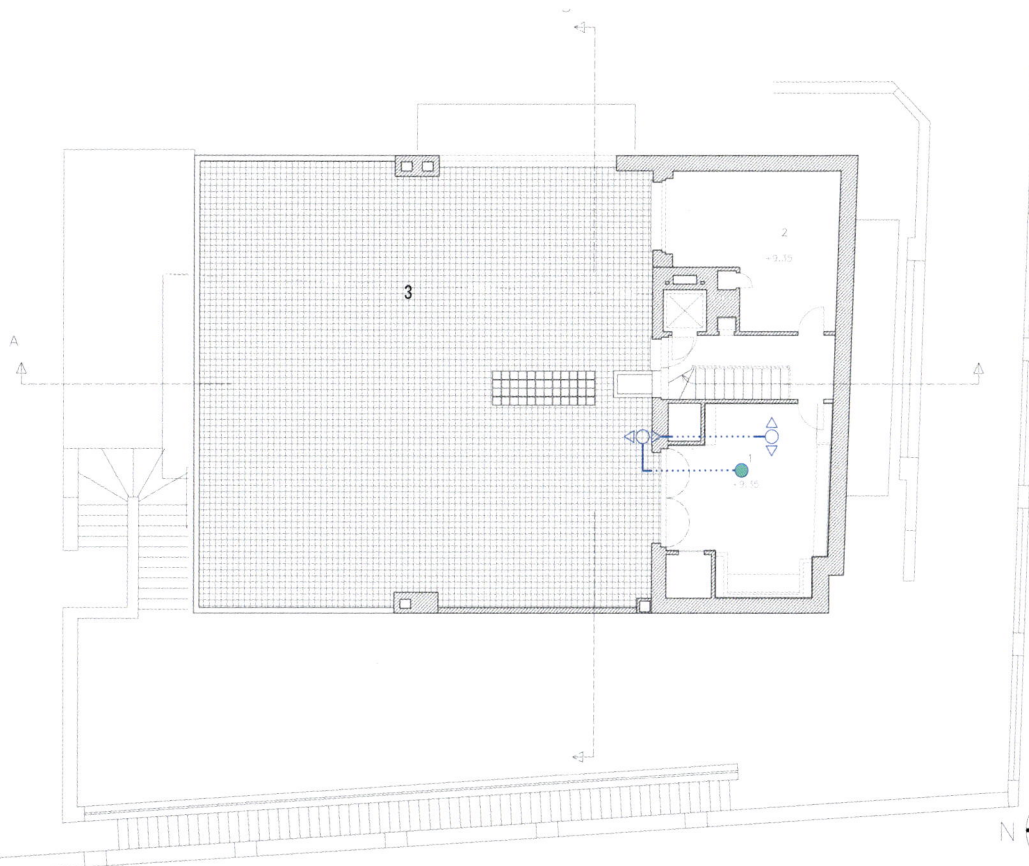

Second floor
1 Summer dining room (Japanese room)
2 Darkroom for photography
3 Roof terrace

Entrance niche with an outdoor bench in
travertine. On the right, plant pot; on the left,
main entrance door

Vestibule on entrance level with dark blue
ceiling. Opening to stairs leading to the main
hall. Very low room height

View from entrance corridor to vestibule and stairs to salon. At the wall large high glossy green emailed ceramic tiles

View in salon to the fireplace with the original
furniture selected by Loos and his client.
Landscaping painting at the wall

"'Here'," he said, 'will be the bright aquarium. [...]
No one understands him. The client wants to pull him
aside, there are important things to discuss. The owner's
favorite place will be here; when he comes home in the
evening tired from work, he'll watch the mute play of
the fish. All the colors will shimmer in the lamplight."
(cit. in C. Loos-Beck, *Adolf Loos - privat*, 1936, p. 20)

View in salon of opposite side with original
furniture selected by Loos and his client.
Landscaping paintings at the wall. Window
above and stair are the connections to boudoir

"There the plates lie on long tables, but they're gray and colorless! I'm disappointed. Loos laughs. They haven't been polished yet. Look at that! He himself gets water and pours it over the gray stone. It's a miracle! The green marble lights up in a deep, dark green; blue, violet, reddish-yellow veins run through it in gentle waves. *It looks like the sea.*"
(cit. in C. Loos-Beck, *Adolf Loos - privat*, 1936, p. 38)

268

View from salon to dining room

View from dining room to open stair to first floor. The left door of the wall cupboard provides access to the kitchen

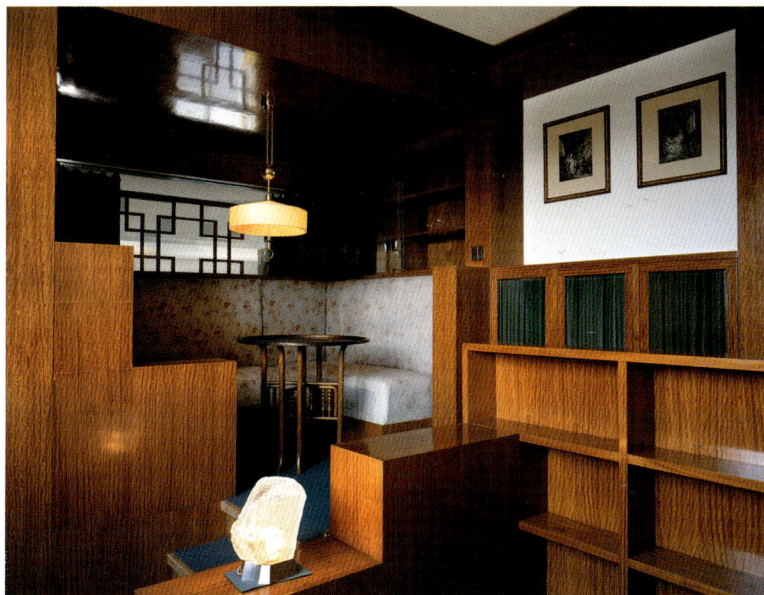

Boudoir higher part, view to salon

Lady's dressing room with white desk
and pale timber wardrobes and wall covering.
Dressing room of the gentleman on the
opposite side of the master bedroom in dark
and hard timber with black inlays on
the surface of his desk

Boudoir lower part with day bed and chair
for relax

View from the working desk of Frantisek
Müller in library

View from open stairway on first floor to master bedroom

Master bedroom. Curtains, wallpaper and the daycover of the bed in the same textile material. Soft and intimate atmosphere

View into Japanese summer dining room on top floor with window to roof terrace

# Khuner Country House

Kreuzberg near Payerbach (Austria)

Paul Khuner
Vienna 6.2.1886 - 3.11.1932
Director of food producing company
Paul Khuner Apartment (1040 Vienna,
Möllwaldplatz 4), 1907, work cat. no. W.57.07
Khuner Garden House (Kreuzberg near Payerbach,
Niederösterreich), 1929-1930, work cat.
no. H.199.29

Hedwig Khuner, born Sommer
Vienna 20.1.1886 - New York August 1974

Section BB
1 Terrace
2 Hall
3 Fireplace
4 Pantry
5 Bathroom
6 View gallery (for breakfast)

Main central hall for living activities with
coves and gallery around. Roof terrace over
traditional gabled roof

**Class**

Country house; new construction and fit out.

**Type of construction / Construction
design**

Basement in quarried stone construction,
above outer walls and the two interior
load-bearing walls: wood block construction.
Interior partition walls: 7 cm strong plaster
planks.
Ceilings: wood-beamed ceilings with
timberboard lining; the pipework for
the bathrooms is above the beams, hence
these surfaces are raised in level.
The wood beams above the ground floor
each protrude 50 cm laterally and the
external wall of the second floor is shifted
outward to this measure; in the interior,
the beams cantilever beneath the lateral
projecting corridors. Central, two-story
living-hall with differentiated room heights
in the adjacent areas.
Flat gabled roof with zinc plate covering
designed as a purlin roof, above all at
the rear a roof terrace.

**Dimensions**

Base area: 16.15 x 19.1 m.
Levels: 6.
Stories: 4.
Living area (without basement and roof
floor): ca 430 sq m.

**Collaborators**

Heinrich Kulka; landscaping: Grete Salzer.

**Work catalog no.**

H.198.29

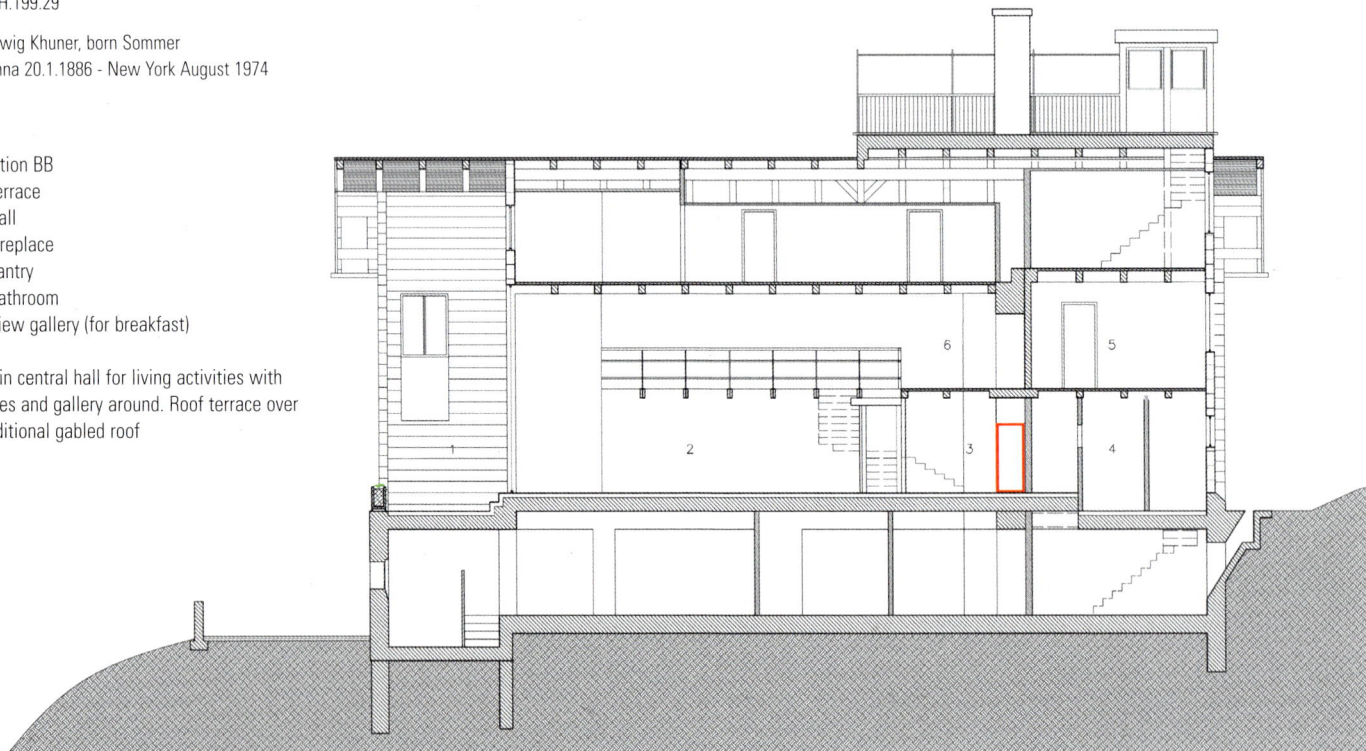

Present view of north facade with large
window opening in front of hall. Terrace
balustrade designed for plants

Terrace in front of hall is lowered by 3 steps, so that it is possible to sit inside and look over the balustrade

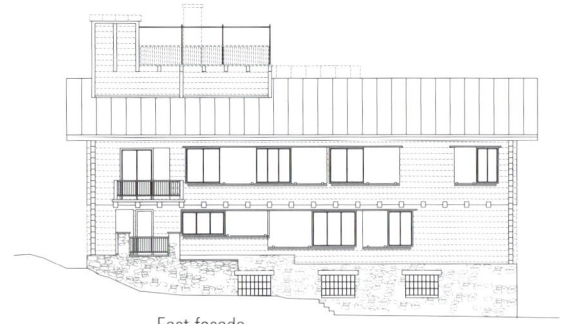

East facade

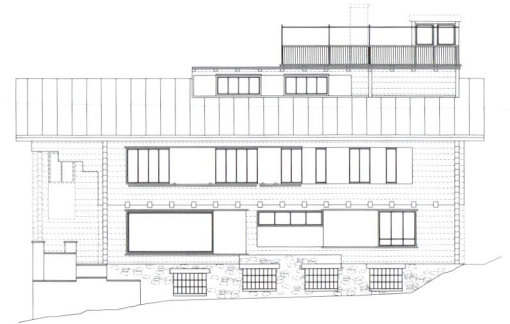

West facade

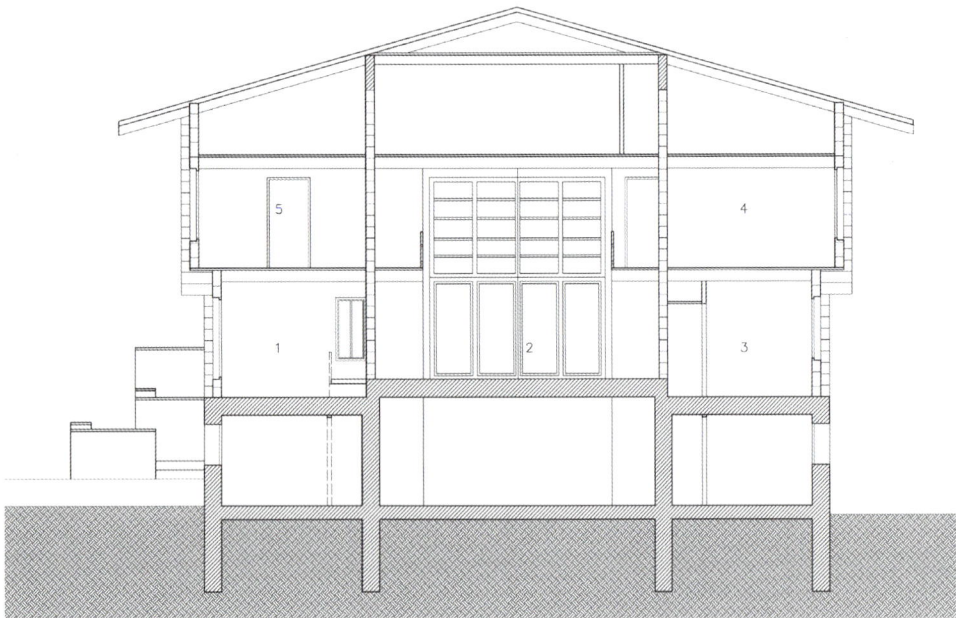

Section AA
1 Gentlemen's room
2 Hall
3 Host
4 Gentlemen's room
5 Son's room

Cross section through hall with front window, that could completely open, with panoramic view of the Alps

0   1                    5

North facade

South facade

Present view of hall with panoramic window

Raised ground floor
1 Entrance
2 Ski room
3 Pantry
4 Kitchen
5 Dining room
6 Library (gentlemen's room)
7 Terrace
8 Host
9 Bathroom
10 Host
11 Vestibule
12 Hall
13 Inglenook

Main level. Concept of living space: hall with piano and sitting facilities for relaxing and communication; dining area and inglenook in a cove. Library (gentlemen's room), vestibule with stairs and kitchen are seperated

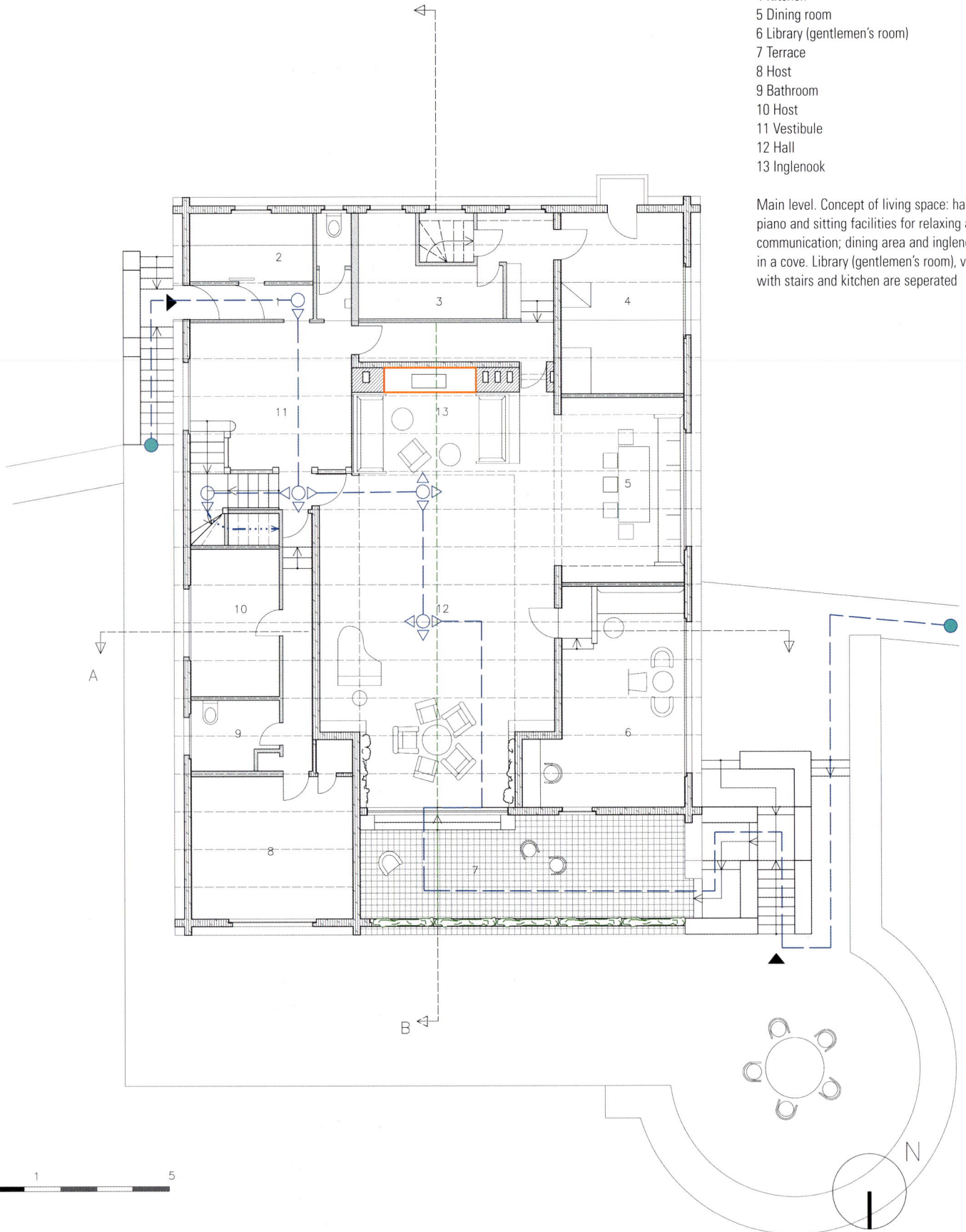

A

B

0    1              5

N

First floor
1 Daughter's room
2 Daughter's room
3 Son's room
4 Host
5 Lady room
6 Gentleman room
7 Housemaid
8 Housemaid
9 Bathroom
10 View gallery (for breakfast)
11 Void

Private rooms accessed by open gallery
to hall

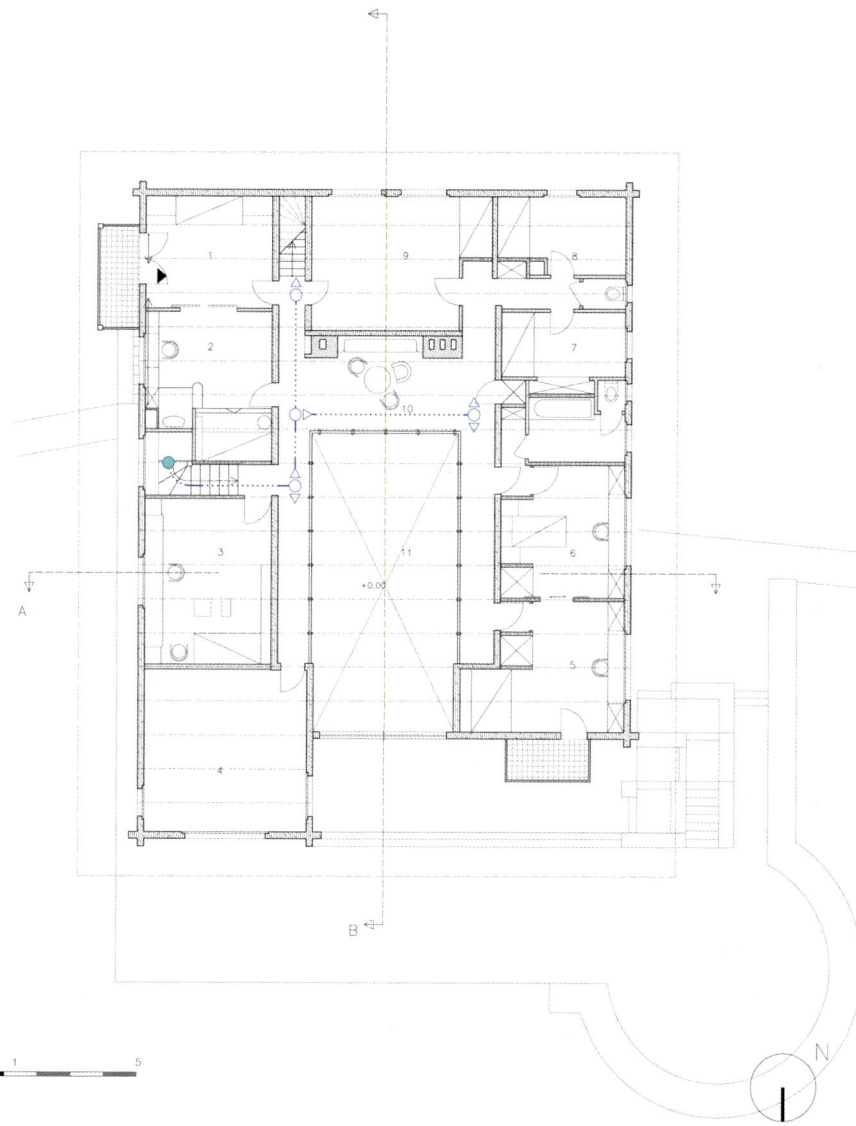

Attic floor

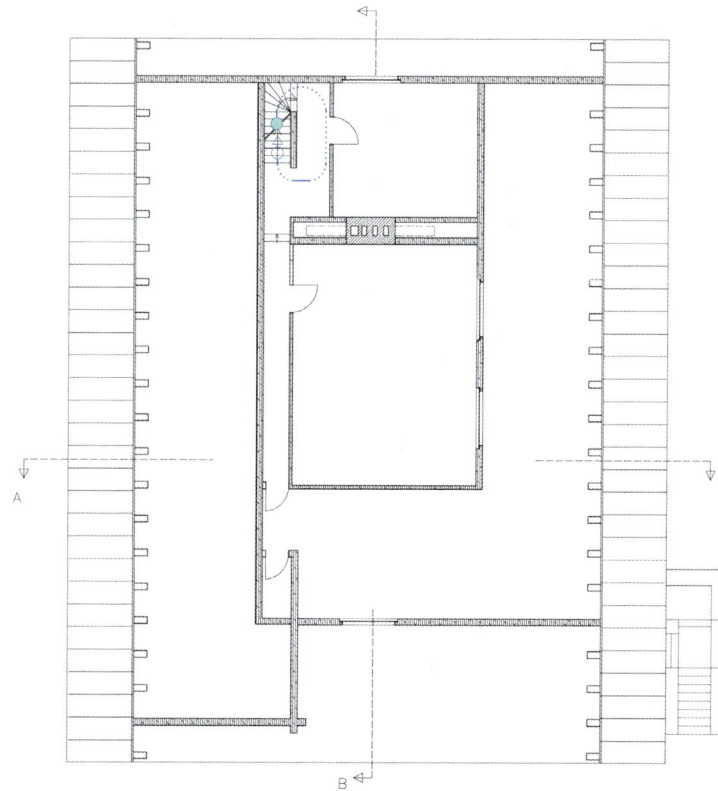

Present view in hall towards inglenook

View in ladies' bedroom, with cove for the bed. Wall covering with references to Japanese culture

View in daughters' room with cove for the bed. Wall covering with references to Japanese culture (grass wallpaper)

View from the gallery towards the hall
with cove for dining and inglenook
Photo by M. Gerlach Jr., ca 1930
(ALA 3174)

"Loos begins to speak before a photo from the Khuner
house. He pulls a matchbox from his pocket: 'Look,'
he cries, 'this is modern architecture! The house of
the future won't be made of reinforced concrete, that has
to be blown up with picric acid to remove it – like what
happened at the last exhibition in Paris – the house of the
future will be made of wood! Like little Japanese houses!
It has sliding walls! Modern architecture is: Japanese
culture plus European tradition!'"
(cit. in C. Loos-Beck, *Adolf Loos - privat*, 1936, p. 104)

View in library (gentlemen's room)
Photo by M. Gerlach Jr., ca 1930
(ALA 3169)

Entrance vestibule with stairs to first floor
Photo by M. Gerlach Jr., ca 1930
(ALA 3167)

# Semi-detached House in Werkbund Settlement

Woinovichgasse 19
1130 Vienna

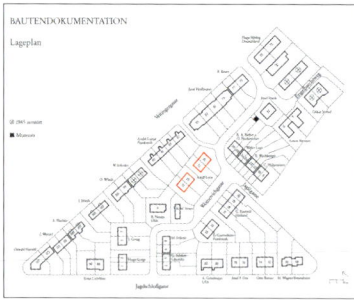

Werkbund Settlement
Organization: Österreichischer Werkbund;
general coordination Arch. Josef Frank
Client: GESIBA - Gemeinwirtschaftliche
Siedlungs-u. Baustoffanstalt

**Class**
Settlement semi-detached house;
new construction and interior fit out.
**Type of construction / Construction design**
Load-bearing solid brick walls with concrete ceilings.
Only outer walls are load-bearing.
Chimneys are integrated into the house dividing walls.
Gallery is constructed with a very thin concrete slab.
Flat pent roof.
*Raumplan.*

**Dimensions**
Base area: 12.40 x 7.60 m (duplex);
6.20 x 7.60 m (house unit).
Clear room heights: living area:
ca 4.00 m; top floor: 2.40 m; entrance,
gallery: ca 1.95 m; kitchen: ca 2.25 m.
Levels: 5.
Stories: 4.
Living area (without basement):
ca 95 sq m.
**Collaborators**
Heinrich Kulka
**Description**
See Chapter 6 "Settlements".

**Work catalog no.**
H.208.30

South facade

Street and garden elevations of semi-detached houses with two stories at the front and three stories at the back

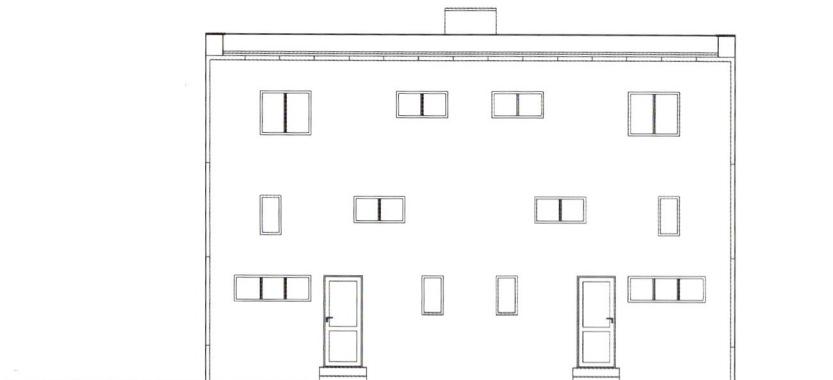

North facade

Present view to street facade with large
window opening in front of living hall. Terrace
balustrade designed for plants

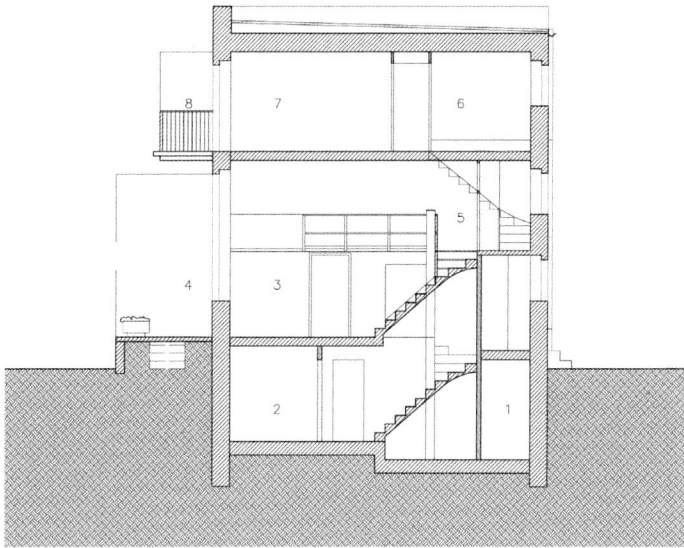

Section BB
1 Heating/Cellar
2 Storage
3 Dining/Living room (Hall)
4 Terrace
5 Gallery
6 Bedroom
7 Bathroom
8 Terrace

Cross section through hall with front window,
and open gallery in mezzanine

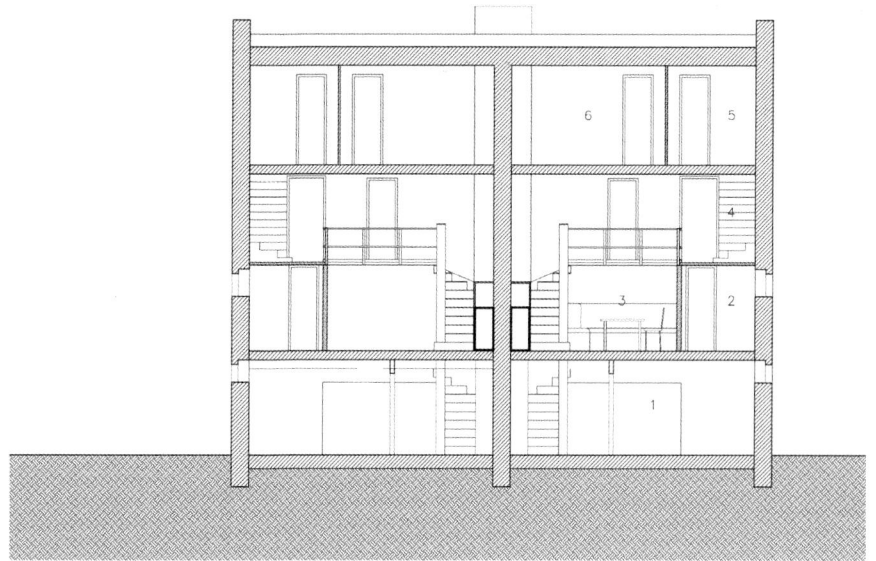

Section AA
1 Laundry-storage
2 Anteroom
3 Dining/Living room
4 Gallery
5 Child bedroom
6 Bedroom

Section through hall with lower entrance
vestibule and open gallery above

Present view to garden facade with kitchen
entrance. Facade covered with Japanese ivy

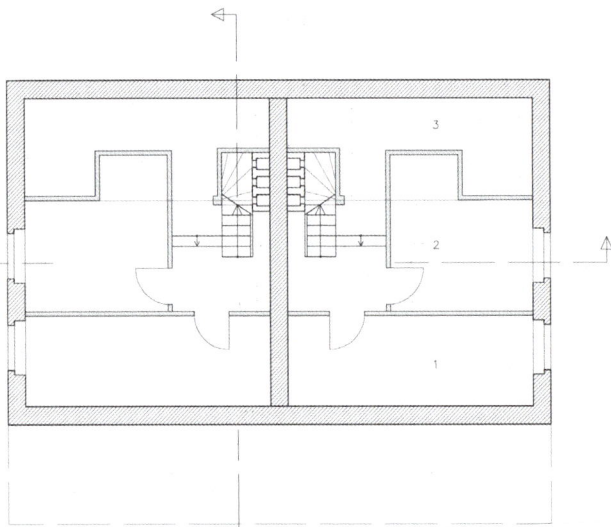

Basement
1 Storage
2 Laundry storage
3 Heating/Cellar

Storage and utility rooms

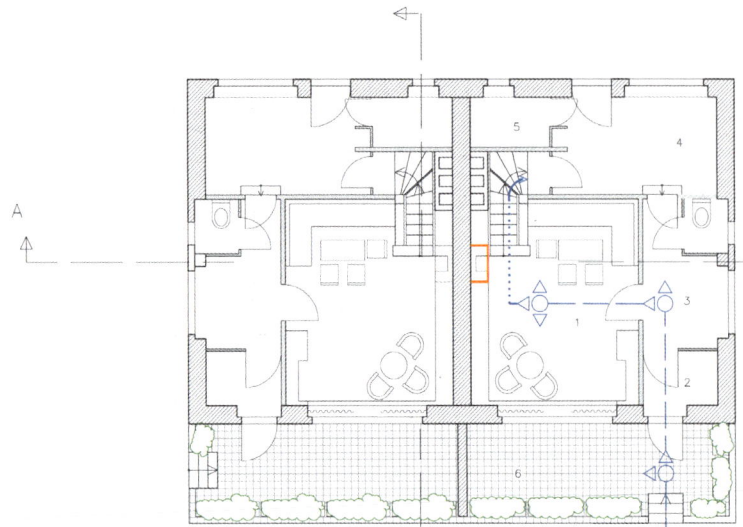

Ground floor
1 Dining/Living room
2 Vestibule/Wardrobe
3 Anteroom
4 Kitchen
5 Pantry
6 Terrace

Main level. Concept of living space: hall with sitting facilities for relaxing and communication, dining area, fireplace and open stairs to first floor. Vestibule and kitchen are separated

Present view of hall with fireplace and dining area

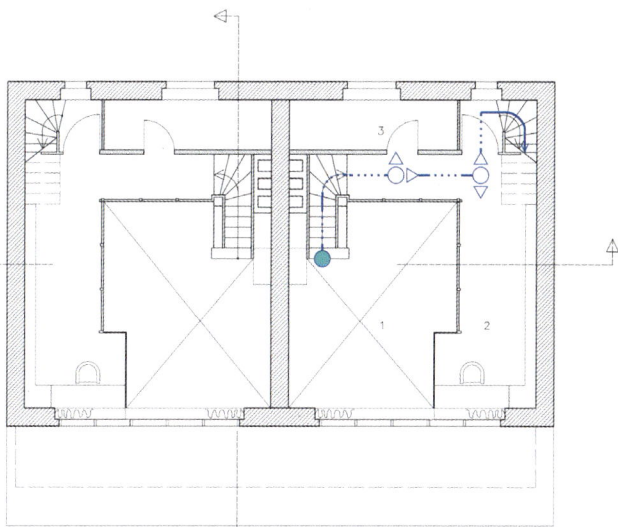

First floor
1 Void
2 Gallery
3 Small room

Open gallery to hall

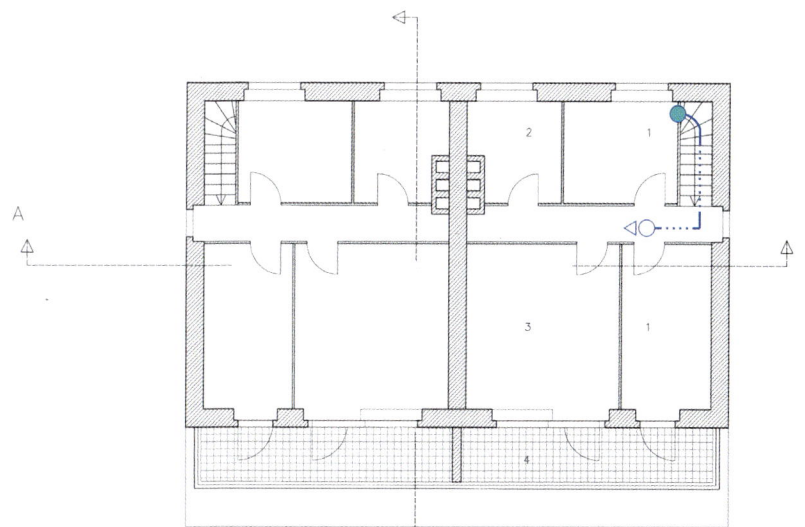

Top floor
1 Child bedroom
2 Bathroom
3 Bedroom
4 Terrace

Private rooms

0    1                    5

Gallery with upholstered contemporary
furniture

Present view of hall from gallery

# Mitzi Schnabl House

Flachsweg 27
1220 Vienna

Mitzi Schnabl
Kärnten 1885 - died after 1955
Houskeeper of Adolf Loos

Friedrich Schnabl
Carpenter

**Class**

Settlement house; new construction.

**Type of construction / Construction design**

Planned: without basement; executed: with full basement.

Originally planned as wood-frame construction; but erected in solid brick construction, the ceilings are wood-beamed.

Overhanging on all sides, a very flat-pitched roof, originally planned as a wood cement roof.

Ceilings with small height differences, originally planned: floor of the living area lowered by a step and the bedroom above it raised by a step in order to gain approximately 30 cm in height for the central living area.

**Dimensions**

Base area: 5.13 x 8.27 m (Loos' plan); 5.61 x 8.6 m (actual construction).

Clear room heights: living area: ca 2.5 m; first floor: 2.54 m.

Levels: 3.

Stories: 3.

Living area (without basement): ca 80 sq m.

**Materials**

No interior decorating carried out by Loos.

**Work catalog no.**

H.216.31

North facade

0   1                5

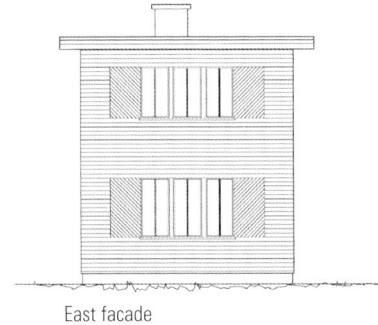

East facade

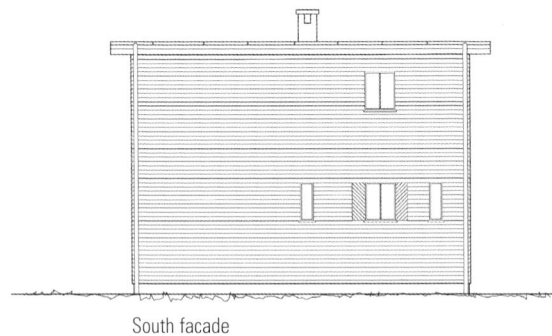

South facade

West facade

Simple box originally designed by Loos in structural timber and timber cladding. Designed as a personal gift by Loos to his longtime housekeeper Mitzi Schnabl

Present view of the house which was built
after Loos died. Construction in brick with
render facade, volume is lifted up because
of the river Danube possible floods

Present view of garden facade

Section AA
1 Cooking/Dining/Living room
2 Vestibule
3 Bedroom
4 Bedroom

Cross section through original design with
a higher living space

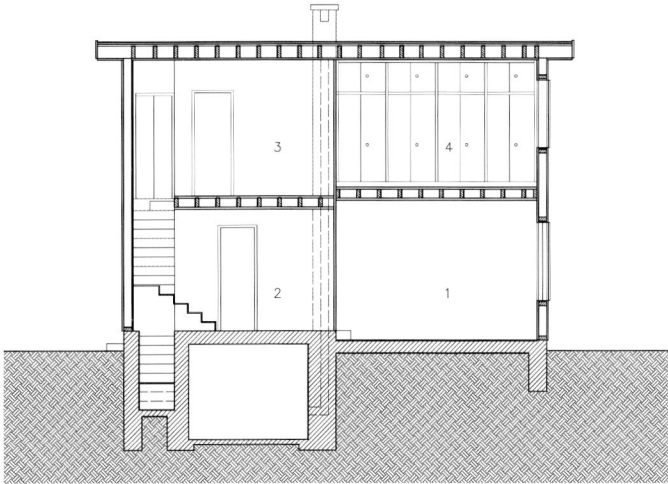

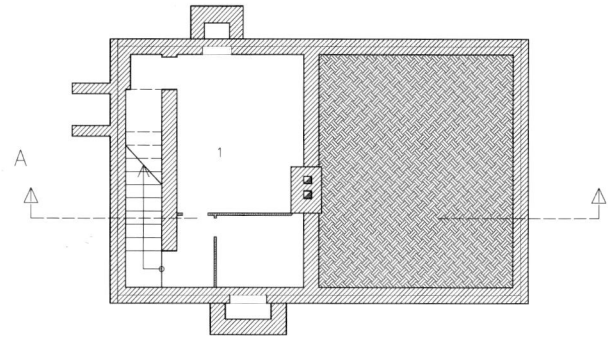

Basement
1 Cellar/Heating/Storage

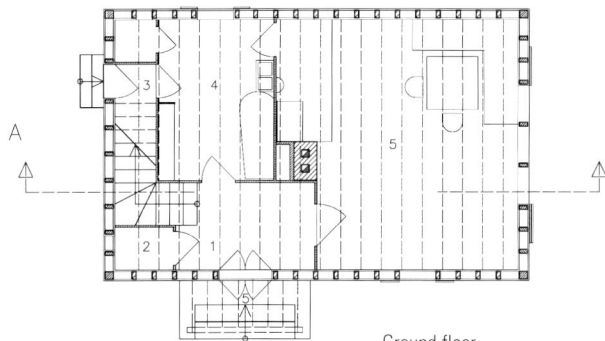

Ground floor
1 Vestibule
2 Wc
3 Pantry
4 Bathroom/Sink/Kitchen
5 Cooking/Dining/Living
6 Entrance

Concept of living space: cooking/dining/living
combined in one central room. Stairs and
a combined kitchen/bathroom are separated

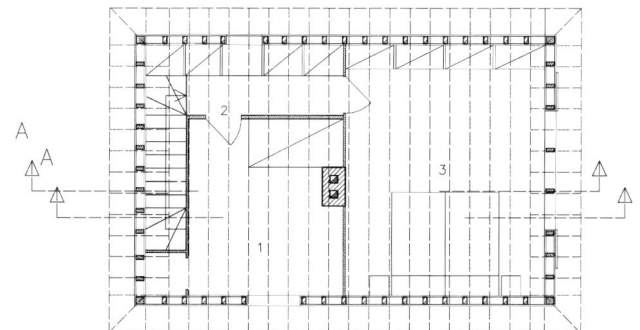

First floor
1 Bedroom
2 Corridor with wardrobe
3 Bedroom

Private rooms

# Annexes

# Chronological List of Loos' Works*

*From Burkhardt Rukschcio, Robert Schachel,
*Adolf Loos - Leben und Werk*, Residenzverlag,
Wien-Salzburg 1987 (2nd ed.), pp. 675-76.

*Works legend*
R = Realised
P = Project only
E = Existing
EP = Existing partly
NP = Not proved

**1897**
1
Ebenstein Tailor Shop (R)
**1898**
2
Goldman & Salatsch Men's Fashion Salon (R)
3
Furnishings for Eugen Stössler (R)
4
Theater for 4000 persons I (P)
5
Kaiserjubiläums-Gedächtniskirche St. Elisabeth
(P)
**1899**
6
Café Museum (R/E)
7
Dr. Hugo Haberfeld Apartment (R)
**1900**
8
Residential building in Brünn (R)
9
Vienna Women's Club (R)
10
Furnishings for Dr. Otto and Auguste Stoessl
Apartment (R)
11
Hugo and Lilly Steiner Apartment (R)
12
Gustav and Marie Turnowsky Apartment (R)
13
Zionist Settlement (P)
14
Theater (P)
**1901**
15
K.K. Priv. Allgemeine Verkehrsbank (previously
Czjzěk exchange office) (R)
**1903**
16
Villa Karma (R/E)
17
Leopold Langer exchange office (R)
18
Adolf Loos Apartment (R/EP)
19
Clothilde Brill Apartment (R)
20
Jakob Langer Apartment (R)
21
Dr. Leopold Langer Apartment (R)
22
Dr. Leopold Langer Apartment (R)
23
Michael Leiss Apartment (R)

24
Ferdinand Rainer Apartment (R)
25
Elisa Reitler Apartment (R)
26
Dr. Gustav Rosenberg Apartment (R)
**1904**
27
Villa Chance (P)
28
Steiner Ornamental Plumage Shop I (R)
29
K.K. Priv. Allgemeine Verkehrsbank, Neubau
affiliate (R)
30
Emanuel and Berta Aufricht Apartment (R)
31
Alfred Sobotka Apartment (R)
32
Moritz Fuchs Apartment (R)
33
H. and Elsa Gall Apartment (R)
34
Dr. Karl Gombrich Apartment (R)
35
N.N. and Annie Wagner-Wünsch Apartment
(R)
36
Georg and Else Weiss Apartment (R)
37
Apartment business premises of
K.K. Priv. Allgemeinen Verkehrsbank (P)
**1905**
38
Hedwig Kanner Apartment (R)
39
Alfred Kraus Apartment (R)
40
Carl Reininghaus Apartment (R)
41
Dr. Hermann and Dr. Eugenie Schwarzwald
Apartment (R)
42
Dr. Ludwig and Clothilde Schweiger Apartment
(R)
43
Josef Wertheimer Apartment (R)
44
Dr. Rudolf Türkel Apartment (R)
45
Theater for 4000 II (P)
46
Wilhelm Beer Villa (P)
47
Mountain house (P)

**1906**
48
Showroom for Siemens & Halske company (R)
49
Steiner Ornamental Plumage Shop II (R)
50
Office of Arthur Friedmann (R)
51
Arthur and Leonie Friedmann Apartment (R)
52
Dr. V. Groser Apartment (R)
53
Emmy Piringer Apartment (R)
54
Hotel Friedrichstraße (P)
**1907**
55
Entrance and staircase (R)
56
Wilhelm and Martha Hirsch Apartment (R)
57
Paul Khnuer Apartment (R)
58
Rudolf Kraus Apartment (R)
59
Arnold and Julius Bellak Apartment (R)
**1908**
60
Ministry of War (P)
61
Arthur Friedmann's garden house (R)
62
Kärntner Bar (R/E)
63
Otto and Olga Beck Apartment (R)
64
R. Fischl Apartment (R)
65
Arthur and Leonie Friedmann Apartment (R)
66
Gravestone (P)
**1909**
67
House on Michaelerplatz (R/E)
68
Leopold Goldman House (R/EP)
69
City plan for Karlsplatz (P)
70
Multi-purpose hall (P)
71
Technical Museum (P)
72
Residential building with statue of rider
(P)

# Selected Bibliography

**Writings by Adolf Loos**

*Das Andere*, Wien 1903.

*Richtlinien für ein Kunstamt*, Verlag Richard Lanyi, Wien 1919.

*Ins Leere gesprochen. 1897-1900*, Editions Georges Crès, Paris-Zürich 1921; English edition: *Spoken into the Void*, in *Spoken into the Void: Collected Essays, 1897-1900*, The MIT Press, Cambridge (MA) 1982.

*Trotzdem*, 1900-1930, Brenner Verlag, Innsbruck 1931.

*Die Potemkinsche Stadt*, in *Verschollene Schriften 1897-1933*, edited by Adolf Opel, Prachner Verlag, Wien 1983 (new edition 1997).

**Books on Adolf Loos (selection)**

Heinrich Kulka, *Adolf Loos*, Löcker-Verlag, Wien 1930 (second edition 1979).

Claire Loos, *Loos privat*, Johannespresse, Wien 1936.

Paul Engelmann, *Adolf Loos*, Architektur und Bauverlag, Wien (facsimile of the original edition Tel Aviv 1946).

Lina Loos, *Das Buch ohne Titel. Erlebte Geschichten einer Wiener Schauspielerin*, Büchergilde Gutenberg, Wien 1953.

Ludwig Münz, Gustav Künstler, *Der Architekt Adolf Loos*, Schroll-Verlag, Wien 1964.

Elsie Altmann-Loos, *Adolf Loos der Mensch*, Herold Verlag, Wien-München 1968.

*Adolf Loos für junge Leute*, exhibition catalogue, Vienna, Museum des 20 Jahrhunderts, Scheller (texts), Gerlach, Marlon (photos), Wien 1970.

Vera Josefa Behalova, *Adolf Loos - Villa Karma*, graduation dissertation, Wien 1974.

Hermann Czech, Wolfgang Mistelbauer, *Das Looshaus*, Löcker Verlag, Wien 1976.

*Adolf Loos 1870-1933 - Neue Wege der Baukunst*, exhibition catalogue, Vienna, Genossenschaftl. Zentralvereinigung Raiffeisen, 1980.

Julius Posener, *Vorlesungen zur Geschichte der Architektur (1750-1933). Arch + 48; 53; 59; 63/64; 69/70. 2 Vorlesungen über Adolf Loos*, Arch + Verlag, Aachen 1980-83.

Burkhardt Rukschcio, Robert Schachel, *Adolf Loos - Leben und Werk*, Residenzverlag, Wien-Salzburg 1982 (2nd edition 1987).

Dietrich Worbs, *Adolf Loos 1870-1933 - Raumplan-Wohnungsbau*, exhibition catalogue, Vienna, Akademie der bildenden Künste (December 1983 - January 1984).

Elsie Altmann-Loos, *Mein Leben mit Adolf Loos*, with an afterword by Adolf Opel, Amalthea, Wien-München 1984.

Hildegund Amanshauser, *Untersuchungen zu den Schriften von Adolf Loos*, graduation dissertation at Salzburg University, VWGÖ, Wien 1985.

*Kontroversen - Adolf Loos im Spiegel der Zeitgenossen*, edited by Adolf Opel, Georg Prachner Verlag, Wien 1985.

*Konfrontationen - Schriften von und über Loos*, edited by Adolf Opel, Georg Prachner Verlag, Wien 1988.

Max Risselada, *Raumplan versus Plan libre - Adolf Loos-Le Corbusier*, Rizzoli International Publications Inc., New York 1988.

Burckhardt Rukschcio, *Adolf Loos - Festschrift zum 60. Geburtstag 1930*, Löcker Verlag, Wien 1988.

*Adolf Loos als Konstrukteur*, exhibition catalogue, Vienna, Institut für Hochbau, Techn. Univ. Wien, 1990.

Adolf Opel, Marino Valdez, *"Alle Architekten sind Verbrecher" - Adolf Loos und die Folgen*, Edition Atelier, Wien 1990.

Beatriz Colomina, *Sexuality and space*, Princeton Papers on architecture, Princeton (NJ) 1992.

Beatriz Colomina, *Privacy and Publicity, modern architecture as Mass Media*, The MIT Press, Cambridge (MA) 1994.

Eva B. Ottilinger, *Adolf Loos - Wohnkonzepte und Möbelentwürfe*, Residenzverlag, Wien-Salzburg 1994.

Leslie Vanduzer, Kent Kleinman, *Villa Müller*, Princeton Architectural Press, New York 1994.

Christian Kühn, *Das Schöne, das Wahre und das Richtige - Adolf Loos und das Haus Müller in Prag*, Bauwelt Fundamente 86, Friedrich Vieweg & Sohn, Braunschweig-Wiesbaden 1989/2001.

Fedor Roth, *Adolf Loos und die Idee des Ökonomischen*, Deuticke, Wien 1995.

Friedrich Kurrent, *Adolf Loos - 40 Wohnhäuser*, Verlag Anton Pustet, Salzburg 1998.

Karel Ksandr, *Villa Müller - Adolf Loos & Karel Lhota*, Argo-Publisher, Praha 2000.

Markus Kristan, *Adolf Loos - Landhaus Khuner am Kreuzberg*, Höhere Graphische Bundes- Lehr- und Versuchsanstalt, Wien 2004.

**Illustrated Books on Loos' Projects (selection)**

Roberto Schezen, Joseph Rosa, Kenneth Frampton, *Adolf Loos - Architecture 1903-1932*, Monacelli Press, New York 1996.

Markus Kristan, *Loos Villen*, Album Verlag, Wien 2000.

Markus Kristan, *Loos Wohnungen*, Album Verlag, Wien 2000.

Markus Kristan, *Loos Geschäftslokale*, Album Verlag, Wien 2001.

**Others**

Hermann Muthesius, *Das englische Haus*, 3 voll., Gebr. Mann Verlag, Berlin 1903-1906 (new ed. 1999).

Hermann Muthesius, *Landhaus und Garten*, Verlagsanstalt F. Bruckmann, München 1907.

Leberecht Migge, *Die Gartenkultur des 20. Jahrhunderts*, Diederichs, Jena 1913.

Le Corbusier, *Urbanisme*, Paris 1925.

Josef Frank, *Die internationale Werkbundsiedlung Wien*, Schroll Verlag, Wien 1932.

Magda Maetz, *Otto Stoessl, sein Leben und seine Jugendwerke*, degree thesis, Wien 1948.

Herbert Steiner, *Die Gebrüder Scheu*, Europa Verlag, Wien 1968.

Karl Kraus, *Die Fackel - Nachdruck der Ausgaben 1/1899-922/1936*, Verlag Zweitausendeins, Frankfurt 1977.

Eduard F. Sekler, *Josef Hoffmann - Das architektonische Werk*, Residenz Verlag, Salzburg 1982.

Cornelia Fritsch, *Der Kritiker Otto Stoessl*, degree thesis, Wien 1985.

Astrid Gmeiner, *Der österreichische Werkbund*, Residenz Verlag, Wien-Salzburg 1985.

Friedrich Scheu, *Ein Band der Freundschaft - Schwarzwald-Kreis u. Entstehung der Vereinigung sozialistischer Mittelschüler*, Böhlau Verlag, Wien 1985.

Friedrich Achleitner, *Aufforderung zum Vertrauen*, Residenz Verlag, Salzburg-Wien 1987.

Jan Turnovsky, *Die Poetik des Mauervorsprungs*, Vieweg Verlag, Braunschweig 1987.

Adolf Krischanitz, Otto Kapfinger, *Werkbundsiedlung Wien*, Beton Verlag, Düsseldorf 1989.

Werner Öchslin, *Stilhülse und Kern - Otto Wagner, Adolf Loos und der evolutionäre Weg zur modernen Architektur*, GTA, Zürich 1994.

Wolfgang Hink, *Karl Kraus, Die Fackel 1899-1936 / Bibliographie und Register*, Saur-Verlag, München 1994.

"Gartenkunst des Jugendstils und der Zwischenkriegszeit - Tagungsbeiträge und Werner'sche Verlagsanstalt", in *Die Gartenkunst*, vol. 2, Worms 1995.

Friedrich Achleitner, *Wiener Architektur*, Böhlau, Wien 1996.

Robert Streibel, *Eugenie Schwarzwald und ihr Kreis*, Picus Verlag, Wien 1996.

Gerhard Weissenbacher, *In Hietzing gebaut*, 2 voll., Verlag Holzhausen, Wien 1996 und 1998.

Heinz Lunzer, Victoria Lunzer-Talos, *"Was wir umbringen", Karl Kraus - Die Fackel*, Mandelbaum-Verlag, Wien 1999.

Leberecht Migge, *Der soziale Garten / Das grüne Manifest*, Gebr. Mann Verlag, Berlin 1999.

Terence Riley, Barry Bergdoll, *Ludwig Mies van der Rohe - Die Berliner Jahre 1907-1938*, Prestel Verlag, München 2001.

Heidi Brünnbauer, *Im Cottage von Währing-Döbling*, Edition Weinviertel, Wien 2003.

Heinz Lunzer, Victoria Lunzer-Talos, *Peter Altenberg - Extracte des Lebens*, Residenz-Verlag, Wien-Salzburg 2003.

Gottfried Semper, *Style in the technical and tectonical arts; or practical aesthetics*, Getty, Los Angeles, 2004 (German original edition: *Der Stil in den technischen und tektonischen Künsten; oder praktische Ästhetik*, 1878-79).

Elana Shapira, *Assimilating with style*, degree thesis, Wien, Universität für angewandte Kunst, 2004.

Susanne Blumesberger, *Helene Scheu - Riesz (1880-1970)*, Praesens Verlag, Wien 2005.

Ursula Prokop, *Jacques und Jacqueline Groag - Zwei vergessene Künstler der Wiener Moderne*, Böhlau Verlag, Wien 2005.

Bruno Taut, *Das japanische Haus und sein Leben (Houses and People of Japan)*, Gebr. Mann Verlag, Berlin 2005.